The
COMPLETE PATENT *kit*

The COMPLETE PATENT *kit*

Second Edition

James L. Rogers

Attorney at Law

SPHINX® PUBLISHING
AN IMPRINT OF SOURCEBOOKS, INC.®
NAPERVILLE, ILLINOIS
www.SphinxLegal.com

Second Edition: 2009

Published by Sphinx Publishing, an imprint of Sourcebooks, Inc.

Naperville Office
P.O. Box 4410, Naperville, Illinois 60567-4410
(630) 961-3900
Fax: (630) 961-2168
www.sourcebooks.com
www.SphinxLegal.com

This publication is designed to provide accurate and authoritative information in regard to the subject matter covered. It is sold with the understanding that the publisher is not engaged in rendering legal, accounting, or other professional service. If legal advice or other expert assistance is required, the services of a competent professional person should be sought.
From a Declaration of Principles Jointly Adopted by a Committee of the American Bar Association and a Committee of Publishers and Associations

This product is not a substitute for legal advice.
Disclaimer required by Texas statutes.

Library of Congress Cataloging-in-Publication Data

Rogers, James L.
  The complete patent kit / by James L. Rogers.
    p. cm.
  Includes index.
 1. Patent laws and legislation—United States—Popular works. 2. Inventions—United States—Popular works. 3. Inventor—United States--Handbooks, manuals, etc. I. Title.

KF3114.6.R642 2005
346.7304'86—dc22
2005021668

Printed and bound in the United States of America
DR 10 9 8 7 6 5 4 3 2 1

Contents

Chapter 21: Relief Available in Patent Infringement Cases 437

Injunctive Relief
Lost Profits
Reasonable Royalty
Interest, Costs, and Fees
Enhancement of Damages

Chapter 22: What to Do if You Are Sued for Patent Infringement 447

Hiring a Defense Team
Response to an Assertion Letter
Obtain a Written Opinion
Deciding What to Do

Chapter 23: Defenses to Patent Infringement 455

Patent and Claim Invalidity
Non-infringement
Novelty
Prior Invention
Obviousness
Inadequate Disclosure
Lack of Utility
Inequitable Conduct
Not in Force
First Sale Doctrine and Exhaustion
Estoppel
Prosecution History Laches
Double Patenting
Experimental Use
Incorrect Inventorship

Chapter 24: Special Defenses to Patent Infringement 477

Antitrust Violations
Statute of Limitations
Laches
Intervening and Prior User's Rights
Medical Procedures
Old or Exhausted Combination

How to Use the CD-ROM

Thank you for purchasing *The Complete Patent Kit, 2ⁿᵈ Edition*. We have included every document in the book on the CD-ROM that is attached to the inside back cover of the book.

You can use these forms just as you would the forms in the book. Print them out, fill them in, and use them however you need. You can also fill in the forms directly on your computer. Just identify the form you need, open it, click on the space where the information should go, and input your information. Customize each form for your particular needs. Use them over and over again.

The CD-ROM is compatible with both PC and Mac operating systems. (While it should work with either operating system, we cannot guarantee that it will work with your particular system and we cannot provide technical assistance.) To use the forms on your computer, you will need to use Adobe Reader. The CD-ROM does not contain this program. You can download this program from Adobe's website at www.adobe.com. Click on the "Get Adobe Reader" icon to begin the download process and follow the instructions.

Once you have Adobe Reader installed, insert the CD-ROM into your computer. Double click on the icon representing the disc on your desktop or go through your hard drive to identify the drive that contains the disc and click on it. Once opened, you will see the files contained on the CD-ROM listed as "Form #: [Form Title]." Open the file you need through Adobe Reader. You may print the form to fill it out manually at this point, or your can use the "Hand Tool" and click on the appropriate line to fill it in using your computer. Once all your information is filled in, you can print your filled-in form.

NOTE: *Adobe Reader does not allow you to save the PDF with the boxes filled in.*

• • • • •

Purchasers of this book are granted a license to use the forms contained in it for their own personal use. By purchasing this book, you have also purchased a limited license to use all forms on the accompanying CD-ROM. The license limits you to personal use only and all other copyright laws must be adhered. No claim of copyright is made in any government form reproduced in the book or on the CD-ROM. You are free to modify the forms and tailor them to your specific situation.

The author and publisher have attempted to provide the most current and up-to-date information available. However, the courts, Congress, and your state's legislatures review, modify, and change laws on an ongoing basis, as well as create new laws from time to time. By the very nature of the information and due to the continual changes in our legal system, to be sure that you have the current and best information for your situation, you should consult a local attorney or research the current laws yourself.

• • • • •

This publication is designed to provide accurate and authoritative information in regard to the subject matter covered. It is sold with the understanding that the publisher is not engaged in rendering legal, accounting, or other professional service. If legal advice or other expert assistance is required, the services of a competent professional person should be sought.

>*—From a Declaration of Principles Jointly Adopted by a Committee of the American Bar Association and a Committee of Publishers and Associations*

This product is not a substitute for legal advice.

>*—Disclaimer required by Texas statutes*

Using Self-Help Law Books

Before using a self-help law book, you should realize the advantages and disadvantages of doing your own legal work, and understand the challenges and diligence that this requires.

THE GROWING TREND

Rest assured that you will not be the first or only person handling your own legal matter. For example, in some states, more than 75% of the people in divorces and other civil cases represent themselves. Because of the high cost of legal services, this is a major trend, and many courts are struggling to make it easier for people to represent themselves. However, some courts are not happy with people who do not use attorneys and refuse to help them in any way. For some, the attitude is, "Go to the law library and figure it out for yourself."

We write and publish self-help law books to give people an alternative to the often complicated and confusing legal books found in most law libraries. We have made the explanations of the law as simple and easy to understand as possible. Of course, unlike an attorney advising an individual client, we cannot cover every conceivable possibility.

COST/VALUE ANALYSIS

Whenever you shop for a product or service, you are faced with various levels of quality and price. In deciding what product or service to buy, you make a cost/value analysis on the basis of your willingness to pay and the quality you desire.

When buying a car, you decide whether you want transportation, comfort, status, or sex appeal. Accordingly, you decide among choices such as a Neon, Lincoln, Rolls Royce, or Porsche. Before making a decision, you usually weigh the merits of each option against the cost. When you get a headache, you can take a pain reliever (such as aspirin) or visit a medical specialist for a neurological examination. Given this choice, most people, of course, take a pain reliever, since it costs only pennies; whereas a medical examination costs hundreds of dollars and takes a lot of time. This is usually a logical choice because it is rare to need anything more than a pain reliever for a headache. But in some cases, a headache may indicate a brain tumor, and failing to see a specialist right away can result in complications. Should everyone with a headache go to a specialist? Of course not, but people treating their own illnesses must realize that they are betting on the basis of their cost/value analysis of the situation. They are taking the most logical option.

The same cost/value analysis must be made when deciding to do one's own legal work. Many legal situations are very straightforward, requiring a simple form and no complicated analysis. Anyone with a little intelligence and a book of instructions can handle the matter without outside help. But there is always the chance that complications are involved that only an attorney would notice. To simplify the law into a book like this, several legal cases often must be condensed into a single sentence or paragraph. Otherwise, the book would be several hundred pages long and too complicated for most people. However, this simplification necessarily leaves out many details and nuances that would apply to special or unusual situations. Also, there are many ways to interpret most legal questions. Your case may come before a judge who disagrees with the analysis of our authors.

Therefore, in deciding to use a self-help law book and to do your own legal work, you must realize that you are making a cost/value analysis. You have decided that the money you will save in doing it yourself outweighs the chance that your case will not turn out to your satisfaction. Most people handling their own simple legal matters never have a problem, but occasionally people find that it ended up costing them more to have an attorney straighten out the situation than it would have if they had hired an attorney in the beginning. Keep this in mind while handling your case, and be sure to consult an attorney if you feel you might need further guidance.

LOCAL RULES

The next thing to remember is that a book that covers the law for the entire nation, or even for an entire state, cannot possibly include every procedural difference of every jurisdiction. Whenever possible, we provide the exact form needed; however, in some areas, each county, or even each judge, may require unique forms and procedures. In our state books, our forms usually cover the majority of counties in the state or provide examples of the type of form that will be required. In our national books, our forms are sometimes even more general in nature but are designed to give a good idea of the type of form that will be needed in most locations. Nonetheless, keep in mind that your state, county, or judge may have a requirement, or use a form, that is not included in this book.

You should not necessarily expect to be able to get all of the information and resources you need solely from within the pages of this book. This book will serve as your guide, giving you specific information whenever possible and helping you to find out what else you will need to know. This is just like if you decided to build your own backyard deck. You might purchase a book on how to build decks. However, such a book would not include the building codes and permit requirements of every city, town, county, and township in the nation; nor would it include the lumber, nails, saws, hammers, and other materials and tools you would need to actually build the deck. You would use the book as your guide, and then do some work and research involving such matters as whether you need a permit of some kind, what type and grade of wood is available in your area, whether to use hand tools or power tools, and how to use those tools. Before using the forms in a book like this, you should check with your court clerk to see if there are any local rules of which you should be aware or local forms you will need to use. Often, such forms will require the same information as the forms in the book but are merely laid out differently or use slightly different language. They will sometimes require additional information.

CHANGES IN THE LAW

Besides being subject to local rules and practices, the law is subject to change at any time. The courts and the legislatures of all fifty states are constantly revising the laws. It is possible that while you are reading this book, some aspect of the law is being changed.

In most cases, the change will be of minimal significance. A form will be redesigned, additional information will be required, or a waiting period will be extended. As a result, you might need to revise a form, file an extra form, or wait out a longer time period. These types of changes will not usually affect the outcome of your case. On the other hand, sometimes a major part of the law is changed, the entire law in a particular area is rewritten, or a case that was the basis of a central legal point is overruled. In such instances, your entire ability to pursue your case may be impaired.

Introduction

The Complete Patent Kit is meant to be an all-encompassing resource for the inventor. However, other individuals—the corporate executive concerned with maximizing value from the intellectual property of a corporation, individuals involved in intellectual property (IP) transactions, companies desiring to launch a product, and people involved in financing IP assets—will also find this book an excellent resource. In addition to covering the actual mechanics of patent procurement, this book covers subjects such as what makes a strong patent, how to recognize patent infringement, and how to commercialize an invention. These are issues that truly can make or break businesses in today's world, where the assets of a company are becoming increasingly based on intellectual property rights like patents.

There are many reasons inventors apply for patents. Inventors want to know that their ingenuity will be protected from copycats. A patent, if properly drafted, can do this. Patents will also make inventions worth more to potential investors. Many startup companies apply for a patent simply to attract capital to fund their companies.

This book is divided up into six sections.

✪ Section 1 deals with important issues prior to making an application for a patent. Small inventors often come to me and want to obtain a patent on an idea. These people are creative and entrepreneurial. They are the backbone of this country's spirit and fuel both innovation and, ultimately, job creation. However, I often find that while they have clearly put a lot of thought into their invention, they have not put too much thought into patent law. Not every inventor needs to write his or her own patent application. In fact, the decision to write one is really a cost-benefit decision. It may also be wise, at times, to let others with more experience at drafting applications do what they do best. However, every inventor does need to know some things about patent law before even considering filing a patent application. This section is geared to provide inventors the knowledge to make informed decisions. Issues covered include the advantages of patent protection, the disadvantages of patent protection, and reasons not to seek patent protection. You will learn how to conduct a patentability search to determine whether an invention is novel and learn about other requirements for patentability. Determining the worth of an invention clearly hinges on whether patent protection can be obtained for such an invention. The issues covered in Section 1 are important for all people involved in an IP transaction that involves potential patent rights to an invention.

✪ Section 2 covers the actual mechanics of patent application drafting and filing and thus will be of particular interest to people who want to procure a patent. However, knowing something about how a patent application is drafted, particularly the claims that define a patented invention, is important for all involved in patent transactions. In addition, this section covers how even individual inventors can preserve foreign patent rights as well as strategies for foreign patent protection. Other types of patent applications, such as the provisional patent application, are also discussed.

✪ Section 3 of this book deals with what occurs between a patent applicant and the U.S. Patent Office after a patent application is filed. I find that many inventors mistakenly believe that once a patent application is filed, they will get a patent. This is rarely the case. In fact, most patent applications are rejected. Section 3 provides strategies for overcoming typical patent office rejections. Again, these concepts are important to know for anyone who wants to determine the worth of a patent.

✪ Section 4 covers things to do after a patent is issued. Subjects such as patent maintenance are discussed. You will also learn how to monitor competitors and recognize patent infringement. Having an understanding as to patent infringement is essential for not only the patent owner who wants to protect patent rights but also for those people who want to have ideas about the risk involved in launching a new product.

✪ Section 5 teaches you how to protect your patent. Whether you're fending off other inventors or responsibly expanding on someone else's idea, you'll need to know the ins and outs of patent infringement cases.

✪ Section 6 details ways to commercialize and make money off your invention. IBM, a large and prosperous company, makes billions of dollars in revenues from licensing many of its products. This is a form of commercialization that is well within the reach of even individual inventors. I have included a flowchart on the next page that will help you see the big picture of the patent process from start to finish. You will learn about all these steps in the chapters to come.

The flowchart shows you where each is discussed.

I welcome your feedback, questions, or concerns. For additional links related to intellectual property law beyond those contained in the Appendices of this book, or to contact me, please visit the following website: www.ypatent.com.

I look forward to hearing from you.

—James Rogers, Registered Patent Attorney

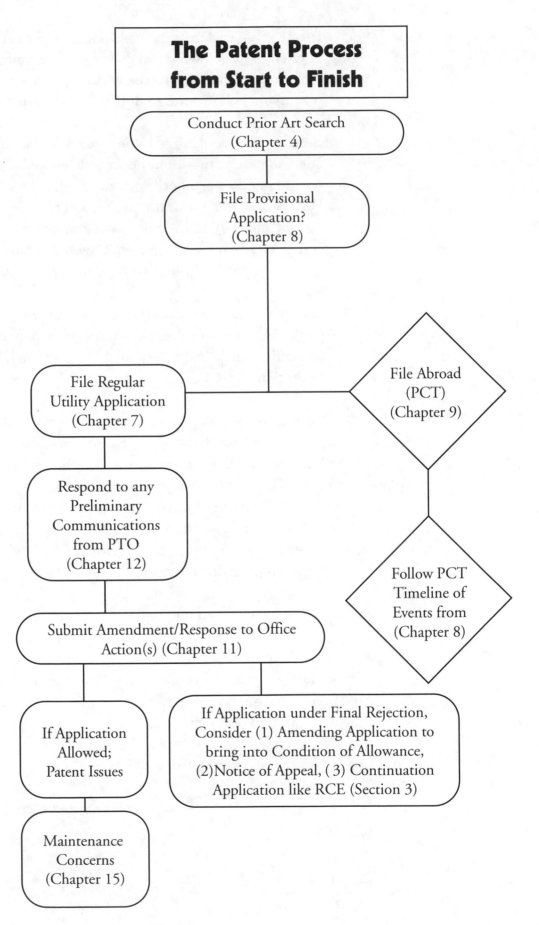

Section I

BEFORE YOU FILE YOUR APPLICATION

Overview of the Patent Process

A *patent* gives you, the inventor, the exclusive right to make, use, or sell your invention. The entire rationale for granting patents to inventors is "to promote the progress of science and useful arts, by securing for limited times to authors and inventors the exclusive right to their respective writings and discoveries," as stated in Article 1, Section 8 of the U.S. Constitution.

THE PURPOSE OF PATENTS

By giving inventors an exclusive right to their discoveries, inventors have a greater incentive to pursue their inventions, since there is a greater likelihood that they will see a return on their investment. Patents are, in effect, a valuable reward given to inventors for all of their hard work in creating something new. By giving inventors a type of *monopoly* on their inventions for a certain amount of time, it is believed that they are more likely to make sacrifices and investments to spend time inventing.

Patents also provide a greater incentive for inventors to make their inventions public through the patenting system. If you know that as soon as you disclose your invention someone could steal it and start using it as his or her own invention, you are probably going to be hesitant about disclosing your invention. In fact, you are probably going to want to keep your invention secret. By giving you protection against this kind of theft as soon as you file your patent application, it is believed that you will be more likely to tell the outside world about your invention. In the eyes of patent law, disclosing your invention to the world adds to the wealth of information in your field. In turn, this leads to future technological improvements and advancements in your field.

FACTORS TO CONSIDER

Deciding whether you should seek patent protection on your invention involves a variety of factors. No single factor is likely to answer this question for you, but there are several factors you should consider.

Drawbacks to Applying for a Patent

On the negative side, be aware that obtaining a patent is not an inexpensive process. Even if you go at it alone, there are some pretty hefty fees associated with the patent process itself. For example, there are fees to file your patent application ($155 for a small entity), as well as search fees ($255 for a small entity), and examination fees ($105) associated with such a filing. If you hire a patent attorney or agent to handle your application process, your fees will be considerably more expensive, ranging in the thousands of dollars just for his or her representation alone.

A patent owner must also pay about $6,000 in *maintenance fees* to keep a patent alive in the United States for its full term. If you want patent protection abroad, you will also have to pay maintenance fees for each country in which you seek to keep your patent in force. In total, it is not uncommon for a person to spend around $10,000–$30,000 for obtaining and maintaining a patent in the United States, depending on the complexity of the invention. By doing things yourself, you will probably cut these expenses in half, but the fees can still be considerable for the individual inventor.

Another thing that you should keep in mind is that obtaining a patent is not an easy process. Your success in obtaining a patent will depend on a host of factors, such as your invention's *novelty* (a term that is defined for you in Chapter 3). Also, the chances of obtaining a patent have been decreasing. The reasons for this decline are believed to be due to an increasing belief by the United States Patent and Trademark Office (PTO) that many patents granted in the past should in fact not have been granted.

Another factor that you should consider is that having a patent on your invention does not necessarily mean that you have anything of value. What will be important instead is whether your invention has value to someone else. If your invention has no value to anyone, then your patent is basically going to be worthless. One thing that I find many inventors and patent attorneys alike do not appreciate is that people in this world do not buy technology; they buy products. For example, when people go to shop for a video game at the local software store, they are not looking to buy the software program behind the game. They want to buy the game itself regardless of the software. So, while a patent on video game software might be a nice thing to have, if there is no one interested in buying this particular video game, then the patented technology alone is not going to have significant value.

However, do not let uncertainty about this deter you. How do you know if your invention is valuable? If your invention already exists or there is already a better product out in the marketplace, then you are probably not going to make money off your invention by obtaining a patent. In Chapter 4, you learn how to uncover *prior art* to determine whether similar products exist in the marketplace. There are also experts who can assist you with valuing your invention. The United Inventors Association (UIA) is a nonprofit organization that will evaluate your invention for a cost of around $312. Their website is www.uiausa.com. Although $300 may seem like a lot of money to you, it is actually quite inexpensive compared to the costs of the patent process. Therefore, such evaluations can be very helpful before you engage in drafting a patent application for your invention.

In deciding whether or not your invention has possible value, one question that you can ask is whether or not innovative features of your invention could possibly give someone a competitive edge in the marketplace. If the answer to this question is yes, then a patent should be filed. What are innovative features? There are different key concepts and questions you should ask yourself about your invention to determine whether it has innovative features.

- ✪ Performance—How well does your invention carry out its intended function?

- ✪ Efficiency—How efficient is my invention?

- ✪ Capacity—Does my invention have higher storage?

- ✪ Structure—Is your invention a new product made up of existing components arranged in a different way that offers new or improved benefits? Is your invention a series of products that are used together to offer a new set of benefits? Is your invention a smaller size, which gives it added benefits? Is your invention made up of a material having a property not normally associated with it (e.g., plastics that conduct electricity)?

- ✪ Function—Does your invention process or store information more efficiently?

Another factor you should consider is whether you will be able to detect infringement if you get a patent on your invention. If your invention is impossible to detect in the marketplace, it may be best to use some other form of *intellectual property* (IP) protection, such as a *trade secret.* Otherwise, you will find that although you have a patent, there is no practical way for you to enforce your patent rights and stop others from using your invention.

Even if an invention has market value, another thing that you should keep in mind is that the patent that protects your invention may be worthless because it is very easy for competitors to design around. This means that all your competitor needs to do in order to avoid infringement of your patent is to choose an equally viable, noninfringing substitute. Whether or not a competitor can do this depends on the *claims* of your patent. *Claim drafting* is discussed in detail later in the book.

One way to counteract this problem is to write claims in your patent that are difficult to design around. Part of the objective of this book is to show you how to draft such claims. However, no matter how great of a claim drafter you become, there is always the possibility that your claims must be drafted narrowly, and therefore, your scope of protection will be very narrow, too. This is because you cannot claim what others have already disclosed, and if a lot has already been disclosed relating to your invention, what you may end up obtaining for a patent are claims drawn to a much narrower aspect of your invention than you thought when you started out. Chapter 4 of this book will be the most useful chapter for you in considering this factor, since it covers how to search for what others have already disclosed about your invention. If, after reading Chapter 4, you find that others in your field have already disclosed so much of your invention that any patent you could obtain would appear worthless to you, then it might be time to reconsider whether you want to obtain a patent on your invention at all.

On the other hand, your technology may also become outdated in a very short time frame. This is often the case with computer programs, which can become out-of-date pretty quickly. In such instances, it will probably not make sense to seek a patent that can take two to three years to obtain. Instead, you may want to consider other types of intellectual property protection, such as *copyrights* or *trade secrets*, which will be discussed in Chapter 2.

Benefits to Applying for a Patent

Do you ever wonder why large companies have so many patents? IBM leads the patent warehouse among all companies. In 2005, it obtained 2,941. The company's overall patent portfolio is stuffed with a staggering 40,000 U.S. patents. So why would a company spend so much money obtaining and maintaining patents? One of the primary reasons is that patents bring in considerable revenue to companies like IBM. Patents can be sold and licensed just as you might sell or rent your house.

The value of a patent to a potential purchaser or licensee arises from what patents can do. A U.S. patent gives its owner the *right to exclude others* from making, using, importing, selling, or offering for sale your invention within the United States, its territories, and possessions. The right to exclude others in this manner can be a formidable right. By having a patent on your invention, it is going to be worth considerably more to someone else than if you do not have a patent. The reasons for this are simple. Any person who might be interested in your invention will not only have to spend money to purchase your invention, but will also most likely need to spend a lot of money to get your invention to the marketplace. Since the purchaser will need to spend a couple hundred thousand dollars to do this, he or she is going to be much more interested in a marketplace that is not already infiltrated with competitors. You can feel more confident about the marketability of your invention and can charge a lot more, as well as sell a lot more copies of a product that is not already out in the marketplace.

Patents also have value beyond their enforcement value. Patents can serve as a deterrent to infringement as well as a bargaining chip in negotiating sales or licenses. To understand the value of this reason for obtaining a patent, think about this. A company with a single patent is probably going to have less chance of entangling another company in some type of patent dispute then a company with one hundred patents. In other words, if your company with one patent on a particular technology goes into a licensing discussion with another company having one hundred patents related to the same technology, you will probably end up being more restricted in what you can do against the company that has one hundred patents. As a result, you are likely to be at a disadvantage. To make it easier, think of patents like spiderwebs. The company with one hundred patents has a larger web than your company with one patent, and as a result it is more likely to entangle you in this web with its myriad patent claims. This is a good reason to obtain patents beyond their direct money-making value in the form of protecting products which can be sold.

NOTE: ***Laws about imported products***—*A special statute (35 U.S.C. §271(g)) also provides that a product imported into the United States will infringe a process patent for making the product if the patented process was implemented abroad.*

In addition to creating *barriers* in the marketplace, there are many other possible factors as to why patents are obtained. Patents can create value in and of themselves. A patent can be licensed. (This is a major method of extracting value from patents, often practiced by very large corporations.) In recent years, revenue through licensing has taken off as a strategy to enhance the wealth of companies. For the individual inventor, wealth can also be achieved through the licensing of a patented invention. In fact, *licensing* is even more important for the individual inventor, because he or she typically will not have the resources to market and sell an invention alone. The best alternative to obtain wealth from the patent is to license it to companies that have the ability to get the invention into the marketplace. A patent can also be sold or even put up for collateral. Patents will probably also lend you credibility if you ever need to obtain financing for your company. A patent offers assurances to potential financial investors that other companies will not want to enter the business niche you have carved out with the claims of your patent. A barrier to a competitor's entry into a market is highly respected by people who can finance your company, such as *venture capitalists*. You will be able to approach such financial parties in a much better light with a patent in hand than if you do not have one.

There have been plenty of inventions that someone may not have considered valuable when invented, but later turned out to be worth a lot of money. One reason for this is that times change, and what may not seem very valuable today could be valuable to someone months or years from now.

WHO CAN APPLY FOR A PATENT

A patent can only be applied for in the names of the *real persons* (the *inventors*) who have conceived the invention that you claim in your patent application. If any person has made any contribution toward the conception of any element in any claim listed in your patent application, then that person must be listed as an inventor in your patent application. It does not matter whether you have contributed 99.9% toward the conception of your invention. If another person has contributed the remaining 0.1% toward the invention, you must apply for the invention with that person if that 0.1% is part of any *claim* in your application. Ordinarily, there must at least be communication—direct or indirect—between those claiming joint inventorship. When two people are totally unaware of each other's work—even if they are employed by the same company—there is no joint inventorship. However, two or more people do not have to begin working on an invention at the same time for them to ultimately be considered joint inventors. The statute that governs this is 35 U.S.C. §1165, which specifies that individuals may be joint inventors even though:

1. they did not physically work together or at the same time;

2. each did not make the same type or amount of contribution; or,

3. each did not make a contribution to the subject matter of every claim of the patent.

Generally, a *joint invention* occurs when two or more persons, collaborating together, each contribute to the conception of the solution that constitutes the invention. *Conception* is the completion of the mental part of an invention. According to the courts, it is the formation in the mind of the inventor, or a definite and permanent idea of the complete and operative invention as it is hereafter to be applied in practice. Conception is complete only when the idea is so clearly defined in the inventor's mind that only ordinary skill would be necessary to reduce the invention to practice, without extensive research or experimentation. To be complete, conception must include every feature of the claimed invention.

Determining whether a person is a joint inventor is highly fact-specific and there is no bright line standard. However, one does not become an inventor either by suggesting a desired end or result, with no suggestions of means, or by merely following the instructions of the person who conceived the solution. Ultimately, to be considered a joint inventor, a person must make a contribution to the conception of the claimed invention that is not insignificant in quality when that contribution is measured against the dimension of the full invention

Another very important thing that you need to remember about inventorship is that an inventor's own statements are inadequate to prove conception, and instead must be corroborated with independent evidence. This independent evidence can be either:

- contemporaneous documents, which must allow a skilled artisan to practice the portion of the invention that the coinventor contributed; or,

- the oral testimony of an independent witness.

NOTE: *__Draft your claims to your benefit__—The fact that only your claims matter for purposes of determining inventorship gives you the option of drafting your claims so that you are the only inventor who has made any contribution to any of them.*

It is important to list the inventors correctly, because the enforceability of your patent is predicated on properly listed inventorship. Incorrect listing of inventors with deceptive intent, is considered to be *inequitable conduct.*

You may be wondering how any future proceeds of your invention will be split among coinventors. The answer is that each inventor will have an undivided one-half interest in the patent. This could lead to unfair results if one inventor has done most of the conceiving of the invention while a coinventor has made only a small contribution. In such a case, it is recommended that you have an agreement between yourself and your coinventor so that any future proceeds are divided according to your respective contributions.

TYPES OF AVAILABLE PATENTS

There are three types of patents that you can obtain from the PTO.

Utility Patent

The first and most common patent is called a *utility patent.* A *utility patent* protects the way an article is used and works. (35 U.S.C. §101.) Unless otherwise noted, the chapters of this book are written on the assumption that you are interested in preparing a utility patent.

Design Patent

The second type of patent you can obtain is called a *design patent.* A *design patent* protects the way an article looks. By and large, most of what applies to utility patents in this book is also applicable to design patents. You will learn more about some specific rules regarding design patents in Chapter 8.

Plant Patent

The last type of patent you can obtain is called a *plant patent,* which, as the name suggests, protects the discovery of new varieties of plants. This is a specialized type of patent that is not very common and is beyond the scope of this book.

WHAT IS PATENTABLE

There are four categories of inventions that Congress deemed to be the appropriate subject matter of a patent:

1. processes;

2. machines;

3. manufactures; and,

4. compositions of matter. (35 U.S.C. §101.)

Process   *Process* means a process, art, or method, and includes a new use of a known process, machine, manufacture, composition of matter, or material. *Process inventions* consist of a series of steps or acts to be performed, namely a model of treating certain materials to produce a given result. It is an act, or a series of acts, performed upon the subject matter to be transformed and reduced to a different state or thing. A process requires that certain things be done with certain substances and in a certain order.

On October 30, 2008, the Federal Circuit decided an important case, *In re Bilski*, which set down new rules regarding the patentability of a process. Specifically, the court affirmed rules previously held in *Gottschalk v. Benson* 409 U.S. 63 (1972) that a claimed process is patent-eligible only if (1) it is tied to a particular machine or apparatus, or (2) it transforms a particular article into a different state or thing. Nicknamed the "Machine-or-transformation test," the court rejected all previous tests including the "useful, concrete, and tangible result test."

Example:

A claimed process which took temperature readings during curing of synthetic rubber and used a mathematical algorithm, the Arrhenius equation, to calculate the time when curing would be complete was held patentable subject matter. While a claim drawn to a fundamental principle is unpatentable, an application of a law of nature or mathematical formula to a known structure or process was patentable. The claim here operated on a computerized rubber curing apparatus and transformed raw, uncured rubber into molded, cured rubber products.

The net results of this decision is to make the patentability of processes, particularly computer processes, more difficult. First, merely using a computer to perform calculations, display results, or gather data will probably not suffice to transform a general computer into a particular machine. Thus running software on general purpose digital computers to convert formats of numbers has been held not patentable (*Gottschalk v. Benson*). A method for performing automatic calculations related to a circuit on a computer is not patentable (*In re Gelnovatch*). However, a general purpose computer programmed to vary the brightness of screen pixels to display images more clearly became a specific purpose computer and was held patentable (*In re Alappat*).

How to turn a computer process invention into patentable material is not entirely clear. The computer would likely have to do more than function as a device to store, display, and/or retrieve data. Instead, it may be programmed to implement a significant aspect of the claimed method or play a significant role in implementing the process. However, limiting your preamble to a "computer-implemented method" is not going to be enough to pass the hurdle. Instead, you may want to incorporate specific hardware limitations into individual method steps. As to a possible alternative to reciting physical hardware in a method claim, consider describing the elements using means-plus-function format. Also consider diversifying your claims using Beauregard claims that cover a computer-readable medium such as a storage device.

Medical Procedures
Although medical procedures can be patented, it does not make much sense to try to patent them. There is a special statute that exempts health care providers from infringement liability for performing medical procedures. (35 U.S.C. §287(c).) However, this same statute does not say anything about medical devices—so you could enforce a patent that covers your medical device.

E-Commerce

Process claims are often seen with e-commerce inventions that can be broadly defined as computer-implemented inventions that are directed to methods of doing business (often selling or buying goods and services) over the Internet. For example, when you go online to bid on some item or book a hotel, that computer-implemented process, without a doubt, has been patented by someone at one point in time.

NOTE: *Pay particular attention to the definition of a process.*
You should pay particular attention to the definition of a process including a new use of a known process, machine, manufacture, composition of matter, or material. Inventors often needlessly assume that because something is old in the art, they cannot patent a newly discovered use for that old thing. For example, if you discover that some old composition for potassium metaphosphate is useful for removing alluvium deposits in water systems, you can patent this newly discovered use. What you would have to do is write a claim directly to that new use. (You will learn how to draft claims in a later chapter.) You would not be able to claim the composition of potassium metaphosphate since that composition has already been discovered, but it is perfectly acceptable to claim your newly discovered use for that old composition.

Machines, Manufactures, and Compositions of Matter

The last three categories—machines, manufactures, and compositions of matter—all define *things* rather than actions. A *machine* is defined as a concrete thing consisting of parts, or certain devices and combination of devices. Examples of machines include cars, telephones, and computers. A *manufacture* is the production of useful articles from raw or prepared materials by giving to these materials new forms, qualities, properties, or combinations. This category is sometimes also referred to as an *article of manufacture*. Examples include things such as desks, cabinets, and screwdrivers. You can distinguish an article of manufacture from a machine because manufactures do not have working parts as their primary feature. A *composition of matter* is a composition of two or more substances and all composite articles, whether they are the results of chemical union, mechanical mixture, or they are gases. In biotechnology, composition of matter includes chemical structures and formulations of drugs, genes, and proteins.

The types of things that you can seek to patent are broad. In fact, the Supreme Court has stated that Congress intended statutory subject matter to "include anything under the sun that is made by man." (*Diamond v. Chakrabarty,* 447 U.S. 303 (1980).)

Combination of Known Elements that Yield Predictable Results

You can also take elements that are already known and combine them in a novel way. This novel combination is patentable. However, not only must the combination be one that has not previously been disclosed, the combination must also be nonobvious to someone skilled in your art. The combination of familiar elements is likely to be obvious when it does not more than yield predictable results. (see *KSR International v. Teleflex, Inc.,* 127 S. Ct. 1727, 1739 (2007).)

Example:

Agrizap owned the '636 patent that related to a method and apparatus for electrocuting pests, such as rats. The invention operated by sensing the presence of a pest with a resistive switch. When the pest made contact with a high voltage electrode and a reference electrode, its body completed an electric circuit that triggered a generator that produced a voltage to kill the pest. Agrizap had sold a commercial apparatus containing every element of the '636 patent, except that it used a mechanical switch instead of a resistive switch to complete its circuit. This commercial apparatus was also sold for more than a year before Agrizap applied for its '636 patent, so that it could be considered prior art under patent laws. Although the commercial embodiment does not disclose the resistive switch, such a switch was disclosed by two other prior art patents. Thus, the use of an animal body as a resistive switch to complete a circuit was known in the art. The court held that the '636 patent was invalid based on obviousness even though no single piece of prior art disclosed each of the elements of the '636 patent.

WHAT IS NOT PATENTABLE

While the Supreme Court stated that "anything under the sun that is made by man is patentable," this famous quotation does have limits.

First, the United States Code requires that the subject matter sought to be patented must be a *useful* invention. (35 U.S.C. §101.) This is technically called *utility* and is discussed throughout the book.

Second, you cannot patent things that you find as they *exist in nature.* For example, if you discovered a new mineral in the earth, you would not be able to patent the mineral unless you made some type of alteration to it (such as by genetic engineering). Similarly, while you would not be able to obtain protection on a new, naturally occurring protein or chemical compound, a patent could be obtained on *purified* forms of the protein or chemical compound. This is the reason that in patents to such compositions you will see words like "a purified," "an isolated," "a substantially pure," or "a biologically pure" product or compound to distinguish them from naturally occurring, nonstatutory subject matter. However, the mere isolation of a product that occurs in nature but is purer than its natural equivalent is unpatentable unless there is an unexpected effect due to such isolation.

Akin to not being able to patent things that exist in nature, courts have also held that you cannot patent *ideas, laws of nature,* and *natural phenomena.* Thus, scientific ideas like Einstein's $E=mc^2$ or Newton's law of gravity would not be patentable. However, while the idea itself is not patentable, a new device by which it may be made practically useful would be.

Printed matter per se is not proper subject matter for protection by patent. An exception exists, however, when the printed matter has physical significance and is incorporated appropriately into a claim. For example, layout marks on a headband or physical demarcations on magnetic storage media have been held to constitute statutory subject matter.

NOTE: *Descriptive material, such as music, literature, art, photographs, and arrangements or compilations of facts or data that are merely stored to be read or outputted by a computer, without any functional relationship to the computer, is not a process, machine, manufacture, or composition of matter.*

LENGTH OF A PATENT

If you obtain a utility or plant patent on your invention, your patent will last for a period of twenty years from the earliest effective U.S. filing date of your patent application. The term for design patents is shorter—fourteen years.

The earliest effective filing date of your application will be the date that you file your first regular U.S. patent application, even if you file an earlier *provisional application* or a subsequent *continuation application.* Both of these types of applications are discussed in later chapters.

WHEN TO APPLY FOR A PATENT

Assuming you have weighed all the factors and have decided that it is worthwhile to seek patent protection on your invention, you should apply for your patent before you disclose your invention to the public. While you will learn that in the United States you can disclose your invention (such as by publishing it in your favorite journal or marketing it) for up to a year prior to the time you file for a patent application, the laws in foreign jurisdictions are usually not going to be as kind. Most foreign jurisdictions bar you from obtaining a patent once you have disclosed your invention to the public. Unless you want to forgo patent rights in foreign countries, apply for your U.S. patent as soon as possible and before you disclose your invention to the public.

THE WORK INVOLVED WITH OBTAINING A PATENT

You will read the term *patent prosecution,* or simply *prosecution,* of your patent application in this book many times. This is different from the prosecution that you might associate with the police, trials, or any breaking of the law. In the world of patents, the term prosecution has to do with not only preparing and filing your patent application, but also what occurs after such filing. It is *all* the work that is involved with obtaining a patent.

After you file your patent application, there will be an exchange between you and the patent office regarding your application. For example, the patent office may send you what is called an *office action,* in which they reject some or all of the claims in your application and then set out a list of their reasons. You will then have to respond to this action in the form of a letter, in which you provide reasons why the PTO is wrong. Alternatively, you will have to amend your claims to bring them in line with what the PTO wants. This type of exchange between you and the PTO is referred to as *prosecution.*

HIRING AN ATTORNEY OR AGENT

As you will see in the chapters to come, probably the toughest job in the patent process is going to be dealing with all of the scientific literature (called *prior art*) that already exists relating to your invention. A knowledge of this prior art and how your invention differs from it will be very important as you distinguish your invention from the prior art. The best person to deal with distinguishing an invention from what others have written in the field is the inventor him- or herself—not a patent attorney or agent who is less familiar with the field pertaining to the invention. In that respect, you not only can write your own application, but are probably the best person to do so.

Choosing a Patent Attorney or Agent

If you later decide that you are running into problems with the prosecution of your application, you can always consult a patent attorney or agent for advice, probably reducing your costs by doing a lot of the work yourself. In fact, if you decide to obtain an attorney or agent to write and prosecute your application even after finishing this book, you will still be ahead in learning about the process of prosecuting your application. This knowledge will keep you better informed about the patent process so that you can make wise decisions in assisting your attorney or agent.

Both patent attorneys and agents are registered with the PTO and are legally capable of representing you before this office and handling the prosecution of your application. The difference between the two is that patent attorneys are also registered to practice law in at least one state. This means that patent attorneys have a qualification that agents do not—they have been prepared in areas of law, such as contracts and the like, that are offered by law schools.

Given that a considerable amount of prosecution of your patent application involves dealing with laws, rules, and regulations, this could give a patent attorney an advantage over an agent when it comes time to argue legal points regarding your application. However, there are also some excellent patent agents who are considerably better versed—particularly in patent law—than most patent attorneys.

Whether you choose a patent attorney or an agent to assist you, you should choose one who has familiarity with your scientific discipline. If your invention relates to the chemical field, it would be better to choose an attorney or agent who has a chemical scientific background and experience in the chemical arts rather than one who has a mechanical background.

You should inquire into his or her level of experience with obtaining patents in your field. The following are legitimate questions to ask:

- How many patent applications have you written in my field?

- How many patents have you obtained?

You should look at the cost of your patent attorney or agent. Patent attorneys will generally cost more than agents. Also, a patent attorney or agent with considerable experience in obtaining patents will be more expensive than one with less experience.

Obtaining a patent involves more than just writing your application. It also involves a lengthy process with the PTO. The length of time will depend on each individual case. Even if an agent or attorney can offer you a ballpark figure of how much the process will cost, you must remember that this is only an estimate given the uncertainty of what type of obstacles you are going to incur as your attorney or agent prosecutes your application.

INVENTION PROMOTION FIRMS

Invention promotion firms are the ones you hear on radio claiming that they will determine the worth of your invention, and then help you patent and market your invention. They usually operate in two phases—first, charging customers about $900 for assessments of proposed inventions; and, then offering further services (e.g., patenting, promotion, etc.) for fees ranging from $5,000 to $45,000. They use sophisticated sales techniques, and always promise huge profits to inventors.

I can not state this emphatically enough—stay as far away from these types of firms as possible! I have received many calls from small inventors who have informed me that such firms have scammed them out of thousands of dollars with nothing to show for it. If you do not believe me, then look up information on a current class action lawsuit against such a firm (*Federal Trade Commission v. International Product Design, Inc.*) for a detailed analysis of how these firms scam people. The defendants in that case used an invention promotion scheme designed to persuade consumers to spend tens of thousands of dollars for worthless services by falsely representing that their ideas have been expertly assessed and have market potential that will likely net them huge profits. In short, if it sounds too good to be true, it probably is. If you hire anyone to help you patent your invention, hire a patent agent or attorney directly and be very cautious of these all-in-one invention promotion firms.

KEEP INVENTING AND IMPROVING YOUR INVENTION

It has been said more than once that the second time around is always easier. If you have come up with one patented invention, you are probably capable of coming up with more. So my advice to you is to keep inventing. Some of your inventions will be worth more than others and hopefully you will come upon that one invention that is the jackpot.

Sometimes your new inventions will be improvements upon your old inventions, which is acceptable. You can patent improvements upon an existing patented invention if there are enough differences to make the improvements patentably distinct. If you want more information on what makes an invention *patentably distinct,* you can look at Chapter 23 where the prohibition against double patenting of an invention is discussed.

Patenting improvements of an existing invention can lead to additional patents for you and possibly more patents that you can then exploit for money. Sometimes these improvement patents are even more successful than the earlier, base technology patents. Moreover, by improving on your earlier existing technology, you will be helping to keep competitors from making these improvements. Your goal should be to create an exclusive technology niche for yourself.

These improvement patents are sometimes referred to as *picket fence patents,* which—as the name suggests—are used to fence in, or surround, your core patent (or even patents owned by someone else if your improvement is on that patented technology). By obtaining picket fence patents, you prevent your competitors from designing around your core technology. This is important because if your competitor finds a way to design around your technology, he or she will be free to sell his or her products without having to worry about your patent rights.

KEEP GOOD RECORDS

You should keep good records of your inventive process. Unlike abroad, the United States is still a *first-to-invent country.* What this means is that you will be entitled to a patent on your invention vis-à-vis any third party who was later in time than you in respect to the inventive process. This is true whether or not the third party got to the patent office quicker than you for the invention. However, the catch is that you must be able to document that you were the first inventor.

There are really two types of records that you should keep. Your first type of record is the *laboratory notebook.* Include everything from test results to your theories or conclusions in your laboratory notebook. There are two very important reasons to do this. The first reason is that such information can become vital toward proving your date of invention if this becomes an issue in a patent dispute years down the line in court. Another important reason is that good records will keep you organized. Few of us have the capacity to recall what we have done years earlier. Keeping good records will allow you to do this.

As you prepare your notebook, it is a good idea to follow these points.

- Date each page.

- Use a bound notebook.

- Do not erase any entries or tear any pages out of your notebook.

- Start your subsequent day's work on a new page.

- It is also a good idea to have each page of your notebook read and then signed by two witnesses. It is best to have people who do not have a close familial relationship to you act as witnesses. Your witnesses should be over the age of twenty-one, and should also be someone who has the necessary technical expertise to understand what you wrote. This is because the witness may be called into court, not to just verify that you made the entry, but also to substantiate the facts and nature of your work.

Two companies that sell laboratory notebooks are:

- Scientific Notebook Company
  www.snco.com; and,

- Fisher Scientific
  https://www1.fishersci.com/index.jsp.

The second type of record that you should keep is something called the *invention disclosure form* that records all information relevant to the conception and development of your invention.

Label any Products You Sell with Your Patent Number
It is very important that you have your manufacturer label all of your products covered by your patent with the word "Patent" or the abbreviation "Pat" together with the number of your patent. If you cannot directly label your product because of the character of your product, then you should label the packaging of your product in this way.

The reason why labeling is so important is because there is a special statute (35 U.S.C. §287) that specifically says you can only recover damages from the time that you give an infringer notice of infringement if your goods are not labeled as specified above. For example, let's say that you fail to label goods covered by your patent claims. Several years later, you discover that Infringer X is selling your product. Since you did not label your product, you have forgone any chance to obtain damages from Infringer X until you actually give notice to him or her about the infringement. You have forgone the chance to collect damages for the several years Infringer X was using your patent without paying you.

NOTE: *If you sell a component that is not specifically covered by your patent claims, but which is used in combination with other components to form a device that is covered by your patent, you should similarly mark the component. In this case, you can say "For Use under U.S. XXXX." You should not specifically state that such component is covered by your patent when it is not because 35 U.S.C. §292 prohibits the marking of a product with a patent number when it is actually not patented.*

FURTHER INFORMATION

There are several main sources of laws that you should be able to consult when you have questions regarding patent prosecution of your application, including the following:

- ✪ *Title 35 of the United States Code.* These are the broad-based laws enacted by Congress that guide the PTO in enacting more detailed laws governing patent prosecution. They are sometimes referred to as the *Patent Laws.* You can find these laws on the PTO website at:
  www.uspto.gov/web/offices/pac/mpep/consolidated_laws.pdf.

- ✪ *Title 37 of the Code of Federal Regulations.* These are often referred to as the *Patent Rules* and are somewhat more detailed than the Patent Laws. These rules can be found on the PTO website at:
  www.uspto.gov/web/offices/pac/mpep/consolidated_rules.pdf.

✪ *Manual of Patent Examining Procedure.* This is referred to as the *MPEP* for short, and is a detailed rule book that you will inevitably consult as you prosecute your application. This is, in effect, the bible of the PTO. If your examiner needs guidance, he or she will consult the MPEP. Therefore, it also makes sense for you to consult the MPEP. This book is so important that you should go online now and start to familiarize yourself with its organization. The MPEP can be found online at: www.uspto.gov/web/offices/pac/mpep/mpep.htm.

Other Tools for the Patent Holder

To maximize the protection and utilization of your patented invention, you should consider various forms of intellectual property protection in addition to relying on the rights provided by your patent. You can use a *trademark* to distinguish products sold under the scope of your patent. *Domain names* can also be used to strengthen your business or product launch. *Trade secrets* will protect information developed in the course of manufacturing and marketing your patented invention. *Confidential agreements* can prevent the loss of your patent rights altogether.

Even if you find that patenting your invention does not make sense from a market viewpoint or you determine that obtaining a patent will be unlikely, this does not mean that you need to give up on making money off your idea. Lots of products have been very successful in the marketplace without patent protection. What makes these products successful is usually due to good marketing. Other forms of intellectual property can be invaluable to such effective marketing. In this section, you learn about various other forms of intellectual property protection that you can use either in conjunction with a patent or in place of patent protection.

COPYRIGHTS

Copyright protection extends to just about any original work of authorship. Things that you can copyright include books, computer software, music, choreography, motion pictures, photographs, maps, three-dimensional objects, and even buildings.

Obtaining a copyright is inexpensive, and you should seek copyright registration for any eligible work. Such protection will be particularly useful for software inventors. Although relatively cheap, remedies for copyright infringement are surprisingly harsh. Not only is there an automatic level of damages called *statutory damages,* which can run as high as $150,000 for each work infringed if the copyright owner elects not to rely upon actual damages, as well as *additional profits* of the infringer, but if someone willfully infringes a copyright—such as by copying or distributing copies of one or more copyrighted works that have a total value in excess of $1,000—that person also risks criminal prosecution.

Software copyright owners should consider supplementing their rights with technology that prevents copying. If you have a copyright on a software invention, you will probably quickly come to realize that stopping people from copying your invention can be a logistical nightmare given new tools like the Internet, where programs can be downloaded and distributed in a matter of seconds. Therefore, you will want to consider some of the new technologies that make such copying more difficult.

Of course, implementing such technological measures does not guarantee that your work will not be copied. As soon as DVDs were encrypted with a program called *Content Scrambling System* (CSS), a program called DeCSS came out that decrypts an encrypted DVD. Still, such anti-copying measures can go a long way in the protection of intellectual property, as there are also special statutes that impose both civil and criminal penalties against people who try to circumvent your anti-copying technology measures.

There are many books and other resources that can help you with copyright registration. A valuable website and very useful resource is the United States Copyright Office at www.copyright.gov.

Copyright vs. Patents

There are several major differences between copyright and patent law.

Fees

The fees for obtaining a copyright are very small (about $35 for your application), whereas the fees for obtaining a patent can be very large. For example, if you hire a law firm to file your patent application, you can expect to pay at least $5,000 just for the preparation. Prosecution of your patent application will cost you even more. In the end, a typical patent can cost between $10,000 and $35,000 or more, depending on the complexity of the invention. Of course, if you do it yourself, this price will be much less.

Difficulty to Obtain

Obtaining a patent is much more difficult than obtaining a copyright. The subject matter that you seek to patent must undergo a rigorous examination procedure with the Patent and Trademark Office concerning issues such as *novelty*. This is not the case with copyrights. In fact, you can copyright something even though you were not the first person to create the work, as long as you have not copied the work from any other person. In patent law, however, there are statutory bars that prevent you from patenting subject matter that was already in existence before your invention.

Term

A work that is created on or after January 1, 1978, is automatically protected under copyright law from the moment of its creation. The term generally lasts for the author's lifetime, plus an additional seventy years. The term for patents is much shorter, generally twenty years.

Ideas

You cannot obtain a copyright on an idea. You are only allowed to obtain protection on the expression of that idea onto some tangible medium. This prevents others from copying and infringing on your exclusive rights. Thus, if you come up with a new business method, you could write that idea onto paper and prevent others from copying the explanation of your method. However, your business method idea alone is not copyrightable. In comparison, the same business method alone could be the subject of a patent.

Independent Creation

A major disadvantage of copyrights in comparison to patents is that a copyright does not prevent someone from independently coming to your same creative expression so long as there has been no copying of your own expression. This is not the case with patents where a patent owner can stop a potential patent infringer even if the infringer is unaware of the patent claims and somehow comes up later on with the same invention.

Example:

Joe thinks of a great poem and writes it down. Amazingly, Anne—without any knowledge of Joe's poem—thinks of the same poem and also writes it down. Under such circumstances, Joe can not sue Anne for copyright infringement because Anne's creation was independent of Joe's work.

Subject Matter

You cannot obtain a copyright on purely *functional objects*. You could not, for example, seek copyright protection for a new type of screwdriver that you have developed. However, the same screwdriver would be proper subject matter for a patent.

Despite the differences, there is an area of overlap between copyrights and patents. In certain cases, it may be possible to both copyright and patent your invention. For example, an ornamental design may be copyrighted as a work of art. The same design may also be subject matter of a design patent, as long as the design is embedded in an article of manufacture. Computer programs are copyrightable and may also be proper subject material for a patent.

TRADEMARKS

A *trademark* is a word, name, symbol, or logo that you affix to goods in order to distinguish yourself as the source of the goods. The purpose behind trademark law is to allow consumers to identify you as the seller or maker of the goods.

What Can Be Trademarked

American trademark law has historically been based on the premise that you must have actually used a trademark on your goods before you can seek *registration* of your trademark. However, this rule has been considerably relaxed. You can now seek to register a trademark even if you have never affixed it to goods that you sell, as long as you have the *intention* of using your trademark in the future.

Nearly any word, name, or symbol can be trademarked, as long as the word is not merely descriptive of your product and the name is not confusingly similar to any other registered trademark.

For example, you would not be able to seek trademark protection for the word "heater" to identify heaters you sell, but you might be able to trademark the word "takomo" for your heaters.

In addition to words, names, and symbols, it is also possible to seek trademark protection on the packaging and design of your product. This is often referred to as *trade dress*.

It is possible to seek a *design patent* on the design of an article. In this respect, there is some overlap between trademark protection and patent law. However, you would not be able to seek trademark protection on any design feature that is functional in nature. A feature is *functional* if its design is essential to the use or purpose of the article rather than just a means to identify the article. If a feature is functional, you will need to apply for a design patent for protection.

Advantages and Disadvantages of Trademark Protection

The cost of obtaining a trademark (about $275 for each class of goods that you want to register your mark) is considerably more than the cost of obtaining a copyright. There is also an *opposition procedure* in which other owners of trademarks can oppose the registration of your trademark. However, the cost and difficulty of obtaining a trademark is still considerably less in comparison to obtaining a patent on an invention.

Given the relatively minor cost of obtaining a trademark (at least in respect to obtaining a patent), obtain a trademark on anything that you think should be trademarked. This includes the name of your business as well as any products that you sell.

As with copyrights, trademarks have an advantage over patents when it comes to the term of protection. In fact, you can protect a trademark for an infinite term as long as you continually renew your mark with the PTO.

TRADE SECRETS

The *Uniform Trade Secrets Act* defines a *trade secret* as:

> *information, including a formula, pattern, compilation, device, method, technique, or process, that: (i) derives independent economic value, actual or potential, from not being generally known to, and not being readily ascertainable by proper means by, other persons who can obtain economic value from its disclosure or use, and (ii) is the subject of efforts that are reasonable under the circumstances to maintain its secrecy.*

This definition is very broad. In essence, a trade secret is any information that provides a *commercial advantage* that is protected because you take steps to keep such information secret.

A number of factors are used to determine whether something is a trade secret. These factors include the following:

- the extent to which your information is known outside of your business;

- the extent to which the information is known by employees inside your company;

- the extent of the measures taken by you to guard the secrecy of your information;

- the value of the information to your business and your competitors;

- the amount of effort or money expended by you in developing your information; and,

✪   the ease or difficulty with which information can be properly acquired or duplicated by others.

Secrecy   As stated above, one of the requirements of a trade secret is that efforts be taken to keep the subject information secret. If you do not take protective measures, the information will likely not be considered to be a trade secret by a court. The protective measures you can take to keep information a trade secret are limited only by your imagination. One measure might be restricting access to the information.

There are a number of things you can do to keep your valuable information a trade secret. Here are just a few of the most important things.

✪   Restrict Access. One of the most important steps you can take to keep information secret is to insist that people who have access to the information sign confidentiality agreements. Restriction measures might include requiring passwords for access to confidential proprietary information.

✪   Label information as confidential. It is important that you show any outsider—such as a court—that you consider your information to be confidential. The measures above will help in this, but you should also label any such information as "confidential." In any confidential agreements that you use, spell out exactly what information you believe to be confidential.

✪   Use confidentiality agreements. As will be discussed later in the chapter, confidentiality agreements require that parties bound to the agreement keep the designated information in the agreement confidential. In any relationship you have with another party that involves confidential or trade secrets, you should use confidentiality agreements. These types of agreements are probably the number one factor that influences courts when determining whether information is a trade secret.

Trade Secret Protection vs. Patent Protection   Given the things you can protect as a trade secret can be virtually limitless (so long as you maintain secrecy), everything that you can patent will also be something you can protect as a trade secret. The question then becomes, which form of protection is better? There is not an easy answer and the choice is really a business decision.

In some circumstances, you may want to choose a trade secret over patent protection. In other situations, you will want to choose trade secret protection *in addition* to patents. Following are some of the factors you should consider in your decision to add trade secrets to your patent portfolio or to substitute patent protection for trade secrets all together.

Term of Trade Secrets

Trade secrets differ from patents in that a trade secret can last forever as long as the trade secret is not divulged to the public. Patents, on the other hand, have a finite duration (twenty years from the date you file your application). However, you need to ask yourself whether you can keep your property a secret. For example, if your secret is revealed to the public by a disgruntled employee, your trade secret will technically no longer be a trade secret.

Independent Discovery

Trade secrets do not offer protection if some third party independently comes up with your invention, whereas a patent on that invention would still afford you rights against that third party. If what you are protecting is something that can be easily determined by *reverse engineering,* trade secret protection can be uncertain. Reverse engineering is a process of taking a completed product and breaking it down so the manner and method of how it was constructed can be determined and duplicated.

Cost of Procurement

Trade secret protection will cost you less money up front. In fact, there are no associated costs other than the business costs associated with maintaining the secrecy of the trade secret. But such costs over the lifetime of your trade secret could actually cost you more than obtaining a patent if you have to take large measures to ensure the secrecy of your invention.

For example, if you engage in licensing your invention, you will need to take steps in the form of confidentiality agreements to ensure that your licensee does not reveal your trade secret to the world. You will also need employees to sign such agreements if they have access to your trade secret. These administrative steps can be quite costly.

Cost of Enforcement

The costs of enforcing trade secrets against a third party are less than the costs of enforcing your patent rights against a third party. Usually, what you are seeking in trade secret litigation is to enjoin a third party from revealing your secret. This will cost much less than a patent infringement action, which is among the most expensive types of litigation.

Recently, there has been some uncertainty in some courts as to whether a court can legitimately enjoin a third party from disclosing a trade secret, because such restraint might violate the First Amendment. This could leave you with the sole remedy of damages against the third party. In the meantime, your trade secret is revealed and you no longer have trade secret protection for your invention.

Ease of Procurement

Obtaining a patent takes, on average, about twenty-five months. However, you can start protecting something as a trade secret immediately. Many inventions—particularly those in the computer software industry—may have a very short product life cycle. If you believe that it will be just a matter of months before your competitor will come out with an entirely different product that will displace your patented product, then you may be better off going with trade secret protection. In fact, your invention may be displaced in the marketplace even before you are able to obtain your patent and start enforcing it.

Risks of Disclosure

This factor can be an argument *for or against* using trade secrets instead of patents, depending on how you look at it. As discussed earlier, the risk of disclosure of information that is subject to trade secret protection is severe. You will probably lose all protection over the information as a trade secret. But there are also some risks to disclosure of an invention that is the subject of a patent. Once people learn about your invention (either when your patent application is published or when it issues), there is some risk that such people can use your disclosed information to make improvements that they can then patent. Such improvements may be patentable and can thereafter be enforced against you.

Moreover, your competitors may find ways to *design around* the claims of your patent. That is, your competitors might be able to come up with a product that escapes the scope of your patent claims. If your claims are not written to encompass such products, your competitors can legitimately sell those products without worrying about patent infringement.

NOTE: *You may be wondering if you can obtain both a trade secret and a patent for your invention. The answer is no. Patent applications are published eighteen months after they are filed. Once your application is published, it is no longer a trade secret—it is now in the public domain.*

CONFIDENTIALITY AGREEMENTS

Confidentiality agreements, otherwise known as *nondisclosure agreements* (NDAs), are contracts that bind one or both parties to an agreement to keep information secret. If a party breaks the agreement, you can then sue that party in court for a *breach of your contract.*

Confidentiality agreements seem to be common buzzwords in any business dealings in the intellectual property world. Mention sharing information with a third party, and one automatically thinks that a confidentiality agreement is a necessity.

There is nothing wrong with immediately considering the use of a confidentiality agreement any time that you disclose information to some third party. However, it will often be impractical, as well as unnecessary, for the individual inventor to insist upon the use of a confidentiality agreement in certain situations. A goal in this section is to explore some of the situations in which you can do away with a confidentiality agreement, as well as those situations in which you should insist upon such an agreement.

When Not to Use Confidentiality Agreements

Once you have a patent on your invention, you can rest assured that your invention is protected. This is why patents exist. Moreover, if you are an individual inventor who is trying to promote your invention to prospective licensees or buyers, the real world will dictate that you not be in a position to insist upon a confidentiality agreement.

In fact, most companies that an individual inventor approaches with respect to his or her invention will not only refuse to sign a confidentiality agreement, but also will insist that the inventor sign some type of waiver on the company's part of any *breach of confidentiality*. Companies often evaluate the inventions of multiple inventors, but will not be interested in most. They do not want to incur the risk that such inventors will sue the company claiming that there was some breach of a confidentiality agreement.

In short, as an individual inventor, you simply do not have the bargaining power. If you want the company to evaluate your invention, you will simply not be in a position to insist that the company sign a confidentiality agreement. However, if you have a patent in hand, you have protection on your invention.

Most people are not in business to look for inventions to steal. Individual inventors often have an unfounded fear that once they reveal their patented invention, someone will run off and start to use the invention. The great majority of companies are more than aware that you can sue them if they try to steal your patented invention. Most, if not all, will respect your patent.

Further, your patented invention will be worth nothing to anyone if you approach your invention with the state of mind that you must go to extremes to keep it secret. Get your invention out there in the marketplace and exploit it. Any risk that someone could run off with your patented concept is far outweighed by what you will lose if you take no steps to exploit your patented invention.

When to Use Confidentiality Agreements

Even though there are times when you can do away with confidentiality agreements, there are situations in which they can come in very handy and at times are a necessity.

After Patent Filing but Before Patent Issues

If you have filed a patent application but have not yet been issued a patent, then you may want to consider insisting upon a confidentiality agreement.

Prior to Filing a Patent Application

If you have not yet applied for a patent on your invention, then you will want to insist upon a confidentiality agreement before you disclose your invention to some third party. Of course, the better approach in this case would be to apply for that patent before you make the disclosure anyway. This ideal situation may not be a choice for you, as you may need to show your invention to an outside contractor to get your invention to work.

If you do disclose your invention prior to filing a patent application without a confidentiality agreement and someone runs off with your idea, you are not out of luck. If you have kept good records as to how you came up with your invention, then you can use those records to still claim *priority of invention*. However, having a confidentiality agreement will make your task much easier.

One of the best reasons for insisting upon a confidentiality agreement at this stage lies not so much in the risk that someone will steal your invention, but rather the risk that you may jeopardize your ability to obtain a patent on your invention. This will certainly be the case for countries abroad. Most countries abroad follow the rule that once you make your invention public (as by public disclosure), you forgo patent protection. By using a confidentiality agreement, you will not be considered to have disclosed your invention to the public.

While the United States still follows a first-to-invent system and allows you to file your patent application within a year of public disclosure, dates can often be subject to dispute. You can use a confidentiality agreement to your advantage if anyone later tries to claim that you made your invention public more than a year prior to your patent application.

Disclosure of More than Your Patented Invention

Confidentiality agreements can be used for any of your *proprietary information*. There is often a lot more than your patented invention that you want to keep secret. For example, a company will also be concerned about information relating to its underlying business operations, such as financial data, which could signal the strength or weakness of a company. A competitor who knows that a company is in a weakened state may want to drive that company out of business.

The point is that you will need to think about whether you may disclose more than your patented invention. This will be particularly applicable to companies (as opposed to individual inventors). Such companies will often have accumulated a lot of proprietary information that could be revealed to a competitor during discussions related to the commercialization of a patented invention. Some of this information may also be patented, but most of it will exist as a trade secret. These companies should insist upon confidentiality agreements that protect such trade secrets.

As companies build up their patent portfolios and proprietary know-how, there is often not a great way to know exactly what is patented and what is not. Most people, even in a large corporation, are not familiar with all of the proprietary information of the company. For this reason, it is wise to make confidentiality agreements a standard practice before entering into any type of discussions with any third party.

Noncompetition Agreements

Noncompetition agreements have a more drastic effect than nondisclosure agreements. In a noncompetition agreement, the employee agrees not to work for competitors for a specified time period after leaving your company. This effect on the employee is clearly much more restrictive than a nondisclosure agreement, which simply requires that your employee not disclose any proprietary information gained while working for you. Since the effect can be so drastic (e.g., restriction on the livelihood of an employee), various states take a rather suspicious eye toward such agreements. But most states do uphold these agreements, so long as they are limited in duration (i.e., not something extreme, like for the lifetime of your former employee, but rather for a limited term, like one year), geographic scope, and subject matter.

To increase your chances that a noncompetition agreement will be enforced by a court, there are some actions that may prove beneficial. First, you may want to consider writing in the agreement that the employee agrees that he or she will be acquiring confidential information, and generally describing its nature. You may also want to consider giving your employee additional consideration for signing the noncompetition agreement, such as a bonus, which will be viewed favorably by a court should you need to enforce the agreement.

NOTE: *Using boilerplate forms—If you have decided that a confidentiality agreement is in order, you need to know what makes a good confidentiality agreement. There are many boilerplate confidentiality forms available. As with any type of legal form, however, you should put some thought into what the agreement says and the significance of the various clauses.*

Factors to Consider in Drafting a Confidentiality Agreement

Here are some important points to keep in mind as you draft your own confidentiality agreement.

State what is being exchanged in return for confidentiality obligations. This is known in the law as *consideration*. Every contractual agreement must have consideration. In other words, when you enter into an agreement with another party, you must give something of value in return for something of value by the other party. This is usually not a problem since the threshold for consideration is not very high. But you should have some clause that sums up what is being given for what. For example, if you look at the sample confidentiality agreements in Appendix E, you will see language like "now," "therefore," and "for and in consideration of the mutual promises, covenants, provisions and agreements contained herein." This language relates to consideration.

If your confidentiality agreement is being used in the employer-employee context, you might use language such as the following for your consideration clause: "The undersigned acknowledges that during his employment he may receive, or gain access to, the proprietary information of the Company, and in consideration for his employment, terminable at will, as a product manager, the undersigned stipulates and agrees as hereinafter set forth."

Identify the technology to be protected. Confidential information can include more than technical information like your inventions, trade secrets, know-how, techniques, source code, testing methods, processes, formulas and research data. It can also include financial and business information, including customer and supplier lists, product and marketing plans, financial records, and personnel data. You should always specify in the agreement exactly what you consider to be your proprietary information that is subject to the confidentiality agreement. Although some courts may find that a general description of confidential subject matter may include specific information that a company regards as confidential, other courts may not hold the same view. The safest bet is to specifically identify the information that you consider to be confidential.

You can do this in a number of ways. If you have a patent on the technology or a patent application, then you should identify the patent or patent application. If the confidentiality agreement relates to trade secrets in your company regarding some type of technology, then you should also identify the technology as specifically as possible. For example, if it will be necessary for you to disclose secret information relating to the operation of your new DNA sequencing machine, then you should specifically identify your DNA sequencing machine in the agreement.

Being specific as to the proprietary information that you regard as confidential serves another purpose, as well. You will aid employees of the other company in knowing exactly what is to be considered confidential. In other words, it will give guidance to members of the organization in ensuring the confidentiality of the information.

Purpose. You may want to include a clause in your confidentiality agreement that states that each party shall not use any confidential information of the other party for any purpose other than evaluation of the contemplated transaction.

Use two-way confidentiality agreements if appropriate. If both parties to the confidentiality agreement may be exchanging confidential material, then you should use a two-way mutual agreement. Doing so will also achieve better harmony between each party because no one will feel left out.

Consider an inadvertent disclosure clause. If you are the company that is required to keep information secret, you may want to consider an *inadvertent disclosure clause* that relieves you of liability for accidental disclosure of confidential information. A sample clause you could use is the following:

> "Neither party shall be liable in damages for any inadvertent disclosure of proprietary information where at least a

reasonable degree of care has been exercised, provided that upon discovery of such inadvertent disclosure it shall have endeavored to correct the effects thereof and to prevent any further inadvertent disclosure."

Avoid indemnification against third party liability. Some confidentiality agreements state that a receiving party must indemnify the disclosing party against the improper disclosure of proprietary information owned by third parties. An example of such a clause might be the following:

> "The receiving party recognizes that certain confidential information may be subject to a duty to other parties to maintain the confidentiality of such information and to use it only for certain limited purposes, and the receiving party agrees to indemnify the disclosing party against any liability to such other parties attributable to any breach of this Agreement."

You should reject any such clause because you simply will have no idea what information is subject to this clause.

Require oral or visual information to be identified as confidential in writing. Sometimes the interaction between two parties will involve a situation where the proprietary information can not be identified in the agreement itself. For example, there may be an exchange of employees to the plants of each company. What may be considered proprietary may actually be something that employees come into visual or oral contact with. The agreement should specify that any such oral or visual disclosures of proprietary information must be declared as proprietary at the time it is disclosed, and that it must also be summarized in a writing that is marked as proprietary and delivered to the receiving party within a reasonable time period.

In large organizations, have contact people responsible for receiving confidential information. It will be a good idea to identify by name any individuals who are responsible for disclosing and receiving proprietary information. This will help to ensure that personnel at the large organization is indeed aware that information is to be kept confidential.

No rights granted. Be wary of letting your confidentiality agreement become a licensing agreement where it could be construed as giving rights to the other party to use your intellectual property. Thus your agreement should provide that nothing in the agreement shall be construed as grating any rights under any patent, copyright or other intellectual property right of the disclosing party, nor shall the agreement grant the receiving party any rights in or to the confidential information other than the limited right to review such confidential information solely for the purpose of evaluation of the contemplated transaction.

Irreparable harm. It is a good idea to have the receiving party to confidentiality admit that improper use or disclosure of confidential information will cause irreparable harm to the disclosing party. This is important because a disclosing party typically enforces a confidentiality agreement by seeking an injunction to prevent imminent disclosure of confidential information. This provision will make it easier to obtain such relief since a showing of irreparable harm is a prerequisite for such relief.

Markings. You may want to require that all information considered confidential be marked as such. However, be careful about including such a clause because it may mean that anything you forget to specifically label as confidential will not be considered confidential.

Need to know. You may want to provide that confidential information will be disclosed only to persons who need to know the information and only to the extent necessary to affect the purposes set out in the agreement. You can further provide that information under the agreement will only be shared with third parties that have an obligation to maintain confidentiality (such as attorneys, accountants, etc.), and an enforceable confidential relationship that is as strong as the provisions in your agreement.

Confidentiality Agreements for the Employee

In addition to the clauses above, there are some other issues that should be contained in a confidentiality agreement signed by an employee.

First, limit your liability for confidential information an employee may bring to you as an employer. An employer will want to ensure that its own liability is limited with respect to confidential information that the new employee will bring into the job. A clause such as the following can be helpful in this respect:

> "The undersigned represents that he does not have in his possession any written materials embodying information known or claimed to be the proprietary or confidential information of any other person, and further represents that he has not removed any written material from the premises of a former employer without the written consent of that employer. The undersigned further represents that to his knowledge his employment with the Company will not require him to use or disclose any proprietary or confidential information of any former employer."

An employer should also place in the agreement the right to let any subsequent employers of the employee know about confidential material that the company regards as proprietary. A clause such as the following can be helpful in this respect:

> "The undersigned agrees that the Company may inform any person or entity subsequently employing him, or evidencing an intention to employ him, of the nature of the information it asserts to be proprietary, and may inform said person or entity of the existence of this Agreement and the terms hereof, and provide to said person or entity a copy of this Agreement."

Employers who hire employees involved in the technical inventing process should require that their employees agree—as a condition of employment—to assign to the employer all rights to inventions conceived by the employee while at work, or in subject matters related to work, or while using any resources of the employer. Failure to do this may lead to unexpected ownership arguments down the line. The last thing you want as an employer is to find one of your employees claiming ownership to some invention that he or she developed while working full-time at your expense.

Also wise is to include assignments of other forms of IP. For example, the employment agreement may require an employee to identify any works that he or she created prior to employment and specifically agree that any IP created during this employment belong to the company. As an example, the contract might include language that specifically states that if the employee uses any software she created before her employment at the company or places it on her work computer, then the company has an irrevocable license to use that software. This type of clause can eliminate the threat of future copyright infringement claims as well as protect the company's profits.

Here are a couple sample clauses that you might use for your employee. (See 81 Cal. L. Rev. 595, 599 (1993) for other possible clauses.)

> "The undersigned agrees that he will disclose to the Company all inventions, improvements, software, processes, ideas, and innovations (hereinafter referred to, for convenience only, as "Discoveries"), made or conceived by him, whether or not patentable or copyrightable, either solely or in concert with others, and whether or not made or conceived during working hours, during the period of this employment, which (a) relate to the existing or contemplated business or research activities of the Company; (b) result from the use of the Company's proprietary information, facilities, or resources; or (c) arise out of or result from work performed for the Company. The undersigned further agrees to keep full and complete records concerning the development of discoveries as above defined and to tender such records to the company upon request."

> "The undersigned hereby assigns to the Company his entire right, title, and interest in and to all discoveries as above defined, which he may develop or originate alone or with others, and the undersigned agrees that all such discoveries and inventions shall be the exclusive property of the Company, and are reserved for exclusive use and benefit of the Company. The undersigned further agrees to assist the Company in obtaining and enforcing patents, copyrights, and/or any other statutory or common-law protection available as to such discovery or invention whether under foreign or domestic law. The undersigned further agrees to execute all documents deemed necessary or advisable by the Company for use in applying for or obtaining patents, copyrights, or any other statutory or common-law protection for such discoveries and inventions, and for enforcing same. The undersigned acknowledges that his obligations under this Paragraph shall continue beyond the termination of

his employment, but that after such termination the Company will compensate him at a reasonable rate for time actually spent at the Company's request for such assistance."

Sample Confidentiality Agreement

You can find two sample confidentiality agreements in Appendix E. These agreements will obviously need to be adjusted depending on the context that you are using your confidentiality agreement. They do not include every provision discussed above and should not be used as boilerplate forms without any thought put into the provisions.

JOINT OWNERSHIP AGREEMENTS

If you own your patent with someone else, you will want to have an agreement with your co-owners relating to your patent rights. Such agreements are commonly referred to as *joint ownership agreements* (JOA).

One of the most significant issues that you will want to resolve in a JOA is how your invention will be *commercialized*. The obvious issue here is how any profits from your patented invention will be distributed.

Without an agreement that specifies how any proceeds will be divided, the law will assume that either you or your co-owner can do whatever he or she wants with the invention without any financial accounting to the co-owner. The United States Code provides that either of the joint owners of a patent may make, use, or sell a patented invention without the consent of and without accounting to the other joint owners. (35 U.S.C. §262.)

Example:

Dave worked for over three years coming up with a new, improved hammer. Tom worked a mere two weeks, but was included as an inventor since he did contribute to one of the patent claims. Even though Tom's contribution was small, Tom could commercialize and collect profits from the sale of the new hammer without any duty to account to Dave for those profits. The solution for Dave should be a joint ownership agreement that spells out how any profits from the commercialization of the invention will be distributed.

Requirements for Obtaining a Patent

This chapter introduces the most important statutory requirements that can bar you from obtaining a patent on your invention. These requirements are absolutely vital for you to understand and may also be somewhat foreign to you at this point in time. The requirements are:

- ✪ novelty;

- ✪ obviousness;

- ✪ written description requirement;

- ✪ enablement;

- ✪ best mode; and,

- ✪ utility.

As you read through this chapter, remember this: your goal is not just to write a patent application and obtain a patent. Instead, your goal is to obtain a high-quality patent for your invention. A *high-quality* patent is one that gives you the broadest protection for your invention and can withstand invalidity attacks from your competitors. The patentability requirements that you will learn about in this chapter are not only necessary from the standpoint of obtaining your patent, but can be used later to attack the validity of any patent that you obtain. These requirements are very important and are referred to throughout the book.

NOVELTY

As the name suggests, *novelty* has to do with whether your invention is new. If your invention is an old concept, then it makes sense that the government will not give you an exclusive monopoly in the form of a patent. Patents are granted to inventors in return for the exchange of new information that can advance the technological body of knowledge in this country. The government is not interested in giving away patents in exchange for information that is already known.

You can think of novelty as requiring that your invention must not have been known before. However, patent law is much more specific about what this term means. You will be at an advantage if you can start thinking about this in terms of patent law. Under patent law, novelty requires that there is no prior art that anticipates your invention.

Prior art is discussed in the next section. You can also find a detailed discussion on each of the prior art sections in Chapter 13. For now, you can limit your understanding about prior art to what is contained in the next section. But if you get a rejection of your patent application on the basis of one of the prior art sections, you will appreciate the more detailed discussion in Chapter 13 (as well as the tips contained there for overcoming such rejections).

If during your search you uncover prior art related to your invention, the next question to ask is, *Does this prior art anticipate your invention?* If the prior art that you uncover does anticipate your invention, your invention is not novel. If the prior art does not anticipate your invention, your invention will be patentable, so long as your invention is not obvious with respect to this prior art. (The meaning of *obviousness* is explained later in this chapter.)

Prior Art   Prior art can include printed material, like patents and publications, or it can include things like public knowledge and use or sale of your invention. Prior art can be a patent or publication that discusses an invention similar or related to yours. It can also be general public knowledge, public use, or public sale of such an invention.

Patents

A U.S. or foreign patent is prior art if it is:

- ✪ issued before your date of invention; or,

- ✪ issued more than one year before your U.S. filing date.

A U.S. patent issued to another is also prior art if its U.S. filing date precedes your date of invention, even if it does not issue until after the filing date (or patent issue date) of your claims under examination.

Publications

A printed U.S. or foreign publication is prior art if it is:

- ✪ published before your date of invention; or,

- ✪ published more than a year before the filing date of your application.

A U.S. published patent application is also prior art if its U.S. filing date precedes your date of invention. The PTO takes the position that Internet materials are printed, so long as they include publication dates. (MPEP §2128.)

Public Knowledge, Use, or Sale of Your Invention

Any knowledge or use of your invention by others in the United States before your invention date constitutes prior art. Any public use or sale of your invention more than one year before the date of your patent application also constitutes prior art. (Chapter 4 fully explains how to search for prior art.)

Anticipation

As stated, the only time that prior art may bar your invention from being patented is when *anticipation* is directly related to how you draft your claims. Lack of novelty is when such prior art anticipates your invention.

You define your invention in the claims sections of your patent application. You will learn how to define your invention by writing claims in Chapter 6. For now, all you really need to know is that each of your claims sets the *boundaries* of your invention.

For example, if your invention is a table, you might have one claim that claims the table with legs and a top. In such a case, you are claiming a table made up of legs and a top. The legs and top are said to be *elements* or *limitations* of your claim, because they are the features that you list in your claim. If you were to have a second claim to the table having legs, a top, and an enamel surface, then this claim would have an additional limitation—the enamel surface.

You look at claims individually for anticipation purposes. A claim is anticipated only if each and every element as set forth in your claim is found, either expressly or inherently, in a prior art reference. In other words, anticipation requires that a piece of prior art (a patent, publication, sale, or use) discloses each and every limitation of your claimed invention. The invention described by the prior art must be shown in as complete detail as is contained in your claim. Additionally, the reference must not only disclose all elements of your claim, but it must also disclose the elements arranged as in your claim. Although the elements must be arranged as required by your claim, identical terminology is not required. (MPEP §2131.)

It is permissible for your examiner to find that a prior art reference inherently discloses an element of your claim, even though the disclosure does not come right out and explicitly state the element.

Example:

Abbott Labs had a claim directed to its new product inhalation anesthetic sevoflurane (a composition claim). Unfortunately it had to recall the product because use of the product resulted in excess acid buildup. However, its scientists soon discovered that adding water to its solution would stabilize Lewis acids. A prior art reference, however, disclosed that water could be combined with sevoflurance but had not realized that doing so would prevent acid buildup. The reference would still prevent Abbott from obtaining a patent on the product because the reference discloses the product inherently. It does not matter here that the properties of the product were not disclosed. Abbott would only be able to patent use claims directed to this new use.

Claim Charts

In considering whether your claims are anticipated and therefore invalidated by prior art, it is helpful to develop a *claim chart*. In a claim chart, you make two columns, one for the invention as described in your patent claim and one for the reference you are considering. When you write the claim in the left column, you divide it into its elements or limitations. On the right side of your chart, you can list the elements that are disclosed in your prior art reference. If your claim reads on the prior art in that it contains all of the elements disclosed in the prior art reference, it is invalid. *Reading on* means that there is a 1:1 correspondence between the items in the two columns of the chart.

If you uncover a prior art reference that has a 1:1 correspondence with your claimed invention, you will need to think of an element to add to your claimed invention that is not contained in the prior art reference in order to differentiate your claimed invention and thereby negate such anticipation. If you find it impossible to do this, then your invention is not patentable the way it is. You will then want to reconsider whether you should even try to obtain a patent on it at this point in time.

OBVIOUSNESS

In addition to a lack of novelty, a claimed invention is unpatentable if the differences between your claimed invention and the prior art are such that the subject matter as a whole would have been *obvious* at the time your invention was made to a person having *ordinary skill in the art* (a person skilled in your field). In short, the PTO can take anything that qualifies as prior art, combine it with any other prior art, and then reject your claimed invention on the basis that it is an obvious invention—even though neither one of such references alone would anticipate your invention.

Obviousness is a potent tool for the examination of your application because the examiner does not have to find that each particular reference, such as one individual science report, anticipates your claim. The examiner *would* have to reject your invention on the basis of a lack of novelty. Instead, the examiner only needs to find that all of the references combined teach or suggest your invention.

Any reference that your examiner uses as prior art, however, must be *analogous* to the art of your invention. A reference is considered analogous and, therefore, available for use in an obviousness rejection, if it is either:

❂   within the field of your endeavor; or,

❂   reasonably pertinent to the particular problem with which your invention was involved.

The requirement that prior art references be analogous to the art of your own invention is a requirement unique to obviousness. It is not a requirement for the purposes of whether a single reference anticipates your invention under the concept of anticipation above. In determining whether a single reference bars your invention under anticipation, the reference may be from an entirely different field than your invention or may be directed to an entirely different problem from the one addressed by you, yet the reference will still anticipate if it explicitly or inherently discloses every limitation recited in your claims.

You will learn much more about obviousness in Chapter 13. Note that not finding any one reference that does not anticipate your invention may end your inquiry for novelty, but not for obviousness purposes. Keep both novelty and obviousness in mind as you do your patent searching in Chapter 4.

WRITTEN DESCRIPTION REQUIREMENT

The *written description* requirement is the first of three requirements under the first paragraph of 35 U.S.C. §112. The second and third requirements, *enablement* and *best mode,* are discussed in the next two sections.

The written description requirement prevents you from claiming subject matter that was not described in your patent application as filed. In fact, it prevents you from doing anything to the claims of your patent application that are not supported by your written description in your application as you file it.

The essential goal of the written description requirement is to clearly convey the subject matter that you have invented. The requirement for an adequate disclosure ensures that the public receives something in return for the exclusionary rights that are granted to you by a patent. The government will give you a patent, but in return, wants you to disclose your invention to the public. This disclosure adds to the scientific body of knowledge that will advance technology.

To satisfy the written description requirement, your patent application must describe the claimed invention in sufficient detail so that one skilled in the art can reasonably conclude that you have possession of your claimed invention. This is done by describing your invention with all of its limitations using such descriptive means as words, structures, figures, diagrams, and formulas that fully set forth your invention.

Possession can be shown by describing an actual reduction to practice of your invention. You could do this, for example, by showing that you constructed an embodiment or performed a process that met all the limitations of your claimed invention and determined that your invention would work for its intended purpose.

Possession can also be shown by proving your invention was *ready for patenting,* such as by the disclosure of drawings or structural chemical formulas that show your invention was complete, or by describing distinguishing, identifying characteristics sufficient to show that you were in possession of your claimed invention.

The PTO has an extensive set of guidelines on the written description requirement, which can be found on their website at: http://uspto.gov/web/patents/guides.htm.

ENABLEMENT

Enablement is another requirement and becomes an issue in more unpredictable fields like biology and chemistry. The test for enablement is whether one skilled in your art would be able to practice your claimed invention without an undue amount of experimentation. The state of the art that is considered is based on the art as it exists at the time you file your application. The fact that the state of art later changes so that one is enabled to practice your invention does not eliminate this rejection if one skilled in your art was not enabled to practice your invention at the time your application was filed.

For some types of inventions, particularly computer-related inventions, it is not unusual for the claimed invention to involve more than one field of technology. For such inventions, the disclosure must satisfy the enablement standard for each aspect of the invention.

Example:

To enable a claim to a programmed computer that determines and displays the three-dimensional structure of a chemical compound, the disclosure must enable a person skilled in the art of molecular modeling to understand and practice the underlying molecular modeling processes. The disclosure must also enable a person skilled in the art of computer programming to create a program that directs a computer to create and display the image representing the three-dimensional structure of the compound.

As long as your specification discloses at least one method for making and using your claimed invention that bears a reasonable correlation to the entire scope of your claim, then the enablement requirement is satisfied.

Determining Enablement

There are many factors that are considered when deciding whether there is sufficient evidence to support a determination that a disclosure does not satisfy the enablement requirement and whether any necessary experimentation is *undue*. These factors include, but are not limited to, the following:

The Breadth of Your Claims. If your claims are narrow in scope, it will be easier to satisfy the enablement requirement. It is more likely that someone can practice your narrowly defined invention without undue experimentation.

The Nature of Your Invention. This is the subject matter to which your claimed invention pertains. The nature of your invention will become a backdrop to determine the state of the art and the level of skill possessed by one skilled in your art.

The State of the Prior Art. This is what one skilled in your art would have known, at the time you filed your application, about the subject matter to which your claimed invention pertains. The state of the prior art will provide evidence for the degree of predictability in the art.

The Level of One of Ordinary Skill. This refers to the skill of one in your art in relation to the subject matter to which your claimed invention pertains.

The Level of Predictability in the Art. The more predictability in your art, the more likely it is that someone can practice your invention without undue experimentation. If one skilled in the art can readily anticipate the effect of changes within your invention's field or subject matter, then there is predictability in the art.

On the other hand, if one skilled in the art cannot predict how your invention's topic matter would react to a change, then there is lack of predictability in the art. For example, in fields like chemistry, there may be times when the well-known unpredictability of chemical reactions will alone be enough to create a reasonable doubt as to whether an invention enables others in your field.

Example:

Wright filed an application with claims directed to processes for producing live, nonpathogenic recombinant vaccines against RNA viruses, the vaccines produced by the processes and methods for their use in preventing infection. The description in the specification, however, provided only a single working example detailing the use of a recombinant vaccine that conferred immunity in chickens against the Prague Avian Sarcoma Virus. The examiner allowed only the narrow claims directed to the subject matter specifically disclosed but rejected as not enabled the broader claims directed to vaccines against all pathogenic RNA viruses in any animal, including humans. The examiner found that a person of ordinary skill in the art would have needed to engage in undue experimentation to practice the claimed invention given the breadth of the claims, the unpredictability in the art, and the limited guidance provided by Wright in the application. The examiner noted that RNA viruses are a very diverse and genetically complex group of viruses, to include the HIV virus, which to date has eluded the scientific community's efforts to develop a vaccine against it. (In re Wright, 999 F2d 1557 (Fed. Cir. 1993).)

The Amount of Guidance or Direction Provided by You

This refers to the information in the application, as originally filed, that teaches exactly how to make or use your invention. The amount of guidance or direction needed to enable your invention is inversely related to the amount of knowledge in the state of the art as well as to the predictability in the art. The more that is known in the prior art about the nature of your invention—how to make it, how to use it, and the more predictable the art is—the less information needs to be explicitly stated in your specification. In contrast, if little is known in the prior art about the nature of your invention and the art is unpredictable, your specification will need more detail as to how to make and use your invention in order to be enabling.

The Existence of Working Examples

A working example is based on work that has actually been performed. The more working examples there are, the more likely someone can easily practice your invention.

The Quantity of Experimentation

Obviously, the quantity of experimentation needed to make or use the invention based on the content of the disclosure also affects the ease at which someone can practice your invention.

Missing Essential Claims

Enablement will bar your application when any critical or essential features to your claimed invention are missing from your claim. Such essentiality will be determined by looking at your application to see if you have recited any feature as being critical to the practice of your claims. If this feature is missing from your claims, then those claims fail the *enablement test*.

Example:

Where the only mode of operation of a process disclosed by Joe in the specification involved the use of a cooling zone at a particular location in the processing cycle, the examiner made a proper rejection of Joe's claims because he failed to specify either a cooling step or the location of the step in the process. (*In re Mayhew*, 527 F.2d 1229 (CCPA 1976).)

Biotechnology Inventions and Enablement

The *Manual of Patent Examining Procedure* (MPEP), Section 2402, Paragraph 1 states that:

> *where the invention involves a biological material and words alone cannot sufficiently describe how to make and use the invention in a reproducible manner, access to the biological material may be necessary for the satisfaction of the requirement for patentability under U.S.C., Title 35, Sec. 112.*

Thus, a deposit of biological material is necessary when the material is essential for the practice of the invention, and:

✪ the material is not known and readily available to the public; or,

✪ when the material cannot be made or isolated without undue experimentation.

Although it may not be necessary to deposit host cell lines or plasmids containing heterologous DNA, even when such DNA sequences and proteins expressed by the DNA sequences are claimed, such deposits should nevertheless be considered. If an error in either the DNA or protein sequence is discovered after an application is filed, an amendment of the claims or specification to correct such an error in the absence of such a deposit may be considered new matter. (*Ex parte Maizel*, 27 U.S.P.Q.2d 1662 (1993).)

However, if an application as filed includes sequence information and references a deposit of the sequenced material made in accordance with the requirements of Title 37 of the Code of Federal Regulations (beginning with §1.801), corrections of minor errors in the sequence may be possible based on the argument that one of skill in the art would have resequenced the deposited material and would have immediately recognized the minor error.

It may also be useful to deposit essential biological materials if the material is only referred to in a publication but is not commercially available. The MPEP states that:

> *those applicants that rely on evidence of accessibility other than a deposit take the risk that the patent may no longer be enforceable if the biological material necessary to satisfy the requirements of U.S.C., Title 35, Sec. 112 ceases to be accessible. (MPEP §2404.01.)*

If at some point during the patent term the material becomes unavailable and cannot be obtained without undue experimentation, the patent would become unenforceable.

You must also make reference to your biological deposit in your specification by indicating:

- the name and address of the depository institution with which the deposit was made;

- the date of deposit of the biological material with that institution;

- the accession number given to the deposit by that institution; and,

- to the extent possible, a taxonomic description of the biological material.

Computer Programs

While no specific, universally applicable rule exists for recognizing an insufficiently disclosed application involving computer programs, the failure to include either the computer program itself or a reasonably detailed flowchart that delineates the sequence of operations the program must perform are subject to challenge by your examiner.

Moreover, as the complexity of functions and the generality of the individual components of a flowchart increase, the basis for challenging the sufficiency of such a flowchart becomes more reasonable, because the likelihood of more than routine experimentation being required to generate a working program from such a flowchart also increase. (MPEP §2106.02.)

BEST MODE

The *best mode* requirement is the third requirement under the statute. (35 U.S.C. §112(1).) The best mode requirement prohibits inventors from disclosing only what they know to be their second-best embodiment, while retaining the best for themselves. In other words, if you know of a preferred way of using and making your invention, you cannot conceal this from the public by leaving it out of your patent application.

There are two factual inquiries to be made in determining whether a specification satisfies the best mode requirement. First, there must be a subjective determination as to whether, at the time your application was filed, you knew of the best mode of practicing your invention. Second, there must be an objective determination as to whether the best mode was disclosed in sufficient detail to allow one skilled in the art to practice it. (*Fonar Corp. v. General Electric Co.,* 107 F.3d 1543 (Fed. Cir. 1997).)

UTILITY

Utility is a patentability requirement that makes sure your claimed invention has an actual real-world use. In most cases, this will not be a concern to you, as most novel inventions are useful to *someone* in this world.

Some types of inventions that plainly lack utility are inventions that do not operate to produce the results claimed. Such inventions are called *inoperative,* and if an invention does not work, it cannot be said to have any utility. These cases are rare, however, and usually revolve around inventions that are incredible, such as speculative claims that some uncharacterized composition cures a wide range of cancers. The PTO may establish a reason to doubt your asserted utility when the written description suggests an inherently unbelievable undertaking or involves implausible scientific principles. (*In re Eltgroth,* 419 F.2d 918 (CCPA 1970).)

While an invention that is inoperative is not useful according to the law, the Federal Circuit has stated that a claimed device must be totally incapable of achieving a useful result in order to have no utility. (*Newman v. Quigg,* 877 F.2d 1575 (Fed. Cir. 1989).) If an invention is only partially successful in achieving a useful result, a rejection of the claimed invention as a whole for lacking utility is not appropriate. (*In re Gardner,* 475 F.2d 1389 (CCPA 1973).)

Special PTO Guidelines in Assessing Utility

The PTO has set out guidelines that an examiner will address in determining whether your invention has utility. These guidelines are particularly applicable to inventions pertaining to the biological arts. The first step in the analysis is to identify what an applicant claims as his or her invention. For example, if the claim states, "a cDNA consisting of the sequence as set forth in SEQ ID No. 1," the applicant is claiming a cDNA.

The next question to ask is whether there is a *well-established utility* for that claimed invention. An invention has a well-established utility if:

✪   a person of ordinary skill in the art would immediately appreciate why the invention is useful based on the characteristics of the invention (e.g., properties or applications of a product or process); and,

✪   the utility is specific, substantial, and credible.

If a well-established utility exists, then utility exists.

Example:

Alec's application teaches the cloning and characterization of the nucleotide sequence of the well-known protein, insulin. Since those skilled in the art at the time Alec files his application knew that insulin had a well-established use, it would be improper to reject Alec's claimed invention as lacking utility on the basis that Alec did not include in his application any statement as to a specific and substantial utility.

If there is no well-established utility, the PTO will look to see whether you have made any assertion of utility for your invention. If there is no such assertion, a rejection under §101 is made.

If any assertion is found in your application, the PTO asks whether such assertion identifies a specific utility. A *specific utility* is specific to the subject matter claimed, in contrast to a *general utility,* which would be applicable to a broad class of the invention.

Example:

Melissa claims a cDNA and asserts in the specification that it can be used as a probe to obtain the full-length gene that corresponds to the cDNA. Melissa also asserts that each full-length gene can be used to make the corresponding protein that can then be used to study the mechanisms in which the protein is involved.

This use would not be considered by the PTO as specific, because it would be applicable to the general class of cDNAs. Any partial nucleic acid prepared from any cDNA may be used as a probe in the preparation and/or identification of a full-length cDNA. Melissa's invention would be rejected for a lack of utility.

Even assuming that a specific utility exists, the PTO will next ask whether the asserted utility identifies a *substantial utility*. A substantial utility is a utility that the PTO defines as a real-world use. Although the PTO does not specifically define this term itself, the PTO gives examples of what does and does not constitute real-world uses. The following are examples of real-world uses:

- ✪ A therapeutic method of treating a known or newly discovered disease.

- ✪ An assay method for identifying compounds that themselves have a real-world context of use.

The following are examples that do not have a real-world use:

- ✪ Basic research, such as studying the properties of the claimed product itself or the mechanisms in which the material is involved (the cDNA example).

- ✪ A method of treating an unspecified disease or condition (in contrast to specific diseases or conditions).

- ✪ A method of assaying for or identifying a material that itself has no specific or substantial utility.

- ✪ A method of making a material that itself has no specific, substantial, and credible utility.

- ✪ A claim to an intermediate product for use in making a final product that has no specific, substantial, and credible utility.

Assuming that your invention does have a specific and substantial utility, the final question that the PTO will ask is whether the assertion of specific and substantial utility is *credible.*

An assertion is credible unless the logic underlying the assertion is seriously flawed or the facts on the assertion is based are inconsistent with the logic underlying the assertion. Basically, the asserted utility must be believable to a person of ordinary skill in the art based on the totality of the evidence and reasoning provided.

An assertion that a claimed invention is useful in treating a symptom of an incurable disease may be considered credible by a person of ordinary skill in the art on the basis of a fairly modest amount of evidence or support. In contrast, an assertion that the claimed invention will be useful in curing the disease may require a significantly greater amount of evidentiary support.

Utility in the Pharmaceutical Arts

In the pharmaceutical arts, practical utility may be shown by adequate evidence of any pharmacological activity. Simply identifying a pharmacological activity of a compound relevant to an alleged pharmacological use provides an immediate benefit to the public, and therefore meets the requirements of §101. (*Nelson v. Bowler,* 626 F.2d 853 (CCPA 1980).)

Example:

A compound's modulation of blood pressure in rats and its stimulation of smooth muscle tissue of gerbil colons constituted sufficient utility. The court stated that "practical utility" is a shorthand way of attributing "real-world" value to claimed subject matter. In other words, one skilled in the art can use a claimed discovery in a manner that provides some immediate benefit to the public. (*Nelson v. Bowler,* 626 F.2d 853 (CCPA 1980).)

Generally, pharmacological activity refers to the properties and reactions of drugs, especially with relation to their therapeutic value. (*Cross v. Iizuka,* 753 F.2d 1040 (Fed. Cir. 1985).)

Courts have routinely found evidence of structural similarity to a compound known to have a particular therapeutic or pharmacological utility as being supportive of an assertion of therapeutic utility for a new compound. (*In re Brana,* 34 U.S.P.Q.2d 1436 (Fed. Cir. 1995).)

Example:

Tom presented evidence in his specification that his claimed compounds had a close structural relationship to daunorubicin and doxorubicin, both of which were known to be useful in cancer chemotherapy. He also presented evidence demonstrating substantial activity of his claimed compounds in animals customarily employed for screening anticancer agents. The claimed compounds were found to have utility.

If reasonably correlated to the particular therapeutic or pharmacological utility, data generated using in vitro assays, or from testing in an animal model or a combination thereof, almost invariably will be sufficient to establish therapeutic or pharmacological utility for a compound, composition, or process. (MPEP §2107.03.)

Evidence of a therapeutic or pharmacological utility also does not have to be in the form of data from an art-recognized animal model for the particular disease or disease condition to which the asserted utility relates. Data from any test that you can reasonably correlate to your asserted utility may be provided.

There is also no requirement that you wait to file your application until you have initiated human clinical trials for a therapeutic product or process. However, if you have initiated human clinical trials for a therapeutic product or process, the PTO should presume that you have established that the subject matter of that trial is reasonably predictive of having the asserted therapeutic utility. This is because before a drug can enter human clinical trials, you must provide a convincing rationale to those skilled in the art (the FDA) that the investigation may be successful. (MPEP §2107.03.)

Utility vs. Enablement Requirement
The requirement of utility under 35 U.S.C. §101 is different from the requirement of how to use the invention under 35 U.S.C. §112(1). The requirement of utility is that some specific, substantial, and credible use be set forth for the invention. On the other hand, enablement requires an indication of how the use (required by utility) can be carried out (i.e., how the invention can be used).

Searching for Prior Art

A *patentability search* is used to seek for patents and publications that constitute prior art with respect to your invention. There are a number of very important reasons why you should do this.

THE IMPORTANCE OF A PRIOR ART SEARCH

First, the search may uncover prior art that is identical to your invention being considered for patenting (i.e., such prior art anticipates your invention). If this is the case, you should not waste the time and money that go into the patenting process.

Second, even if the prior art that you uncover does not anticipate your invention, the prior art may be so close to your invention that any patent you might obtain would be so limited that it would not be worth anything.

Third, if you decide to go ahead and draft a patent application and engage in the patent process, the patents and other prior art uncovered during your search will help you develop technical prose for writing your own application and refine the scope of your claims to be presented.

Fourth, even if you are lucky enough to get a patent issued because your examiner fails to uncover a prior art reference—examiners will do their own limited search—that you did not take the time to uncover, one of your competitors will find that reference later on and hold your patent invalid based on that reference. But if you take the time now to uncover that reference, you will have the ability to design your claims so that the reference does not invalidate your patent.

The next two chapters show you how to write a patent application. Reading through prior art patents relating to your field of art now will help you write a better application later.

SIMPLE SEARCHES FOR FREE

The use of other patents as references is not limited to what patentees describe as their own inventions or to the problems that they address. Patents are part of the literature of the art, relevant for all they contain and what follows from them. Therefore, the search for prior art patent references should not only be a big part of your search, but you should pay attention to everything that is contained in the patents (not just the claims).

Use the PTO Site

Probably the best way to search for and access U.S. patents for free is by going to the PTO website and searching for U.S. patents. You can do this by following these steps.

- ✪ Go to the PTO home page at www.uspto.gov.

- ✪ At the PTO website, there is a sidebar with "Patents" listed.

- ✪ Select "Search" under the heading "Patents." This will then bring you up to a web page where you will see the heading "Issued Patents" on the left side and "Patent Applications" on the right.

You will also notice on this web page that there are three options for your patent search. You can either do a "quick search," "advanced search," or "patent number search."

If you click on "quick search," you will bring up a page where you can input two terms and thereby search for those two terms in all U.S. patents. This is a *Boolean* search. You will notice that your search can be limited by *fields*.

You will notice that you can search all fields or limit your search of your two terms to particular fields, such as the title, assignee name, inventor name, as well as a host of other fields. You will also notice that you can select specific years or all years dating back to 1790 for your search.

NOTE: *You can save any of the pages that you bring up by hitting "File" at the top of your browser and then "Save as." You can also save any image by right-clicking on your mouse and then hitting "Save as." This will allow you to view these pages later on while you continue your search.*

The advanced search is much like the quick search. However, it allows you to search more than two fields and additional terms at the same time. Try to conduct an advanced search. Advanced searches let you become very specific in your searches. There are many fields by which you can limit your search. Examples include the patent number (PN), class (CCL), title (TTL), and abstract (ABST). Searching by classification of the patent is very useful since patents from 1790–1975 are only searchable by either patent number and current U.S. classification on the PTO site. Any other type of search will only bring up patents issued from 1975 to the present (although this is still a lot of information).

Suppose that you are interested in searching for patents issued on January 8, 2002, for tennis racquets and motorcycles by the inventor Julie Newmar. Your text search might look something like this: "ttl(tennis and (racquet or racket))isd/1/8/2002 and motorcyclein/ newmar-julie."

Your last search option on the PTO website is to do a *patent number search*. This requires you to know the number of the patent that you want to find. This will probably be of less use to you as you are searching for prior art relating to your invention, as you are probably not aware of any patent numbers concerning your invention. However, if you do know the patent number that you want to look up, this is the quickest way to obtain that patent.

One disadvantage of using the PTO website is that although your search option gives you the choice to search all years, it is somewhat deceiving. Patents issued prior to 1976, can only be searched for by patent number or current U.S. classification. Thus, when you enter your Boolean terms, you are only really searching patents from 1976 to the present. This is a serious limitation that you should be aware of, since older patents are just as good prior art as more recent patents. By searching only the PTO database, you might leave gaps in your search. Nevertheless, the PTO database is the best starting site for your money—it's free.

NOTE: *As you uncover prior art patents, read the entire disclosure of the patent to see whether it anticipates your invention. Be careful not to fall into the trap of thinking that only the claims of a patent can by used to anticipate your invention. You may be particularly inclined to do this after reading Chapter 6, which states that claims define your invention. For anticipation purposes, however, your examiner is free to use everything he or she finds in a patent or any other prior art reference.*

U.S. Published Applications

United States nonprovisional utility and plant applications are published eighteen months from the earliest filing date for which benefit is sought. (35 U.S.C. §122(b).) Having your application published is actually beneficial, because you are entitled to receive a reasonable royalty dating back to your publication date, with respect to any claims that are infringed as of the publication date, so long as those claims have been substantially unaltered from the publication date to your patent issuance date.

Your application will normally be published in the form it exists at the time that you file your patent application. Amendments that you make to your application will generally not be reflected in your published application unless you supply an electronic copy of your application containing the amendment within one month from the date you file your application or within fourteen months from the earliest filing date for which benefits are sought, whichever is later. (37 C.F.R. §1.215.)

Early Publishing or Request Not to Publish

You may request early publication of your U.S. patent application. If you make such a request, you must submit an early publication fee at the time that you submit your application.

Requesting early publication will usually speed up the publishing of your application by a couple of months before the normal eighteen-month publishing date. This could be advantageous because your reasonable royalty for infringement of your claims may then extend back several months. However, requesting early publishing is your decision. If you want to make the request, you need to indicate this in your *application data sheet* and pay the required fee. (See Chapter 7.)

The PTO also gives inventors the right to request that their patent application not be published. Some inventors are concerned about publishing the contents of their patent application. To keep your patent application from being published, you must certify that your invention has not and will not be the subject of a patent application in another country or under a multilateral international agreement that requires publication.

You can revoke your request not to publish at any time. If you do file your invention abroad, you must notify the PTO within forty-five days from the date your application is filed in a foreign country so that the PTO can publish your application here in the United States. If you fail to do this, your application will go abandoned.

My recommendation is to let your application publish eighteen months after it is filed. As stated above, if you allow your application to be published, you are entitled to receive a reasonable royalty back to the publication date, with respect to any claims that were infringed as of the publication date, and where those claims must have been substantially unaltered from the publication date to the patent issuance date. If you do not publish your application, you forgo this reasonable royalty.

Searching for a U.S. Publication

Published applications are the predominant form of prior art used by examiners. Therefore, you absolutely must include a search for both U.S. and foreign published applications during your search. For example, you can search foreign published applications from March 15, 2001. You will see that the PTO writes this as 15 March 2001, which is the same way that you will see dates abroad written (the day followed by the month and the year).

Foreign Patents   The definition of what constitutes prior art with respect to patents is as follows.

A *U.S. or foreign patent* is prior art if it is:

○   issued before your *date of invention* or

○   issued more than one year before your U.S. *filing date.*

A *U.S. patent issued to another* is also prior art if:

○   U.S. *filing date* precedes your *date of invention,* even if it does not issue until after the filing date (or patent issue date) of your claims under examination.

This definition includes foreign patents, so you must include a search for foreign patents during your search. As with U.S. patents, your examiner is not restricted to the information conveyed by the patent claims, but may use any information provided in the specification that relates to the subject matter of the patented claims. You will need to read the entire patent.

The *European Patent Office* (EPO) has a very good website at www.european-patent-office.org. If you hit "Search Engines and Site Index" on this page, you will find several databases. One of the databases that you can choose is "esp@cenet—Free Patent Searching," which will bring you to a page where you can search patents worldwide. There are also options where you can search specific countries abroad.

The EPO site also offers a way to obtain documents that were filed during the prosecution of a European patent application, much like with the PAIR system at the PTO. (See Chapter 10.) What you need to do to accomplish this at the EPO site is to click on the "epoline" icon on the sidebar and then hit "File Inspection." All you will need now is the European patent application number that you want information about, which you can type in the provided box. The nice thing about this site is that you can immediately display each document for printing without even having to order the document to be sent to you.

International Applications

A typical way to file foreign applications is through the *Patent Cooperative Treaty* (PCT). These applications are published eighteen months from their priority date in the *PCT Gazette*, which can be accessed electronically through the Intellectual Property Digital Library website (www.wipo.int/ipdl) of the World Intellectual Property Organization. This can serve as yet another useful free website to search for prior art on your invention. You will learn more about foreign filing in Chapter 9.

Other Publications

Patent publications are not the only type of publications that can be used against your own patent application. Publications also include references like journals and even product catalogs. In fact, even articles posted on the Internet can be used as prior art references against your own patent application. This means that a thorough prior art search should include these other references too.

Many science journals can now be accessed online in addition to at the library. For example, if you are interested in journals relating to the medical field, a good site to go to is the *National Center for Biotechnology Information* (NCBI) site at www.ncbi.nlm.nih.gov. This site has a list of journals with links to full text websites for the journals. The site also has a database called *Pub Med* that allows you to search for articles in all the journals according to your inputted search terms.

All companies have catalogs that list what they sell. Many of these catalogs can be read directly online by visiting the company website. If they cannot be read directly online, you can go to the website of the company and request that a catalog be sent to you.

> ### *Author's Note: Start simple*
> Although it may seem obvious, one of the best ways to search for prior art references is through your favorite search engine.

FEE-BASED SEARCHING

In addition to the PTO free website, there are various fee-based search engines. One website that you may find helpful is www.delphion.com (formerly www.patents.ibm.com). To use most of the best features on this site, you must become a paid subscriber.

A very powerful fee-based search engine is called *Dialog,* which you can find at www.dialog.com. The fees can be considerable based on your usage. However, Dialog is probably the most powerful search tool around for intellectual property. You can search for everything from patents to literature concerning your invention. Dialog takes some time to learn, but their customer assistance is very good. If you do learn Dialog, you will be equipped to do some of the most powerful prior art searching possible.

Two other very useful fee-based databases are Westlaw (www.westlaw.com) and Lexis (www.lexis.com). Both allow you to search for patents. In addition, they both have very good public information databases where you can gather a lot of information about your competitors. You will need to sift through all of the legal searching options, since these two databases really started as tools for only attorneys. Still another fee-based database you might want to check out is Micropatent (www.micropat.com).

Paying Another to Do a Search for You

Another option that you have is to pay someone to do a prior art search for you. You can find such searchers by looking for them on the Internet or in various intellectual law journals and magazines. One such magazine is called *Intellectual Property Today,* which you can find online at www.iptoday.com. Another popular journal among patent agents and attorneys is called the *Journal of the Patent and Trademark Office Society,* which you can find at www.jptos.org.

If you do not have the time to do a search yourself, you should consider paying someone to do a search for you. However, you should keep in mind that you not only can do a search for prior art yourself, but you are perhaps the best person to conduct the search.

USING THE CLASS/SUBCLASS CLASSIFICATION SYSTEM FOR YOUR INVENTION

As previously mentioned, you can conduct searches based on the class/subclass of your invention. Conducting such searches at the PTO website is beneficial because it will pull up patents issued prior to 1975. It is also useful because these searches can pull up much more possible prior art than if you conduct searches based on text alone.

Here is how the class/subclass classification system works. Technology is divided in three major disciplines:

1. chemical;

2. electrical; and,

3. mechanical.

Each of these disciplines is further subdivided into subtechnologies. For example, *electrical* is subcategorized into five subtechnologies:

1. communications;

2. computers;

3. physics;

4. optics; and,

5. system components.

These subtechnologies are further divided into classes. For example, the communications subcategory of electrical has classes such as Class 379–Telephony and Class 348–Television. Finally, these classes are again further divided into subclasses. For example, Television has subclasses such as TV displays and receivers. The title and definition of each class and subclass are text searchable.

All the classes and subclasses are contained in something called the *Manual of Patent Classification*. A version of this manual can be found online at the PTO website. You can find it by going to the PTO homepage (www.uspto.gov) and clicking on "how to guides" at the top of the page and then by clicking on "classification."

Try searching for "fishing nets" using this system. In the search box on the right type in "fishing nets" and click "search." The result returns Class 43 "Fishing, Trapping and Vermin Destroying."

Clicking on the hyperlink to Class 43 will pull up a page with a definition of this class, cross-reference to other classes as well as all the subclasses in this class. For example, the Subclass 4 "fishing" is listed as a subclass under the definition of the class and it refers to apparatuses and methods for hooking and gathering fish.

Notice that there is a red "P" next to this subclass. By clicking on this you will automatically retrieve all U.S. patents in this subclass. This is known as a *classification search*. It allows for a complete search of patents issued in any particular subclass. Another important thing it allows you to do is to search and view patents issued prior to 1976. Doing a quick and advanced search from the PTO patent site, which you did previously, will only pull up patents issued after 1976.

If you would like to see a list of all the classes in the *Manual of Patent Classification*, click on "class number and titles" in the upper left-hand corner of the page. Moreover, if you click on the "go" you will find the subclasses. For example, click on the "go" for Class 15 "scrubbing, brushing and general cleaning" and you will see that its Subclass 3 is "machines."

Example:

Suppose you want to do a text search for "radio sunglasses." One way you could perform your search would be to search for the terms "radio" and "sunglasses" together or you could do a broader search by searching for the term "radio" or "sunglasses." You could even do a broader search for say truncated versions of "sunglasses" by doing an advanced search (see above) for "sunglass$." As you pull up results, you should scan the titles of the patents and note the particular class/

subclass of the pertinent patents. Doing such a search will pull up three classes. These are:

1.   Class 381 "audio";

2.   Class 455 "telecommunications"; and,

3.   Class 351 "eye examination and vision correction."

With these classes in hand, you can now go to the *Manual of Patent Classification*. This will allow you to identify other pertinent classes/subclasses and their associated patents. In addition, you can check cited references in the patents you have found.

DOCUMENTING YOUR SEARCH

As you conduct your prior art search and you run into any reference that you feel is related to your own invention, you should incorporate such a reference into a typed master list. It may be easier to keep this list on a word processor so that you can manipulate it later on. All references that may have a bearing on the patentability of your own invention must be disclosed to the PTO in an *information disclosure statement* (IDS). By compiling a list of any such references now, your job of submitting an IDS will be much easier later on.

Your master list should have the following four headings:

1.   *U.S. Patents*—Place only U.S. patents that you find during your search under this heading.

2.   *Foreign Patents*—Place only foreign patents that you uncover during your search.

3.   *Publications*—Under this heading, place your science publications and any published patent applications that you find.

4.   *Other References*—Use this heading to place any miscellaneous references that you find, such as company brochures or anything else that does not fit into one of the other headings.

SECTION II

FILING YOUR APPLICATION

Drafting Your Patent Application

At this point, you should have completed your prior art search. You are hopefully starting to get a feel for what must be included in a patent. If this is the case, you are off to a good start with drafting your patent application, since issued patents contain the information that is included in the application. The only difference between an issued patent and a patent application is the order of the information.

PARTS OF YOUR APPLICATION

The recommended ordering of your application is stated at 37 C.F.R. §1.77(a) and also in the MPEP. (MPEP §601 and §608.01(a).) According to these sections, your application should include the following parts:

- ✪ utility application transmittal form;

- ✪ fee transmittal form;

- ✪ application data sheet;

- ✪ specification;

- ✪ drawings; and,

- ✪ executed oath or declaration.

This chapter discusses your specification and drawings.

HOW TO GO ABOUT DRAFTING A PATENT APPLICATION

You should thoroughly understand this chapter as well as the next before you move ahead to draft your patent application. They provide a logical order in which to draft your application. However, the patent application drafting process is not etched in stone. There are many ways to arrive at your intended goal of a well-drafted application. If you are the type of person who absolutely needs to work on a section in logical order, draft your patent application as described in this chapter. However, once you are familiar with all the steps, you may find an approach that works better for you. One approach that many patent practitioners take as they draft their patent application is as follows:

First, understand your invention in the context of the prior art. As an inventor, you are the best person to fully understand your invention in the context of the prior art. If, for some reason, you do not have a firm grasp on how your invention is novel with respect to other inventions in your field, you need to stop and finish this task. Identify any key references to ensure that these references do not anticipate or render your own invention obvious as you draft the claims of your own invention.

After thoroughly understanding your own invention in the context of the prior art, it will be helpful—particularly in the case of mechanical inventions—to prepare any necessary drawings of your invention. The drawings will help you immensely as you prepare your written description, which, as you will soon see, is closely interconnected with the drawings. In your drawings, assign numbers to each element that is illustrated by the drawings. A good way to do this is to start with the numeral 10 and continue using increments of two (e.g., 12, 14, 16). This will allow you to use the unassigned odd numbers in the event you wish to add another element later.

Prepare one or two independent claims, reciting only those essential features necessary to make your invention novel and nonobvious. These claims should represent the backbone of your invention and recite only those elements that prevent anticipation of your invention. After you have prepared these independent claims, prepare other claims dependent from the independent claims, which add further elements or features that elaborate on or further specify the nature of the elements recited in the independent claims. (All of Chapter 6 is devoted to writing claims.)

Prepare the other parts of your patent application (e.g., background, etc.) as described in the next section of this book.

DRAFTING YOUR SPECIFICATION

As provided by 37 C.F.R. §1.77(a), your *specification* consists of the following parts in the following order:

- ✪ title of the invention;

- ✪ cross-reference to related applications;

- ✪ statement regarding federally sponsored research or development;

- ✪ reference to a *sequence listing,* a table, or a computer program listing an appendix on a compact disc and an incorporation by reference of the material on the compact disc;

- ✪ background of your invention, which includes both the field of your invention and a description of related art;

- ✪ brief summary of your invention;

- ✪ brief description of the several views of your drawings;

✪   detailed description of your invention;

✪   claims that must commence on a separate sheet (see Chapter 6);

✪   abstract; and,

✪   DNA sequence listing (only applicable to biotechnology invention).

NOTE: *In addition to these sections, you will sometimes see a "Copyright Notice" section that you can place right after the title of the invention. The notice is required if you use copyrights anywhere in your specification. Your section heading and notice should look like the following:*

Copyright Notice

A portion of the disclosure of this patent document contains material to which a claim for copyright is made. The copyright owner has no objection to the facsimile reproduction by anyone of the patent document or the patent disclosure, as it appears in the Patent and Trademark Office patent file or records, but reserves all other copyright rights whatsoever.

You should make the listed items the section headings of your specification. Each one of these section headings should be in uppercase and without underlining or bold type. If one of the listed sections is not relevant to your invention, you can simply write "Not Applicable" next to the section heading or simply leave out the section altogether.

Appendix C contains a sample patent application. You will notice that various section headings that are not applicable to the particular patent have been left out.

Your specification should be written using one-and-a-half spacing or double-spacing. You must use paper that is either 8½ x 11 inches or size A4. You should number your pages, preferably centered at the bottom of the page.

Look again at the sample patent application contained in Appendix C. You will notice that the paragraphs of the specification, other than the claims and abstract, are numbered. By numbering your paragraphs, you will find it much easier to make any amendments to your specification by using replacement paragraphs.

The paragraph numbers should consist of at least four numerals enclosed in square brackets, including leading zeros (e.g., [0001]). The numbers and enclosing brackets should appear to the right of the left margin as the first item in each paragraph and should be highlighted in bold. A gap of four spaces should follow the number. You do not consider section or paragraph headers as part of your paragraph for numbering purposes, nor would you consider any tables or formulae.

Author's Note: Find what works for you.

Although I am presenting this material in step-order fashion according to how you arrange your patent application under the MPEP, you should realize that the order you draft your application is not etched in stone. In fact, many patent drafters find that drafting some claims before they do any other part of the application is much easier. I think this can actually be helpful, because claim drafting really focuses your thoughts on what is essential to your invention. Once you have focused on writing a few claims, you can come back to the other parts of your application, such as the detailed written description, and fill in the details. As you might recall from Chapter 3, details are required to fulfill all of your disclosure requirements, such as the written description requirement.

Whether you proceed to write your claims first or draft your application in the order presented here, I would suggest that you read both this chapter and the following one before you start doing any work on drafting your application. You should have a good idea of what is required for your application before you start drafting.

STEP 1: TITLE OF THE INVENTION

The title of your invention should appear at the top of the first page of your specification, unless you have included it in your application data sheet (discussed in Chapter 7). The title should be as short and specific as possible. It should be general in scope but not so general that it fails to describe broadly the invention claimed.

The title of the invention has been used by the Federal Circuit to assist in claim interpretation. It is important that the title capture the gist of your invention.

STEP 2: CROSS-REFERENCE TO RELATED APPLICATIONS

You should include a cross-reference to any related applications that you may have filed unless you have included this information in your application data sheet (discussed in Chapter 7).

Examples of related applications that you might cross-reference are any other U.S. or foreign applications from which you are claiming priority.

NOTE: *The sample patent in Appendix C has no cross-reference to related application section because the patent upon which this application is based had no cross-reference to any related applications.*

STEP 3: STATEMENT REGARDING FEDERALLY SPONSORED RESEARCH AND DEVELOPMENT

If your invention is sponsored by the federal government, you must include a statement to the effect that: "the invention was made with Government support and the Government has certain rights in the invention." This requirement has to do with the *Bayh-Dole Act,* which requires certain requirements be met (one of which is this statement requirement). If these requirements are not met, the consequences can be severe with the government potentially being able to take title to your invention.

Author's Note: U.S. government contract
If you have a contract with the U.S. government for experimental, developmental, or research work, and you come up for a subject invention that is conceived or first actually reduced to practice while performing work under your government contract, you may be under what is referred to as a *patent rights clause*. This clause may be in your contract with the U.S. government. Under such a clause, you must comply with specific notice and disclosure requirements or else all rights in your invention can be lost. Failure to comply with time requirements can result in the government obtaining title to your invention. *Time requirements* are provided by the Federal Acquisition Regulation (FAR) at 48 C.F.R. §27.303. Among the requirements is that you must give notice in writing of each of your subject inventions within two months after an inventor discloses it in writing to any of your personnel responsible for patent matters. If your contract with the U.S. government cannot be characterized as being for experimental, developmental, or research work, then you should object to inclusion of a patent rights clause in your contract.

STEP 4: REFERENCE TO A SEQUENCE LISTING, TABLE, OR COMPUTER PROGRAM LISTING

A computer program listing, a nucleotide, an amino acid sequence listing submitted under 37 C.F.R. §1.821(c), or a table that has more than fifty pages of text, may be submitted on compact disc. A computer program listing that is over three hundred lines *must* be submitted on compact disc.

A *computer program listing* is defined as a printout that lists—in appropriate sequence—the instructions, routines, and other contents of a program for a computer. A compact disc is defined as a Compact Disc—Read Only Memory (CD-ROM) or a Compact Disc—Recordable (CD-R). If you decide to or are required to submit a compact disc with your application, you must follow the requirements set forth in 37 C.F.R. §1.52(e). One such requirement is that your specification must incorporate by reference the material on the compact disc, which is done in this section heading.

NOTE: *If none of this is applicable to your own invention, you can simply leave out this section heading. The sample application contained in Appendix C has no such heading.*

STEP 5: BACKGROUND OF THE INVENTION

Begin the background of the invention with a statement of the field of art to which your application belongs. This statement goes into what is called the *technical field*.

Technical Field

If you have problems drafting the technical field, the PTO states that you can simply paraphrase the applicable U.S. patent classification definitions of your invention's subject matter. So, if you have determined the most relevant class/subclass for your invention, you can use the class definitions to help you draft your field of invention.

NOTE: *Look at the field of the invention for the sample patent application contained in Appendix C on page 579. The statement starts off with the words "the present invention relates," followed by the words "more particularly." This is a good example of how you should write your statement.*

The first part of the statement after "relates" is a broad characterization of your invention, and the second part after "more particularly" characterizes the most important feature of your invention. In other words, you start off your statement with a broad characterization that is similar to the class of your invention, and then you end your statement with a more specific characterization that is equivalent to the subclass of your invention. If your invention relates both to a device *and* method, both should be included in the technical field.

Description of Related Art

The next part of the background section should be a *description of related art,* including any prior art references that you have uncovered in your prior art search from Chapter 4. (This section can also be titled "Background Art.") This section should begin by showing the prior art, namely the type of product or method that your invention will be better than. You should then address the problems associated with this prior art product or method, and the fact that there exists a need to overcome these problems.

Example:

You have just come up with a way to label nucleotides nonradio-actively, and you believe this will be of great use to the scientific community in using such nonradioactive nucleotides for assays due to their increased safety. You could start off your Description of Related Art section by introducing radioactive nucleotides of the past and their various uses by the scientific community. You would then describe the associated problems of using such radioactive nucleotides by explaining that their use is often very hazardous. You might also explain that, because of this, their use in the laboratory is often very slow and cumbersome. You would want to keep emphasizing that there exists a need for safer nucleotides that is crying out to be solved.

If you follow this format of identifying all of the problems of any prior art invention, you can really start making an argument for the nonobviousness of your invention over the prior art. (Nonobviousness is discussed at length in Chapter 13.) The reader should come out of your background section with the feeling that the prior art has lots of problems. Your reader will then be impressed when he or she moves on to the rest of your specification and finds out that your invention has solved all these problems.

The length and detail of your background section will really depend on how much prior art you wish to discuss, as well as the scope of the claims that you are trying to patent. If you are presenting very broad claims to an invention, then you should prepare a rather detailed background section explaining many of the deficiencies and problems of the prior art. However, if you are claiming a very narrow invention, then you can get right down to business and simply note the specific problem of the prior art that your invention is going to solve.

NOTE: *Take a look at the "Description of the Prior Art" for the sample application in Appendix C. You can see that this section is very short. This most likely means that the claims are going to be narrowly drawn to an invention that solves the problem of carriers that have not been very easy to ship and store in the past.*

Author's Note: Take a balanced approach.
There is a current school of thought that patent disclosures should be drafted with a minimum profile—in fact, some recommend for disclosures not to even include a summary of the invention—to avoid limiting your invention. However, the background section is important because it helps people see how your invention makes a contribution to what has already been done (the prior art). This can be helpful not only for your examiner, but also to a judge or jury if you are defending your patent in court. The best approach is a balanced one. Have a background section that discusses something about the prior art, but do not write a treatise. Just get right down to business and point out what is out there and how your invention is better. A good rule of thumb for a majority of applications is a background section that is two to three paragraphs in length. One paragraph can identify a prior art reference, another can go into the problem with that reference, and your last paragraph can identify your solution to that problem.

STEP 6: BRIEF SUMMARY OF THE INVENTION

Your *brief summary* (sometimes called the *disclosure of invention*) should be comparable to the scope of your broadest claim. (Drafting your claims is discussed more thoroughly in Chapter 6.) However, your brief summary should be written in clear prose rather than in the patentlike language that you will use in drafting your claims. In other words, your summary should be written in a way that a nontechnical person, who may have difficulty interpreting claim language, can easily understand.

One technique that you can use in writing the summary of your invention is to take the broadest claim that you draft and rewrite that claim in plain English. You can then also include any of your alternative embodiments—which will also be dependent claims in your "claims section" discussed in the next chapter—as aspects of your invention. For example, you might use the phrase "in one aspect, the invention features." Be careful, however, about using the phrase "the invention is" outright. Stating outright that your invention is such and such may unnecessarily limit your invention because you are telling the reader that " my invention is this." It is much better to use a phrase like "in one aspect, the invention features" or "in one embodiment, the invention features."

Some patent drafters also include objects of the invention in the summary section. Such objects will typically address the short-comings included in the background section by now stating the advantages provided by the current invention that address each of those shortcomings. An example might be "1) It is, therefore, an object of this invention to provide a screw that is less costly to make. 2) It is a further object of this invention to provide a screw that is more easily turned." To end an objects of the invention paragraph, some drafters include a type of tie-all statement such as, "the sub-ject invention results from the realization that a less expensive, more easily turned screw is effected by..." The goal of this statement is merely to get the reader to see how your invention is achieving your stated goals.

If you do include an objects of the invention paragraph, you should still add a restatement of your broadest claim and aspects of your invention as stated above after this paragraph. Whether you specifi-cally use an objects of the invention paragraph or not, you should know what the objects of your invention are so that you can con-tinually make out a case in your patent the advantages of your invention. It just may be wise from a patent perspective not to label these advantages as "objects" because some courts in the past have interpreted some dominating statements as limiting your invention to only those objects, particularly where you write your objects incor-rectly and include structural limitations. An otherwise infringing product, lacking one to all of your stated advantages or not fulfilling one to all of your stated objects, may be regarded as noninfringing. For these reasons, I recommend that you stay away from using "objects" in your summary section although you will likely see many patents with such wording.

Example:

In his disclosure, Gentry stated "another object of the present invention is to provide a console positioned between the reclin-ing seats that accommodates the controls for both of the reclining seats." In his later patent infringement suit, where the alleged infringer did not include the controls for the reclining seats, the court held there was no infringement because Gentry had limited his claimed invention to controls on a console between reclining seats due to "objects" and other statements made in his specification. This was true even though Gentry's claim said nothing about "controls" at all. If the goals had, however, not stated structure (i.e., "console") but rather goals, then this result would probably have been different.

Since drafting your brief summary is often done in conjunction with or after you draft your broadest claims, you can save this section for later and complete it after you have drafted your claims, if you prefer.

STEP 7: BRIEF DESCRIPTION OF THE SEVERAL VIEWS OF THE DRAWING

You must briefly describe each figure of the drawing. Each figure should be described in a separate paragraph (e.g., Figure 1, Figure 2, etc.). Then later in your detailed description of your invention you will describe your invention in reference to each of these figures.

Typically, one will use the entire term "Figure" or capitalized "FIG." rather than "Fig.," both in the brief descriptions of the several views of the drawing and when referring to the figures again in the detailed description.

Look again at the sample application in Appendix C. Since the invention is relatively easy to picture in that patent, there are not very many different views or figures presented. However, it is better to be overinclusive than underinclusive. You will learn shortly that your drawings work with your detailed description section and must provide enough detail and clarity so that someone skilled in your art can make and use your invention.

STEP 8: DETAILED DESCRIPTION OF THE INVENTION

This section is the real meat part of your patent application. Your specification should be drafted using language from your claims (another reason to draft some claims first before completing other sections of your patent specification). Often, claims are copied into your specification, and then broken down into more readable sentences.

The first thing that you should know about your *detailed description* (often referred to as the *description* or *best mode for practicing the invention*) is that it must be complete and detailed enough so that a person who is skilled in your field (or your art) can make and use your invention without extensive experimentation. This requirement is referred to as the *enablement requirement*. (35 U.S.C. §112, Paragraph 2.)

> ***Author's Note: A special note for computer-related inventions***
>
> To ensure that you have met the enablement requirement for computer software inventions, you should include a computer program listing. (You will also need to comply with the requirements of Step 4 regarding the submission of your listing.) At a minimum, you should include a detailed flowchart so that a person skilled in your field would be able to write your program without undue trial and error.
>
> For computer-related inventions, the PTO provides guidelines at MPEP §2106 that you should look at. Those guidelines provide that the disclosure must, "enable a skilled artisan to configure the computer to possess the requisite functionality, and, where applicable, interrelate the computer with other elements to yield the claimed invention, without the exercise of undue experimentation."

As stated earlier, the enablement requirement demands that your invention be described in such full, clear, and concise terms as to enable a person skilled in your field to practice your invention. This does not mean that you have to detail what is already well known in the art concerning your invention.

In fact, Section 608.01(h) of the MPEP specifically states that:

where elements or groups of elements, compounds, and processes, which are conventional and generally widely known in the field of the invention described, and their exact nature or type is not necessary for an understanding and use of the invention by a person skilled in the art, they should not be described in detail.

However, the MPEP goes on to state that:

where particularly complicated subject matter is involved or where the elements, compound, or processes may not be commonly or widely known in the field, the specification should refer to another patent or readily available publication which adequately described the subject.

Example:

Suppose that you have just come up with a protein in the biological field. Part of your invention involves the cloning of the gene that expresses that protein. Since the cloning of a gene is now well known in the biological field, you would not need to provide instruction on the steps of cloning. You could simply state that cloning techniques are well known by persons skilled in the biological arts. However, it would still be safer in this case to incorporate by reference some texts that teach how to clone.

NOTE: *Remember to be cautious. If you are not sure whether some feature of your invention is well known in your field, you should either incorporate by reference patents that adequately describe this feature or write into your detailed description an adequate disclosure of this feature. It is extremely important that you provide a complete and adequate disclosure of features that are necessary to enable your invention.*

If you do not incorporate such necessary material into your application now, you will forever be barred from putting such material into your application later and will still rely on your application's filing date for prior art purposes. This is because the PTO will not allow you to add new matter to your patent application later. Your claims will also fail for lack of enablement, if such claims are directed to any subject matter for which you have not provided a full disclosure on how to make and use your invention.

Incorporating Material by Reference

When you refer to other patents, scientific journals, and the like to indicate the background art, you can rewrite what was said in those references directly into your background section. In the alternative, you can incorporate the reference directly into your specification without having to rewrite everything that has been said in the reference. This is known as *incorporation by reference.*

Incorporation by reference provides a method for integrating material from various documents into your patent application by citing such material in a manner that makes clear that the material is effectively part of your application as if it were explicitly contained therein. The information that you incorporate by reference into your application becomes as much a part of your application as if the text was repeated directly into your application, provided you make a proper incorporation by reference.

Any reference that you are using to indicate the background of the invention or the state of the art is considered to be nonessential subject matter by the PTO. You are allowed to incorporate by reference nonessential subject matter from a wide range of sources, including both patents and nonpatent publications.

To incorporate by reference, you must make sure that you include an identification of the reference (e.g., patent, publication, or application). If you want to incorporate only specific parts of the reference, you must also identify just those parts.

Example:

The details of the handle assembly are set forth in column 5, lines 62–100, of U.S. Patent 4,133,196; the disclosure of which is incorporated by reference.

You can also incorporate by reference only part of the material from the reference that you want to include in your own patent application.

Example:
The disclosure of a valve on page 5, lines 5–35, of application No. XX/YYY,YYY, is hereby incorporated by reference.

NOTE: *The preferable method of incorporating a co-pending application by reference is to provide the names of all the inventors, the title of the application, and the patent's filing date.*

Another thing that you should know about incorporating by reference is the following:

If the material that you want to incorporate by reference is considered to be *essential material,* the PTO limits the types of references that you can incorporate by reference. In other words, if the material that you want to incorporate by reference into your specification is necessary to describe your invention, provide an enabling disclosure of your invention or describe your best mode, it is considered essential material by the PTO. (MPEP §608.01(p).)

The PTO will only allow you to incorporate by reference essential material from U.S. patents or patent publications. You may also incorporate by reference certain U.S. patent applications (those that do not incorporate essential material by reference), but not foreign applications, patents, or publications.

You do not, however, need to worry too much about improperly incorporating essential material into your specification space. You can later amend your disclosure to include the material incorporated by reference directly into your specification. The amendment must be accompanied by an affidavit or declaration stating that you mistakenly tried to incorporate the amendatory material by reference into your application.

However, the consequence of failing to incorporate material (or write such essential material directly into your specification) that is necessary to enable your invention is much greater. Your claimed invention may be invalid. Do not be afraid to incorporate references into your specification. Make your description as complete as possible.

Provide Written Support

While you must be complete in your detailed description, you should *not* discuss why your invention works. There is no requirement that you provide an explanation of the underlying mechanism of your invention.

An important issue with respect to your detailed description relates to what is referred to as the *written description requirement*. Under this requirement, your detailed description must provide clear, written support for all of the terms that you use in your claims. In other words, your detailed description section is like a dictionary for your claims.

The reader must be able to find information about any features that you mention in your claims by looking through your detailed description. If the reader cannot find any such information, then you have not provided a sufficient basis for your claims, and they will fail for lack of written description. You can help to avoid written description problems by writing as complete and full disclosure of your invention as possible in your detailed description section.

Disclose Best Mode

Enablement and written description issues can be some of the toughest issues to overcome with your patent application. Another important issue that does not come up as often is the *best mode requirement*. The best mode requirement simply means that your description must disclose the embodiment of your invention that you consider to be the best mode for practicing your invention. In other words, you are not allowed to hide from the public the best way to carry out your invention. For example, if you are aware of a specific material that will make possible the successful reproduction of your invention but do not disclose it, speaking instead in terms of broad categories, the best mode requirement has been violated.

Disclose Utility

You should also include statements in your application as to why you believe your invention is useful. *Statements of utility* are particularly important in the more unpredictable arts, such as biotechnology and chemistry. In fact, if your application relates to such arts, it would be a good idea to read about the utility requirement in Chapter 3 so that you know about some of the problems that you could encounter if you do not assert a specific and credible utility in your application.

Writing Your Detailed Description

Having discussed the requirements of enablement, written description, best mode, and utility, it's time to look at the actual mechanics of writing your detailed description. Your description should be written in easy-to-understand English. Short paragraphs are better than long ones. Also, particularly in mechanical inventions, your description section must work in conjunction with your drawings.

Look at the sample application contained in Appendix C. You will see the format of a typical written description for mechanical inventions. A mechanical invention is used as an example because these types of inventions are very common in patent law. The style and format of writing your description will vary depending on the type of art to which your invention pertains. The best thing you can do is to look at a lot of patents relating to your invention to get a feel for a standard format.

Examine the detailed description in Appendix C on page 579. The detailed description refers to the different views of the drawings by specifying the numbers of the figures and the different parts by use of reference numerals. For example, the description starts off with a reference to the entire inventive part (the folding carrier) and assigns it the number 12.

You may also notice that the sample application not only details many physical characteristics of the folding carrier, but also includes cooperative relationships, functions performed, and results attained. For example, after supporting member 18 is described, there is an explanation of how the carrier works (how it is attached to the car, how the carrier is moved from an extended to a collapsed position, etc.). This helps satisfy the requirement of sufficiency of disclosure and provides a basis for broad claim coverage.

NOTE: *It is typical and advisable to start the numbering of your parts with a number such as 10 (or in this case, 12), or a number that is at least larger than the number of figures contained in your drawings, in order to avoid any confusion between your reference number and the figure numbers in your drawings. It is also advisable to skip numbers as you sequentially identify parts of your invention. If you look at the sample patent, you will see that the numbers increase by two (e.g., 14, 16, 18, 20). Skipping numbers in this manner will leave you some unused numbers (the odd numbers in this case) to assign to any parts that you want to add later.*

If your invention has any alternate embodiments of your invention, you should discuss these in your detailed description.

Example:

You invent an improved latch that slides by the use of a handle. If alternative embodiments exist (the handle takes on different shapes that are used for sliding the latch), you should include these in your detailed description. Instead of assigning completely different reference numbers for the alternate embodiments of the handle, you could give your main embodiment of the handle the number 20, and then identify the second embodiment with the number 20(a), the third embodiment of the handle with 20(c), and so on.

If any parts or features of your invention are critical to the operation of your invention, then you must set forth all such elements. Be careful about emphasizing the importance of any characteristic of your invention unless it is truly a critical aspect of your invention. If you emphasize any feature of your invention as critical to your invention, you will have to include such feature later on in your claims. As you will learn in Chapter 6, adding limitations to your claims actually narrows the scope of your claims.

You can include tables and mathematical formulas in your detailed description, or you can submit such material as formal drawings. You are not allowed to include graphical illustrations, diagrammatic views, flowcharts, or diagrams in your detailed description, but must instead submit such material as formal drawings.

The detailed description usually ends with some type of statement explaining that the embodiments of your invention that you have disclosed are not intended to be *limiting* features. Look at the sample application in Appendix C on page 579. It states that, "Since certain changes may be made in the foregoing disclosure without departing from the scope of the invention herein involved, it is intended that all matter contained in the above description and depicted in the accompanying drawings be construed in an illustrative and not in a limiting sense." You can use this same language in your own patent application or any similar type of language that you find in your review of other patents during your prior art search.

Good Drafting Techniques

There is a general trend within the PTO toward using your detailed description in construing the terms of your claims. Keep this in mind as you draft your detailed description.

- ✪ Avoid closed-ended phrases like "the invention" or "all embodiments of the invention." These phrases have been interpreted to expressly limit the claims. (*SciMed Life Systems v. Advanced Cardiovascular Systems*, 242 F.3d 1337 (Fed. Cir. 2001).)

- ✪ Use open-ended phrases, such as "one embodiment of the invention, among others." Also, use permissive language like "may" or "can."

- ✪ Disclose alternative embodiments of your invention. Disclosing only one embodiment in a consistent manner serves to "implicitly define" claim terms. The best way to add alternative embodiments to your invention is to try and think of how your competitor might try to design around your invention. Think of different ways to practice your invention and to cover these alternatives in your detailed description. If there are other types of elements or features that can be substituted to perform a particular type of feature that you already mentioned, then describe this alternative feature. This is particularly true when you use certain claims called *means-plus-function claims* (discussed in the next chapter). If you claim a means for attaching a door and your disclosure mentions only a hinge as a way to attach this door, you will be limited to doors attached by hinges or their equivalents, unless you have described other ways that your door can be attached.

✪   Be careful that your alternative embodiments do not limit alternative structures. This can happen when your alternative embodiments limit your invention to the commonalities found among your different embodiments.

Example:

Joe's description, in describing "passage," stated that "other non-smooth geometries may be used" and "the second section of the bore may be conical." Ultimately, the court could decide that the word "passage" must include only "nonsmooth" and "conical" passages.

✪   Keep in mind that when you discuss prior art elements, you may be excluding those prior art elements from your claimed invention.

✪   Use clear and concise language. You should strive to use words and terms that have a clear and unambiguous meaning. If there is any doubt about the meaning of a claim term, then include its definition in your written description.

✪   If your invention includes an element that is novel due to a numerical parameter, describe the operable range of this parameter. First, describe a broad range that encompasses the operable limits of your invention without encompassing the prior art. Second, describe a narrower numerical range that captures preferred embodiments. Third, describe the narrowest numerical range that captures your most preferred embodiment. Doing so will aid in preventing any would-be infringer from trying to limit your claims to a specific numerical value or overly narrow range. If you are relying on your numerical range to support the patentability of your invention, you should also describe the benefits of your specified ranges over the prior art, since inventions that rely on numerical ranges are often held as obvious matter of *routine optimization*. If you fail to state the importance of your range, you may have to submit a declaration later on to establish that the range produces unexpected results beyond those that would be expected by routine optimization.

✪ When referring to embodiments of your invention, it is best to state "an embodiment" or "one embodiment," or similar words, so it is clear that all embodiments of your invention are not being described. This way, you will be less likely to unnecessarily limit the scope of your invention if you need time to enforce your claims against a potential infringer. Also, the word "preferred," or even better, the phrase "for example," can be useful when drafting your specification. Use of this phrase may help in ensuring that would-be infringers do not try to limit your terms by their stated meaning. For example, if your claims recite a "first panel connected to a second panel," and you state in your detailed written description that the first panel is "bolted to" the second panel, a would-be infringer may try to argue that your claimed patent connection must be limited to being secured by a bolt. One way to help you in avoiding such a situation might be to say "the first panel connected to the second panel, for example, by a bolt" in your description, so as to indicate that you are not limited to connection by a bolt.

Author's Note: Present Invention

Be careful of using the phrase "the present invention" or even "preferred embodiment." Using a phrase like "the invention," you may unnecessarily limit the scope of your invention for infringement purposes. Most patent drafters are now stating that you should avoid all use of the phrase "the invention" except maybe in your summary section where you might state, "In one aspect, the invention features..."

✓ Use this type of language	✓ Avoid this type of language
✓ "an embodiment," "one embodiment of the invention, among others..." "may," "can"	✓ "all embodiments," "the embodiment," "the invention is," "the present invention" "is"

STEP 9: CLAIMS

This section of the specification is discussed in detail in Chapter 6.

STEP 10: ABSTRACT OF THE DISCLOSURE

Your *abstract of disclosure,* or simply *abstract,* should start on a separate page in your application and should be limited to a single paragraph, not to exceed one hundred fifty words. This is the place where you let your reader quickly ascertain the nature of the subject matter of your invention.

Your abstract should include everything that is new in the art to which your invention pertains. If your invention is an improvement of an old apparatus, process, product, or composition, your abstract should include the technical disclosure of the improvement.

Where your invention pertains to a machine or apparatus, your abstract should include its organization and operation. However, extensive mechanical details should not be included. In fact, your abstract should not be any more limiting than your broadest independent claim. This is because some courts have used the abstract in limiting your claims. The MPEP provides an example of an abstract as follows:

> *A heart valve, which has an annular valve body defining an orifice and a plurality of struts forming a pair of cages on opposite sides of the orifice. A spherical closure member is held within the cages and is moved by blood flow between open and closed positions in check valve fashion. A slight leak or backflow is provided in the closed position by making the orifice slightly larger than the closure member. Blood flow is maximized in the open position of the valve by providing an inwardly convex contour on the orifice-defining surfaces of the body. An annular rib is formed in a channel around the periphery of the valve body to anchor a suture ring used to secure the valve within a heart.*

STEP 11: SEQUENCE LISTING

NOTE: *This section is only applicable to those applicants who are filing patent applications that contain nucleotides (the basic building blocks of our genetic material), or amino acids (the building blocks of our protein cellular machinery). If you are not filing such a biotechnology invention, then you do not need to read any further here. In fact, the material is probably not going to make much sense to you if you are not familiar with biotechnology inventions. You can simply leave this section out of your patent application or write "Not Applicable" underneath the section.*

For those of you who are filing for biotechnology inventions, you will need to be aware of the sequence listing rules provided in 37 C.F.R. §1.821. These rules provide that if your application contains a sequence of at least ten or more nucleotides (four or more of which are specifically defined) and/or at least four or more amino acids (four or more of which are specifically defined), then you must include a paper or compact disk copy disclosing the nucleotide or amino acid sequence listing as provided in the rules. "Specifically defined" means any nucleotides other than "n" or amino acid other than "Xaa," or, in other words, naturally occurring. It does not matter if the sequence you are describing is publicly known. You must still file a formal sequence listing if those sequences meet the length and definition requirement above.

The sequence rules further provide that each sequence in your sequence listing must be cited with an identifier (e.g.,"SEQ ID NO: 1," "SEQ ID NO: 2," etc.) at each place in your specification, claims, figures, or abstract where your sequence is shown or discussed. Identifiers for figure sequences may be included in the "Brief Description of the Drawings," rather than the drawings themselves, if their connection can be clearly interpreted. However, if what you are describing is a fragment of a larger sequence that is included in your formal sequence listing, you do not need to create a separate sequence listing for such fragments. In your application, claims, or figures, you should simply identify such fragments as part of your larger sequence (e.g., "residues 1–25 of SEQ ID NO: 4"). Each discrete fragment of a sequence having a gap, however, must be displayed as separate sequences in your sequence listing. For example, if a chemical moiety has several strands of protein attached to it, each protein sequence should appear in the sequence listing separately, without showing the chemical moiety.

NOTE: *If you fail to comply with the formal sequence rules at the time you file your patent application, this failure will not prevent you from obtaining a filing date for your patent application. Instead, the Office of Initial Patent Examination (OIPE) will issue you a* Notice to File Missing Parts *along with a* Notice to Comply with Requirements for Patent Applications Containing Sequence Disclosures *about two months from the date you file your patent application. You will have two months from this notice to file the correct listing, although this deadline can be extended by five additional months—seven months in total—by filing for extensions of time and paying the necessary fees.*

DRAWINGS

You are required to provide drawings of your invention when such drawings are necessary to understand your invention. (35 U.S.C. §113.) If you file your application without drawings and the PTO considers that drawings are necessary for an understanding of your invention, your application will be considered incomplete and you will not obtain a filing date. Your drawings must also show every feature of your invention specified in your claims. (37 C.F.R. §1.83(a).)

In most cases, you will need to prepare drawings for your invention. The rules that govern the formalities of your drawings are specified in 37 C.F.R. §1.84. If your drawings do not conform to all of these rules upon submission, they will be considered *informal*. You will be notified of such informalities in a Notice of Draftspersons Patent Drawing Review, which is a form usually attached to the first *official office action* that you receive from the PTO. This notice will list all of the defects in your drawings.

You can wait to correct such defects right up to the time when or if your application is allowed. However, once you receive a Notice of Allowance, you must correct such defects within three months. This is an absolute cutoff date. No extensions are allowed. (A *Notice of Allowance* is a paper from the PTO that tells you that your patent application has been approved and that a patent will soon be issued.)

Formal Drawings

You can take a chance and submit informal drawings with your application and wait to see if your application is allowed before spending the money to provide formal drawings. However, it is best to submit formal drawings with your application for the following reasons:

- ✪ Your application will be published eighteen months from the time you file your application, unless you have certified that you are not filing abroad and do not want your application published (not recommended). Your drawings must be of sufficient quality for publication. If your drawings are not of sufficient quality, examination of your application will be delayed. Submitting formal drawings will ensure that your drawings are fit for publication.

- ✪ Formal drawings will make a better impression on your examiner.

- ✪ Drawings are a very important part of your obligation to teach persons skilled in your art how to make and use your invention without undue experimentation (enablement), and also your obligation to provide a written description for your claimed invention. By submitting carefully prepared drawings now, you are less likely to make costly errors later. Remember that you will never be able to add features to your drawings that are not disclosed in your specification. This is because the PTO will consider it *new matter*. You are never allowed to add new matter to your application and still rely upon your earlier application filing date.

- ✪ If you wait to submit formal drawings until after you receive a Notice of Allowance, you will have only three months to do it. Doing it initially will save you stress and time.

- ✪ The PTO will issue your patent a few months sooner if you have already filed formal drawings before a Notice of Allowance.

Unless you have some specialized drafting experience, you will most likely need to hire a professional draftsperson to complete formal drawings for your invention. There are, however, good drawing programs like Microsoft®Visio® Technical edition that can be useful in preparing your own informal drawings. Using some of these programs in conjunction with following rules set out by the PTO in 37 C.F.R. §§1.81–1.84, it may be possible for you to complete formal drawings yourself. However, in practice, even most patent attorneys and agents hire professional draftspeople to complete the drawings for a patent application. You can find a professional draftsperson by doing a search on the Internet or by consulting technical journals such as the *Journal of Patent Office Society* or *Intellectual Property Today*.

Whether you hire someone to prepare your drawings or prepare them yourself, make sure that all claimed elements are shown in your drawings.

Drawing Rules   Even after you receive formal drawings back from your draftsperson, you should check them for accuracy. Check to make sure they meet the requirements for drawings discussed in this section. (37 C.F.R. §1.74.)

Go from General to Specific

A good practice tip is to present your drawings in order of general to specific. In other words, your first drawing should be one of your invention as a whole with each of the required elements. You will see that this technique of going from general to specific applies equally to your claims. There is good reason for this commonality because claims, as well as your detailed written description, should work in conjunction with your drawings. Good drawings should actually visually parallel your claims.

Views

You should provide as many views of your invention as are necessary to make the understanding of your invention clear. The views may be plan, elevation, section, or perspective views. Detail views of portions of elements, on a larger scale if necessary, may also be used. Having too many views (figures) can never hurt.

All views on the same sheet of your drawings should stand in the same direction and, if possible, stand so that they can be read with the sheet held in an upright position.

The figures or views on the sheets of your drawings should be labeled in consecutive Arabic numbers (FIG. 1, FIG. 2, FIG. 3, etc.).

You should not crowd your figures all onto one page. Use as many sheets as you need to keep your figures spaced apart enough so they do not look crowded. If you do place more than one figure per sheet, you should arrange the figures so that the numbers increase from top to bottom. Of course, the numbers should also increase from sheet to sheet.

Drawing Sheets

Your drawing sheets must be on paper that is flexible, strong, white, smooth, nonshiny, and durable. Only one side of the sheet may be used for the drawing. The sheets must be either 8½ x 11 inches or size A4. The sheets that contain the figures of your drawings should be labeled in consecutive Arabic numbers, followed by a forward slash, and then the total number of sheets you are submitting. Therefore, if you are submitting six sheets of drawings, you would label the first sheet as "1/6," the second as "2/6," and so on. These numbers should appear on the top center of each sheet, just outside the margin. The drawing sheet numbering must be clear and larger than the numbers used as reference characters to avoid confusion. Your draftsperson should do this for you if you are having your drawings professionally prepared.

Identification of Drawings

It is a good idea to identify each sheet of your drawings, so that if any of your sheets become disorganized, the PTO can easily put the sheets back together. You should place this identification on the front of each sheet, centered within the top margin. The identification should include the title of your invention, inventor's name, and *application number* (or *docket number* if an application number has not been assigned to the application). One way to create a docket number is to use your last name (or first couple of letters of your last name) followed by a number that corresponds to how many applications you have filed.

You can type the identifying information onto a label and then affix this label directly to your drawing sheets. If you type directly onto your drawing sheets, you may damage your sheets. For example, if your name is Jane Doe, you might include the following information on a label and then affix it to your sheet.

Applicants: Jane Doe
Serial No.: Not Yet Assigned
Title: SLIDING LATCH
Docket No.: DOE1

Reference Numbers

You should include reference numbers specifying where on your drawings each of the parts or features are located that were introduced in your detailed specification. These numbers must match the numbers you used in your detailed description. These numbers should start at 12 or a number larger than your highest figure number and increase by two or more, so that if you ever need to add a reference number in between, you will be able to do so without having to place an added reference number out of incremental sequence.

You should draw a line from each of your reference numbers to the feature or part that you are designating. The line should start just off (not touching) each reference number from about the imaginary center of the reference number and extend and touch the feature or part that you are identifying. The lines that run from your reference numbers can be straight or curved, but should never run into each other.

You can see this by looking at Fig. 2 from the sample patent application contained in Appendix C on page 579. The only time that the line extending from a reference number should not touch the part it is referring to is when the reference number is used to designate an entire assembly of parts, as with reference number 12 in Fig. 2. You will notice that the line extending from 12 also has an arrow pointing to the assembly, and any line that you use to designate such an assembly should also have an arrow.

If you place more than one figure on a drawing sheet, you may be tempted to draw two lines from one reference number to the same feature. Although this may be convenient, you should not do this, but rather use two of the same reference numbers with two separate lines, since the figures should be self-contained.

Photographs (black-and-white)

Photographs are not usually submitted in drawings unless there is some special reason for doing so, such as when the photographs are the only practicable medium for illustrating your invention. Photographs are typically submitted in biological inventions for electrophoresis gels, blots, autoradiographs, and the like.

Color Drawings or Photographs

Because of reproduction problems, the PTO sets down quite a few rules that you must follow if you want to submit either color drawings or color photographs. These rules are contained in 37 C.F.R. §1.84(a) for color drawings and 37 C.F.R. §1.84(b) for color photographs. In each case, you are required to submit a petition to the PTO.

Copyright Notices

A copyright notice (e.g., "© 2003 John Doe") may be placed adjacent to copyright material in your specification. Remember to include an additional separate section heading at the start of your specification as discussed previously.

If your copyright notice appears in your drawing, the notice must be limited in print size from 1/3 inch to 1/4 inch, and must be placed within the sight of the drawing, immediately below the figure representing the copyright material.

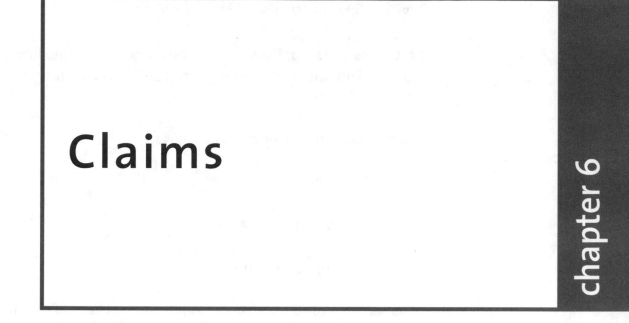

Claims

This chapter covers the claim section of your specification. A separate chapter has been devoted to explaining how to draft your claims because it is a lengthy and important topic.

CLAIMS FORMAT

Your claims section must begin on a separate sheet of paper, and it must start with one of the following phrases:

- ✪ "I claim" (use this if you are the sole inventor);

- ✪ "We claim" (use this if you are filing an application in which there is more than one inventor); or,

- ✪ "The invention claimed is" (this can be used whether you have one or more inventors).

On the next line of your claims portion, number your claims using Arabic numerals (i.e., 1, 2, 3). If you have just one claim, you would write the number "1," followed by the claim. If you have more than one claim, you would continue numbering the claims in order. Look at the sample application in Appendix C for the format of your claims. You should see that there are twelve claims in the sample patent 4,518,108.

A claim contains three separate parts:

1.   the preamble;

2.   a transitional phrase; and,

3.   the body of the claim.

This section provides a detailed explanation of each of the three parts.

Preamble   Following the appropriate numeral, start your claim with a capital letter—typically "A" or "An"—and then the product or method that you are claiming. This portion of your claim is known as the *preamble*.

The *preamble* of a claim is an introductory statement, usually in single paragraph form, that should recite at least the statutory class of the invention (e.g., apparatus, composition, process), but it may recite more. Look at claim 1 of the sample patent application in Appendix C. You will see that the claim starts off with the phrase "A folding carrier mountable on an automobile or the like." This is the preamble. The phrase starts off with the word "A" and then cites an apparatus ("a folding carrier"), which is the statutory class of the invention.

If the body of your claim fully sets forth all the limitations of your claimed invention and your preamble merely states, for example, the purpose or intended use of your invention, then your preamble will not be considered a limitation and will be of no significance in construing your claim. However, any terminology in your preamble that limits the structure of your claimed invention must be treated as a claimed limitation.

In general, it is a good idea to consider anything you write in your preamble as potentially limiting your claim. So be careful how much you add in the preamble because it may limit the scope of your claim when you try to enforce your claim against a potential infringer.

Example:

Dr. J obtained a patent with a claim to a method of "treating or preventing macrocytic megaloblastic anemia" by administering a combination of folic acid and vitamin B "to a human in need thereof." Dr. J later sued R for infringement based on an over-the-counter dietary supplement marketed by R that contained folic acid and vitamin B. R's product was labeled and sold for maintenance of blood homocysteine levels, but did not state that it was useful for the treatment or prevention of macrocytic megaloblastic anemia. The court held no infringement, noting the importance of the fact that the preamble set forth the objective of the method and that the body of the claim required that the method be performed "to a human in need thereof." The court explained that the preamble was a statement of the intentional purpose for which the method must be performed. The presence of this language in the actual body of the patent seemed to tilt the scale toward treating the preamble as a limitation since it gave life and meaning to the preamble's statement of purpose. In this case, Dr. J would have been better off drafting the claim more broadly by simply using a preamble such as "a method comprising."

Sometimes, however, having such a limitation can actually work to your advantage, especially if you need to distinguish your invention based on the prior art.

Example:

Dr. P's patent was directed to a method for treating sunburn using a composition containing a fatty acid ester of ascorbic acid. Dr. P sued M alleging that M's prescription skin composition infringed its claim. M defended on the basis that P's claim was invalid as anticipated by a patent that disclosed all of the ingredients of P's patent and disclosed the use of these compositions for topical application to the skin and hair. The treatment of sunburn, however, was not disclosed. A higher court disagreed that the patent was anticipated since P's claim was directed to a new use (treating sunburn) for an old composition and disagreed that the treatment of sunburn was inherent in the prior art patent. One reason why the court construed the preamble limitation as part of the claim was that the claim body provided "topically applying to the skin sunburn" a fatty acid. This arguably brought the preamble into the body of the claim.

The lesson here is that drafting patents is complicated and indeed an art. You will need to review the prior art. If you want your preamble to become limiting to the scope of your patent claim, then you should add the limitation to the preamble and also incorporate phrases such as "administering to a person in need thereof," which will link or connect the preamble to the body of your claim. Your best protection, however, is to include a variety of claims with different scopes; one broad and one with the limiting preamble. More will be said later on in this chapter about using a variety of claims in your patent application.

Transitional Phrase

The *transitional phrase* is an introductory clause between the preamble and body of the claim. It indicates where the background ends and the body begins, and defines how to interpret the claims. The commonly used phrases are "comprising," "consisting essentially of," and "consisting of." Each one of these phrases is important to understand because its use determines how broad your claim will be. Each phrase defines the scope of your claim with respect to what unrecited additional components or steps, if any, are excluded from the scope of your claim.

NOTE: *Sometimes you will see "comprising," "consisting essentially of," and "consisting of" in the body of your claim. When such phrases appear in a clause of the body of your claim, rather than as a transition phrase immediately following the preamble, they limit only the element set forth in that clause; other elements are not excluded from your claim as a whole. (Mannesmann Demag Corp. v. Engineered Metal Products Co., 793 F.2d 1279 (Fed. Cir. 1986).)*

Open-Ended Transitional Phrases

The word "comprising" is frequently used because it is open-ended in that it does not exclude additional, unrecited method steps or elements. *Comprising* is a term of art used in claim language that means that the named elements are essential, but other elements may be added and still be within the scope of the claim. Such an open-ended claim is infringed if all the recited elements are found in the infringing product, even if additional elements are also found. In other words, an accused product or method will infringe upon a product or method claim having the transitional phrase "comprising" even if it employs additional steps.

Example:

A claim that recites a device as comprising elements A, B, and C would be infringed by a device having elements A, B, C, and D. The claim is interpreted as "my invention is at least the following, but it may include more."

Sometimes you will see the word "including" or "which comprises" instead of "comprising." All are equivalent to each other. The use of the transition phrases "comprising" or "including" are the best types of transition phrases that you can use in drafting your patent claims because your coverage is broadest.

However, sometimes the PTO will not give the broad coverage that you normally get by using the transition clause "comprising." For example, your detailed description may not enable such broad coverage. Also, it is easier for prior art to anticipate a broad claim than a claim with more elements. So if you write a claim comprising only two elements, hoping to capture potential infringers whose products contain those two elements, it will be easier for a prior art reference to anticipate (teach each and every element) elements A and B rather than elements A, B, and C.

Closed Transitional Phrases

"Consisting of" is a transitional phrase that is much more limiting when it comes to what you are claiming. The use of the word "consisting" when used as a transitional phrase excludes any element that you have not specifically claimed. Thus, if your claim is to a gadget consisting of elements A and B, any potentially infringing product must contain only elements A and B or their *equivalents* and nothing else.

Author's Note: What Is the Doctrine of Equivalents?

A very important concept in patent law is called the *Doctrine of Equivalents*. This doctrine comes into play if and when it comes time for you to sue someone for infringement of any one of the claims of your patent.

In essence, the *Doctrine of Equivalents* says that not only can you sue someone for infringing upon the literal meaning of a limitation in your claim, but also for any equivalents of that limitation. By equivalents the law means insubstantial differences of that limitation. This is deemed fair because it is difficult for mere language to capture every type of minor variation.

Partially Open-Ended Transitional Phrases

A third type of transitional phrase that can be used in claim drafting is the phrase "consisting essentially of." This transitional phrase is used to denote a partially open claim. It occupies a middle ground between closed claims that are written in *consisting of* format and fully open claims that are drafted in a *comprising* format.

This transitional phrase is sometimes seen preceding a list of ingredients in a composition claim or a list of steps in a process claim. By using the phrase "consisting essentially of," you signal that the invention necessarily includes the listed ingredients or steps and is open to unlisted ingredients or steps that do not materially affect the basic and novel properties of the invention.

An ingredient or step has a material effect if the effect is of importance or consequence to those persons having the typical and ordinary skill in your art. For example, if your invention is a chemical composition, then you might ask whether the addition of some other element to that composition would have any importance in respect to the properties of that composition. If the answer is no, then a claim using "consisting essentially of" would encompass that additional element. If the answer is yes, then the element would be outside the scope of the claim and escape literal infringement of that claim.

Although *consisting essentially of* is typically used in the compositions of matter, there is nothing wrong with using this term as modifying language for method steps. In such a case, the claim can only include steps that do not materially affect the basic and novel characteristics of the claimed method.

Example:

1. A process of producing a completely hardened metal structural element provided with a fracture of an intended course consisting essentially of:

   (a) subjecting the surface of the completely hardened structural element at least along a portion of the intended course of the fracture and in traverse limitation thereto to a high energy radiation to selectively embrittle the metal; and,

   (b) splitting the elements along the intended course of the fracture.

While a *consisting essentially of* may help you to capture potential infringers who try to include steps that do not materially affect the basic and novel characteristics of your invention, this type of claim can sometimes run into problems with prior art just as with the broader *comprising* format.

To see this, say there is prior art that has the additional elements of (c) and (d), so that the prior art contains elements (a), (b), (c), (d). So long as (c) and (d) do not affect the basic and novel characteristics of the process, you would not be able to argue that your claimed invention is different from the prior art for anticipation purposes. You *would* be able to argue this if you had written the claim in the *consisting of* claim format.

By writing a claim with *consisting essentially of,* you are in effect saying, "I'm claiming my listed steps, plus any other steps that do not affect the basic and novel characteristics of my method." You would need to amend your claim in such a situation to the more restricting transitional phrase of *consisting,* or else you would be infringing upon this prior art and the PTO would reject your claim.

For purposes of searching for and applying prior art, if you do not spell out clearly in your specification what the basic and novel characteristics are, *consisting essentially of* will be construed as equivalent to *comprising.* (MPEP §2111.03.) Moreover, if you contend that additional steps or materials in the prior art are excluded by the recitation of *consisting essentially of,* you have the burden of showing that the introduction of additional steps or components would materially change the characteristics of your invention.

> ***Author's Note: Which transitional phrase should you use?***
> While there is no definitive answer as to which transitional phrase to use, it would be rare for a patent application not to contain at least one claim having the broadest "comprising" transitional phrase. Broad is better from the standpoint of the number of possible infringers that you can capture later on. However, while using a broad transitional phrase like "comprising" will indeed capture more potential infringers of your claim, it will also make it easier for your examiner to find prior art that anticipates your claim.

Body of Your Claim

The third part of your claim is called the *body of your claim.* This is where you set out either the process steps (if you are claiming a method or process) or the structural limitations (if what you are claiming is a structure). These steps or limitations are what define and make up the invention for which you seek protection.

Look again at Claim 1 of the sample patent application on p.587. The start of Claim 1 from the sample follows with the start of the body of the claim in italics.

1. A folding carrier mountable on an automobile or the like, said carrier comprising:

   (a) a frame;

   (b) a carrying member pivotally mounted to said frame said carrying member movable about a first axis between an operative extended position and a collapsed position, said carrying member and said frame being in a substantially side-by-side relationship when said carrying member is in its collapsed position, a foot of said carrying member positioned to contact the automobile when said carrying member is in its operative extended position.

In this claim, there are structural limitations set out in the form of (a), (b), et cetera. To make the reading of these limitations easier, each of the elements or limitations is set out in a separate paragraph.

You should also notice that the structural elements making up this folding carrier are not set out alone but are rather interrelated to the other structural elements set out in the claim. Your claim must end with a period, and you may not use a period in your claim anywhere except at the end of your claim.

TYPES OF CLAIMS AND HOW TO DRAFT THEM

For ease of discussion, the classes of claims are divided into the following headings—Apparatus, Compound, Composition, and Process claims. All of these types of claims come within the scope of 35 U.S.C. §101. This division is the most common way most patent attorneys refer to them.

The thing that you must keep in mind as you write your claims is that each claim must fall into a separate statutory class. Think of claims as an individual oasis. Claims are separate and distinct from each other. When it comes time for your examiner to examine your application, he or she will look at each of your claims independently for patentability purposes. Similarly, when it comes time for you to enforce your claims for infringement purposes, you will look at each one of your claims separately to determine whether infringement exists.

While you can include more than one statutory class of claims in a patent application, you cannot include two separate classes within the same claim. The only exception to this rule is a *product-by-process claim*. This claim has been determined to be a separate statutory claim class. (This class of claim is discussed more fully later in this chapter.)

Apparatus Claims

Apparatus claims are one type of product claim that covers a device. For example, the following would be considered an apparatus claim:

1. A decorative figure assembly, comprising:

    (a) a non-fluid filling material;

(b) a plurality of individual closure means each for closing a bag;

(c) a plastic torso bag containing a first portion of said filling material and having an open end being closed by a first of said plurality of closure means;

(d) a plastic head bag containing a second portion of said filling material and having an open end being closed by a second of said plurality of closure means;

(e) two plastic arm bags containing third and fourth portions, respectively, of said filling material and each having an open end being closed by a third and a fourth of said plurality of closure means, respectively; and,

(f) a plurality of coupling means for coupling said torso bag to said head bag, to said arm bags, and to said leg bags, wherein said head bag, said arm bags, and said leg bags are coupled by said plurality of coupling means to said torso bag and form a figure proportioned to a costumed human.

A claim to an apparatus covers what a device is. As you can see from the previous example (Claim 1), there are *elements* or *limitations* (a–f) that define the structure of the decorative figure assembly. The claim in this case ends with a *wherein* clause. Such *wherein* or *whereby* clauses are typical in apparatus claims and usually tie in the important elements of the apparatus and state the advantage or what is accomplished by the apparatus. Such *whereby* clauses can be instrumental in getting claims allowed without necessarily adding limitations to your claims. For example, pointing out the advantages of your invention in a *whereby* clause may strengthen your case to negate an obviousness rejection.

Claims directed to an apparatus must be distinguished from the prior art in terms of *structure* rather than *function*. You should claim an apparatus in terms of its structure, not by what it does.

The only time that you are allowed to come close to describing something by its function is when you use a special type of claim drafting format called a *means-plus-function clause.* (More detailed information about means-plus-function clauses is discussed later in this chapter.)

Compound Claims

If you are claiming a chemical compound, a typical way to phrase your claim is to say, "A compound of the formula:" and then draw the formula that you are claiming. Such claims are commonly referred to simply as *compound claims.* The format of this claim is exactly like a conventional format except that it lacks a transitional phrase like "comprising."

If you do not know the formula or structure of the compound that you are claiming, you may claim your compound by listing its physical and chemical characteristics. This is sometimes referred to as *fingerprinting.*

A second way that you may claim a compound of unknown formula is by claiming it in terms of the process by which it is made (product-by-process claim). For example, it would be proper to claim "A chemical compound produced by a process comprising the steps of:" and then list all of the steps.

Composition Claims

Composition claims define a composition as a combination of chemical components. Such claims may not be directed to naturally occurring substances because such substances are unpatentable under 35 U.S.C. §101. Claims directed to *newly* discovered compositions of matter that are products of nature must be prefixed with the phrases such as "a purified," "an isolated," "a substantially pure," or "a biologically pure" product or compound (such as a purified protein) to distinguish them from naturally occurring, unpatentable subject matter.

You will often see *ranges* cited in a composition claim. One thing that you need to keep in mind is that such ranges are anticipated by prior art that intersects anywhere within your cited range. Thus, if your claim cites 0.2–0.4% molybdemum (Mo) and 0.6–0.9% Nickel (Ni) as your composition, this claim will be anticipated by a reference that discloses 0.25% by weight Mo and 0.75% Ni. (*Titanium Metals Corporation of America v. Banner,* 778 F.2d 775 (Fed. Cir. 1985).)

If your claimed composition is physically the same as the composition cited in prior art and you are simply stating some new property or use of the composition, the prior art will render your claim unpatentable. Thus, you would not distinguish yourself from prior art merely by citing the glass transition temperature of a copolymer that was not cited in the prior art since this is merely citing a new physical property of the same composition. (*In re Spada*, 911 F.2d 705 (Fed. Cir. 1990).)

Process Claims

There are two types of *process claims*. The first type is a claim that defines how to make something such as an apparatus, composition, or compound. Such a process claim may consist of a single step or many steps.

The second type of process claim is one that defines how a machine operates or how to operate on a composition, material, or article to make it do something. The second type of process claim is commonly referred to as a *method claim* although the word "process" is good form because it is the word used in the relevant statute.

> ***Author's Note: Infringement of process or method claim***
> A process or method claim is not infringed unless the accused process substantially follows the patented methods and employs all of the steps or stages of the patented process in the United States (*Pelligrini v. Analog Devices Inc.*, 2005). However, a *Special Statute Regarding Infringement Process Abroad* (35 U.S.C. §271(g)) provides that a product imported into the United States will infringe a process patent for making the product if the patented process was implemented abroad. Process claims can be somewhat inconvenient to enforce because the infringer may be the end user of the device and thus often a customer rather than a competitor. Also, the claim must be operated, or the composition, material, or article operated upon in the United States in the same manner as required by the claims. You should try to include other types of claims in your application in addition to process claims if possible.

An example of a process claim could read as follows:

1. A purified polynucleotide having a nucleic acid sequence selected from the group consisting of SEQ ID NO:1, SEQ ID NO:2, and SEQ ID NO:3.

2. An expression vector comprising the polynucleotide of Claim 1.

3. A host cell transformed with the expression vector of Claim 2.

4. A process for producing and purifying a polypeptide, said process comprising the steps of:

   (a) culturing the host cell of Claim 3 under conditions suitable for the expression of the peptide and

   (b) recovering the polypeptide from the host cell culture.

This last claim, a process claim, is taking the host cell that was claimed in Claim 3 and performing process steps on the cell to obtain a protein.

Author's Note: What Is a Markush Group?

A *Markush Group* is a group of related items joined by the word "and." Inventions in metallurgy, refractories, ceramics, pharmacy, pharmacology, and biology are most frequently claimed under the Markush format. However, purely mechanical features or process steps may also be claimed this way.

A Markush group, incorporated in a claim, should be closed, that is, it must be characterized with the transitional phrase "consisting of," rather than "comprising" or "including." The Markush group can be broadened somewhat, however, by the transitional phrase "consisting essentially of" to include traces of materials outside the specified group.

You can see that the transitional phrase "consisting of" is used. Look at Claim 1 that states, "SEQ ID NO:1, SEQ ID NO:2, and SEQ ID NO:3." While Claim 1 could have been made into three separate claims by claiming each sequence separately, the use of a Markush group does the trick itself with one claim. Typical examples of claims using the Markush format can be found in the PCT International Search and Preliminary Examination Guidelines at www.wipo.int/pct/en/texts/pdf/ispe.pdf.

In a process claim you must set forth all the active steps with verbs ending in "-ing," or else your process claim will be rejected as being vague and indefinite.

Example:

Alison wrote two of her claims as follows:

1. A process for using monoclonal antibodies of Claim 4 to isolate and purify human fibroblast interferon.

2. A process for using monoclonal antibodies of Claim 4 to identify human fibroblast interferon.

These claims are properly rejected under 35 U.S.C. §112 on the basis that they cite a use without the reciting of any active "-ing" process steps. (*Ex parte Erlich,* 3 U.S.P.Q.2d 1011 (1986).)

Product-by-Process Claims

There is one type of hybrid between a product and process claim that is authorized called a *product-by-process* claim. In this type of claim, the process referred to is the process of *making* a product, not the process of using a product.

While a product-by-process claim format may appear to cross the line between improperly combining two statutory classes of invention, it is acceptable because a product-by-process claim merely uses one statutory class of invention (e.g., process limitation) to define or fingerprint another statutory class (i.e., the product). (*Ex parte Lyell,* 17 U.S.P.Q.2d 1549 (1990).) If you include a product-by-process claim in your application, you should also include a product claim if possible.

There are some disadvantages of a product-by-process claim when compared with a product claim.

- ✪ Product-by-process claims are harder to infringe than a product claim alone. This is because a product-by-process claim is infringed only by the claimed product made through a substantially identical process as the process recited in your product-by-process claim. However, if you have a product claim, your product claim will be infringed by the same product made by a different process. In other words, the process serves as an added limitation of a product-by-process claim when it comes to infringement analysis.

✪ Even though product-by-process claims are defined by a process, determination of patentability is based on the product itself. If the product in the product-by-process claim is the *same as* or *obvious from* a product of the prior art, the claim is unpatentable even though the prior product was made by a different process.

✪ Product-by-process claims may also run into problems with the written description requirement. This may be particularly true in the biological and chemical arts when the invention is some chemical composition that is claimed by describing the process used to obtain it. The problem with such a claim is that the written description requirement usually requires that the chemical composition be more precisely defined as by structure, formula, or chemical name.

If you include a product-by-process claim and your process is itself novel and nonobvious, you should also include a claim directly to your process in your application. If your product claim is not allowed, you will be able to patent your process claim.

DRAFTING DEPENDENT CLAIMS

A dependent claim is a claim that refers back to and further restricts a single preceding claim. There are many reasons for including dependent claims in your application. Here are several of them.

✪ A dependent claim saves you from repeating all of the elements of the main claim (the claim from which the dependent claim depends).

✪ A dependent claim shall be presumed valid even if it is dependent upon an invalid claim. (35 U.S.C. §282.)

Dependent claims are a good way to add additional claims to your application if you want to add some significant element or feature to a claim that you have previously written. If your main, broader claim is held invalid, your dependent claim will be evaluated on an independent basis and is presumed valid until proven otherwise.

✪   Thus, if a potential infringer finds a prior art reference that anticipates your broad main claim and is successful in invalidating it (but not your narrower dependent claim), you will still be able to enforce your narrower dependent claim.

✪   Of course, independent claims also stand on their own and you would be able to achieve the same result by writing your dependent claims as independent claims. However, you are charged an extra fee for each independent claim that you file in excess of three independent claims. Filing dependent claims will therefore not only save you from repeating all of the elements of an independent claim but it will also save you money.

✪   By further restricting your invention with the use of dependent claims, there is greater likelihood that one of your dependent claims has all of the features in an accused infringer's product. Although the accused product will also infringe the broader independent main claim in your application from which your dependent claim depends, you may gain a psychological advantage with a judge or jury who is able to clearly see how the accused product matches up to your claim.

A dependent claim may depend from an independent claim or from another dependent claim. There is no limit to the length of a chain of dependent claims. However, you should group all claims dependent from the same independent claim directly after that claim. Also, any dependent claim that you write must further restrict the claims on which it depends.

Example:

Inventor Joe claimed an electrical circuit in the following manner:

I claim:

1. An electrical circuit comprising, in series, a 10–20 amperes DC current source of variable content, an 8–10 ohm resistor, and a 3–8 uf capacitor.

2. An electrical circuit according to Claim 1, wherein the resistor is a 5–10 ohm resistor.

The second dependent claim is rejected by the PTO since it broadens rather than restricts Claim 1. (The ohm range of the resistor is increased from an 8–10 range to a 5–10 range.) The PTO is this detailed regarding your claims.

When you draft a dependent claim, your dependent claim is considered to include all of the limitations that you have placed in the claim from which your dependent claim depends as well as any additional limitations that you add in your dependent claim. This has the practical effect that any time the main claim is not infringed, then your dependent claim will never be infringed. In fact, the PTO defines a dependent claim as one that shall not conceivably be infringed by anything that would not also infringe the basic claim. This makes sense because main claims are less restrictive and, therefore, are more encompassing than dependent claims.

Since the transitional phrase "consisting of" is a close-ended phrase, if you use it in the main claim, you are not allowed to add new elements to its dependent claim. You are allowed to add new information to your dependent claim that further defines a preexisting element contained in the prior claim, but you cannot go as far as to add a new feature to your dependent claim.

There is no rule against using a dependent claim that is in a different statutory class from the main independent claim. For example, if your main independent claim is a product claim, you are allowed to use a dependent claim that is a process of using the product of your main claim.

You should draft enough dependent claims to cover all possible permutations that are useful in your invention. Thus, if you invent a new medical devise and some of its useful feathers are A, B, and C, then you should have three dependent claims to A, B, and C. However, you should also include four additional dependent claims to A+B, A+C, B+C, and A+B+C.

Multiple-Dependent Claims

Sometimes, but not often, you may want to refer back to not only one preceding claim, but to several other claims. When you do this, you are creating what is called a *multiple-dependent claim*. As with dependent claims, a multiple-dependent claim must further restrict the claims on which it depends.

While multiple-dependent claims are permissible, you must always refer to the prior claims in the alternative. Examples of properly worded multiple claims are:

"A gadget according to Claims 3 or 4, further comprising..." or

"A gadget as in any one of the preceding claims, in which..."

Examples of unacceptable multiple dependent claim wording are:

"A gadget according to Claim 3 and 4, further comprising..." or

"A gadget according to Claims 1–3, in which..."

You should avoid using multiple-dependent claims, as there is a multiple-dependent claim surcharge. The number of claims upon which the filing fee is based increases considerably as a result of multiple dependency.

NOTE: *A multiple-dependent claim may not depend on any other multiple-dependent claim. (For more information on multiple-dependent claims, see MPEP §608.01(n).)*

MEANS-PLUS-FUNCTION CLAUSES

There is a special statute that states that an element in a claim for a combination may be expressed as a means for performing a specified function, without recital of the structure, material, or acts disclosed in the specification. As noted earlier, when discussing apparatus claims, this is the only time that you are allowed to describe something in a claim by its function rather than by function. To create a *means-plus-function clause,* a structure is followed by the word "means" rather than by its specific structure. If you return to the apparatus claim example on page 113, there are two means-plus-function clauses in that claim—elements (b) and (f):

✪   (b) a plurality of individual closure means...

✪   (f) a plurality of coupling means for coupling said torso bag...

If you use a means-plus-function format in your claim, you must remember to always include more than one element in your claim. In other words, you cannot write your claim with a single means plus a statement of function and nothing more. The reason for this is that the statute that authorizes this type of format requires the claim be a *combination.* (35 U.S.C. §112).

A means-plus-function element can be incorporated in the preamble of a claim, as well as in the body. It can appear in combination with other means-plus-function elements or in combination with nonfunctional elements. It can even be applied as an element of a claim in *Jepson format* (discussed later). If you are using more than one means clause in your claim, it is often helpful to distinguish between the clauses by stating "first means" to refer to the first means clause and "second means" to refer to the second means clause, and so on.

In order to make sure that your apparatus claim is not anticipated by prior art, you must recite at least one feature that differentiates your apparatus from any prior art apparatus. You cannot avoid anticipation by claiming some novel function that your apparatus does. A recitation with respect to the manner in which your apparatus is intended to be used does not differentiate your claimed apparatus from a prior art apparatus if the prior art apparatus teaches all the structural limitations of your claim. Conversely, the mere fact that a prior art device performs all the functions recited in your apparatus claim does not mean that such prior art anticipates your claim if there is any structural difference.

Example:

Evan's claims were drawn to a disposable diaper having three fastening elements. A prior art reference disclosed two fastening elements that could perform the same function as the three fastening elements in Evan's claims. Evan's claims would not be anticipated by the reference since the reference did not disclose the separate third fastening element.

When you use a means-plus-function clause, the PTO (or a court later on in an infringement suit) will look to your specification for structures that you have listed that carry out the function of your means-plus-function clause. Structures that you have disclosed in your specification that are clearly linked or associated to your cited function will be considered corresponding structures. After you obtain a patent on your claims, any infringer who uses a corresponding structure to the one that you have cited in your specification will be an infringer of your means-plus-function claim. The reverse side of this is that any corresponding structure in the prior art will also anticipate your means-plus-function claim.

Equivalents   If you read the statute closely, you will see that it also talks about *equivalents thereof.* This means that the PTO (or a court later on in an infringement analysis) will not only look to the corresponding structures that you have disclosed in your specification, but also any equivalents.

Factors that the PTO will look to in order to determine whether a prior art element is an equivalent include:

✪   whether the prior art element performs the identical function specified in your claim in substantially the same way and produces substantially the same results as the corresponding element disclosed in your specification;

✪ whether a person skilled in the art would have recognized the interchangeability of the prior art element for the corresponding element disclosed in your specification; and,

✪ whether there are insubstantial differences between the prior art element and the corresponding element disclosed in your specification. (MPEP §2183.)

The reason that you are given equivalents is so that you do not have to fill up your patent specification with a laundry list of everything you can think of that might be an equivalent to your invention. This prevents a would-be infringer from using your invention later just because they thought of some equivalent structure that can carry out your means-plus-function clause. Again, the reverse side of this is that the PTO can look for equivalents to anticipate your claimed element.

Using a means-plus-function clause can actually be more limited than simply writing your claims without such clauses. When you use a means-plus-function clause, equivalents are determined with respect to the actual means that you have shown in your specification. In determining the equivalents of an element not written in means-plus-function format, however, any and all equivalents of that element are examined.

If you use a means-plus-function clause, an equivalent structure cannot embrace technology developed after the issuance of your patent, whereas you can use such equivalents to find infringement under the doctrine of equivalents. For these reasons, if you include some of your elements in means-plus-function format, it is wise to include other claims in which your elements are not in such a format, if possible.

Advantages   While there are some limitations of using means-plus-function type claims, these types of claims can find their use in patent application drafting. Since the statute that provides the basis for a means-plus-function clause specifically states that such a claim is to be constructed to cover both the disclosed structure in your specification as well as its equivalents, use of a means-plus-function clause may provide you some insurance against recent court limitations that have been placed on the doctrine of equivalents. Writing a wide range of claims with varying scope can often be your best way to capture potential infring-ers of your patent later on down the road.

If you do include a means-plus-function claim in your application, be sure to disclose at least one structure in your specification for carry-ing out the function in your means-plus-function clause. If you fail to do this, you run the risk that your claim will be invalid on the basis of indefiniteness or lack of enablement unless one of ordinary skill in the art would have understood the precise structures, materials, or acts for performing your claimed specific function from the applica-tion disclosure.

JEPSON CLAIM FORMAT

Sometimes a claim is written in a form in which the preamble recites all the elements or steps that are already known about your inven-tion. After this preamble, the claim goes on to list those elements or steps that you consider to be the improvement of your invention. This style is referred to as the *Jepson claim format*. The following claim is an example:

Example:

In an electromagnetic energy shield having a volume resistivity to be effective as an electromagnetic shield comprising a resin matrix loaded with particles coated with silver in an amount of about 40 to 80 volume percent, the improvement being that the silver-coated particles are a maxim size in the range of from 0.5 to 40 mils and wherein the resin is compressible.

A disadvantage of Jepson style claims is that you impliedly admit that the subject matter recited in the preamble (i.e., up to "the improve-ment being") is old in the art. (*Application of Ehrreich*, 590 F.2d 909 (1979).) For this reason, if you use Jepson claims in your application, you have a clear point of novelty that you want to emphasize and include other claims in non-Jepson format. In general, most patent practitioners do not use Jepson claims even though it is the only type of claim that the PTO recommends.

GENERAL CLAIM DRAFTING RULES AND TECHNIQUES

Your specification must include at least one claim that states with precision what you consider to be your invention for which a patent is sought. However, in practice, your specification will always include more than one claim. It would be risky to include just one claim because if that one claim were to be held invalid, you would have nothing to enforce. If you include other claims in your specification— even if some of your claims were held invalid later on—you would still have other claims to rely on. The fact that one or more claims may be held to be invalid does not mean that other claims are automatically invalid. Claims stand or fall on their own and each claim is considered separate from the other claims.

Although there is no particular rule, an application ordinarily will have at least one or two independent claims characterizing the invention as an apparatus, at least one independent claim directed to the anticipated commercial embodiment of your invention, another claim or two as a method, if appropriate, and a sufficient number of dependent claims to comprise a claim total of at least twenty.

After twenty claims, you will be charged an extra fee for each additional claim that you submit. (The fee was $25 per claim in excess of twenty at the time of publication.) You are also charged an extra fee for each independent claim in excess of three that you submit. (The fee was $105 per claim for a small entity at the time of publication.) Often you will see only three independent claims in an application unless your invention is particularly complex or some other reason justifies adding more.

Draft Broad Claims

If you draft broad claims, it is harder for someone's invention to avoid infringing on your claims, meaning that you have a broader scope of protection. To do this, you should use an open-ended transitional phrase such as "comprising" if it is possible to do so. By using an open-ended transitional phrase, you will capture an infringer whose product has elements A, B, C, and D, even if your claim recites only elements A, B, and C.

Another way that you can make sure a claim is written as broad as possible is to include as few elements in your claim as possible. This may seem counterintuitive. You do *not* make claims broader by adding detail. Adding more elements or limitations to a claim will actually limit the claim in as far as the types of products that it can encompass. Your broadest claim should recite the core elements of your invention.

NOTE: *Infringement of a claimed combination requires the presence of each claimed element or its equivalent in the accused structure.*

Another way to make your claims as broad as possible is to pay attention to the language that you use to describe features in your claim. You should use language that is broad rather than limited.

Look at the sample patent in Appendix C. One could recite "a folding bicycle carrier" rather than simply a "folding carrier," but you can probably see that by including the word "bicycle," your patent protection might be limited only to bicycle folding carriers. This could be a problem if your would-be infringer comes along and uses your folding carrier to carry suitcases.

To find the language that you want, go to dictionaries and other patents in your field to see if you can pick up better terms for your words. The use of words like "about," "approximately," and "substantially" are also a wise choice instead of reciting specific parameters such as dimensions.

NOTE: *Your broadest claim—the one that restricts your invention the least—should appear as Claim 1. In other words, as you add claims, you must add limitations that further restrict what exactly you are claiming as your invention. You should never place such further restricted claims above any prior less-restricted claims.*

Make Sure Your Claims Are Not Anticipated

While you should write broad claims, you should also draft them so that they are not *anticipated* by the prior art. As stated in Chapter 3, a claim is anticipated by a prior art reference only if each and every element as set forth in your claim is found, either expressly or inherently described, in that prior art reference.

In times past, patent attorneys and agents would often write very broad claims and then let the PTO worry about whether such claims were anticipated by any prior art. This was a convenient way to draft claims because you could let the PTO do a lot of your work in as far as uncovering prior art. You could also push the limits of the PTO in your quest to obtain the broadest claims possible.

The good old days of submitting the broadest claims possible in a patent application and then letting the examiner do the work in determining how you would need to restrict such claims in order to get around prior art are gone. This is no longer a great strategy due to a famous court case known as *Festo.* (*Festo Corp. v. Shoketsu Kinzoku Kogyo Kabushiki Co.,* 344 F.3d 1359 (Fed. Cir. 2003). The *Festo* decision is actually a case that is worth understanding. The decision affects the previously mentioned doctrine of equivalents, which allows a patent holder to obtain a range of equivalents for each cited element in a claim even though such equivalents were not specified in the patent application. Under *Festo,* if you file a broad claim and then during prosecution you amend this claim, you may give up your right to the doctrine of equivalents, at least with respect to the elements that you have narrowed. What this means for you as a patent drafter is that it is no longer a good strategy to throw in a bunch of broad claims because you think you can sit back and let your examiner tell you later on how to restrict such broad claims just enough to overcome prior art that the examiner might find. What will occur if you follow such a course of action is that your examiner will find prior art, forcing you to make amendments to your broad claims in order to get them approved. However, by amending your claims, you have now potentially eliminated any chance of using the doctrine of equivalents against a potential infringer later if you are successful in obtaining a patent. A better strategy to engage in would be for you to conduct a very thorough review of the prior art before you draft your claims and file claims that are broad in scope but which also have a pretty good chance at clearing the prior art without needing amendment. This way you will get your broad claims and not forgo the doctrine of equivalents later.

Author's Note: Life after Festo

In light of the *Festo* case, many patent attorneys are now going as far as to advocate that patent drafters file very narrow claims and later on amend such claims if necessary to broaden them in light of a search by your examiner. I am not sure that I would personally advocate such a strategy because any amendment to your claims will raise the question as to whether *Festo* applies to such an amendment. I think the correct strategy is to do your homework. Gone are the days when you can just throw unrealistically broad claims into a patent application. You should submit claims that have a good likelihood of getting approved without amendment. If you want to push the limits, you can submit an unrealistically broad claim. However, also make sure that you include more restricted claims in your application that you are pretty sure should not be anticipated by the prior art. This way you will hopefully at least end up with several claims that have not been amended and do not fall in to the *Festo* trap.

Given that amending your claims can now have adverse consequences, your prior art search has become all the more important. You should be aware of the prior art concerning your invention and draft claims so that they are not overly broad or anticipated by this prior art. If you do want to draft overly broad claims that really push the limits, you should also include claims that are narrower in scope. This way, if you are forced to amend your overly broad claims, you still might be allowed your narrower claims that you have not amended and will thereby be entitled to a range of their equivalents.

Drafting claims is, in effect, a balancing act. While you do not want to draft overly broad claims that will likely force you to make amendments to the claim, you do want to draft claims as broad as possible without reading on or being anticipated by the prior art. By drafting your claims as broad as possible in this manner, you will be able to capture as many potential infringers as possible. At the same time, by drafting your claims so they do not read on the prior art, you will be less likely to have to amend your claims during prosecution and will not give up any equivalents to any elements that you have amended.

Author's Note: Narrowly drafted claims
In any case today, you should include narrowly drafted claims targeting specific markets or applications. By including narrowly drafted claims, the likelihood the claim will be rejected either by the patent office or in court declines tremendously. Claims directed to specific applications may also allow patent searchers by potential licensees to more likely find your patent. The protection that your patent offers will also be much clearer. Having a patent issue quicker because it is filed with initial narrow claims can also be useful to more quickly secure venture capital funding to keep you afloat. You can always then file a continuation application (discussed in later chapters) to pursue broader patent coverage for the broader claims that you do not include in your initial application.

Narrowing Your Claim

As stated above, if your claim reads on prior art, you need to narrow it. One approach to narrowing your claim is to simply review your disclosure and find some aspect of your embodiments not shown, nor obvious, in view of the prior art, and then add it to the claim you are drafting.

The problem with just finding any feature in your disclosure that may be new and nonobvious from the prior art is that such a feature will likely be very easy for your competitors to design around. In other words, your competitors will only have to omit your added new feature to escape a charge of infringement. Moreover, since the new feature is likely to be something that has no real value for their invention, your competitors will probably also not care whether or not their products omit the feature.

A much better approach is to narrow your invention with an element that goes to the heart of your invention in solving a problem. For example, suppose you invent a new blood pressure protector that covers blood pressure cuffs and prevents the transmission of disease-causing agents from one patient to the next. After doing your prior art search, you find many patents and several products which also disclose blood pressure cuff protectors. The heart of your invention, though, is that you have two cutouts in your protector lining that line up with the Velcro adhesive strips on your blood pressure cuff. By exposing the Velcro, your blood pressure cuff is able to be used to secure itself around a patient's arm. Surprisingly, you find that doing this gives much better blood pressure readings than using the prior art blood pressure cuff liners, which do not have the cutouts. Using a problem-focused approach to narrowing your claim to distinguish it from the prior art, you should add this problem-solving feature as a limitation in your claim to the protector. The claim you might write in this example would be:

> *An enclosure for a blood pressure cuff comprising of a sleeve having a front side, a back side, and an opening at one end to insert said blood pressure cuff; and, said sleeve having an aperture on said front panel and an aperture on said back side, wherein said front and back apertures are aligned so as to expose the surface area of means used to attach said blood pressure cuff, wherein said blood pressure cuff is self-attaching when used for measuring a patient's blood pressure.*

Using Antecedent Basis

Make absolutely sure that all of the terms and phrases that you use in your claims have *antecedent basis* (support) in your detailed description. If your claims do not have support, then your claims will be rejected for a lack of written support.

> **NOTE:** *Make sure that you use language in your claims that is consistent with the language of the disclosure part of your application. This practice will help ensure that your claims are supported by the specification.*

Another issue that frequently arises with respect to lack of antecedent basis is when you state phrases like "said lever" or "the lever" in your claim, but you have never previously introduced "lever" into your claim. To avoid this problem, use words like "a" and "an" when you are first introducing elements that you are citing in a claim. After you have introduced an element by the words "a" or "an," you then typically refer back to the previously introduced element using the words "the" or "said."

If you try to introduce an element or limitation in your claims with the word "said," your claim will fail for indefiniteness. Fortunately, the problem can be easily cured by amending your claim to include the proper antecedent article.

Essential Features

If you have stated in your specification some feature that is critical to your invention, you must include this critical feature somewhere in your claims. Such essential matter may include missing elements, steps, or structural cooperative relationships of elements described by you as necessary to practice your invention.

In addition to including all the essential features of your invention in your claims, you should interrelate all these essential elements or your claim may be rejected as being vague and indefinite.

Claim Limitations to Avoid

You should avoid drafting your claims by excluding what you *did not* invent rather than by particularly and distinctly pointing out what you *did* invent. Such phrases are known as *negative limitations* and can lead to problems in your claims. Statements in your claim that try to sum up your invention by saying what it does *not* constitute are likely to lead to a rejection as being vague and indefinite. You should always state what you are claiming in the positive.

Also avoid the phrase "at least one of" where you want to claim in the alternative. If you desire to claim in the alternative, then it is better to claim "at least one of the following," and then list the categories that may be joined by "and." For example, "Part X includes at least one of the following: A; B; and Z." Better yet, you could claim "Part A includes at least one of the following: A; B; or Z," to make clear that you mean either one of the three rather than all three together. Otherwise, you may unnecessarily and without intention limit your claim.

Use of Trademarks in Your Claims

The use of trademarks to identify the source of materials is permitted in claims, as long as the trademark is in all capital letters. However, avoid using a trademark alone to describe anything in your claim.

Draft from Broad to Narrow

The whole idea to drafting claims is to obtain the broadest coverage for your invention as possible. As previously explained, you can do that by drafting broad claims. But what if your broad claims are rejected by your examiner? Where are you left after that? You will have to make an amendment to your claim to restrict or narrow its scope. By making amendments to your claims, you will give up the possibility of suing anyone for using any equivalents of your amended elements.

Include a Variety of Claim Types

To avoid losing the ability to go after an infringer for using equivalents, draft a variety of claims with varying degrees of scope. Again, you should place your broadest claims at the beginning and your narrower claims at the end. It is also wise to include a variety of claim formats if possible. If you have a new product, you should also include any possible process claims relating to that product.

There are several advantages to using multiple statutory types. First, drafting such claims will make it more difficult for a potential infringer to invalidate your patent later on. For example, if you have invented a new apparatus, you should include claims not only to the apparatus, but also methods of using the apparatus and methods of making the apparatus if possible. In the event that prior art is later uncovered that discloses the apparatus, your claims to the methods may nevertheless be novel and nonobvious.

Second, using multiple statutory types may avoid the need for claim amendments that can give rise to prosecution history estoppel. For example, if the examiner asserts prior art that discloses your apparatus but not its method of using the apparatus, your method claims may be allowed without amendment. In that way, the range of equivalents available for the allowed method claims will not be limited by prosecution history estoppel under the *Festo* case. Using various statutory classes will also make it easier to target different classes of infringers. For example, your method claims may allow you to go after end users, whereas your method of making the apparatus will probably come in handy against manufacturers. Both the end users and manufacturers will probably be direct infringers of your apparatus claims.

It is also a good idea to include an independent claim that is narrowly drafted to cover a preferred embodiment of your invention. Such a claim may include a number of elements that are each novel so that there is a high probability of patentability over known prior art. Such a narrowly drafted *picture claim* will likely be allowed by your examiner without amendment and thus be allowed its range of equivalents that would not exist with a claim that has been amended.

You should also make sure that your claims cover all disclosed and contemplated embodiments of your invention. Go back to the disclosure part of your application and ensure that you have claims that cover each of your disclosed embodiments. If you disclose such embodiments but fail to claim them, then you can be deemed to have surrendered such unclaimed but disclosed embodiments under a case known as *Johnson & Johnson*. Using means-plus-function claims can help you claim all of your disclosed embodiments since elements described with means-plus-function terminology will be construed to encompass all structures in your disclosure as well as their structural equivalents.

Author's Note: Prosecuting Inventions

The PTO will only allow you to prosecute one invention at a time in a patent application. Do not let this deter you from including all aspects of your invention. You will be allowed by the examiner to restrict out any claims that are considered to be distinct enough to constitute a separate invention in a "restriction requirement" from your examiner. But restricting out such separate inventions can actually be beneficial in that no one will later be able to argue that such restricted inventions are patently indistinct from your elected invention.

Vary Claim Terms

Perhaps the most important thing that you can learn from this chapter is that variety is best when drafting your claims. Not only should you use a variety of claim types and vary the scope of your claims from broad to narrow, you should also think about varying your claim language for the elements of your claim. If you later get barred on one claim term, this will possibly prevent you from being barred on every other claim that uses the same term. Of course your claim terms need to find support in your disclosure (where you should also use this variety of term drafting). As you draft your claims, think about how your competitors will use various equivalents to get around the language of your claims and try to ensure that such equivalents will be captured by your claims.

Include Your Invention in Combination

When inventors come up with some improved feature of a product, patent attorneys will typically include at least one claim to the improved feature in combination with old features that make up that product. Such claims are referred to as *claims to the combination*. In other words, if you invent a new carburetor for a car, you will want to claim the car that has your improved carburetor as a combination.

The reason that you should include a claim to the car as a whole has to do not with infringement but rather with future royalties. Future infringers will likely want to sell a car with your improved carburetor. If your patent only contains claims to the carburetor, such future infringers will infringe your patent if you use the comprising language with your claims to the carburetor. (Remember, *comprising* means that all the infringer's product needs to contain is each and every element of your claim. If a carburetor is in the car, that will constitute infringement.) However, your future royalties will not be based on the sales from the car but rather on sales from that carburetor in the car. To get future royalties on the sale of the car, you will need to include a claim to your carburetor in combination with other features that make up the car.

This does not mean, however, that claims to your improved feature alone are not important. You should also include claims to any elements of your combination that you can claim. Some patent drafters forget to do this, and it can lead to disaster later when it comes time to pursue a potential infringer of your patent. One instance when it can lead to disaster is when you want to go after someone who is selling your improved carburetor as a component to the public to replace worn out carburetors. If you do not have a claim to the carburetor alone, your patent may not cover such a sale. The manufacturer of the carburetor will argue that its sale of the carburetor alone does not contain each and every element of your claim to the carburetor in combination with other features that make up your car. By adding the other features of the car, the manufacturer escapes direct infringement of that combination claim. And since you have no claim to the carburetor itself, the manufacturer may escape patent infringement altogether.

Useful Technique for Drawing Good Claims

While there is no one right way to go about drafting your patent claims other than by putting time and care into writing your claims and studying the way others have written claims, here is one technique that may assist you.

As stated before, you will want to start your claims with your broadest claim. As a first step in drafting your broadest claim, list all of the fundamental elements of your invention. You should include enough such elements to just distinguish your invention over the prior art, but no more. Decide which elements of your invention are absolutely necessary for operability and clear it against the prior art.

Example:

Suppose that you are the first person to come up with the idea of a table. Your essential elements would probably be:

1. a top (since tables need tops);

2. legs (since tables probably need legs); and,

3. some way to secure your legs to the top (you would not want to specifically delineate rivets or some other specific means at this time).

Having listed all of the appropriate necessary elements, you could now write an independent claim that might go as follows:

1. A table, comprising:

    (a) a top portion or surface and

    (b) one or more legs that are secured to said top portion or surface.

You could then proceed to further limit your broad claim by adding dependent claims that add limitations corresponding to the different embodiments of your table. For example, you might want to specify how the top portion is attached to the legs. You might also want to specify the shape of your elements in Claim 1. Some possible dependent claims you might write are the following:

1. The table of Claim 1 wherein said one or more legs are secured to said top portion or surface by a hinge.

2. The table of Claim 1 wherein said top portion is substantially rectangular.

Although this is a very simplified example, it serves to show that you need to think broadly with the fewest elements possible to begin. You then add more limitations in your dependent claims. After you have finished this, you can write additional independent claims. Your additional independent claims might cover any novel process that you can also claim. It is also a good idea to write an independent claim that covers the embodiment of your invention that you are going to actually use commercially.

Completing Your Application

chapter 7

In Chapter 5 you learned that your application has the following parts:

- utility application transmittal form;

- fee transmittal form;

- application data sheet;

- specification;

- drawings; and,

- executed oath or declaration.

At this point, you have completed drafting your specification and your drawings. This chapter covers how to complete the remaining parts of your application. You can take pride that you have already prepared your application for all practical purposes. The rest of the work that follows is more akin to procedural matters, but is important nevertheless.

In addition, this chapter discusses how to complete your *Information Disclosure Statement* (IDS). Although an IDS is not a formal part of your application, it is recommended that you complete your IDS now and submit it along with your application for reasons that are discussed in this chapter.

> ### *Author's Note: Consider filing a provisional patent application.*
> Before you go through the expense of filing a regular utility patent application, consider filing a provisional patent application (discussed in the next chapter). Provisional patent applications are easier and less costly to file than a regular utility patent application. However, if you do file a provisional, you will need to file your regular patent application within one year from the date that you file your provisional application.

To get started, the very first thing that you will want to include in your application materials is a cover sheet in which you tell the PTO exactly what you are enclosing in your envelope. Your cover sheet should look like the one contained in Appendix G. Next, you should complete the *Utility Application Transmittal Form.*

UTILITY APPLICATION TRANSMITTAL FORM

The utility application transmittal form should be downloaded from the PTO website (www.uspto.gov) in order to ensure that you are using the most recent version. Information on this can be found in Appendix G.

> ### *Author's Note: Transmittal Form*
> To obtain the transmittal form, as well as any other required PTO form, click on "patents" and then "forms." You will find two versions of a "utility patent application transmittal"—a regular PDF and an editable PDF. The editable version is nice because you can type in all of the required information and then print it out. However, the PTO does not let you save the form with the data you have inputed. So, if you are going to electronically send it to the PTO you will need to rescan your

printed PDF form and then upload this PDF version as an attachment for any electronic filing to the PTO.

To complete the application, follow these steps.

✪ At the upper right corner, fill in your docket number (this is your own internal reference number that you create to keep track of your application), your name as the inventor, the title of your invention, and the express mailing number you will use to send your application. (See the section on "Sending Your Patent Application" on page 154.)

✪ You should check item 1, fee transmittal form, to indicate that you are including this form with your application.

✪ You should check item 2 if you are claiming small entity status. If you are filing your application as an individual inventor and have not yet assigned your application, you will check this box. By claiming small entity status, you will be entitled to half the regular fee that the PTO charges to file an application. This reduced fare is available for three types of inventors:

- an independent or sole inventor;

- a small business that is defined as a business that employs five hundred or fewer employees (the number of employees is defined as the average number of individuals employed by the business on a full-time, part-time, temporary, or other basis for each of the pay periods for the past twelve calendar months (13 C.F.R. §121.106)); and,

- a nonprofit organization either in this country or abroad.

Neither of these three classes of inventors can have assigned or be under any obligation to assign their invention to an entity that does not classify as a *small entity* in order to qualify for this special fee status.

– Caution –

Do not make any attempt to try and deceive the PTO about your small entity status if you do not qualify as a small entity. Any attempt to fraudulently establish status as a small entity is considered fraud upon the PTO, which can result in the invalidity of your issued patent. (For more information about small entity status, see 35 U.S.C. §41 and 37 C.F.R. §1.27.)

- ✪ You should check item 4 if you are including drawings with your application, and indicate how many sheets of drawings you are submitting.

- ✪ You should check the applicable box to indicate that you are submitting a declaration. If this is your original application and not a continuation, you should check the box labeled "Newly Executed."

- ✪ Check box 6 indicating that you are submitting an application data sheet.

- ✪ Boxes 7–8 will only apply if you are submitting a CD-ROM, CD-R, or sequence listing.

- ✪ If you have assigned your application, you can send in the assignment papers with your application and would correspondingly check box 9.

- ✪ Box 10 has two boxes that probably will not apply to you. The first box concerns a statement made under 37 C.F.R. §3.73(b), which would be used for assignees who wish to take some action concerning a patent. The second box concerns a power of attorney that your attorney will check if you have engaged counsel to file your patent application on your behalf.

- ✪ Box 11 concerns translations of patent applications and will probably not apply to your situation.

✪   You should check box 12 if you are submitting an Information Disclosure Statement (discussed on p. 149), as well as the box labeled "Copies of IDS Citations" to indicate that you are submitting copies of your listed references.

✪   Box 13 should be checked if you are submitting a preliminary amendment. Preliminary amendments are used to make changes to a patent application. You will learn more about these types of amendments later in the book and do not need to concern yourself with this at this point.

✪   You should check box 14 to indicate that you are submitting a return postcard. This will only be applicable if you are mailing rather than electronically filing your application.

✪   If you are making any priority claim to a previously filed foreign patent application that you have filed for your invention, you may need to submit a certified copy of the foreign application and check box 15.

Author's Note: Patent Application Priority Documents
The USPTO, EPO (European Patent Office), and JPO (Japan Patent Office) now allow patent application priority documents to be exchanged between the offices electronically. The USPTO will automatically attempt to electronically retrieve a copy of an EPO or JPO priority document, to which priority is claimed in your U.S. application. For applications filed prior to July 28, 2007, however, you must file a request or an authorization form for the USPTO to retrieve a copy of the priority document (use Form PTO/SB/38 *Request to Retrieve Electronic Priority Application(s)*). If you are doing the reverse and you want the USPTO to release a copy of an unpublished U.S. application to a participating intellectual property office, then you should submit form PTO/SB/39.

✪   If for some reason you are requesting that your application not be published, you should check box 16.

✪   Check box 17 if there is any other type of document that you are submitting along with your application that is not listed on the transmittal form. Again, if there are no other documents, simply leave this box unchecked.

✪ If this is your original or first application in the United States, you do not have to worry about box 18.

✪ Fill in the information concerning your correspondence address unless you have a customer number, in which case you would simply affix your customer number label to the area indicated on the form.

You can obtain a customer number by going to the PTO website and filling out Form PTO/SB/125 (Request for Customer Number). Within a few weeks after you send in the form to the PTO, you will receive small barcode stickers that have your customer number. You can use these labels on all future filings with the PTO.

✪ Print your full name and sign the form.

FEE TRANSMITTAL FORM

Include a fee transmittal form (PTO/SB/17 (10–07)) in duplicate after your utility transmittal form. You can also fill out a *Patent Application Fee Determination Record* and attach it behind your fee transmittal form. These forms can be found on the PTO website. Some things to note when completing your fee transmittal form include the following:

✪ In item 1, you should check the box authorizing the Commissioner to charge any indicated fees and credit any over-payments to your deposit account number if you have such an account set up with the PTO.

✪ You should also check the box labeled "Charge any additional fee(s) or underpayments of fee(s) under 37 CFR 1.16 and 1.17," which will notify the PTO that you want any other fees that you may incur with respect to your application to be charged to your deposit account.

Deposit accounts are very convenient because you can charge any fees associated with the prosecution of your application to your account. If you so authorize at the time you pay your fee, the PTO will also charge any deficiency or credit any overpayment to your account. If at any time you authorize any fee to be charged against your account and there are insufficient funds to cover such a fee, then the PTO will charge you a surcharge in addition to the fee.

If you are an individual inventor who is planning on filing a single application, then the trouble of setting up a deposit account will probably not be worth obtaining one. However, if you plan on filing additional applications in the future, a deposit account may be worth setting up with the PTO.

Provisions exist in which you can establish for a small fee ($10) a *deposit account* with the PTO in order to cover fees associated with the handling of your application. However, a minimum amount of $1,000 is required to establish such an account and a monthly service charge is incurred for balances below the $1,000.

✪ You should check the box labeled "Small Entity Status" if you qualify as a small entity.

✪ Under item 2, you should indicate the type of payment you are making if you are submitting your payment to the PTO along with your application (i.e., not charging your deposit account). If you check the box labeled "Credit Card," you should fill out a credit card payment form PTO-2038. This form is listed in Appendix G. You should attach this form directly behind your fee transmittal. This form is self-explanatory. If you need further help with the form, there are instructions on the PTO website. Under 104 The Complete Patent Kit the "Request and Payment Information" heading, you should state "basic filing fee" as a description of request and payment information.

Fee Calculation   This is the section of your fee transmittal where you calculate out how much money you owe the PTO for various fees.

✪   Under item 1, you should enter the appropriate fee next to the "utility filing fee" box. (This fee was $155 for small entities at the time this book was published. You will also need to enter the appropriate search fees ($255) and examination fees ($105) for small entities.) You should carry these figures over to the subtotal box.

✪   Under item 2, you will need to figure out your total number of claims in your specification, the total number of independent claims, and the total number of multiple-dependent claims.

✪   Each independent and dependent claim in your application will count for one claim. If you have included any multiple-dependent claims, you will need to count up all of the claims to which the multiple-dependent claim refers to in order to figure out how many claims to add to your total.

    If you have used any multiple-dependent claims in your application, you should submit a separate form provided by the PTO called a *Multiple-Dependent Claim Fee Calculation Sheet*. Download this form as instructed in Appendix G. This is to ensure that you are using the most recent PTO version. You should attach it after your *Patent Application Fee Determination Record*.

    Claims in proper multiple-dependent form are considered to include all of the claims to which they refer. If you have any other claims that depend on a multiple-dependent claim, those claims also count for the number of claims referred to in your multiple-dependent claim.

✪   In item 3, you will need to include the appropriate extra fee ($130 for a small entity at the time this book was published) for each additional sheet of your patent specification that exceeds one hundred sheets of paper.

✪   In item 4, you should include any other applicable fees.

APPLICATION DATA SHEETS

You should fill out an *Application Data Sheet* (SB14EFS-WEB) in the forms section at the PTO website. There are also instructions that accompany this form (SB14 EFS-WEB Instructions), which you should follow to guide you through the form. In short, an *application data sheet* is simply a form where you list out information concerning your application. Not every part of the data sheet will apply to your situation. If a section does not apply, you are permitted to simply leave that section blank. In other words, you only need to fill in the situations that are applicable to your own application.

OATH OR DECLARATION

An *oath* is a statement signed before a notary, while a *declaration* is a statement warning you about willful false statements. While you do not have to file an oath or declaration at the precise time you file your application to obtain a *filing date,* it is highly recommended that you complete your oath or declaration now. If you wait to file it, you will receive a Notice Missing Parts, and you will also incur a surcharge for late filing. Every oath must include a statement that acknowledges the duty to disclose to the PTO all information known to you to be material to patentability. (37 C.F.R. §1.63(b)(3).) You should use PTO Form PTO/SB/1209 *oath or affirmation,* which is also available in the forms section at the PTO website.

INFORMATION DISCLOSURE STATEMENT

Each individual associated with the filing and prosecution of a patent application has a duty of candor and good faith in dealing with the PTO. This includes a duty to disclose all information known to that individual to be material to patentability. (37 C.F.R. §1.56.)

The way that you comply with your duty to disclose information to the PTO is through an *Information Disclosure Statement* (IDS). The USPTO provides a form you should use for your IDS (SB08A for page 1 and SB08B for page 2), as well as associated instructions for completing the IDS (SB08A EFS-Web Instructions).

There is no limit to the number of IDS submissions that you can make. For example, you could submit an IDS now with your current application, and then if you later discover a material reference, you can include that reference in a second IDS, which you would simply call a *Supplemental IDS*.

It is very important to be diligent in forwarding to the PTO any information that you believe may be material. When a failure to meet the disclosure duty is found to be a result of fraud, bad faith, or other misconduct on your part, the failure will prevent your patent from being granted. Alternately, if your patent is granted before such misconduct is discovered, the courts can hold all of your patent's claims to be invalid and your patent unenforceable if such misconduct can be shown later.

In order to comply with your disclosure duty, you should submit the most recent IDS form that the PTO has available. Instructions on how to download this form from the PTO website are in Appendix G. Behind your IDS, you should also submit a form that the PTO provides to list all of your references (*Information Disclosure Statement Cover Letter*). Again, because you will not know your examiner's name or Group Art Unit at this point, you can simply state "Not Yet Assigned."

If you have met all of the requirements for your IDS, your examiner will consider each of the references that you have listed on your citation list form and initial next to each of the references that the examiner has considered. Your examiner will send you a copy of the citation list with his or her initials next to the references considered in the next office action that you receive from the PTO. Any items that have not been considered by your examiner will have a line drawn through the citation.

Electronic Submission

The PTO allows applicants to electronically file an IDS. As with the filing of your patent application, I recommend that you use electronic filing because it will make your life easier. You should download and complete Form PTO/SB/08A EFS-Web entitled *Information Disclosure Statement by Applicant,* which is listed on the PTO website forms section just as you would if you were to file your application by mail.

To file your Information Disclosure Statement using EFS-Web, select the document description "Information Disclosure Statement Letter" under the category "IDS/References" and upload your completed IDS in PDF format.

Time to Submit Your IDS

Submit your IDS along with your application, because the longer you wait after submitting your application, the more you must do in order to get the PTO to consider your IDS and the more you are going to have to pay. The following four stages in your prosecution illustrate this.

1. If you submit an IDS within three months from the date you file your application or prior to the mailing date of the first office action on the merits (not procedure) by the PTO, whichever is later, the PTO will consider your IDS without any charge.

2. If you file your IDS after the time in stage 1, but prior to a final action or Notice of Allowance, you must either provide a certification or pay a fee specified in 37 C.F.R. §1.17(p).

   If you opt for the certification instead of paying the fee, you must certify (and this means it must be true) that the references you are submitting to the PTO became known to you or anyone else involved with the prosecution of your application no more than three months prior to the time you are submitting these references (i.e., the mailing date of your IDS).

   In the alternative, you can certify that such references were cited in a counterpart foreign application (such as in an international search report you receive during the prosecution of your foreign application) no more than three months prior to your submission.

   A counterpart foreign patent application means that a claim for priority has been made in your U.S. application and foreign application based on it or that the disclosures of your U.S. and foreign patent application are substantively identical.

NOTE: *Under this certification, it does not matter whether you actually knew about any information cited before receiving a piece of information like a search report. What matters is what is stated in the search report.*

You can use either one of the certification statements below. Simply place the applicable certification statement into your IDS and you can avoid paying the required fee.

(a) *I hereby state that each item of information contained in the information disclosure statement was first cited in any communication from a foreign patent office in a counterpart foreign application not more than three months prior to the filing of the information disclosure statement; or,*

(b) *I hereby state that no item of information contained in the information disclosure statement was cited in a communication from a foreign patent office in a counterpart foreign application, and, to the knowledge of the person signing the certification after making reasonable inquiry, no item of information contained in the information disclosure statement was known to any individual designated in Section 1.56(c) more than three months prior to the filing of the information disclosure statement.*

If some of the references that you list were cited in a communication from a foreign patent office not more than three months prior to the filing of your IDS, and others were not known more than three months prior to filing your IDS, then you can simply create two lists in your IDS and make each certification under its appropriate list of references.

3.   If you file your IDS after a final office action or a Notice of Allowance, but before paying the issue fee, then you must submit both the required certification under stage 2 and the fee set forth in 37 C.F.R. §1.17(p). You are no longer permitted a choice at this stage. If you are unable to make the certification because it is not true, then you should file a *Request for Continued Examination* (RCE) of your application.

4. If you want to submit an IDS after paying your issue fee, your only option is to withdraw your application from issue so that you can file your IDS in a continuing application.

What to Include in Your IDS

Your IDS must include the following:

✪ A list of all U.S. and foreign patents, U.S. patent applications, publications, and any other information submitted for consideration by the PTO (hereinafter individually or collectively referred to as documents or references).

Example:

The duty of disclosure requires reporting to the PTO any co-pending U.S. applications that contain information material to the examination of the application in question. A copy of the relevant co-pending application (or a copy of the relevant parts of that application) must be provided in your IDS. (37 C.F.R. §1.98(a)(2)(iii).) If you have a co-pending application, whether in the United States or abroad, with similar claims to the ones in your current application, you should submit that co-pending application. In a recent case, the Federal Circuit said that not only must you disclose references cited in any related patent applications, but you must also disclose any communications with the PTO that you had in your related patent applications. Remember, the duty is on you to let the PTO know about information that concerns the patentability of your present application. It is far better to be safe and include more than to include less and be sorry later.

✪ A legible copy of each foreign patent and each publication (or the portion of the publication that is material). For any unpublished pending U.S. patent applications that you cite, you should also include a copy of that application or the portion that is material to patentability. However, when the disclosure of two or more patents or publications listed in your IDS are substantively cumulative, a copy of just one of the patents or publications may be submitted, provided you state that the other patents or publications are cumulative.

✪   A concise explanation of relevance for any documents listed that is not in the English language. You have quite a bit of flexibility in your explanation, and you may simply point out similarities as well as differences between the reference and your claims. However, you must bring to the examiner's attention the reference's relevant teaching.

– Caution –

If you can get a hold of an English translation of the non-English reference, it is best to submit this. Even the costs of translation can save you a great deal of expense sometime down the road should someone try to argue that you engaged in inequitable conduct with the PTO by not bringing to its attention such a reference. By having the reference translation into English, you will be in a better position to say that nothing was hidden from your examiner.

Your explanation can also be fulfilled by submitting an English-language version of any search report or action that cites such non-English reference and that indicates the degree of relevance found by the foreign office.

How to Cite References Included in Your IDS

✪   U.S. patents—Identify by inventor, patent number, and issue date;

✪   U.S. patent application publication—Identify by applicant, patent application publication number, and publication date;

✪   U.S. application—Identify by inventor, application number, and filing date;

✪   Foreign patents and published foreign patent applications— Identify by the country or patent office that issued the patent or published the application, an appropriate document number, and publication date indicated on the patent or published application; and,

✪   Publications—Identify by publisher, author (if any), title, relevant pages of the publication, date, and place of publication.

Supplemental Information Statements

As stated, there is no limit to the number of IDS submissions that you can make. In fact, under your duty of good faith and candor, you must let the PTO know about any material references that you discover up until the time that your patent issues.

An example of a supplemental IDS follows. In this common example, the applicant has already received a first office action from the PTO, but a final rejection has not yet been received. Therefore, the applicant can either pay a required fee in order to get the PTO to consider the references or can opt for one of the two certifications previously explained. Since in this case the references became known to the applicant through a European Search Report issued in one of applicant's foreign filed applications for the same invention, the applicant has opted to make certification in order to avoid paying a fee. Be sure to include forms PTO/SB/08A and B, which lists any of your supplemental references, behind your supplemental IDS.

Supplemental Information Disclosure Statement

Sir:

The documents listed on the enclosed Form PTO/SB/08A and B have come to the attention of the Applicant.

I hereby state that each item of information contained in the information disclosure statement was first cited in any communication from a foreign patent office in a counterpart foreign application not more than three months prior to the filing of the information disclosure statement.

Respectfully submitted,

_____

John Smith, Applicant

COVER LETTER

It is a good idea to include a *cover letter* that simply tells the PTO what they are receiving from you. A blank cover letter that you can fill out is included in Appendix G. If you are mailing your application instead of using electronic filing, your cover letter should appear at the top of your stack of papers. None of your papers should be stapled. However, it is a good idea to place a clip around all of your papers so that they do not become disorganized either en route to the PTO or while at the PTO.

POSTCARD

If you are mailing your patent application, you should include a self-addressed, prepaid postcard with your patent application. Your self-addressed, stamped postcard is useful because it can serve as evidence of what you have sent to the PTO. Keep it in your records once the PTO sends it back to you.

On the front of the postcard, print your name and address and place a stamp on it. On the back of your postcard, list each document that you are including in your package to the PTO. The back of your postcard can be organized as follows:

Serial No.: Not yet assigned	The following papers have been received:
Filed: Herewith	(1) Utility Application Transmittal
Title: (Insert title)	(2) Fee Transmittal Form (in duplicate)
	(3) Fee Determination Record
Inventor(s): (Insert names)	(4) Multiple Dependent Fee Worksheet
	(5) Declaration (executed)
	(6) Information Disclosure Statement
Docket No.: (Insert #)	(7) IDS Citation List (2 pages)
Express Mailing #: (Insert #)	(8) Postcard

IF YOU MAIL YOUR PATENT APPLICATION

People are in the patent arena to protect their inventions. One of the simplest ways to protect your invention is to obtain the earliest effective filing date for your invention. For that reason alone, it is recommended that you use Express Mail to send your patent application.

While it is possible to send your application by first class mail, your filing date will be the date that your PTO actually receives your application. However, if you send your application by Express Mail, your filing date will be the date that you actually deposit your application with the United States Postal Service.

To obtain the advantage of Express Mail, make sure that you fill in the "date in" box on your express mailing label. You should also include somewhere on your correspondence to the PTO an express mailing form where you certify the date that you have deposited your papers with the post office. This statement appears on all of the forms that you will use in Appendix G.

You can use Express Mail for any other type of paper you send to the PTO during the prosecution of your application.

Electronic Submission as an Unregistered Filer

The USPTO allows electronic filing of your patent application. Filing electronically is not only encouraged by the PTO, it is also a lot easier than mailing your application. You can file as an *unregistered filer* by doing the following:

- ✪ Go to the USPTO home site (www.uspto.gov) and click on the "patents" like on the left-hand side of the page and choose "file online in EFS-web."

- ✪ Choose to file as "EFS-web unregistered e-filers."

- ✪ Insert your last and first name as well as your email address and choose "new application."

- ✪ Check the box "new utility application."

✪   As you continue through the process, you will be allowed to insert information concerning your utility application and attach all necessary documents.

The PTO offers tutorials on filing your application electronically. In fact, if you go to www.uspto.gov/ebc/portal/tutorials.htm you will be able to try before you file your PCT application. This feature allows you to practice filing an application without actually submitting one.

Electronic Submission as a Registered Filer

The PTO also allows you to file your application as a *registered filer,* which is more complicated but has its advantages. As a *registered filer,* you will be able to monitor the status of your filing later on after your filing by using the PTO's *Patent Application Retrieval Information System* (PAIR). You will also be allowed to file subsequent papers later on, which are required in prosecution of your patent application.

Registration takes some time to set up. You must first obtain what is called a *customer number.* You obtain a customer number by filling out a *request for customer number form,* which can be downloaded from the "electronic business center" ("EBC") page at the PTO website (www.uspto.gov/ebc). After you have filled out the form you should then fax it to the Electronic Business Center Help Desk at 703–308–2840. The PTO will send back to you a n*otice of customer number assignment,* as well as labels carrying that customer number.

After you have obtained your customer number, you should complete a *Certificate Action Form* and have that form notarized. You must then mail the form to:

Mail Stop EBC
Commissioner for Patents
P.O. Box 1450
Alexandria, VA 22313

You can download the *Certificate Action Form* by going to the EBC page on the PTO website and then clicking on "downloads."

After the PTO receives your Certificate Action Form, it will send you two codes that will uniquely identify you. The first code is called an *authorization code,* and the second is called a *reference number.* At this point, you are ready to electronically submit your patent application. All you need to do is download the EFS software. This download can again be found at the EBC page by clicking on "downloads," and then on "EFS filing software."

Filing your patent application can be a little daunting at first, particularly for users who are not experts at computers. However, I believe that the benefits outweigh any trouble that you may encounter. There is also an extremely helpful telephonic technical assistance center at the PTO called the Electronic Business Center (EBC), which is available from Monday through Friday. This center can be reached by calling 866–217–9197.

Digital Certificates

Within one hundred twenty days of receipt of your authorization code and reference number, you will need to download your *digital certificate* to your computer from the Electronic Business Center (EBC). If you do not download your digital certificate in the allotted times, your codes will expire.

Once you have your digital certificate, you will still need to use it once every ninety days. This is because as you use it, it automatically gets renewed by the PTO. You can copy your digital certificate onto other computers, but these copies must also be used once every ninety days in order to self-renew.

After downloading your digital certificate, you should also create self-recovery codes in case something happens to your digital certificate. This will allow you to recover your digital certificate later if you need to. You can create self-recovery codes by going to the PTO website at: http://sas.uspto.gov/ptosas.

DO A FINAL CHECK AND MAKE A COPY OF YOUR APPLICATION

☐   Cover Letter.

☐   Utility Application Transmittal.

- ☐ Fee Transmittal Form. (After you complete this form, make a copy of it so you can submit it in duplicate.)

- ☐ Fee Determination Record Form.

- ☐ Multiple-Dependent Fee Worksheet. (If you have any multiple-dependent claims, you should complete this worksheet.)

- ☐ Specification. (Indicate in the cover sheet the number of pages.)

- ☐ Drawings. (Indicate in your cover letter whether you are submitting formal or informal drawings.)

- ☐ Declaration. (Indicate in your cover letter whether your drawings are executed or unexecuted. Since there is really no reason why your drawings should be unexecuted unless you have not been able to obtain a coinventor's signature at this time, you will most likely indicate "executed.")

- ☐ Information Disclosure Statement.

- ☐ IDS Citation List. (Indicate the number of pages you are sending.)

- ☐ Postcard if mailing your application. (Be sure to place a stamp on the front of the card.)

Before you put all of your papers into a legal size Express Mail envelope to send, make sure that you copy all of your papers, including your postcard (front and back) and your completed Express Mail label. If you are electronically filing your patent application, you will also be given the opportunity to print out your application, which you should do so.

File each of these copied papers into a separate folder. Most patent attorneys and agents use a three-part folder. Use one part of the folder for your copied application, one part for correspondence that you will receive from the PTO, and the third pocket for correspondence that you send to the PTO.

If you are mailing your patent application, your patent application should be sent to the following address:

Mail Stop Patent Application
P.O. Box 1450
Alexandria, VA 22313

Preparing Other Types of Applications

There are other kinds of applications you may file during the patent process besides utility and process patent applications. This chapter discusses when, how, and why you would file these applications.

DESIGN PATENT APPLICATIONS

There are three types of designs:

1. a design for an ornament, impression, print, or picture applied to or embodied in an article of manufacture (surface indicia);

2. a design for the shape or configuration of an article of manufacture; and,

3. a combination of the first two categories.

Note that each of the three types of designs has in common the embodiment of the design in an article of manufacture. This is an important distinguishing feature because a claim to a picture, print, impression, et cetera, that is not applied to or embodied in an article of manufacture cannot be patented. (MPEP §1504.01.)

Differences from Utility Patents

Review U.S. Patent No. 296,039 in Appendix D. You will notice that many parts are different from utility patents.

One of the first things you may notice is that design patents are much shorter than utility patents. The main reason for this is that there is no detailed, written description in a design patent. In design patents, the drawings substitute for the detailed, written description.

Another important feature is that a design patent includes only a *single* claim. This claim has a peculiar format that applies only to design patents. The single claim should normally be written as follows:

> *The ornamental design for [the article that embodies your design or to which the design is applied] as shown and described.*

One good thing about this is that you are not going to have to spend a lot of time drafting your claims for a design patent.

Additional differences between a design and utility patent include the following:

- The term of a design patent is fourteen years from the date of the patent grant whereas the term of a utility patent is twenty years from the effective U.S. filing date of the utility patent.

- Utility patent applications may claim the benefit of a provisional application, but design patent applications may not.

- An RCE is not available for a design patent (discussed later).

- Design patent applications are not subject to the publication rules that are applicable to utility patent applications.

- An international application naming various countries may be filed for utility patents under the *Patent Cooperation Treaty* (PCT), but no such provision exists for design patents.

- Foreign priority can be obtained for the filing of utility patent applications up to one year after the first filing. This period is six months for design patents.

Design Patent Specifications

For the most part, everything that you learned about utility patents is also applicable to the necessary sections of your design patent application. Your design patent specification should include the following sections:

- ✪ *Title.* Your title must designate the particular article on which your design is embedded and the title must correspond with your claim. For example, the design on the sample patent in Appendix D is embedded on a grille, so this is the title of the patent (Patent No. D296,039).

- ✪ *Cross-Reference to Related Applications.* This is the same section as covered for a utility patent. You do not need to include a cross-reference to related applications if you include the cross-reference in your application data sheet.

- ✪ *Statement Regarding Federally Sponsored Research or Development.* Just as with a utility patent, you must include this section if it is applicable.

- ✪ *Description of the Figure or Figures of the Drawing.* This is the same as for your utility patent.

- ✪ *Drawings.* Every design patent application must include either a drawing or a photograph of the claimed design. As your drawing or photograph constitutes the entire visual disclosure of your claim, it is of utmost importance they be clear and complete. (Photographs are only acceptable in applications in which the invention is not capable of being illustrated in an ink drawing or where the invention is shown more clearly in a photograph. You must also comply with 37 C.F.R. §1.84(b) if you want to submit photographs.)

  You should make sure that you include a sufficient number of views to disclose the complete appearance of the design, which may include the front, rear, top, bottom, and sides. In addition to all the rules covered for a utility patent application, you should also look at the rules in MPEP §1503.02 for design patents.

✪   *Single Claim.* As previously stated, your design patent has only one claim. The claim must be in the form "The ornamental design for [the article that embodies your design] as shown and described." Take a look at the sample patent in Appendix D for this format.

Design Patent Application

You should include the following items for a complete design patent application:

✪   *Design Application Transmittal Form.* Instructions on obtaining the most recent version from the PTO website are included in Appendix G. One item that is new to you is item 14. You are entitled to obtain an expedited examination of your design patent application if you make the claim here and pay the specified fee in 37 C.F.R. §1.17(k), which was $900 at the time of publication of this book. If you want to claim expedited procedure, take a look at MPEP §1504.30. You will need to complete a request for expedited examination (Form PTO/SB/27) and a statement indicating that you have completed a pre-examination search concerning your design patent.

✪   *Fee Transmittal Form.* Include a fee transmittal form. (See Chapter 7 for additional information.)

✪   *Application Data Sheet.* Submit an application data sheet. (See Chapter 7 for additional information.)

✪   *Specification.* Include your drafted specification.

✪   *Drawings or Photographs.* Include any drawings or photographs of your design that are necessary.

✪   *Executed Oath or Declaration.* Include a completed declaration. (See Chapter 7 for additional information.)

✪   *Information Disclosure Statement and Citation List.* Complete an IDS just as you would for a utility patent application.

As with filing a regular utility patent application, I recommend that you use electronic filing. However, if you are mailing your design patent application, you should send your design patent application to:

Mail Stop DESIGN
Commissioner for Patents
P.O. Box 1450
Alexandria, VA 22313

If you are requesting an expedited examination of your design patent application, then include the word "Expedited" before "Design" in the address.

PROVISIONAL APPLICATIONS

A *provisional application* is a U.S. national application for a patent filed under 35 U.S.C. §111(b). A provisional application can be filed for both utility and plant patent applications. However, you cannot file a provisional application for a design patent application.

A provisional application is considered expired twelve months after you obtain a filing date for the application, and it is not subject to revival after this time. If this twelve-month period falls on a Saturday, Sunday, or federal holiday, the provisional application will expire on the succeeding business day.

Claiming Priority to Your Provisional Application

Sometime within the twelve months before your provisional application is due to expire, you must file your regular utility patent application that claims priority to your previously filed provisional application. This way you will obtain an effective filing date for your regularly filed application, which dates back to the filing date of your provisional application.

You make this claim to priority in your application data sheet that you fill out for your regular U.S. filed application. If you do not make your claim in your application data sheet, you must specifically state in your regular application that you claim priority. To do this, write as the first sentence of your application,

This application claims the benefit of U.S. Provisional Application No._____, filed _____

It is recommended that you make a claim of priority in your specification as well as in your application data sheet, although it is not necessary.

Filing a Provisional Application

There are several reasons that either alone or in combination may make filing a provisional application a good idea.

✪ A provisional application is easier to complete than a non-provisional utility application because you do not need to submit any claims. You also do not need to file a declaration, nor do you file an IDS. Thus, if you are up against any immediate deadline to obtain your filing date, you will have an easier time completing a provisional application than a regular U.S. application.

✪ Provisional applications cost less to file than regular U.S. applications. Therefore, if there is the possibility that you may later decide to abandon your invention within a year after you file your provisional application, you could just let your provisional application expire.

✪ A provisional application's one year lifetime does not count in the twenty-year lifetime of a patent. In effect, you are given a twenty-one-year period for the filing date of a provisional application before expiration of your patent.

This one-year, free patent term protection can be particularly advantageous if you really are not in a rush to have your patent application examined and issued. That might be the case, for example, when you want as much time as possible to try to commercialize your invention. For example, pharmaceutical inventions are particularly difficult to commercialize. If you need time to develop your invention into products that can be sold and make you money, then it probably does not make much sense to rush ahead and obtain a patent. The term of your patent will start to be used up all while you do not even have any products in the marketplace.

If your situation is the case that your invention can be commercialized quickly, then you may want to consider filing a regular patent application. This may be particularly true for electronic and software inventions that not only can be commercialized fairly quickly, but also have a relatively short commercial life (i.e., a new product is out that replaces your product even before your patent expires).

✪   Provisional applications are not published. This could have some advantages. Since the application is not published, you can gain up to an extra twelve months when you have to file your regular patent application in addition to those eighteen months after you file your regular application before your application is published. This can be advantageous to keep your invention out of the eyes of any competitors for a little longer.

The fact that provisional patent applications are easier to prepare than a regular application should not be the sole reason to file one. If you need some more time to polish the look of your patent application, the filing of a provisional patent application may be the way to go. You can file your provisional and then have up to one whole year to get your regular patent application prepared. But be careful on just what types of changes you need to make. Provisional patent applications, just as with regular applications, must comply with all the patentability requirements discussed in Chapter 3. In other words, your claimed invention must be supported in your written description and you must meet the enablement requirement. You must adhere to the same rules as you prepare your disclosure. And although you do not need to submit claims with your provisional application, you should submit some claims with your provisional patent application. If you do not have in your mind some claims now, you may find as you prepare those claims for your regular application that they do not have support in your previously filed provisional patent application. If your later filed claims do not have support in your previously filed provisional application, you will not be entitled to rely upon your earlier provisional filing date for those claims. This has gotten many applicants into problems.

Example:

Joe filed a provisional patent application on certain drill bits and then followed up with his regular patent application within a year as required. The claim in Joe's regular application claimed a certain angle and ratio of the drill bit. Joe's claim was rejected by the PTO on the basis of a prior sale of drill bits by Joe more than one year prior to the filing date of the regular application. Joe argued that the examiner's rejection was improper because Joe was relying upon the filing date of his earlier provisional patent application, which was filed less than a year after the sale. The examiner again rejected Joe's claim on the basis that the provisional application did not support the claimed angle and ratio, and therefore Joe could not rely upon the earlier filing date of the provisional patent application. If Joe had only recognized that he would want to claim this angle and ratio at the time he filed his provisional application, perhaps he would have included support for the claim in his disclosure. This is a time when filing a provisional is worse than filing a regular application because it lulled Joe into believing that he could rely upon the date of his provisional patent application for claims that he wanted to make.

Completing Your Provisional Application

If you decide to file a provisional application, you should submit the following items to complete the filing of your provisional application:

❂   a cover sheet identifying the application as a provisional application for patent. Use the downloading instructions provided in Appendix G. If filing electronically, choose the document description "Provisional Cover Sheet" (SB/16), rather than "Transmittal of a New Application";

❂   a fee transmittal form (PTO/SB/17) along with the appropriate filing fee ($105 at the time of publication of this book);

❂   an application data sheet (see Chapter 7);

❂   a specification (you do not need to prepare claims for your specification; however, if you submit claims, they will become part of your specification);

✪   any drawings necessary to understand your invention; and,

✪   a return postcard.

NOTE: *Your provisional application specification should be as complete as possible (just as with completing your regular U.S. application). In order to obtain the benefit of the filing date of your provisional application later, the claimed subject matter in your later filed regular U.S. application must have support in your provisional application.*

As with a regular patent application, provisional patent applications can be electronically filed, which I recommend that you use. However, if you are mailing your provisional patent application, you should mail it to:

> Box Provisional Patent Application
> Assistant Commissioner for Patents
> Washington, DC 20231

CONTINUATION APPLICATIONS

A *continuation* is a second application for the same invention that was formerly claimed in a prior non-provisional application and filed before the prior application becomes abandoned or patented. You must have at least one inventor in common with your prior application in order to file a continuation from that prior application.

Filing a Continuation Application

Although your claims in a continuation are directed to the same invention as your previously filed non-provisional application, you can change the scope of your claims. It is not unusual to file a continuation application just prior to the issuance of a patent, so that prosecution based on the original disclosure will be able to be continued. This is valuable when a competitor may attempt to design around your patent in order to avoid literal infringement by adopting minor variants. In such a situation, it may be possible to revise the continuation application claims to cover the variant literally, considerably enhancing the scope of your protection.

A second situation in which you may want to file a continuation is when your examiner has allowed some of your claims but rejected others. In such a situation it may be better to pursue the rejected claims in a continuation and take a patent now for your allowed claims. To do this, you should cancel your rejected claims in your present application and file a continuation in which you pursue your rejected claims.

A third situation in which you may want to consider filing a continuation is when all your claims have been rejected by your examiner and you wish to use a continuation to get in another shot.

NOTE: *What you can do after a final rejection can be quite limited. By filing a continuation, you can get your amendments entered into your new continuing application. However, also note that you can achieve this same purpose by filing an RCE (discussed on page 178). The filing of an RCE may also be less expensive because you do not need to pay for any excess claims that you previously paid for prior to the filing of the RCE.*

Example:

Nicholi receives a Final Rejection from the PTO requiring a response by June 10, 2006. On August 10, 2006, Nicholi decides to file a continuation along with a one-month extension of time rather than responding to the outstanding action.

Since Nicholi obtained a one-month extension of time, the continuation is co-pending with the original application, and thus takes on the original filing date.

A properly filed continuation contains the following parts:

- ✪ *Cover Letter.* Complete a cover letter for your continuation just as you would if you were filing a regular U.S. patent application.

- ✪ *Utility Patent Application Transmittal.* Complete this as you would for your original application. In box 18, make sure that you check the box labeled "continuation." Also be sure to include the prior information about your parent application.

🟦 *Fee Transmittal.* You will need to complete a fee transmittal just as you did with your original application.

🟦 *Credit Card Payment Form.* If you are paying by credit card, you should complete this form just as explained in Chapter 7.

🟦 *Application Data Sheet.* You should complete another application data sheet just as you do for an original application.

🟦 *Specification.* Your disclosure in your continuation must be the same as your parent application. Usually what patent attorneys and agents do is to refile an exact copy of the specification filed in the parent application and then submit a *preliminary amendment* along with the continuation. (See Chapter 11 for more information on preliminary amendments.)

The preliminary amendment serves to update the specification with any changes made during prosecution of the parent application (changes that do not add any new matter). You must file an amendment to reflect the changes made during prosecution of your parent application because these changes do not automatically carry over in a Rule 53(b) application. The submission of a preliminary amendment is considered useful because it lets the examiner more clearly see the changes you are making to your specification. This often gives your examiner a greater comfort zone that you are not adding any new matter to your specification.

If you prefer, you can also rewrite your specification with all of the changes and simply submit it as your new continuation application without having to complete a preliminary amendment. This is easier than filing a preliminary amendment along 124 The Complete Patent Kit with your application and is recommended, at least with respect to your claims for the additional following reason:

A published application does not generally include any amendments (even preliminary) that you make to your application. In addition, you are only able to obtain a reasonable royalty for the infringement of any of your published application claims if those claims remain substantially unaltered from the date they are published to the date they are patented. Thus, if you submit a preliminary amendment including changed claims, you cannot obtain a reasonable royalty for the infringement of such claims if they are patented because they would not have been included in your published application. However, if you submit those new claims as part of your continuation, then you would be able to seek a reasonable royalty for later infringement of those claims so long as you do not substantially alter them before patenting. By including any new claims right in your continuation, you increase the chances that you may seek prepatent damages for such claims.

CONTINUATION-IN-PART APPLICATIONS

A *continuation-in-part application* (CIP) is filed during the lifetime of an earlier non-provisional application, repeating some substantial portion or all of the earlier non-provisional application but adding matter not disclosed in it. (MPEP §201.08.) Thus, a CIP is a continuing application that discloses the same or a substantial part of the subject matter as the parent application, but also includes *new matter* not contained in the original or parent.

CIP applications are useful for updating an application with new technical developments that have arisen during prosecution. The original filing date is retained for subject matter common to the two applications—the new matter receives the later filing date of the CIP application.

A CIP must have at least one common inventor with the original parent application. This means that the parent application may have been filed by a sole applicant, whereas the CIP is filed by that applicant along with other applicants. However, the parent applicant could be filed by joint inventors, whereas the CIP is filed by just one of those inventors.

When to File a CIP

CIPs must be filed while the parent applications upon which they rely are still pending. CIPs are typically filed when an inventor comes up with new, but related features to a previous invention, which were not disclosed in the previously filed patent application. What inventors do in this situation is file a CIP that contains all of the disclosure from the previously filed patent application, along with new matter to the undisclosed features. In that CIP, a claim of priority will be made back to the previously filed patent application so that this earlier filing date will remain for all of the old material in the CIP. Any new matter will have as its filing date the filing date of the CIP. At this point, the old application can be abandoned in favor of the newly filed CIP. This can save on the expenses of having to maintain two separate patent applications (i.e., one application for the old disclosure and one application for the new disclosure).

While CIPs can have their purpose, in some circumstances it may actually be better to file a new patent application with the new disclosure rather than a CIP. Here are some instances in which filing and maintaining two separate patent applications rather than filing a CIP may actually be a better idea.

Patent Term

Recall that patent terms run from the earliest effective filing date of a patent. By claiming priority in a CIP, the patent term will run from the date from which you make a claim of priority. If the new matter that you seek to add in a CIP truly can stand on its own in that it is not anticipated by your earlier filed application, you may be better off just to file this new disclosure as a separate patent application without a claim of priority back to the original application. Otherwise, you are shortening the patent life for the disclosure of the CIP.

– Caution –

If the new material you seek to add is anticipated by your prior application, you will need to make a claim of priority back to your application because your application could be used as prior art against your new filed application if you fail to do so. However, when your new material is obvious in light of the prior application, an obvious rejection can be overcome by asserting common ownership so long as co-pendency exists.

Ownership

When someone assigns ownership of a patent, such assignments typically encompass any future CIPs. So if you have previously made an assignment, say to your prior employer, and have now come up with a new but related invention, you are better off filing a completely separate patent application. Otherwise, your prior employer may be able to claim that it owns the rights to your CIP.

Unsupported Claims

A prerequisite for CIPs is that at least one claim must find support in the disclosure of the parent application. If you make claims in your CIP that are unsupported by your parent application (remember, claims must be supported by the disclosure of the original application in order to capture that earlier date), you may open yourself up to an accusation of inequitable conduct. This could be asserted against you to invalidate your patent. So if none of your claims are not entitled to a claim of priority, do not assert a claim of priority in a CIP. Instead, file a separate patent application.

Fees

The PTO charges a stiff fee for claims of priority made more than sixteen months from the priority date claimed in a prior application, or four months from the parent filing date.

Filing a CIP   All CIPs must follow the rules in 37 C.F.R. §1.53(b). A properly filed CIP should contain the following parts:

- ✪ *Cover Letter*. Complete a cover letter for your CIP just as you would if you were filing a regular U.S. patent application.

- ✪ *Utility Patent Application Transmittal*. Complete this as you would for your original application. In box 18, make sure that you check the box labeled "continuation-in-part (CIP)." Also be sure to include the prior information about your parent application.

- ✪ *Fee Transmittal*. You will need to complete a fee transmittal just as you did with your original application.

- ✪ *Credit Card Payment Form*. If you are paying by credit card, you should complete this form just as explained in Chapter 7.

✪   *Application Data Sheet.* You should complete another application data sheet just as you do for an original application.

✪   *Specification.* As with a continuation, you have two choices. You can file a duplicate copy of your original patent specification and add your new matter, or any other changes, with a preliminary amendment. Alternatively, you can simply submit your CIP as a new rewritten patent application that reflects all of the changes that you want to make. If you have your old application on word processing, it is easier to take your old application and work your new matter into this application and then file this updated application as your CIP.

You should update your cross-references section of your specification so that you have made specific reference to your earlier filed application. (MPEP §201.09.) In your claims section, make sure that you have at least one claim that is supported by the disclosure of your parent application. This is required if you want to be able to make a claim of priority back to that originally filed patent application.

If you have a new best mode to carry out your invention, make sure you update your specification to reflect this best mode.

✪   *Declaration.* Your CIP must be accompanied by a new oath or declaration executed by all of the inventors. (See Chapter 7 for information about how to complete a declaration.)

✪   *IDS.* In any CIP application, there is an explicit duty to disclose all information known to be material to patentability that became available between the filing date of the prior application and the national or PCT international filing date of the CIP application. If any such references have come to your attention, you need to submit them on your IDS and also list them in your citation list.

DIVISIONAL APPLICATIONS

There is a good chance that you may have to file a *divisional application.* Such applications are necessary when you file your regular

U.S. application, and the PTO determines that your application has claims directed to more than one separate invention. In such a case, the PTO will issue you a restriction requirement in your first office action. This requires you to elect one of your claimed inventions and file your other claimed inventions in separate patent applications. These separate patent applications are known as *divisional applications*. You must file these divisional applications while your parent application is still pending in order to take on the priority date of the parent application.

Divisional applications of utility or plant applications filed on or after May 29, 2000, are filed under 37 C.F.R. §1.53(b). This means that a divisional application is assigned a different file application number from its parent application. The filing of your divisional application will have no affect upon the prosecution of your parent application. Both applications can issue into separate patents.

Filing a Divisional Application

The following should be included in your divisional application:

❂ Cover Letter

❂ Utility Patent Application Transmittal—This is the same transmittal that you submit with regular utility application. (see Chapter 7.) In box 18 of the transmittal, check off the box labeled "divisional."

❂ Fee Transmittal—This is the same as for your regular application.

❂ Credit Card Payment Form—Include this form to pay by credit card just as you would for your regular application.

❂ Application Data Sheet—This is the same data sheet covered in Chapter 7. Under the "Application Type," you should indicate "divisional" rather than "regular." You should fill in the appropriate classification of your divisional application, which can be found in the office communication of your parent application in which the restriction requirement was made.

❂ Specification—The MPEP states that your divisional should set forth at least that portion of your earlier application that is germane to the invention that you are now claiming. If a portion of your earlier disclosure is not relevant to the claimed invention of your divisional, you should delete that matter from your divisional application.

The MPEP also states that while you may rewrite your parent application using different phraseology, you are not allowed to depart in substance or variation from your originally filed application when writing for your divisional application. Therefore, patent attorneys and agents usually refile an exact copy of their specification as filed in the parent application and delete claims or subject matter not pertinent to the divisional using a preliminary amendment. (See Chapter 11.) However, as with a continuation and CIP, you may decide that it is easier to simply rewrite your specification on your word processor as a new application that incorporates the changes you want to make. This will save you from completing a preliminary amendment.

✪   Drawings—You can use the drawings that you prepared for your regular application in your divisional.

✪   Declaration—You can simply copy the declaration that you submitted in your prior application and submit it as your divisional declaration because you are not disclosing anything new from what you filed in your parent application.

However, if are you adding claims that are directed to subject matter described but not claimed in your prior filed application, then you should file a supplemental oath or declaration. (37 C.F.R. §1.67(b).) A supplemental declaration form should be downloaded from the PTO website to ensure the most recent version. See Appendix G for detailed instructions.

✪   Information Disclosure Statement and Citation List—You should submit another IDS with your divisional application. However, you do not need to make copies of any reference that was previously submitted and considered by the examiner in your earlier application. (37 C.F.R. §1.98(d).) Simply alert your examiner in your IDS to the list of previous documents and state that since such documents were previously submitted, you are not resubmitting copies of the documents now. However, you should state that you still want the examiner to consider these previously submitted documents in your current IDS. You should also submit a citation list of these documents, which your examiner will send you back with his or her initials indicating that these documents have been considered.

If you have learned of any new material references since you filed your original application, you should include these references in your current IDS, submit copies of these references, and include them on your citation list.

REQUEST FOR CONTINUED EXAMINATION

A *Request for Continued Examination* (RCE) is simply a request that your current application continue to be examined. You can file an RCE for a utility or plant patent application. However, you cannot file an RCE for a design or for a provisional application.

In order to file an RCE, prosecution of your application must be closed. Prosecution of your application is considered *closed* if you have been mailed a final office action, a Notice of Allowance, or your application is under appeal.

You file your RCE by filing a *submission* and the fee set forth in 37 C.F.R. §1.17(e), which was $405 (small entity) at the time of publication of this book. A *submission* includes such things as an amendment to your written description, claims, drawings, new arguments, or new evidence in support of patentability. A submission also includes the filing of an IDS.

An RCE is *not* a new application. Everything that occurred in the prosecution of your parent application will simply be carried over to your RCE. Your RCE is assigned the same application number as your originally filed application. You can think of an RCE as a type of amendment in your current application. If you timely file your RCE, the PTO will withdraw the finality of your office action and your submission in the RCE will be considered.

Filing an RCE   A properly filed RCE should include the following:

✪   Cover Letter—Complete a cover letter for your RCE just as you would if you were filing a regular U.S. patent application.

✪   RCE Transmittal—Instructions for downloading a copy of this transmittal are included in Appendix G.

- In box 1, you must indicate what you are filing for your submission. This can be a submission (e.g., amendment) that you previously filed.

- In box 2, you will notice that you are allowed to request that prosecution of your RCE be suspended for a period of up to three months. Unless you absolutely need the extra time, do not request suspension, because your suspension period will be deducted from your patent term.

  If you do request suspension of prosecution, you still must fulfill all of the requirements for your RCE. Do not expect to request a suspension of prosecution in your RCE with the hope that this will give you time to reply to a final office action. This will not happen.

- In box 3, you should check the appropriate box that indicates how you are paying your fee. If you need an extension of time to reply to a previous outstanding office action in your application, you should check the box for extension of time and pay the applicable fee. Extensions of time are discussed in Chapter 10.

  NOTE: *You do not need to pay for a fee for any excess claims that you previously paid for prior to filing your RCE.*

- Be sure to sign your RCE and also fill out the certificate of mailing.

✪   Credit Card Payment Form—Include this form if you are using your credit card to pay the required fee.

✪   Your Submission—This will normally include an amendment or reply to your previous final office action. However, a *submission* might also include other types of papers, even an IDS. For example, you might want the PTO to consider some reference after prosecution of your application has closed. You could use an RCE with an attached IDS to do this.

✪   Information Disclosure Statement—If you are aware of any material references that you have not previously brought to the attention of your examiner, you should submit an IDS along with your RCE.

An IDS will be considered without you having to make a certification or pay a fee, so long as your IDS is submitted prior to the mailing of a first office action on the merits in your RCE. You generally will receive your first office action within two months from the date that you file your RCE. The three-month period that you have to file an IDS in a Rule 53(b) application does not apply to an RCE. This means it is even more important that you file any IDS along with your RCE if you need to do so.

Filing Your RCE Electronically   You can file your RCE electronically. Choose document description "Request for Continued Examination" located in the "Amendment" and "Petition" categories.

Questions should be directed to EBC Customer Service Center at 866–217–9197 (toll-free) or 571–272–4100 or by sending an email to ebc@upto.gov.

CLAIMING PRIORITY TO EARLIER APPLICATIONS

One nice thing about continuing applications is that they can take on the effective filing date of their parent application. If your original application was filed in June 1, 2005, and you file a continuing application in February 1, 2006, the effective filing date for your continuing application will be June 1, 2005, as long as you meet the rules for claiming priority.

The earlier filing date is referred to in patent law as the *effective filing date* of the continuing application rather than its *actual filing date*. Having an earlier effective filing date than the date on which you actually file your patent application can be advantageous with respect to prior art references that could potentially anticipate your invention.

Benefiting from an Earlier Application

There is no limit to the number of prior applications through which a chain of continuing applications may be traced to, but there are three main requirements that must be met in order for you to obtain benefit to an earlier filed application.

1. There must be at least one common inventor between your current application and the application to which you seek benefit. It is also an important requirement of a CIP that at least one inventor of the new subject matter disclosed in a CIP be an actual inventor of the prior art subject matter disclosed in the parent application (35 USCA §120 (2005); 37 C.F. R. §1.78(a)(4)(2005)).

Example:

Inventors A and B invent a new desk with chairs and drawers and file a patent application. Later, coworker C invents different types of drawers for the desk. A CIP is filed, adding the new subject matter of the drawers naming inventors A and B of the parent application along with C as the inventorship in the CIP. However, if neither A nor B had any input in conceiving the new drawers, then this method is incorrect. This is a situation where the CIP does not meet the requirement for a continuing application to include at least one inventor named in the parent application as an inventor in the new subject matter. Such an application is not a true CIP and is not entitled to the filing date of the prior application. In fact, the prior application is prior art to the CIP.

---

2. Your currently filed application must have co-pendency with your earlier filed application. *Co-pendency* means that your continuing application must have been filed before the

patenting, or before abandonment or other termination of your previously filed application.

3. You must make a specific reference to your earlier filed application in the first sentence of your description in your continuing application following the title. You can also make this specific reference in your application data sheet. (See Chapter 7.)

Sometimes your pending application is one of a series of applications wherein your pending application is not co-pending with the first filed application in the series, but is co-pending with an intermediate application entitled to the filing date of the first application. If you desire your pending application to have benefit of the first filing date, you must make specific reference not only to the intermediate application but also to the first application. (MPEP §201.11.)

Your reference in your specification can state the following:

This is a _____ [insert the type of continuing application] of Application No.

_____ [insert the Application Number of the parent application], filed _____.

You should also include the status of your previously filed parent application (whether it is patented or abandoned) if you know it. For example, if your previously filed application is now a patent, you can state the following:

This is a _____ of Application No. _____ , filed _____ , Patent No. _____.

As another example, if your previously filed application was abandoned, you can state the following:

This is a _____ of Application No. _____ , filed _____ , now abandoned.

For utility or plant applications (including reissues) filed on or after November 29, 2000, any claim of priority must be made within four months from the actual filing date of your current application or sixteen months from the filing date of your prior application, whichever date is later. (37 C.F.R. §1.78 and MPEP §201.11.)

There may be cases in which you decide either not to claim priority of a prior application, or to cancel your claim to priority by amending your specification or submitting a new application data sheet to delete any references to prior applications. Remember that the term of the patent will be measured from the earliest effective filing date of your application. If you are making reference back to several continuing applications and an originally filed application, your effective filing date will be the date you filed your original application, and your patent term will run from that date. However, if you refrain from making reference back to your earlier filed applications, then your patent term will start later.

While it is easy to say that you should consider not making a claim of priority to earlier filed applications in order to increase your patent term, you usually do not have this luxury. It is common to rely on an earlier filing date for prior art purposes because usually several years do not go by without prior art becoming a problem in your later filed application.

However, you may want to consider refraining from making a reference to an earlier filed application so as to extend your patent term if your invention is a pioneer in your field rather than just an improvement. This is because the pioneer invention presumably will encounter a minimum amount of relevant prior art. On the other hand, if the invention is an improvement, it may be better to claim an early priority date so as to limit its prior art exposure.

You can obtain the earlier filing date of a parent application only as to the subject matter that is common to both your continuing and parent application.

Another thing that you should note is that if your earlier filed application is fatally defective because of an insufficient disclosure (e.g., lacks enablement, written description, etc.), then your current application is not entitled to the benefit of the earlier filing.

Filing Your Application Abroad

As stated in Chapter 1, a U.S. patent will give you the right to exclude others from making, using, selling, offering for sale, or importing within the United States, its territories, and possessions the subject matter that is covered by the patent. A patent will *not* give you the right to exclude others from these acts if they are carried out in foreign countries. Given the importance of the possible foreign market for your product, you need to consider the possibility of making foreign applications for patents abroad.

PATENT COOPERATION TREATY

A well-known procedure to gain patent protection in many countries is a procedure under the *Patent Cooperation Treaty* (PCT). The PCT enables you to file one application called an *international application* in a standardized format in English with the PTO and have that application acknowledged as a regular national filing in as many member PCT countries as you designate. PCT is so common for foreign patent protection that most of this chapter will be directed to its workings.

Advantages and Disadvantages

There are many advantages of filing your application under the PCT to gain foreign protection. Some of the more important ones follow.

✪   By filing a PCT application, you will not need to hire foreign associates in each of the countries where you seek a patent right now. All you will need to worry about is meeting the requirements of filing your one PCT application. However, you will need to hire foreign associates when it comes time for you to enter the national stage in each country that you do want to pursue patent protection. By thirty months from your claimed priority date, you will need to file national stage applications under the PCT. (35 U.S.C. §371.)

✪   The cost of filing your application is considerably cheaper than paying for the filing of individual patents in each country that you seek protection right at the start. You have up to thirty months to decide whether you want to file a national stage application in the foreign countries you designate at the time you fill your PCT application. During this thirty month period, you can evaluate the potential strength of your patent application and evaluate financial, marketing, and commercial considerations.

✪   The PCT gives you the benefit of an international search report with respect to prior art on your invention. This can give you a good idea whether your invention will be patentable before you go to the considerable expense of patenting your invention in each of the foreign countries that you designate and even whether you should continue prosecution of your U.S. application.

OVERVIEW OF THE PCT PROCESS

There are four divisions or conceptual entities that work together to process your PCT application. These divisions are conceptual because in reality, each of these four divisions can reside in as few as two actual governmental bodies—the PTO and *World Intellectual Property Organization* (WIPO).

Receiving Office

The first division is called the *Receiving Office* (RO), which is the office where you file your PCT application. The PTO will act as a Receiving Office for your application so long as at least one of the applicants (this can include assignees) is a resident or national of the United States.

The RO grants an international filing date to your application, collects fees, handles any informalities in your application, and monitors all corrections. The RO will transmit a copy of your application, called the *search copy* (SC), to the *International Searching Authority* (ISA). The RO will also forward your original application, called the *record copy* (RC), to the *International Bureau* (IB). The RO will keep its own *home copy* (HC) of your application.

International Bureau

The second division is called the *International Bureau* (IB). The basic job of the IB is to publish your application and act as a central coordinating body for your application. The function of the IB is actually performed by the *World Intellectual Property Organization* (WIPO) in Geneva, Switzerland.

After publication of your PCT application (between about eighteen and nineteen months from your priority date), the IB notifies each national office that you designate of your desire to proceed with a patent application in that designated country. The IB also forwards to each designated office a copy of your PCT application, a copy of the International Search Report, a copy of any amendments you have made under PCT Article 19, and a copy of any priority document.

> ***Author's Note: A published application is not a patent.***
> Some people mistakenly believe that when a PCT application is published the published application means that they have patent protection. This is easy to do because these publications look like patents. However, this is incorrect. To get patent protection, you will need to file that PCT application in each of the countries that you want patent protection. In other words, you will need to enter the national phase of each country for which you want patent protection. (You will learn how to do this later in this chapter.) You may also have noticed that U.S. patent applications are published. What this effectively means is if you file a PCT application and then later enter the United States, you will get two applications for your same invention published, one after you enter the PCT stage and later when you enter the U.S. stage.

International Searching Authority

The third division is called the *International Searching Authority* (ISA) whose job is to conduct a prior art search of your invention. You can elect the PTO as your ISA.

It is also possible to select the *European Patent Office* (EPO) as your ISA. Many PCT applicants have historically selected the EPO as their ISA, since you can obtain a PTO search later, when you enter the national stage examination in the United States.

By selecting the EPO to conduct a search for you now, you can obtain the benefit of having more than one search done for you. This can be beneficial to you in accessing the strengths of your patent application. Also, choosing the EPO as your ISA will allow you to choose the EPO to do a preliminary examination for you during the PCT process.

Although there are reasons for selecting the EPO as your ISA, it is recommended that solo inventors and others on a budget go the conservative route by selecting the United States as their ISA. This will be a cheaper and less burdensome way for such inventors to go. You should also note that the EPO is not a competent ISA to search for business method-type inventions, since business methods are not patentable in Europe.

The ISA will search for relevant prior art pertaining to your invention and then present the results of this prior art search to you in the form of a search report and an ISA written opinion as to the patentability of your invention. This typically occurs around sixteen months from the date of your first patent application filing (i.e., your priority date). The search report (but not the written opinion) will be published along with your PCT application as well any amendments made to your PCT application under Article 19. Publication typically occurs around eighteen months from your priority date (i.e., your first patent application filing).

Any patent documents that the ISA lists on your international search report are identified by the two-letter country code of the country issuing or publishing the document as well as a code for identifying the kind of patent document. The codes for identifying the kinds of patent documents can be found on the WIPO website at www.wipo.int/scit/en.

International Preliminary Examining Authority

The fourth division that can be involved with your PCT application is called the *International Preliminary Examining Authority* (IPEA). This entity will only become involved with your application if you make a demand for preliminary examination of your application. The PTO can serve as an IPEA for all applications filed in the PTO as an RO and also for those PCT applications filed in other receiving offices for which the PTO has served as an ISA. The job of an IPEA is to issue an international preliminary examination report. This report is then communicated to each of the elected offices by the IB.

In summary, by the time of the PCT process is completed, a PCT application file can contain all of the following items:

1. a receiving office file (the *home copy*);

2. a searching authority file (the *search copy*);

3. a file at the International Bureau (the *record copy*);

4. a request for international preliminary examination (*chapter II demand*); and,

5. an international preliminary examining authority file (the *examination copy*).

PRESERVING FOREIGN FILING RIGHTS

Shortly, this chapter will take you through the PCT timeline of events. It is important for you to note now that the first application that you file in the process does not have to be your PCT application. In fact, the typical route is to file your U.S. patent application (either a provisional or a regular application) first, and then within twelve months, file your PCT application.

However, there are alternate ways of entering foreign protection. For example, it is possible to simply file a PCT application first and then designate the United States in your application as one of the countries that you would like to enter the national stage at a later date.

Most, if not all, inventors want to preserve foreign patent protection rights for their invention. Yet when these same inventors come to a realization of the actual costs of going foreign, most of them quickly later determine that they simply cannot afford to go foreign. Foreign patent protection is very expensive. The reason for this is that when you go foreign, you start to incur not only patent protection costs in the United States, but now you are also incurring patent protection expenses in each of the foreign countries that you would like to protect your invention. The costs can be in the hundreds of thousands of dollars for big companies that want worldwide patent protection.

Having alerted you to the costs of foreign patent protection, every inventor can preserve their foreign rights through the PCT. Probably the least expensive way for solo inventors and others on a budget to preserve foreign rights (as well as even to defer U.S. patent costs while they evaluate the marketability of their invention) is to file a U.S. provisional patent application on their invention first. Within one year, these inventors should file a PCT application that claims priority back to that earlier filed provisional patent application. Then, within the thirty months of the PCT process, the inventors can use the PCT application to enter regular patent protection in the United States, as well as any other foreign PCT contracting state that they choose. Following this foreign protection route will be the least expensive for solo inventors. If, as is usually the case at thirty months, your invention (as well as your budget) simply does not permit you to file for protection abroad, you can simply not enter any foreign stages, but you can still enter the United States for protection at this time.

NOTE: *The PCT system was reformed, and applications filed after January 1, 2004, must follow the new system. These instructions follow the reformed system.*

PCT TIMELINE

The PCT process is very time sensitive and can best be understood in the form of a time outline. The process is divided into two stages. The first stage is the *international stage* (or Chapter I of the PCT), and the second stage is called the *national stage* (or Chapter II of the PCT). The national stage is the stage in which you enter the actual individual filings in each of the countries you have designated to obtain a patent. A visual timeline is provided below, taking you through the process.

NOTE: *The time periods highlighted below are absolute cut-off dates. This means that, for purposes of your own calendar, you should be taking the necessary action a couple of months before each of these dates.*

Chapter I You begin at *time zero,* which is when you file your regular U.S. application. This will set your *priority date* for PCT purposes if your U.S. application does not itself rely on any previously filed application for priority purposes. All of the PCT time periods that are hereinafter mentioned are keyed off of your priority date.

File Your PCT Application No later than twelve months from your previously filed U.S. application, you must file your PCT application. Your PCT application should contain the following parts:

✪ Cover Letter—It is a good idea to include a cover letter in which you let the PTO know what you are sending for any of your communications with the PTO. You can use the cover letter that is in Appendix G or type your own similar letter.

✪ Transmittal—Instructions on obtaining a transmittal from the PTO website are in Appendix G.

• In Part I, be sure to fill out and sign the express mailing label section.

• In Part II, check the box for a "new international application" and be sure to list your earliest previously filed application for which you are claiming priority (this is usually the date that you filed your prior U.S. application). You should also check box C and fill in your relevant information for your priority application. If your application is identical to the one that you previously filed with the PTO, you should check the appropriate box in item D.

- In Part III, check box E to indicate that you are submitting a fee calculation sheet (Form PCT/RO/101 annex).

  NOTE: *Dates are written a little bit different when you are dealing with anything abroad. When writing dates in your PCT application or any associated correspondence, you should first indicate the day, then the name of the month, followed by the year. You should then ideally repeat this order in parentheses using just numbers. For example, June 10, 2006, would be written as follows: 10 June 2006 (10.06.06).*

✪ Request (Form PCT/RO/101)—Blank PCT request forms and instructions on how to complete the form can be found at the WIPO's website www.wipo.int/pct/en/forms/index.htm. Several of the more important boxes in that form are discussed. Boxes not discussed are either self-explanatory or in all likelihood will not apply to your situation. However, you should consult the detailed instructions on completing the form at the WIPO site.

  NOTE: *Covering every nuance of PCT is not within the scope of this book and consultation with a patent attorney experienced in foreign practice is recommended if you seek worldwide protection for your patent.*

- Boxes II and III. List the applicants and inventors. In the United States, inventors will be the applicants since patent applications in the United States must be applied for in the name of each inventor. But that is not necessarily the case for contracting states abroad. Also, to be able to file your PCT application with the PTO as the Receiving Office (RO), at least one of the applicants/inventors must be a resident of the United States.

- Box IV. You will leave this box blank if you are filing the request yourself and have no legal representative listed.

- List any previously filed applications for your invention in order to obtain their priority date.

You should also check the box requesting that the receiving office (RO) prepare and transmit to the International Bureau (IB) a certified copy of any earlier filed applications. Rule 17 of the PCT Regulations states that you must submit a certified copy of the priority document to the IB within a specified time. So if you have previously filed a U.S. application with the PTO (as assumed in the foreign filing route being discussed) as your RO, then you should check the appropriate box indicating that you request the PTO to prepare and transmit to the IB a certified copy of your earlier application(s).

• This is where you choose your International Searching Authority (ISA). As discussed earlier in the chapter, sole inventors and others on a budget should choose the United States as the ISA. It will be less expensive and require less work. However, you also can choose the EP as your ISA. If you are absolutely sure that you will be seeking foreign protection or you are on a larger budget, then you may want to choose the EPO as your ISA. The benefits for choosing the EPO are outlined in MPEP §1840 and include such reasons as:

♦ the EPO search fee need not be paid upon entering the EP as a designated office and

♦ the European Patent Office search will provide you with the benefit of a European art search that may be different from the search already conducted by the PTO with respect to your previously filed U.S. application. This gives you the benefit of an international search, which can highlight any problems with your invention before you go to the expense of foreign filing.

There is also a space to indicate whether you want the results of any previous international search to be used. So if the PTO has performed a search on your previously filed U.S. application, you should indicate that you want this search to be used. This can save you money since international searching authorities provide for a reduced search fee when there is a corresponding prior national non-provisional application.

- Box VIII. There are several declaration forms that are optional on your part in submitting with your request. However, completing these declarations can be useful depending on the countries that you later plan to seek patent protection because it may speed up filing for patent protection in those contracting states. For example, if the United States were to be a contracting state that you want to enter in thirty months, a declaration of inventorship might be helpful to fill out now and submit it along with your request. If you do want to fill out any of these declarations, you have thirty months from your priority date to do so to get them in your PCT application. Otherwise, you will need to deal with any such forms when it comes time to enter the national phase of the states you are interested in seeking patent protection.

- ✪   PCT Fee Calculation Sheet (Form PCT/RO/101 Annex)—You should check the PTO website for any changes in fees since they change regularly. (Go to www.uspto.gov and click on the site index, click "Fees, USPTO" and then the "Current FY 2005 Fee Schedule" and then "PCT Fees-International Stage.")

- ✪   Specification/Drawings—Make a copy of your U.S. specification and drawings that you previously submitted to the PTO. The only difference here is that you should make sure that you use A4 paper rather than 8½ x 11 inches.

- ✪   Any Required Sequence Listing—(See Chapter 5 for information about sequence listings.)

Mailing Your PCT Application

You should send your PCT application using Express Mail. To be absolutely safe, also try to send your application and any other PCT papers that you file soon enough so that you ensure it arrives before your absolute cut-off date. While U.S. law gives you the date that you deposit your Express Mail papers with the post office, PCT Rule 20.1(a) provides for marking the date of actual receipt on the request. (MPEP §1805.) To obviate any possible disagreement about which law is right, see if you can get your papers in so that they arrive no later than your absolute cut-off date.

Send your application to the following address:

Mail Stop PCT
Commissioner for Patents
P.O. Box 1450
Alexandria, VA 22313

Electronic Filing of Your PCT Application

As with filing a regular U.S. patent application, the United States allows you to file your PCT with the USPTO as the receiving office. To do this go to the USPTO website (www.uspto.gov), click on "patents" on the left-hand side of the page, and choose "file online in EFS-web." You will need to file as "EFS-web unregistered e-filers" unless you have taken the necessary steps to register yourself as a registered filer (see Chapter 7). Insert your name, as well as your email address, and choose "new application." Next, check the box "international application for filing in the U.S. receiving office." As you continue through the process, you will be allowed to insert information concerning your PCT application and attach all necessary documents. The PTO offers tutorials on filing your application electronically. In fact, if you go to www.uspto.gov/ebc/portal/tutorials.htm you will be able to practice filing an application without actually submitting one.

> *Author's Note: Electronic filing*
> If you are filing your patent application with the IB as your Receiving Office, WIPO allows you to send your application electronically using its *PCT SAFE* software. This can be found at its site (www.wipo.int/pctsafe/en). The WIPO site and PCT SAFE is also a good source for required forms for a PCT application. An easier place to access the required forms is at the PTO's website www.uspto.gov/web/offices/pac/dapps/pct. If you go to that link, you can select the link "forms" on the right-hand side of the page. The required forms are divided up into "Chapter I," "Chapter II," and "National Stage." The form numbers are listed in Appendix G.

Chapter II

Chapter II is simply an arbitrary name used in the PCT that marks a phase of the PCT process that applicants can elect to pursue.

Preliminary Examination Demand

The preliminary examination demand was, until recently, something that everyone did because it was required if you wanted to delay the time for when you had to start filing national stage applications to thirty months. However, all applicants are now automatically given thirty months from the time they file a PCT application to the time a national stage application needs to be filed regardless of whether a demand for preliminary examination has been made.

The only exception to this rule is for a couple of PCT contracting countries (e.g., Brazil and Serbia), which still require that applicants file a demand for preliminary examination and enter Chapter II if they want to wait the full thirty months to file for patent protection. These handful of exceptions can be found at www.wipo.int/pct/en. So if you have patent desires in these countries, you still do need to enter Chapter II or start seeking patent protection there before nineteen months from your priority date.

What does this all mean for you? Well, in most situations, you will not need to worry about Chapter II at all. You can simply skip this section and go down to the thirty-month time period below, which is the time to enter the national stage in those countries that you want patent protection.

In some circumstances, entering Chapter II by filing a demand for preliminary examination may be useful. For example, you should file a demand if you want to make changes to your PCT application. You make such changes by filing Article 34 Amendments with your demand for preliminary examination. Also, some applicants file a demand for a preliminary examination because it will trigger yet another examination and the issuance of an International Preliminary Examination Report on the patentability of your invention. This report is a nonbinding opinion whether your invention appears to be *novel,* to involve an *inventive step* (which means the same as nonobvious), and is *industrially applicable.* What this demand does is in effect give you another bite at the apple to amend your application so as to clear up any problems that you may have encountered from the written opinion from Chapter I concerning novelty, inventive step, or industrial applicability. Remember that you want to clear up any problems before you enter national phase filing in the countries that you intend to seek patent protection. The reason for this is that you will in all likelihood encounter the same type of problems or objections to your application at the time that you go to file in the national phase. But if you encountered no problems during Chapter I, then save yourself the expense and time and not file a demand for preliminary examination.

If you do decide to file a demand for preliminary examination, you must do it no later than three months from the time you receive your International Search Report (ISA) from Chapter I or twenty-two months from your priority date, whichever is later. In other words, you do not need to get your demand in at the same time (by nineteen months) you would if you were seeking delay in those handful of countries (e.g., Brazil and Serbia). However, this nineteen-month time period is still a good date to keep in mind if you want to file a demand in order to submit amendments to your application during a Chapter II phase.

A good tutorial on filing a preliminary examination can be found at the USPTO website at www.uspto.gov/ebc/portal/efs/dct_pct_ demand_tutorial.pdf. Your demand should be filed on PCT Form PCT/ IPEA/401 along with a fee transmittal sheet, Form PCT/IPEA/401 (Annex). Consult the WIPO instructions for a more detailed explanation. Some of the key boxes are discussed as follows:

- Box IV. If you are filing a demand because you want to change your application under Article 34, you should so indicate here and also include your amendments.

- Include a PCT calculation sheet along with your demand.

- Mail your demand and appropriate fees to the specific IPEA that you desire to prepare your International Preliminary Examination Report. The PTO will act as an IPEA for U.S. residents and nationals even if the EPO served as your ISA. To use the PTO as your EPEA, send your demand to:

Mail Stop PCT
Commissioner for Patents
P.O. Box 1450
Alexandria, VA 22313

If your international search report was prepared by the EPO, you can also request the EPO as your IPEA. If you elect this choice, you should mail your demand to:

European Patent Office
Erhardtstrasse 27
D-80331 Munich
Federal Republic of Germany

National Stage   Before the expiration of thirty months from your priority date, you will need to enter the national stage in each of those countries that you intend to seek patent protection abroad. So this means that well before this date, you need to consider how to accomplish this task. Although it is conceivable that you could do this alone, even experienced patent attorneys in the United States will engage foreign counsel to assist with foreign filings. The reason for this is that filing foreign protection abroad can differ dramatically from U.S. practice. For example, if you are going to enter Europe for patent protection, you will need to hire an associate from Europe who has experience for filing applications in the EPO. Although it is possible to simply file what you previously filed in the United States with the EPO, it is always a good idea to have a European associate review and change the application before filing it in the EPO.

> **Author's Note: Entering the national stage**
> Entering the national stage before thirty months is a prerequisite and can be an unforgiving rule. There are few ways to reenter the national stage and keep your priority date if you miss this deadline. In the United States you might try to revive the application based on unavoidable delay (unintentional is not available because 35 U.S.C. §371 allows for revival for failure to comply with national stage requirements only when the failure was "unavoidable." This is a tough standard to meet, so your best policy is to file national stage applications before this thirty-month period is up.

Some of the differences in practice between the USPTO and EPO include the following. The EPO takes a much more rigid view of claims finding support in the specification. Also, claim language like "comprising" is typically replaced by claim language like "characterized by." European laws also give one additional month to enter the national stage (so you will have thirty-one months, rather than the thirty months to enter a filing there).

Author's Note: Finding a foreign associate

Ideally, the best way to find a foreign associate is to get the name of one that someone else has used in the past and recommends to you to use in the future. The EPO website maintains a searchable database for foreign associates, which you can find at www.european-patent-office.org/reps/search.html. Another useful website to find patent agents in the United Kingdom (UK) can be found at www.cipa.org.uk.

You can also contact the patent department in a U.S. law firm. Firms that have intellectual property departments will also have foreign associates that they use for foreign filings. They will more than likely be delighted to give names of such contacts since they usually expect that any business they refer will be returned in their favor by the foreign firm.

Entering the National Stage in the United States

You may be using your PCT application as a means to enter the United States for patent protection on your invention. This may be the case, for example, if you filed for patent protection in the United States with a provisional patent application, then filed a PCT application within twelve months, and now thirty months later you want to start patent examination of your invention in the United States.

You have two options for entering the national phase in the United States at the thirty-month time period. The first route is to file a national stage application under 35 U.S.C. §371. The second route is to file a continuation or continuation-in-part application from the PCT application under 35 U.S.C. §111(a). Both routes must occur while your PCT application is pending or before the thirty-month national stage filing deadline prescribed by 37 C.F.R. §1.495.

The first option is generally referred to as a *national stage perfection route* and is governed by both PCT and U.S. procedure and rules that are summarized in Sections 1893–1896 of the MPEP. The second option is generally referred to as the *bypass route* because all of the requirements of national stage filing under §371 are bypassed in favor of U.S. rules and regulations pertaining to §111(a) filings.

A discussion and comparison of these two routes can be found in Sections 1893–1896 of the MPEP. The main differences between filing a national stage application under 35 U.S.C. §371 under method (1) and a national application under 35 U.S.C. §111(a) under method (2) are as follows:

- Filing Fees—The filing fees are different. For a national stage application, you should consult 37 C.F.R. §1.492 for your filing fee whereas for a national application under 35 U.S.C. §111(a) you should consult 37 C.F.R. §1.16 for your filing fee.

- Certified Copy of Priority Document—You will not ordinarily need to submit a certified copy of any application for which you are claiming priority if you choose to enter the national stage under 35 U.S.C. §371 so long as you have previously submitted such certified copy in your PCT application. However, you will need to submit a certified copy of your priority document (including the PCT application) if you file a regular U.S. application under 35 U.S.C. §111(a).

- Claiming Priority—The rules for claiming priority are slightly different. When you enter the United States via the national stage route (option 1), you do not need to claim priority to the PCT application that you filed leading up to your national stage application. However, you will need to make a claim of priority either in your application data sheet or the first sentence of your specification to any other applications that your PCT application itself relies on for priority. (This must be done within four months from the date on which the national stage commenced or sixteen months from the filing date of the prior application.) The reason that you need not make a claim of priority to your PCT application is because your national stage U.S. application takes on the same filing date as your PCT application. However, if you file a regular U.S. application (option 2), you will need to make a specific claim of priority to your filing date of your application, which you previously filed.

○ Certified Copy of any Priority Document—If you choose the national stage perfection route, you do not usually need to file a certified copy of a priority document, from which priority was originally claimed in the PCT application in order to perfect a priority claim made under 35 U.S.C. §119(a) or 35 U.S.C. §365(b). Such priority document is automatically transmitted from the International Bureau (IB) to all states designated in the PCT Request if properly instructed by you at the time of filing the Request. On the other hand, you must file a certified copy of the priority document at some point during the pendency of the U.S. national application to perfect a priority claim if you choose the bypass route. Regardless of the route chosen, if a national application priority claim extends back to a U.S. application, whether to a first-filed provisional application under 35 U.S.C. §119(e), to a non-provisional application under 35 U.S.C. §120, or to an earlier international application designating the United States under 35 U.S.C. §365(c), such priority must be properly identified either in an application date sheet or at the beginning of the specification in accordance with 35 U.S.C. §119 or §120.

○ Filing Date—Obtaining a filing date is much easier under the bypass route since all you need to file is your specification and any required drawings just as you would need to do to obtain a filing date if you were to file a regular U.S. patent application. As with any such non-provisional filing under 37 C.F.R. §1.53(b), the filing fee and oath/declaration are not essential to obtaining a filing date, since such items can be supplied later in response to a Notice to File Missing Parts. In fact, you can submit such items up to six months from the mailing date of the Notice to File Missing Parts with the payment of extension fees. This is a big advantage and the reason most applicants choose the bypass route. The option of deferring payment of the filing fee is not available under the national stage perfection route, and you must file an oath or declaration in order to establish a filing date.

✪   Managing Documents—National stage perfection applications are initially reviewed and processed by administrative personnel from the PCT Branch. During the initial stages, a U.S. file wrapper is created and the international prosecution of the PCT application is imported into such file wrapper, thereby forming the foundation for the U.S. prosecution. All of the documents generated during the International Stage (PCT Chapters I and II) and forwarded to the PTO are supposed to find their way into the newly created U.S. file. However, it is not an infrequent occurrence that certain documents will be missing from the file and reported as not received by the PTO.

✪   Amendments—Further, if the PCT application is amended extensively under PCT Article 34 during Chapter II of the international phase, it may be more beneficial to choose the bypass route over the national stage perfection route. Amendments made during the prosecution of the PCT application are directly incorporated into the bypass application. In other words, the bypass continuation application, as you will file it, is a clean copy that includes all previously made amendments. In contrast, national stage applicants must file the original PCT application and introduce amendments via separate documentation.

Which route should you choose? In general, you will find the bypass route to be safer unless you really familiarize yourself with PCT procedure. But you should weigh the advantages and disadvantages of each route to determine which route is best for you.

Entering the United States through the Bypass Route
If you choose the bypass route, you should file a clean specification that indicates at the beginning of the specification that such application is a continuation of at least the PCT application. Any Article 19 and Article 34 amendments to the specification and claims made during the international phase should be incorporated into the body of the application prior to filing, such that the bypass

route application shows no sign of, or is clean of, amendments. Basically what you are doing if you choose the bypass route is to file a completely new patent application that incorporates everything done in your PCT application just as you would if you were to draft a regular U.S. patent application. As discussed, you will need a proper claim of priority in your application to your earlier filed PCT application.

> ### Author's Note: Making a proper claim of priority to a PCT application
> If your application claims benefit to an international application, the first sentence of your specification must also be amended to indicate whether the international application was published under PCT Article 21(2) in English.

Example:

Before abandonment of his PCT application, Joe files a 35 U.S.C. §111(a) U.S. non-provisional application. Joe should write the following as the first sentence of his specification:

> This application claims priority to International Application PCT/EP90/00000, with an international filing date of [date], published in English under PCT Article 21(2).

Entering the United States through National Stage Perfection

National stage perfection applicants must start with the original application as filed with the PCT Request and as amended under Article 19 as a foundation. Upon entry into the U.S. national phase, any Article 34 amendments made during PCT Chapter II can be effected by a preliminary amendment or by submitting copies of annexes to the IPER. Such annexes must be line-by-line substitute sheets of the originally filed PCT application as amended under Article 19 (if applicable), which should not present a problem if everything was filed and published in English. If not in English, the translated PCT Article 19 and the translated annexes to the IPER must correspond, as line-by-line replacement sheets, to the original non-English PCT application.

You will need to submit the following parts to the PTO in your application for national stage entry:

- ✪ transmittal letter;

- ✪ declaration;

- ✪ fees; and,

- ✪ IDS.

Transmittal Letter and Necessary Items Specified in the Transmittal (Form PTO-1382)

This form is listed in Appendix G. You need to complete this special transmittal form because you need to specifically identify that you are filing a national stage application under 35 U.S.C. §371. If you do not do this, your application will be treated by the PTO as a regular nonprovisional application. (35 U.S.C. §111(a).)

Check box 3, indicating that you request the commencement of national examination procedures.

Make sure that a copy of your international application (PCT) has been provided to the PTO. A copy should be provided to each designated office by the IB about eighteen months from your priority date. The IB then mails you confirmation (Form IB/308). You can rely on this confirmation instead of providing a copy of your international application to the PTO.

If for some reason you filed your PCT application in a language other than English, you must provide a translation (item 6).

Declaration

You should also include a declaration (item 9). If you do not submit this now, the PTO will send you a *Notice of Missing Requirements* giving you one month to submit it.

Fees

You must also include a basic national fee (item 21). This national fee is not extendable and your application will go abandoned in the

United States if you do not pay this fee before the time has expired for you to commence the national stage (thirty months from your priority date). (37 C.F.R. §1.492.)

However, be sure to check the PTO website for the most current fees. National stage fees are always subject to change. Remember you absolutely must include at least the amount of the basic national fee due or your application will go abandoned.

Electronic Filing of National Stage Applications
As with the initial PCT application, applicants can file the national stage application electronically, as well. Entering the national stage application under 35 U.S.C. §371 using the electronic filing system will allow you to check and edit your application prior to filing.

Information Disclosure Statement (IDS)
You should complete and file an IDS now just as you would if you were filing your regular U.S. non-provisional application. (See Chapter 7.)

If your application is accepted for entry into the national stage, you will be mailed Form PCT/DO/EO/903 indicating acceptance of your application as a national stage filing. (35 U.S.C. §371.)

Entering Europe through the PCT
Next to the United States, Europe is one of the primary markets you should consider if you decide that you can afford the expense of foreign patent protection. The European Union comprises some twenty-seven member states, which creates some unique problems. After you file your PCT application, you can enter into as many of these countries within thirty months from your priority date that you want to. However, a better option is to file your PCT application, and then enter into a European phase application with thirty-one months. If you are successful in getting a European patent, you can then validate this Euro-PCT application in every European member state where you want protection.

Amending Your PCT Application
It is possible to amend your PCT application even before you enter the national stage for each of your designated countries. PCT Article 19 amendments are exclusively amendments to your claims. You have two months from the mailing date of the International Search Report by the ISA or sixteen months from your priority date—whichever occurs

later—to make an amendment to the claims of your application. Your amendments must be filed with the International Bureau, whose duties are performed by the World Intellectual Property Organization (WIPO) in Geneva, Switzerland, and are published. Since the national laws of some designated offices may grant provisional protection on your invention from the date of publication of your claims, you may want to take advantage of this opportunity under Article 19 to polish your claims before such publication.

You also have the right to make amendments to your claims, description, and/or drawings during the Chapter II examination phase. (PCT Article 34(2)(b).) Such amendments are often done in response to the written opinion that you receive during Chapter I of the PCT process (these amendments, as discussed previously, are best filed with your demand for preliminary examination).

Such an opinion might tell you that your application does not comply with formal matters or point out substantive matter, such as your claims are not directed to inventions that have novelty, inventive step, and industrial applicability. Any amendments you make must be made by submitting a replacement sheet for every sheet of your application that differs from the sheet it replaces unless the entire sheet is cancelled. You must also include a description of how the replacement sheet differs from the replaced sheet. (MPEP §1878.02.)

NOTE: *You can always make amendments to your application at the time you enter the national stage of your designated country according to the amendment practice for that designated state.*

Additional Information

The MPEP devotes its entire Chapter 18 to the PCT. You can also find the text of the *PCT Applicant's Guide,* a monthly PCT newsletter, a weekly PCT gazette, downloadable PCT forms, and other information about the processing of international application at the WIPO's website: www.wipo.int/pct/en.

The PCT Help Desk provides information and assistance on the PCT process and can be reached at 571–272–4300 between the hours of 9:00 am and 4:30 pm (EST), Monday through Friday.

OTHER FOREIGN FILING ROUTES

The procedure recommended for filing a PCT application within one year of filing your U.S. patent application is a common way to file your patent application abroad. However, there are alternate routes to foreign filing. One such alternative is to forgo the PCT process altogether and file individual foreign patent applications in the countries where you desire patent protection. A second alternative route to foreign protection is to file your PCT patent application as the first application for your invention. Under this second route, you will still be able to enter the United States prior to thirty months and obtain the filing date of your PCT application. Some of the alternatives are discussed in more detail in the rest of this chapter. However, a complete discussion of every foreign route and nuances of each route are beyond the scope of this book. Consult with a patent attorney with experience in foreign patent protection if your goal is to seek foreign patent protection on your invention.

File in Each Foreign Country or Region Individually

One alternative route to the one presented earlier is to file in each of the foreign countries that you desire patent protection. This is, in effect, what you are doing in the PCT process. However, the PCT process gives you added time to make individual foreign filings in each of the countries that you designate. Also, your individual national filings in each of your designated states are usually less burdensome and therefore less costly when you enter such states by way of the PCT. This is because many of these states will rely on things that have already occurred in your PCT application—like your international search. If you know that you will be selling your invention in only one or two specific countries abroad, then foreign filing individually in each of those countries may be a good idea as opposed to a PCT application.

For European countries, there is a procedure in which you can file a single application in Europe in order to gain patent protection for each of the European countries that you desire protection. If you go this route, you will be issued a European Patent. This patent, like the publication of a PCT application, does not confer any rights per se. You will next need to file that published patent application with each of the European countries that you desire patent protection. As with a PCT application, filing a single European application can save you some costs if there are many European countries that you desire patent protection.

Foreign Filing License

If your invention was made in the United States, a *foreign filing license* is necessary to apply abroad. If a foreign filing license is required but not obtained for your invention, you can be barred from obtaining a U.S. patent on that same invention. Since the United States is by far the largest marketplace for your invention, this is something that you never want to happen.

When you apply for a U.S. patent, you will usually be granted a foreign filing license by the PTO when you receive your filing receipt several months later. If you look on your filing receipt, you will see the phrase "Foreign Filing License Granted" and the date printed on it. Even if the PTO did not grant you a foreign filing license on your receipt, you would automatically be entitled to the license six months from your filing date. However, if you foreign file before you apply for a U.S. patent application, you will have no filing receipt from the PTO granting you a foreign filing license. In such a case, you will need to petition the PTO for a foreign filing license before you file your foreign patent application. Consult MPEP §140 for how to go about submitting a petition to the PTO for a foreign filing license.

Before you file your PCT, you must obtain a filing receipt from the PTO granting you a foreign filing license or else allow six months to elapse. However, there is a safety net with PCT applications if for some reason you have not obtained a foreign filing license before you file your PCT application. It is current practice to construe your PCT filing as petition for the license that should normally be granted. (MPEP §1832.)

If, for some reason, you do not obtain a foreign filing license before you foreign file, there is a procedure to petition for a retroactive foreign filing license (so long as your error occurred without deceptive intent). However, you do not want to be placed in such a circumstance.

Author's Note: Foreign nationals listed on a U.S. patent application

If a foreign national is listed on a U.S. patent application, you should also make absolutely sure that this inventor's country of residence does not require clearance prior to filing an application in the United States Many countries abroad are much more harsh than the United States if a patent application is applied for abroad without obtaining necessary clearance or filing first in that foreign country. Such countries may even impose criminal penalties.

File Your Foreign PCT Application First

It is a perfectly acceptable practice to file your PCT application before you file your domestic U.S. application. If you have done this and want to enter patent protection in the United States at the thirty-month PCT time period, you have two routes to achieve this. The first route is to file a national stage application under 35 U.S.C. §371. The second route is to file a continuation or continuation-in-part application from the PCT application under 35 U.S.C. §111(a). Both routes must occur while the PCT application is pending and/or before the thirty-month national stage filing deadline prescribed by 37 C.F.R. §1.495.

FIle Both a U.S. Application and a PCT Application at the Same Time

If you have the money, it is also possible to file both a regular U.S. application as well as a PCT based off an earlier-filed provisional application. In such a case, you will have two applications going at the same time—your U.S. case and your PCT case. This is a little different than the case of D above because you are not using your PCT application to enter the United States thirty months later. You already have your U.S. case filed. However, nothing would prevent you from entering the U.S. stage through your PCT, which could come in handy if something went wrong with your U.S.-filed application.

Paris Convention

As early as the 1800s, countries—including the United States—acknowledged the need for international cooperation on patent rights with the signing of a multilateral treaty, known as the *Paris Convention*. The *Paris Convention* provides that each signatory country grant a period of one year to any application of a member state after their initial patent application to apply for protection in all of the other member states. This provision offered a number of new advantages. Most importantly, it prevents a foreign patent member patent office from applying intervening prior art that would otherwise prevent a patent. It also allows applicants time to asses the economic viability of their inventions before applying in other member states to determine whether patent protection is warranted. Although the Paris Convention has undergone a number of revisions since the 1800s, it is a viable treaty today.

Claiming Priority to an Earlier Foreign Application

One of the most important rights afforded by the Paris Convention is the right to claim priority to an earlier filed patent application in another country that is a member of the treaty. This is very important because just as with your right to claim priority to an earlier filed provisional application, you can overcome intervening prior art between the filing of your earlier filed priority application and your currently filed application. Here are some important rules to keep in mind to make claims of priority to earlier filed foreign patent applications.

If you file a foreign patent application first and later file your regular U.S. non-provisional application, you have one year from the date of your foreign filing to claim priority to your previously filed foreign application. (35 U.S.C. §119 and MPEP §201.13.) You cannot obtain the earlier effective filing date of applications filed in every foreign country, but for most foreign countries you can. (You can find a list of recognized foreign countries in MPEP § 201.13.)

NOTE: *If you file a design patent application abroad, you only have six months to make your claim of priority.*

In computing your twelve-month time period (or six-month time period in the case of design patent applications) to claim priority, the first day is not counted.

Example:

You file an application in Canada on January 3, 2006. You may file your U.S. non-provisional application on January 3, 2007, and still claim priority to the earlier filing date of your Canadian application.

This twelve-month period (or six-month period in the case of designs) is from the date of the earliest foreign filing and not from any subsequent foreign filings (unless the first filing has been withdrawn or abandoned for some reason).

Example 1:

You file an application in France on January 4, 2006, and an identical application in the United Kingdom on March 3, 2006. You then file in the United States on February 2, 2007. You are not entitled to a right of priority at all. You are not entitled to the date of the French application because this application was filed more than twelve months before your U.S. application. You are not entitled to the benefit of the date of the United Kingdom application since this application is not the first one filed.

Example 2:

You file a regular U.S. patent application on January 1, 2006. Later you discover that your invention is related to embodiments that you did not disclose in your patent application and you file a continuation-in-part (CIP) application on December 23, 2006. You want to gain foreign patent protection and file a PCT application on your invention (including the new embodiments) on December 15, 2007. In this case, you cannot get priority at all in your PCT application because your first filed application (the U.S. application) is more than twelve months from the PCT filing date. Although the CIP is within twelve months from the PCT filing date, it is considered as a second patent application filing for the invention so you also cannot claim priority to it. In this scenario, you may have been better off filing a new patent application rather than a CIP in order to gain priority to it.

If the last day of the twelve months is a Saturday, Sunday, or federal holiday within the District of Columbia, then you may still make your claim of priority even if you file your U.S. non-provisional application on the next succeeding business day.

In order to make a claim of priority to your previously filed foreign application, there must be an identity of inventors between your U.S. application and your previously filed foreign application. (See MPEP §201.13 for the exact requirements that must be fulfilled in order to make a proper claim of priority.) This is a little different from a domestic claim of priority (a claim of priority from one U.S.

application to a previously filed U.S. application in which only one inventor needs to be the same).

Just as with earlier filed domestic application, the disclosure of a foreign application may be insufficient (e.g., lacks enablement, written description, etc.) to support a priority claim for a later filed application in this country. Thus, your foreign application must be written just like your U.S. application (e.g., must be enabling, pass the written description requirement, etc.).

You make your foreign priority claim just as you would with a domestic priority claim, as explained in the last chapter, by including a specific reference to the foreign application. You can make this reference in your specification, your application *Transmittal Letter,* your *Application Data Sheet* or even in your *Declaration.* You must identify the foreign application by specifying its application number, the foreign country and the day, month, and year of its filing. The various application numbers should be presented in proper form. (Consult MPEP §201.14(d) for how to properly cite the application numbers of various foreign countries.)

You must also file a certified copy of your foreign application with the PTO. (35 U.S.C. §119(b).) This means that you must submit a copy of your foreign application (the specification and drawings) as filed in that country. The copy must include a certification by the patent office of the foreign country in which it was filed.

The foreign application does not need to be translated at the time you file your later domestic application. Your examiner will only request translations if the filing date of your foreign application comes into issue. (MPEP §201.15.) If you are later required to provide a translation, the translation must be filed with a statement that the translation of the certified copy is accurate.

If the benefit of a foreign filing date based on a foreign application is claimed in a later filed application (i.e., continuation, continuation-in-part, division) and a certified copy of the foreign application as filed has already been filed in a parent application, it is not necessary to file an additional certified copy in the later application. (MPEP §201.14(b).)

Some Special Considerations when Drafting an Application to Be Filed Abroad

In PCT prosecution, the international application is eventually translated into the language of the designation country for national prosecution. In the alternative, if you have filed the application directly in a foreign country, this country application is usually filed in the designation country's language, although some countries permit filing in English with prompt translation for prosecution. Such a directly filed application is typically a translation of the last U.S. priority application. So whether you use PCT or directly file, you usually can expect a translation of your patent application at some point in time. The translations process, as well as particular rules of foreign countries, means that there are some special considerations you may want to consider when drafting your U.S. patent application in English if you know that it will be filed abroad.

First, for translation ease, consider the following:

1. Since abbreviations may be difficult for a translator, use the term "Figure" or the capitalized abbreviation "FIG." rather then "Fig."

2. Use short sentences, and avoid run-on sentences.

3. Use extensive formatting and indentation to provide clear separation of portions of claim.

4. Do not incorporate by reference. If the material is important to your invention, then disclose this.

5. Keep a parts list. If you keep a parts list, when you are writing your description, you will use the same word. It is better to keep your language consistent, rather than using different words to mean the same thing in different sections of your application. This way, you can make sure that everything is translated the same way.

6. If your application requires a number range, you should give the low end, the high end, and some samples in the middle. If the ranges are critical for your application, you must compare numbers outside the range with numbers inside the range.

As to particular rules, keep the following in mind:

1. In the United States, one often uses Roman letters to designate related or like elements (e.g., "Figure 1A is an enlarged view of the tip of screw of FIG. 1"). Many countries do not permit Roman letters. So you are better off using numerical suffixes instead of letters (e.g., "Figure 1–1 and Figure 1"). In the alternative, just sequentially number your figures. The same thing goes for designated alternative embodiments. ("left and right sides of 80A and 80B" could be said as "left and right sides of 40–1 and 40–2").

2. Some countries prefer that claims include reference numerals, just as you use when writing your specification. Where a claim element refers to more than one feature of a given embodiment, the reference numbers should also be separated by a comma. (e.g., "arms (80, 82, 84)"). Where claim elements refer to features of different embodiments, the reference numerals for the different embodiments should be separated by semicolons (e.g., "arms (80, 82, 84; 160, 162, 164").

Filing a Design Patent Application Abroad

You cannot use the PCT process to file a design patent application. However, it is now possible to obtain a single registered *Community Design* covering all European Union countries. The registration of design applications will be overseen and administered by a newly formed section of the *Office of Harmonization of International Markets* (OHIM). This office is in Alicante, Spain, and its website is http://oami.eu.int. The registered Community Design will provide a cheaper and less complex route for obtaining registration across all fifteen member states. The registration process allows multiple designs to be filed in one application for a relatively low per-design cost. There is no examination process, and the registration is typically issued within about three to six months of filing.

Author's Note: Registered design
The term *design* refers to the appearance of the whole or a part of a product resulting from the features of, in particular, the lines, contours, colors, shape, texture, or materials of the product itself, or its ornamentation.

A registered design protects designs for up to twenty-five years. A *registered community design* confers on its holder the exclusive right to use the design and to prevent any third party from using the design, without the holder's consent in all of the European Union countries. The *use* of a design includes the making, asking, offering, putting on the market, importing, exporting, or use of a product in which the design is incorporated or to which it is applied, or stocking such a product for those purposes. Use is not dependent on an infringer having prior knowledge of the registered design.

Where to Go for More Information about the PCT Process

A lot of information about the PCT process can be obtained from the WIPO website at www.wipo.int/pct/en. The most comprehensive guide is called the *PCT Applicant's Guide* (www.wipo.int/pct/guide/en). Finally, the PCT help desk at the PTO is also a very useful source for answering your questions about the PCT process. Their telephone number is 571–272–4300.

SECTION III

AFTER FILING YOUR APPLICATION

chapter 10

The PTO's Response to Your Patent Application

After you have submitted your patent application, it is stamped with a provisional serial number and the current date. This will become the official filing date of the application. The application is then forwarded to the *Office of Initial Patent Examination* (OIPE) of the PTO to confirm that it contains all the necessary parts.

Your application is then sent to the Licensing and Review Branch, which determines whether it is a candidate for a secrecy order or whether it is drafted to certain subject matter, such as nuclear materials. Your application is then assigned to a *group art unit*. A filing receipt identifying the inventors, the title of the invention, the serial number, and the filing date is issued to you by the Applications Branch.

NOTE: *Issuing the filing receipt ordinarily occurs three or four months from the date of filing the application. Your application is then assigned to an examiner who has expertise in the area of technology related to your invention. Your application is examined for compliance with all legal requirements, and your examiner makes a search through both U.S. and foreign patent documents and literature to make sure that your invention is novel, nonobvious, and meets all the necessary* *disclosure requirements. The examiner will then notify you in writing of his or her decision in a document that is referred to as an office action.*

Relatively few applications are allowed by the examiner as filed. In most cases, one or even all of the claims will be rejected on some legal ground. If you have received an action from the examiner that rejects some or all of your claims, you must either change or cancel some of your rejected claims or persuade the examiner why he or she is wrong.

NOTE: Rejection *is a term that the PTO uses when your claims are not allowed because your subject matter as claimed is considered unpatentable by the PTO.*

Objection is a term that the PTO uses when the form of your claims is considered improper. Rejections are about substance, while objections are about forms.

The practical difference between a rejection and an objection is that a rejection, involving the merits of the claim, is subject to review by the Board of Patent Appeals and Interferences. On the other hand, an objection may be reviewed only by way of petition to the Commissioner if you disagree with the reasoning of your examiner. (MPEP §706.01.)

CORRESPONDING WITH THE PTO

You will find that you can use the same address that you sent your patent application to for other correspondence with the PTO. However, for certain types of correspondence with the PTO, using an appropriate *mail stop* designation before the PTO address will speed up handling of your correspondence. Some of the more common mail stop designations are listed in Appendix A. For example, to submit an amendment to the PTO, you would address your amendment to:

Mail Stop Amendment
Commissioner for Patents
P.O. Box 1450
Alexandria, VA 22313

The PTO also maintains a central facsimile number, which is 571–273–8300. The PTO has actually been encouraging the use of fax for correspondence lately, given inherent problems with mail. Faxing correspondence to the PTO can significantly expedite the handling of your correspondence.

Certain correspondence can never be faxed to the PTO. Examples of papers that cannot be faxed include:

- new patent applications;

- any correspondence being submitted for the purpose of obtaining an application filing date; and,

- drawings (unless being submitted with issue fee payment).

Examples of correspondence that can be faxed include:

- amendments;

- Information Disclosure Statements;

- terminal disclaimers;

- Notices of Appeal and appeal briefs; and,

- RCEs under 37 C.F.R. §1.114.

If you do send your correspondence to the PTO by fax, you should include a *Certificate of Transmission* stamped or written right onto the first page of your papers that states the following:

I hereby certify that this correspondence is being facsimile transmitted to the Patent and Trademark Office (Fax No. 571 -____-____) on _____ [date] _____ [printed name of person signing] _____ Signature.

By using a *Certificate of Transmission,* the PTO gives you the date that you actually start sending your transmission as a filing receipt date.

When you send papers by fax, a return receipt will be automatically generated, which will include the number of pages received as well as the date and time the facsimile was received. Additionally, the return receipt will include an image of the received cover page. The return receipt will be automatically sent to your facsimile machine, as long as your facsimile number is properly programmed in the sending facsimile machine and your facsimile machine is available to receive a fax immediately following the original transmission.

For papers that can be faxed, the receipt date that you are given is the date that the entire fax transmission is received by the PTO, unless such date is a Saturday, Sunday, or federal holiday. In this case, the receipt date will be the next succeeding day that the PTO is open for business.

Example:

A fax transmission from California starting on Friday at 8:45 pm Pacific Standard Time (PST) that takes twenty minutes would be completed at 9:05 pm (PST), or 12:05 am Eastern Standard Time on Saturday. If a Certificate of Transmission is used with the fax, then your fax is deemed to have reached the PTO on Friday. If you do not take advantage of the Certificate of Transmission, the receipt date will be Monday (if this is not a federal holiday). Due to the time zone difference, the fax is not actually sent to the PTO until Saturday, and the receipt date carries over to the succeeding business day.

You can find more information about faxing correspondence to the PTO at the MPEP §502.01.

If you have filed your patent application electronically as a registered e-filer, many subsequent types of communications that you may need to file with the PTO can also be filed electronically.

CHECKING THE STATUS OF A PATENT APPLICATION THROUGH PAIR

The PTO now offers something called its *Patent Application Information Retrieval System* (PAIR), which you can use to access a lot of information about a patent and, in some cases, even patent applications. You can access the PAIR system by going to what is called the patent *Electronic Business Center* (EBC) page at the PTO website. This page can be found at www.uspto.gov/ebc.

There is a public and a private side to PAIR. The public side is something that everyone in the world can see about issued patents and published patent applications. The private side of PAIR is something that only applicants and their attorneys can see about their own patent applications, which have been filed before such applications have been published. What does this mean for you? If you want to check PAIR for information about an application that you know a competitor has filed, you will need to wait until that application has been published before you can see the information by using PAIR. However, it is possible to check the status of your own patent application before it is published through the private side of PAIR. However, if you are not really in the business of filing many patent applications, then setting up access to the private side of PAIR will most likely not be worth your time.

How to Set Yourself Up to Use the Private Side of PAIR

Using the private side of PAIR will only be useful if you are going to file a patent application and want to be able to check the status of that application and its associated filings before it is published. Although this can be useful, setting yourself up for the private side of PAIR can take some work and time. If you only plan to file a single patent application with the PTO in the near future, setting yourself up with PAIR will probably not be worth your time.

Setting yourself up with the private side of PAIR is discussed in Chapter 7, so you should consult that chapter for the details on how to set your self up for the private side of PAIR if you do not mind all the work.

Using the Public Side of PAIR

Once a patent application is published (generally eighteen months after it is filed), you will have access to the filings with respect to that application. If you know the patent number of a patent from a competitor, you can bring that patent up by going to the PTO site and doing a search for the patent. (See Chapter 4.) With PAIR, you can get a lot more information about the patent.

One of the most useful things that you will be able to find out from PAIR is everything that occurred between the applicant for that patent and the PTO during the time that the applicant was trying to obtain that patent. This period of time when the applicant is busy trying to get the PTO to issue a patent is often referred to as the *prosecution stage* of the patent application. All of the documents that are filed relating to that patent application are accumulated together by the PTO into something called a *file wrapper*. By using PAIR, not only will you be able to see the dates and names of each document in the file wrapper, but you will be able to order that file wrapper so you can analyze any of those documents.

To use the public side of PAIR, go to the EBC page at the PTO site (www.uspto.gov/ebc) and click on the "Patent Application Information Retrieval" icon on that page. You will now have three methods to search. You can enter:

1.   a patent application number;

2.   a patent number; or,

3.   a patent application publication number.

Try entering a patent number for a patent that you want to search. What you will find if you do this is a page with a lot of biographical information about the patent. In addition, you will see the entire file history contents for that patent.

LENGTH OF TIME TO OBTAIN A PATENT

On average, you can expect it to take two to three years to obtain a patent. The actual time it takes for you to get your patent depends, however, on a host of factors. For example, if during the examination of your patent application you take a long time to respond to office actions you will inevitably not get a patent as quickly. The time it takes to obtain a patent will also depend on the type of technology involved. For example, biotechnology inventions will be on the upper end of the scale, whereas mechanical inventors typically obtain patents much more quickly (usually twelve to thirteen months). There is a way to get a patent sooner with a *Petition to Make Special,* which is discussed in the next section.

> ***Author's Note: Design patents.***
> Design patents are much quicker to obtain. Design patents issued between 2000–2007 were pending for an average period of time of 16.2 months.

PETITIONS TO MAKE SPECIAL

There are a host of reasons why you may want to try to speed up the examination (and, therefore, issuance) of your patent application. Some of the major reasons follow:

- ✪ If you plan to license your patented invention, your ability to attract potential licensees may be stronger with either a patent in hand or notice from the PTO that your patent application has been allowed. The same rationale applies equally with attracting potential investors in any company you may be forming. Patents simply look good to investors.

- ✪ Because your patent term will be measured twenty years from your application filing date and not the date that your patent actually issues, it is to your advantage to try and keep examination of your patent application as short as possible and have your patent issue as soon as possible. The time you spend in the examination phase is using up the term of any patent that you may obtain.

❁   Patents cannot be enforced against potential infringers until they issue. Therefore, it is to your advantage to get your patent as soon as possible so that you can quickly go after potential infringers.

It is possible to speed up the examination of your application by filing what is known as a *Petition to Make Special*. This can sometimes save you several months in the examination process. There are a host of reasons for which you can file this petition. Some of these reasons are deemed so important by the PTO that you do not even need to file a fee with your petition. Other grounds, while important, still require you to file a fee.

Petition to Make Special—No Fee

The following grounds can be used in a *Petition to Make Special* and do not require a special fee.

❁   You are over the age of 65.

❁   Your health is such that you might not be able to assist in the prosecution of the application if it were to be examined in its normal course.

❁   Your invention would materially enhance the quality of the environment.

❁   Your invention would contribute to the development of energy resources or to the more efficient utilization of energy resources. (Examples include developments in fossil fuels, nuclear energy, solar energy, and inventions relating to the reduction of energy consumption in combustion systems, industrial equipment, and household appliances.

❁   Your invention relates to superconductivity.

Petition to Make Special—Fee

The following grounds can serve as the basis for a *Petition to Make Special,* but require you to pay a fee (37 C.F.R. §1.17(h)).

❁   A prospective manufacturer will not manufacture or increase present manufacture of your invention unless a patent for the invention is granted. (See MPEP §708.02 for what you must specifically allege in your petition.)

✪ There exists an infringing device or product actually on the market or a method in use. (See MPEP §708.02 for what you must specifically allege.)

✪ Your invention relates to HIV/AIDS or cancer.

✪ Your invention can be used to counter terrorism.

✪ Your invention relates to safety of research in the field of recombinant DNA.

✪ Your application is a new application in which a pre-examination search has been made. This type of petition to make special is known as *accelerated examination*. Your *Petition to Make Special* must be filed prior to the examiner's first action. The petition must be accompanied by a search report based on a search conducted by an attorney, a professional searcher, the inventor, or a foreign patent office. One copy of each reference considered most closely related to the subject matter of the claims should also be submitted. In addition, there must be a detailed discussion of the references, pointing out how the claimed subject matter is distinguished from them. Finally, the field of the search must be listed in the petition.

✪ Biotechnology applications for small entities. You must state that the subject of your patent application is a major asset of your small entity and that development of the technology will be significantly impaired if examination of your patent application is delayed, including an explanation of the basis for making the statement.

– Caution –

Be careful about certifying that a prior art search has been made if you go this route. It is recommended that you hire an outside patent attorney or professional search firm to conduct your search if you go this route just so that you cover yourself if anyone later on raises questions about your search. Falsely certifying that a prior art search has been made when it has not can result in a finding of inequitable conduct after your patent is issued, which will leave your entire patent unenforceable.

Accelerated examination costs applicants two to three times more than a traditional patent prosecution. The prosecution process is also more demanding. However, the benefit is that applications should receive a final decision from the PTO in less than a year.

- ✪ Accelerated examination is only for inventors willing to spend the money and extra time needed for this type of examination. The applicant must do a thorough search of prior inventions in the field and identify every single claimed limitation on its own invention in the prior art. Also, a *patentability report* is required. This report must explain how each claim in the application is patentable over the prior art. This is a big difference to your typical patent application where you only need to disclose any prior art you are aware of. This requirement that you search for prior art can come back to haunt you later on if you do obtain a patent and some litigator challenges your patent in court on the basis that you should have disclosed something you should have disclosed to your examiner, but did not find in your research.

- ✪ You—or your counsel—will also be required to work in close consultation with your patent examiner. Typically, you should be prepared for several interviews with your examiner over a relatively short period of time.

- ✪ If your technology involves something like mechanical inventions where the average wait time is on the lower range (twelve to thirteen months), filing for accelerated examination is not going to gain you a lot of time. Moreover, biotech and Internet companies typically do not want a patent published or issued until the latest possible date, so a three to four year pendency is actually to their benefit.

In sum, accelerated examination is not for most inventors. Only if there is some compelling reason that you need a patent to issue very quickly—such as where you need a patent to obtain financing—should you even consider this process.

Author's Note: Expedited examination requirement
Product designs typically have a short shelf life, which means that obtaining issuance of a design patent is typically more of a consideration for the patent filer. Expedited examination of design patent applications is handled under MPEP §1504.30. One of the prerequisites to filing expedited examination is that the applicant must conduct a pre-examination search and include an information disclosure statement. An expedited examination fee is also required.

FIRST OFFICE ACTION

After you file your patent application, your application will be examined and you will receive back your *first office action* (OA). The first office action will either allow your claims or, more typically, reject some or all of your claims. After you receive your OA, record the due date that you should send a response back to the PTO on your calendar. Also, mark your calendar a month prior to this due date so that you are sure to start working on the response well before the actual due date.

In 2007, the average time was 31.3 months from the time that an application was filed to the time a first substantive office action, either rejecting or allowing a patent application, was received. However, the time it will take for you to obtain a first office action (OA) will depend on the technology center handling your application. A chart of the average time after filing before first office action is included below. As an example, take a look at inventions for "electronic commerce" handled by Tech center 3620. In 2007, patent applicants could expect that it would take, on average, 3.8 years before a first office action was mailed by the PTO from this tech center. But if you go toward the end of the chart, you will see that for "glass and paper making" inventions handled by tech center 1730, the time was 1.3 years from the date the application was filed. So the time period is variable depending upon your technology.

Average Time after Filing before First Office Action

Tech Center	Description	Months	Years
3620	Electronic Commerce	45.4	3.8
2140	Computer Networks	40.0	3.3
2130	Cryptography Security	36.4	3.0
2190	Interprocess Communications	35.9	3.0
2160	Database and File Management	35.0	2.9
2620	Television and TV Recording	33.5	2.8
2610	Digital Communications General	32.7	2.7
1740	Metallurgy	30.2	2.5
1610	Pharmaceutical Formulations	29.9	2.5
1760	Food Technology	29.9	2.4
2120	Miscellaneous Computer	28.9	2.4
3730	Medical Instruments	28.5	2.4
1640	Immunology Receptor/Ligands	28.5	2.3
2180	Computer Architecture	27.5	2.2
2110	Computer Architecture	26.9	2.2
1630	Molecular Biology	26.6	2.2
3760	Body Treatment	25.9	2.1
1620	Organic Chemistry	24.8	2.0
3680	Machine Elements	24.1	2.0
1710	Synthetic Resins	24.0	2.0
3710	Amusement	23.5	2.0
1750	Chemical Products	23.5	1.9
3630	Static Structures	23.1	1.9
1650	Fermentation Microbiology	22.8	1.9
1770	Stock Materials	22.8	1.8
3650	Material Handling	22.2	1.8
3750	Fluid Handling	22.0	1.8
1720	Fluid Separation	21.9	1.7
2890	Semiconductor Electrical	20.4	1.7
3660	Computerized Vehicle	20.4	1.7
3720	Manufacturing Devices	20.0	1.7
3610	Surface Transportation	19.9	1.6
2820	Semiconductors	19.7	1.6

Tech Center	Description	Months	Years
3740	Thermal	19.4	1.6
2830	Power Generation	19.2	1.6
2810	Semiconducturs	19.1	1.6
3670	Wells Earth Boring	18.8	1.6
2870	Liquid Crystals	17.8	1.6
2950	Photocopying	16.8	1.5
3640	Aeronautics	16.0	1.4
1660	Plants	15.0	1.3
1730	Glass and Paper Making		1.2
2900	Designs		

Author's Note: First office action
The average time to a first office action in a design patent is fifteen months after filing. Design applications typically take about two years to issue from the time they are filed. Although this is a much shorter time frame than for a utility patent application, the length of time to obtain design patents has been strongly criticized by the industry since designs can go out-of-date so rapidly. By the time a design patent has issued, many product designs have already been replaced in the marketplace.

YOUR RESPONSE OR REPLY

After an office action, you as the applicant or patent owner, must request reconsideration by your examiner with or without an amendment if your action is adverse in any respect. In most cases, you will present your reply in the form of an amendment. (The specifics of drafting an amendment appear later in this chapter.)

Whether you submit arguments or an amendment as your reply, you must distinctly and specifically point out the supposed errors in your examiner's action. You must respond to every ground of objection and rejection in the action.

You must also point out the specific distinctions you believe render your claims patentable over any references that your examiner is applying against you. For example, if the issue surrounding your rejected claims is novelty, then you must point out the patentable novelty of your amended claims in the "Remarks" section of your amendment. A general allegation that your claims are patentable without *specifically* pointing out why is not a sufficient reply. (MPEP §714.02.)

You should also point out the justification behind any amendments that you have made to your specification. In other words, you should point out that any changes you have made are supported by your original disclosure as filed (and therefore do not constitute new matter).

Length of Time to Respond

By statute, you are given up to six months to respond to any action that the PTO sends you. This is an absolute cut-off period and cannot be altered by the PTO. This means that even if you can buy another extension of time, you will not be able to use such extension to avoid abandonment of your application if it means that your response is after six months from the mailing date of your office action.

The PTO typically sets a three-month period to respond to your office action, unless the action relates to a preliminary matter. If this is the case, the PTO typically gives you only one month to respond. This three-month time period to respond is often called a *shortened statutory period*. It is called shortened because, as stated, a statute sets a longer six-month absolute cut-off period to respond to actions from the PTO. However, this same statute gives the PTO the right to set shorter time periods. Your action will tell you the shortened statutory period that the PTO has set for response to your action. Keep in mind, however, that even though you may be able to buy more months, you can never respond later than six months.

The actual time it takes you to reply to your office action is calculated from the date stamped or printed on your office action to the PTO's date of receipt (or, if you use Express Mail, the date of deposit with the post office).

When the PTO says that you have three months to respond to an action, this time period is calculated by months. The PTO does not take into account fractions of a day, unless it has given you one month to respond. Then you are given at least thirty days to send in your response.

When the last day that you have to respond to an action falls on a Saturday, Sunday, or federal holiday, the time period in which you can file your response is extended to the next business day that the PTO is open for business. This rule does not, however, apply when you are using an extension of time.

This is a lot to remember, but if you file your responses at least several days before the due date, you will not have to worry about whether you are filing your response on the absolute cut-off date.

Extensions of Time

The PTO allows applicants to respond late to office actions through a mechanism of purchasing extensions of time. *Extensions of time* are paid for in packages of one month, two months, three months, four months, and five months. (37 C.F.R. §1.136(a).) Five months is the maximum amount of time that you can buy. No cause or reason is needed to make an automatic extension of time. The PTO is very liberal on granting you such extensions as long as you pay the necessary fee.

Extensions of time can and usually are made retroactively. Thus, you are allowed to wait until the final day necessary to respond with your extension of time before sending in your response.

One thing that you should keep in mind with extension of time is that you are never allowed to request an extension that will take you past six months from the mailing date of an office action from the PTO that requires you to do something. (There is a statute that says you must make your response within six months from the mailing date of the office action.)

Another thing that you should keep in mind is that extensions of time are not available for the following more obscure types of things that you could get involved with during the prosecution of your application:

- reexamination;

- interference proceedings;

- reply briefs;

- ✪ requests for an oral hearing in an appeal;

- ✪ response to a decision by the Board of Patent Appeals and Interferences; and,

- ✪ any action from the PTO that specifically states that you cannot seek an automatic extension of time.

Failing to Respond on Time

If you fail to reply to an office action or fail to file a complete and proper reply within the fixed statutory period, then your application becomes abandoned. An *abandoned application* dies and it can no longer issue into a patent, unless you are able to win a petition to revive your application. (See Chapter 15 on how to file a *Petition to Revive.*)

If you cannot revive your application, your only alternative is to pay a new filing fee and file a new patent application for your invention. This can be a fatal course of action because your priority date will now be the date that you file your subsequent patent application. Any prior art that exists before this date could prevent you from obtaining a patent on your invention.

Your examiner is authorized to accept a timely reply by you to a nonfinal office action that is made in good faith and is substantially complete except for an inadvertent omission. (37 C.F.R. §1.135(c).) Such inadvertent omissions include unsigned amendments or amendments that present additional claims but do not include the fees necessary for such claims. In such circumstances, your examiner may consider your reply adequate to avoid abandonment and give you a shortened statutory time period of one month to correct your omission.

SUPPLEMENTAL REPLIES

Sometimes you make a reply only to realize later that you forgot to add something to your reply or you wish to update your reply with new information. It is possible to submit such information in a *supplemental reply.* However, your examiner has the right to refuse it if it *unduly interferes* with the preparation of the office action that your examiner may be working on in respect to your original reply.

An extension of time under 37 C.F.R. §1.136 is not necessary when submitting a supplemental reply to an office action if you have already completed a timely first reply. (MPEP §710.02(e).)

CONSIDER AN INTERVIEW WITH YOUR EXAMINER

An interview is the personal, telephone, or video conference appearance by you, your agent, or your attorney with your examiner. Interviews prior to your first office action are typically not allowed except in the case of continuing or substitute application. However, such interviews are allowed when the examiner determines that such an interview would advance the prosecution of your application.

An interview after *final rejection* (see the next section) may be granted by your examiner, although you have no automatic right to one at that stage in your application. The usual time that you will be asking for an interview is after you receive your first office action. You can request in your action reply that your examiner defer taking any further action on the case until you have had a chance to confer with your examiner in Washington, D.C.

You should arrange for an interview in advance either by letter, fax, or telephone. You must usually arrange to go directly to the PTO in Washington D.C. to conduct a face-to-face interview with your examiner. However, there are certain sites outside of Washington, D.C. where a video conference can be held.

Personal face-to-face interviews are generally the best. By meeting your examiner face-to-face, you will learn a lot more about your examiner's concerns than you will learn about over the phone.

Although interviews are a very useful way for you to present arguments to your examiner in order to get your application into allowance, you need to prepare for your interview. Before your interview, you should complete and send to your examiner the *Applicant Initiated Interview Request Form* (Form PTOL-413A). In this form, you need to provide basic information as well as a brief description of the arguments that you plan to submit at the interview. You also need to check whether or not you intend to show or demonstrate any exhibits at the interview. At the conclusion of your interview your examiner will give you a copy of the *Examiner Interview Summary Form* (Form PTOL-413). In the case of telephone or video interviews, this copy will be mailed to you. This summary form is used to document what occurred during the interview. It is your responsibility to make sure that the substance of the interview becomes of record. You do this by making sure that this form is complete. Under MPEP §713.04, a complete and proper recording of the substance of any interview must include at least the following items:

- a brief description of the nature of any exhibit shown or any demonstrated conduct;

- identification of claims discussed;

- identification of specific prior art discussed;

- identification of the principal proposed amendments of a substantive nature discussed;

- the general thrust of arguments made by you and your examiner;

- a general indication of any other pertinent matters discussed; and,

- the general results or outcome of the interview.

FINAL REJECTION

After your examiner gives you a proper *final rejection,* you no longer have any automatic right to further prosecution of your application. The things that you can do after final rejection are quite limited.

In general, you are restricted to making only those amendments to your claims that will bring your application into condition for allowance or in better form for an appeal of your examiner's decision if you have filed a Notice of Appeal. Changes that you can make after final rejection usually include things like canceling some of your rejected claims or adopting suggestions by your examiner.

If you are submitting a reply to your final rejection in the form of an amendment, you do so under 37 C.F.R. §1.116. If you want to make only arguments and no amendment, then your reply is filed under 37 C.F.R. §1.113. (You can still use the amendment form provided in the next chapter to do this, just change the heading to "REPLY UNDER C.F.R., Title 37, §1.113" and make your arguments in the "Remarks" section.)

You may have to obtain more than one extension of time in order to keep your application from being abandoned after a final rejection.

Example:

You are mailed a final rejection on October 20, 2005, setting a three-month statutory shortened period to respond. Your response, filed on February 20, 2006, together with an automatic one-month extension of time, is timely. If your response does not result in allowance of your application by the PTO, you could file a second response on March 20, 2006, together with a two-month extension of time. While you must pay for the full two-month extension, you will receive a credit for the one-month extension that you have already paid. You can keep obtaining extensions of time up until the statutory six-month cut-off date of April 20, 2006 (in this case).

Your reply after final action does not place your application in condition for allowance, so the period set for your reply will simply continue to run until you file a reply that does. Of course, if you do not do this by the six-month deadline, your application will go abandoned.

If you have run up against a dead end with respect to your examiner in getting your application allowed and the six-month statutory deadline is approaching, you will need to consider some other options in order to keep your application alive. One possible option is to file a continuing application, such as a *Request for Continued Examination* (RCE) under 37 C.F.R. §1.114. (As explained in Chapter 8, you will need to accompany your RCE by a *submission*. This will usually mean that you will need to submit a proper reply to your outstanding office action, as well as the requisite fee.)

Another possible option with respect to final office actions is to try to have your examiner remove the finality of the office action. Most people are not aware of this, but examiners have the right to do this as discussed at MPEP §706.07(d–e).

Notice of Appeal

Another option that you have after a final rejection is to appeal your examiner's decision. To do this, you will need to file a Notice of Appeal and the requisite appeal fee. Appeals will require that you obtain the assistance of an experienced patent attorney or agent in this field. However, you can and should file a Notice of Appeal to preserve your right to appeal if you want to pursue this option. By filing a Notice of Appeal, you will stop the statutory period for abandonment of your application. Instead, new time periods begin with respect to what you must do concerning your Notice of Appeal.

NOTE: *If you have submitted an amendment at or near the end of the statutory period, you should always accompany your amendment with a Notice of Appeal. If you do not do this, your application may go abandoned even before your examiner has considered your amendment after final action.*

When an Office Action Is Improper

Under the current practice at the PTO, any subsequent action that you receive from your examiner on the merits will be made final. There is one exception to this rule, however. If your examiner introduces a new ground for his or her rejection that was neither necessitated by your amendment of your claims nor based on information that you filed in an information disclosure statement during the allotted time period, then a final rejection is improper. (37 C.F.R. §1.97(c).)

Example 1:

An important claim in Joe's patent application is rejected in a first office action on the basis of obviousness over prior art. In his response, Joe argues that his claims are not obvious in respect to the references cited.

In a second rejection, the examiner continues the rejection and adds a further rejection based on §102(a) citing a prior publication that teaches each of Joe's limitations in his claim. This final rejection is improper because the newly added rejection made by the examiner was not necessitated by anything that Joe had done in his response.

Example 2:

Joe's claim is rejected in a first official action for the same reasons as in Example 1. In his response, Joe amends his claims to add a new limitation and argues that this new limitation makes his invention nonobvious.

The examiner issues a final rejection that is based now on a §102(e) publication that was found in a new search. Since Joe's amendment of adding a new limitation forced the examiner to conduct a new search that revealed the publication, this second action is a proper final rejection.

Some special rules as to when a final rejection can be made apply to continuing applications. If you file a continuation, the first action that you receive in that application can be made final when all the claims of the new application are drawn to the same invention claimed in the earlier application and would have been properly finally rejected in that earlier application. Making a first office action final in a continuing or substitute application, however, is never proper when such application contains material that was presented in the earlier application after final rejection, but was denied entry either because new issues or matters were raised that required further consideration.

If you believe that your examiner has incorrectly made a final rejection in your application, you should raise the issue with your examiner. If your examiner still disagrees and you think you are right, your only option is to file a petition for review of your examiner's decision. (37 C.F.R. §1.181.)

Length of Time to Respond to Final Rejection

You will be given a three-month shortened statutory period for responding to the final rejection. However, it is to your advantage to submit a first reply prior to the expiration of two months from the mailing date of your final office action. If you do this, your shortened statutory period will expire at the later end of three months or on the date that the PTO mails you an *advisory action*. Thus, a variable reply period is established if you get your first reply to the PTO within two months from the date of your final office action. (MPEP §706.02(f).)

Example:

A final rejection is mailed to Joe on June 30, 2005, setting a three-month shortened statutory period to respond. Joe responds to the final rejection by submitting an amendment along with arguments as to why his changes overcome the examiner's rejection within two months from June 30.

Joe's examiner mails out an advisory action that states Joe's response does not place his application in condition for allowance and reaffirms the final rejection. If that advisory action was mailed out after three months from June 30, then the shortened statutory time period will be considered to expire on the date the advisory action was mailed.

If Joe now makes a second reply, any extension of time that Joe needs to pay for will be calculated from the mailing date of the advisory action and not from the time period originally set forth in Joe's final rejection.

Your examiner will consider any reply that you submit after final rejection quickly, usually within ten calendar days from the time you submit your reply. You can expect a response from your examiner usually within thirty days from your amendment.

ADVISORY ACTION

An *Advisory Action* (Form PTOL-303) is sent to you by your examiner to acknowledge receipt of your reply to your final office action when your reply is prior to filing an appeal brief and does not place your application in condition for allowance. This form is used by your examiner to advise you of the disposition of your proposed amendments to your claims and of the effect of any argument or affidavit that you submitted that did not place your application in condition for allowance.

APPEAL OF YOUR EXAMINER'S DECISION

If any of your claims have been rejected twice by the PTO or you have been given a final rejection in your patent application, you have the right to appeal the decision to the *Board of Patent Appeals and Interferences.* You must, however, make your appeal within the time allowed for your response, given any extensions of time that you can obtain. You must also pay an appeal fee. The PTO will still charge an appeal fee, even if your amendment ends up not being entered by your examiner.

Your decision whether to appeal a rejection of your claims will depend on whether further prosecution is either undesirable or not possible and you believe there is some likelihood of success in reversing the rejection of at least one important claim. If your application contains some allowed claims, a better course of action may be to respond to the final office action by cancelling the rejected claims in favor of their presentation, with or without amendment, in a continuation application. This will place your pending application (with your allowed claims) in condition for allowance. Prosecution can now proceed on your disallowed claims in the continuation application.

Only questions affecting the merits of the claims—prior art and sufficiency of disclosure issues—are appropriate for decision by the Board. Formal objections or purely procedural matters will not be ruled on in a Board decision. Such matters should be undertaken by petition to the Commissioner prior to the appeal process.

Appeals to the Board of Patent Appeals and Interferences is a subject that is beyond the scope of this book. You will want to consider obtaining the assistance of a patent attorney or agent who has experience in making such appeals. However, understanding some of the critical dates can at least preserve your right to appeal.

- ✪ *Notice of Appeal.* You must file a Notice of Appeal in writing within the period for response to your pending final office action, and this period may be appropriately extended if necessary. The Notice of Appeal stops the time clock with respect to abandonment of your application.

✪ *Appeal Brief.* You must file an *Appeal Brief* in triplicate within two months from the date that your Notice of Appeal is received by the PTO, or within the time allowed for reply to the action from which the appeal was taken, if this time is later. If you fail to file your appeal brief in a timely fashion, your application will go abandoned as of the date that your brief is due if you have no allowed claims in your appeal. If you have claims that were previously allowed by your examiner, your application will be returned to your examiner as to those allowed claims.

The time for filing your appeal brief can be extended automatically. This time period is also not a shortened statutory period, so you can even take extensions up to five months under 37 C.F.R. §1.193(a), which gives you more than a six-month period to reply. (MPEP §710.02(e).) More information about appeals to the Board of Patent Appeals and Interferences can be found at their website www.uspto.gov/go/dcom/bpai/index.html.

✪ *Examiner's Answer.* After you have filed your appeal brief, your examiner has the right to file an *examiner's answer*. This is a written statement in answer to your brief. The examiner may not set forth new grounds of rejection in the answer unless your examiner reopens prosecution on such new grounds.

✪ *Reply Brief.* You may file a *reply brief* within two months of the date of the examiner's answer. (37 C.F.R. §1.193.)

✪ *Oral Hearing.* If you believe that a hearing is necessary or desirable for a proper presentation of your appeal, you have the right to request an oral hearing accompanied by the appropriate fee within two months from the date of your examiner's answer. You will be notified as to the time and place of your hearing.

✪ *Board's Decision.* After the Board of Patent Appeals and Interferences has considered the record, including your appeal brief and the examiner's answer, it will write its decision either affirming your examiner in whole or in part or reversing your examiner's decision. The Board also has the right to set forth a new ground of rejection. A copy of the Board's decision will be mailed to you and the original will be placed in your application file.

Request for Reconsideration

You have the right to request reconsideration by the Board of its decision within one month from the date of the decision. In the event that the Board makes a new rejection of one or more of your appealed claims, you have the right to either ask that the Board reconsider the new rejection or you can have the new rejection considered by your examiner just as if you were prosecuting a new application. If your rejected claims are not allowed by your examiner, then you have the right to make a brand-new appeal before the Board with respect to such rejection. If you do not appeal, the Board will make its original decision final.

Judicial Review

If you are dissatisfied with a final decision of the Board of Patent Appeals and Interferences, you may appeal the decision either to the U.S. Court of Appeals for the Federal Circuit or to the U.S. District Court for the District of Columbia. You have two months from the date of the Board's decision to do this.

The hearing at the district court is a *de novo* (or fresh) hearing, whereas an appeal to the Federal Circuit is based on the PTO prosecution history. A *de novo* appeal to the district court requires much more work than an appeal to the Federal Circuit, but is advantageous if the prosecution history is inadequate to support your case. If based on a strong record, an appeal to the Federal Circuit can be advantageous, as Federal Circuit judges are more experienced in patent issues.

NOTICE OF ALLOWANCE OR ALLOWABILITY

If, after examination of your application, your examiner concludes that you are entitled to a patent, you will be mailed a Notice of Allowance, also called a Notice of Allowability (Form PTOL-37). If your examiner believes that the record as a whole does not make clear the reasons for allowing your claims, the examiner may also attach a separate written *Statement of Reasons for Allowance*. You have the right, but are under no obligation, to file a statement commenting on such reasons for allowance.

When the Notice of Allowance is mailed, the examiner relinquishes jurisdiction of the application, which is forwarded to the issuance branch of the PTO for final processing and printing. Any papers you submit to the PTO following issuance of the Notice of Allowance should be accompanied by the *batch number* printed on the Notice of Allowance.

In situations in which informalities such as drawing corrections are noted on your Notice of Allowance, you must make corrections within three months from the mailing date of the notice. No extensions of time are permitted to do this. (MPEP §710.02(e).)

PATENT TERM ADJUSTMENTS

Under some circumstances the PTO will add more time to the twenty-year (for plant and utility patents) and fourteen-year (for design patents) patent term. Particularly where an invention is worth a lot of money, even a few days of extra patent term can provide great financial benefits to a patent holder. The PTO sets out complex PTA calculation rules in Chapter 2700 of the MPEP. Examples of each of these circumstances are more particularly noted as follows.

✪   If the PTO fails to initially act on your application within fourteen months of its filing date (or that date on which your application fulfills the requirements for entering the national stage if you have filed a PCT application), then the PTO will need to extend your patent term. The term of a patent may be adjusted one day for each day past this deadline if the PTO misses this deadline.

Not all communications you receive from the PTO are considered actions that stop the fourteen-month time clock. For example, preliminary examination communications such as a Notice of Incomplete Nonprovisional Application (PTO-1123), a Notice of Omitted Items(s) in a Nonprovisional Application (PTO-1669), a Notice to File Missing Parts of Application (PTO-1533), a Notice of Informal Application (PTO-152), a Notice to File Corrected Application Papers Filing Date Granted (PTO-1660), or a Notice to Comply with Requirements for Patent Applications Containing Nucleotide Sequence and/ or Amino Acid Sequence Disclosures (PTO-1661) are not considered actions by the PTO that will stop this fourteen-month clock. (These types of actions are discussed further in Chapter 12.)

✪ The PTO fails to issue a patent within three years of the actual filing date of your application. Note that for utility patents that have a twenty-year term, this rule effectively guarantees you a term for your patent of seventeen years, as long as you are diligent in the prosecution of your application. Consult 37 C.F.R. §1.702(b) for more information on this three-year rule.

✪ Delays caused if an interference is declared between your application and the patent application or patent of another. This can occur when there is controversy about whether you or someone else was actually the first to invent what you are claiming to be your invention. You can consult 37 C.F.R. §1.703(c) for more information about this circumstance.

✪ If your application becomes subject to a secrecy order, the PTO will need to add time to your patent term for the period during which your application is under the secrecy order. (37 C.F.R. §1.703(d).)

✪ You have filed a Notice of Appeal to the Board of Patent Appeals and Interferences and the Board or federal court has rendered a decision in your favor. (37 C.F.R. §1.703(e).)

✪ Having complied with all of the requirements necessary for issuance of your patent, the PTO fails to issue your patent more than four months after the date that you have paid your issue fee.

In calculating any *patent term adjustment* (PTA), any overlaps in time caused by the above circumstances are counted only once.

Any term adjustments that you are entitled to receive due to the previously listed failures of the PTO are reduced by your own failures. The PTO calls this a failure to engage in "reasonable efforts to conclude prosecution" and reduces any term adjustment according to the days that you lack such efforts.

The PTO lists a host of examples in which you have failed to engage in reasonable efforts. (37 C.F.R. §1.704(c).) You have failed to engage in reasonable efforts if you do one of the following:

- ✪ Take longer than three months to respond to a notice from the PTO making any rejection, objection, argument, or other request. This three-month period is measured from the date the notice was given or mailed to you by the PTO. From this time until the date that you make your response (considered to be on the day that the PTO receives your response if you mail or fax it, or the date you deposit it in the mail if you use Express Mailing procedures), any term adjustment will be reduced on a day-by-day basis.

- ✪ Submit a reply that omits something (i.e., fails to respond to a pending issue).

- ✪ Pay your issue fee late. In addition, if you file formal drawings with an issue fee payment, your PTA is reduced by the number of days from the filing of the formal drawings to the date of an office action or notice in response to them, or four months, whichever is less. This is why you should consider filing drawings that meet the requirements of 37 C.F.R. §1.84 with your initial patent application or with an otherwise responsive filing such as a response to a notice to file missing parts or a response to an office action.

- ✪ Fail to file a petition to withdraw a holding of abandonment or to revive an application within two months from the mailing date of a notice of abandonment.

- ✪ Submit a preliminary amendment less than one month before the mailing of an office action or Notice of Allowance that requires the mailing of a supplemental office action or Notice of Allowance.

✪   File a continuing application, in which case the period of adjustment shall not include any period that is prior to the actual filing date of the application that resulted in the patent.

✪   Supplemental responses—unless expressly requested by an examiner—and papers that do not comply with the amendment practice rules listed at 37 C.F.R. §1.121 reduce PTA by the number of days from the initial reply to the filing of the supplemental or corrected reply. An Information Disclosure Statement (IDS) filed by itself is treated as a supplemental reply, so try to file the IDS with a reply before the first action.

Contesting Calculation of Term Adjustment

You will be notified by the PTO of any adjustment to the term of your patent if your patent application is approved at the time the PTO sends you a Notice of Allowance and Issue Fee Due (Form PTOL-85).

A correction in the PTA reported in your notice of allowance must be requested by filing a request for reconsideration of PTA under 37 C.F.R. §1.705(b) before you pay your issue fee. Such a request also requires a detailed factual statement stating all pertinent dates, the correct PTA, the bases for the correct PTA, and any delays caused by you as the applicant that will reduce the PTA. In addition there is a processing fee, which was $200 at the time this book was published.

Your issue notification and issued patent will include a second statement of PTA, which will reflect any changes to PTA resulting from events following mailing of your notice of allowance. Any request for reconsideration of the PTA indicated in your patent must be filed under 37 C.F.R. §1.705(d) within two months of your issued patent and must include a detailed, factual statement as described above. Such a request cannot request PTA correction on the basis of issues that could have been raised in response to the notice of allowance.

The rules concerning PTA are very complicated. For more information go to 35 U.S.C. §154(b), 37 C.F.R. §1.701–705 and MPEP §2730–2736. In addition, there is a PTA help line at the PTO that can be reached at 571–272–7702.

PAYMENT OF ISSUE AND PUBLICATION FEE

Within three months from the date of your Notice of Allowance, you must pay an issue fee in the amount shown on your Notice of Allowance (small entities get half off). No extensions of time are allowed to do this.

You should use the special fee transmittal form provided with your Notice of Allowance with your payment. If you fail to pay the issue fee on time, your application will go abandoned.

In addition to an issue fee, your Notice of Allowance may also require that you pay a publication fee if your application was published. This fee must also be paid within three months from the date of mailing of your Notice of Allowance. As with your issue fee, you cannot extend the date for paying your publication fee.

Amending or Modifying Your Application

Amending an application is common. You may notice errors in the bibliographic information that you have provided to the PTO after your have filed your application, or you may want to update biographical information, such as your address. You can make such changes by submitting a new *Application Data Sheet* with the updated information.

You may also notice errors (like spelling mistakes, incorrect citations) in the various sections of your specification. You can correct such changes via an amendment to your specification.

You may also decide that you want to add or delete claims, or vary the scope of your existing claims, either because you seek broader coverage for your invention or you need to do so in order to respond to an office action from your examiner and thereby bring your application in condition for allowance. You can make such changes to your claims via an amendment to your claims, as long as such amendments have support in the disclosure of your original filed application.

You may also need to make changes to your drawings either because you did not submit formal drawings at the time you submitted your application, or because there are errors in your existing formal drawings.

In order to overcome rejections to your claims, you will find that amendments are almost inevitable. Your response to such rejections will take the form of amendments to your claims combined with arguments in support of why your application, as now amended, is ready for allowance. The subject of this chapter is the format of your amendment. The substantive arguments and strategies for overcoming your rejection are discussed in the next chapters.

> *Author's Note: Be careful about amending your claims and remarks.*
> As stated earlier, you should be careful about amending your claims, because you will lose any range of equivalents as to elements that you have amended. In fact, under the principal of *prosecution history estoppel,* you can later be estopped from successfully asserting that your narrowed claim is extendable under the Doctrine of Equivalents to cover subject matter that was surrendered not only by your narrowed claim but also with respect to:
>
> 1. narrowing arguments or remarks that you make in your amendment;
>
> 2. concessions or acquiescence with your examiner;
>
> 3. cancellation of a claim; and,
>
> 4. addition of a new claim.

In short, be careful what you do and say in an amendment concerning your originally filed claim scope coverage.

Because you will lose any range of equivalents for those elements that you make amendments to, you may want to now more seriously consider opposing your examiner's push for you to make amendments. This, however, is not an easy thing to do and will entail making arguments in your remarks section to try and convince your examiner that your claims are patentable as you have written them.

The other thing that you can do is to file an appeal of your examiner's rejection. This was touched upon in the last chapter. The actual process of making an appeal, however, is outside the scope of this book and will require you to obtain the assistance of a patent attorney or agent with experience in making such appeals. The cost, however, could be worth it for the broader coverage of your invention that you could obtain if you win.

MAKING AMENDMENTS TO YOUR APPLICATION DATA SHEET

If you want to correct, modify, or augment information that you previously provided in your *application data sheet,* you should submit a supplemental application data sheet. This requires that you simply submit another application data sheet with all of the information that you provided in your prior application data sheet, along with any additions underlined and any eliminations ~~struck through~~.

In addition to biographical data, you may want to use a supplemental application data sheet to make more substantive changes to your patent application. For example, if you file a CIP and forget to claim priority to your originally filed patent application, you can submit a supplemental application data sheet to correct the problem.

At the time this book was published, the PTO did not have a supplemental application data sheet form on its website, and it is not acceptable to use the initial application data sheet form on the PTO website. A form that you can use to submit your required information is contained in Appendix G. It is basically the same form that you used when submitting your initial application data sheet except for two minor changes. First, the heading now reads "Supplemental Application Data Sheet." Second, the footer has been modified to read "supplemental" in place of "initial." You should type in your application number followed by the filing date of your application and the date that you have prepared your supplemental application data sheet (this can correspond to the date that you Express Mail your supplemental data sheet to the PTO).

WHEN YOU CAN AMEND YOUR SPECIFICATION

When you make amendments prior to any official action by the PTO, your amendments are referred to as *preliminary amendments*. You may need to do this if you have forgotten to add something to your specification when you filed your application.

Preliminary amendments do not enjoy the status as part of your original disclosure unless they are referred to in the first oath or declaration that you file. This is an important point to keep in mind if you run into written description problems in any office action later on. In order to negate any written description rejection, you will need to rely upon your disclosure as originally filed. The written description requirement and responding to office actions are discussed more thoroughly in Chapter 14.

Although preliminary amendments are those amendments submitted prior to the date you received your first office action, you should submit any preliminary amendments as soon as possible after you file your application. This is because once your examiner has started to prepare his or her first office action, entry of a preliminary amendment submitted by you may be disapproved if it unduly interferes with the preparation of your examiner's office action. However, your preliminary amendment will be approved if it is filed no later than three months from the filing date of your application. (MPEP §714.03(a).)

You can also make amendments to your application after you receive a first action from the PTO. Such amendments are usually necessary in order to overcome some rejection in your action. (37 C.F.R. §1.111.)

After Final Rejection   After you receive a final rejection of your application, your rights to amend your application are restricted. (37 C.F.R. §1.116.) The PTO is of the opinion that after a final rejection is made, prosecution of your application should ordinarily be concluded. Therefore, you should not have the unrestricted right to make amendments, as it will create a lot of new work for the PTO. However, you are permitted to submit an amendment that cancels all your rejected claims or otherwise places your application in condition for allowance.

After Notice of Allowance   You do not have an automatic right to amend your application after the PTO mails you a Notice of Allowance. However, the PTO will generally consider such amendments after a Notice of Allowance if they are needed for proper disclosure or protection of your invention, and require no substantial amount of additional work on the part of the PTO. (37 C.F.R. §1.312.)

One type of amendment that you may want to make after Notice of Allowance is one in which you consolidate all your previous versions of pending claims from a series of separate amendment papers into a single clean version. This can be useful for patent printing purposes. You will learn how to do this in the next section. No amendments should be filed after the date you pay your issue fee.

FORMAT OF YOUR AMENDMENT

Your amendment should be divided into the following separate sections, which should each commence on a separate page.

- ✪   *Cover sheet.* The first section of your amendment should include a cover sheet that provides all the necessary information about your application (application number, filing date, etc.). This cover sheet should also include a table of contents to the rest of the parts of your amendment by indicating on what page of your amendment each of the sections begins.

- ✪   *Amendments to the Specification.* The next section of your application (which must start on a separate page) should include any amendments made to your specification. This includes any amendments made to your abstract. However, it does not include amendments made to either your claims or drawings.

- ✪   *Amendments to the Claims.* The next page of your application should include any changes that you want to make to your claims.

- ✪   *Amendments to the Drawings.* If you have any changes that you need to make to your drawings, you must begin on a separate page entitled "Amendments to the Drawings."

✪ *Remarks.* The next part of your amendment papers is a *Remarks* section. This is where you should restate any objections/rejections that your examiner has made in your office action and where you specifically deal with each and every one of those objections/rejections. This part of your amendment contains your arguments for allowance of your application. You will learn about arguments that you can make with respect to objections and rejections in the coming chapters.

Your remarks must address all issues raised by the examiner, pointing out errors in the examiner's position and supporting patentability of you claims as they will appear following entry of your amendment.

The remarks should also summarize the changes that you have made and confirm that no new matter is added to your specification. If you are adding any new claims or amending any of your claims, you should specifically point out where those claims are supported in your original application as you filed it.

The less superfluous material that you say in your remarks section, the better. You should be brief and to the point. Anything that you say in your amendment can be held against you later on as an admission.

Author's Note: Make sure your amendments match your written description.

You cannot make amendments to your patent application that are not supported by your original application's disclosure.

Example:

In July 2005, Harry filed a patent application for his invention of a floating pool stool. On August 20, 2007, Harry discovered that the footrests as shown in his drawings were not included in his description or set forth in the claims, and Harry wanted to claim the stool with footrests. Harry can amend his claims to include the footrests only if he also makes an amendment to include the footrest in the detailed description of his invention. If Harry does not also make an amendment to include the footrests in the description, the claimed footrest will not be supported by the written description.

Cover Sheet Your amendment must start with a cover sheet that provides the appropriate application information (e.g., application number, applicant, filing date) and serves as a table of contents to your amendment by indicating on what page of the amendment each of your sections begins. An example of a cover letter that serves as the first page of your amendment is on page 256.

IN THE UNITED STATES PATENT AND TRADEMARK OFFICE

_____

_____

Amendment

Dear Sirs:

In response to the Office Action of October 10, 2008, please amend the above-identified application as follows:

- Amendments to the Specification begin on page 2 of this paper.

- Amendments to the Claims are reflected in the listing of claims that begins on page 3 of this paper.

- Amendments to the Drawings begin on page 4 of this paper.

- Remarks/Arguments begin on page 5 of this paper.

Amendments to the Specification (Outside the Claims)

To amend your specification outside your claims, you must do two things. First, you must identify for the PTO the paragraph to be modified. You can do this by identifying the paragraph number or even by identifying the page and line of the paragraph that you want to modify. After you have identified the paragraph that you are interested in modifying, you must next show all the changes relative to the previous version of that paragraph. You do this by underlining any new added text and striking through any material that you are deleting relative to the first version. However, where you are deleting five or fewer consecutive characters, you should use brackets (e.g., deletion of the number "4" must be shown as [4]).

Example 1:

You want to add the word "melted" in a paragraph of your specification. If you numbered your paragraphs when drafting your specification, you can easily refer to any specific paragraph in your specification by number in order to amend it. Suppose that the paragraph number you want to replace is [0071]. You can now create a section heading in your amendment entitled as follows:

In the Specification:

Please replace paragraph [0071], with the following rewritten paragraph:

In this construction, the electric heating elements are positioned directly beneath the iron grid bars and melted fat is carried off in grooves formed in the upper surfaces of the bars.

Note that when you replace a paragraph, your amended paragraph takes on the same number as the paragraph you are replacing. If you want to replace your paragraph with more than one paragraph, your added paragraphs should be numbered using the number of your original paragraph for the first replacement paragraph, followed by increasing decimal numbers for the second and subsequent added paragraphs. For example, your original paragraph [0071] might be replaced with paragraphs [0071], [0071.1], and [0071.2].

Example 2:

You have not numbered your paragraphs in your patent application and now you notice that there is a mistake in your disclosure. At the time you wrote your disclosure, you referenced a patent application. However, this application has now turned into a patent and you want to update this fact in your application. Although you have not numbered your paragraphs, the paragraph falls on page 55 and is the first paragraph on that page of your application. You can do the following:

In the Specification:

Please replace the first full paragraph on page 55 with the following amended paragraph:

In another embodiment, mononuclear phagocyte cells according to PCT Publication No. WO 97/09985 and U.S. patent <u>6,267,995</u> ~~application Serial No. 09/041,280~~, filed March 11, 1998, are injected into the site of injury or lesion within the CNS, either concurrently, prior to, or following parenteral administration of Cop 1-activated T cells, Cop 1 or a Cop 1-related peptide or polypeptide.

In addition to amending paragraphs, you are permitted to amend entire sections of your patent application. As with replacement paragraphs, you do this by identifying the section you want to replace and rewriting the section with markings to show all the changes relative to the previous version of that section that you submitted. In fact, you could also submit an entirely new specification with changes. Again, you would need to show any changes with strikeouts of deleted matter and underlining for added matter relative to your previous specification.

Amendments to the Claims

Your claims may be amended in any of the following ways:

- ✪   by canceling particular claims;

- ✪   by presenting new claims; or,

- ✪   by rewriting particular claims.

The format of making changes to your claims is very similar to the format for making changes to your specification in that you will underline material that you want to add and strike through material that you want to delete. For deletion of five or fewer consecutive characters, double brackets should be used. All of your claims should be presented in ascending numerical order.

One difference between amending paragraphs in your specification and amending claims is that you must write the number of the claim that you are amending, followed by the current status of that claim. Status is indicated in a parenthetical expression after your claim number by one of the following:

- ✪ (original)—This means that the claim you are listing is the original way that your claim appeared when you filed your patent application. In other words, this claim has not undergone any changes since you filed it in your original application.

- ✪ (currently amended)—This means that you are making some modification to your current claim.

- ✪ (previously presented)—This means that you previously amended this claim. Although the claim is not the same one that you filed with your original patent application, it is not undergoing any changes in this current amendment. You have simply rewritten the claim in a clean form with the same number in this amendment.

- ✪ (canceled)—When you cancel a claim, you do not rewrite the claim. Consecutively canceled claims can be aggregated under this parenthetical status (e.g., Claims 1–5 (canceled)).

- ✪ (withdrawn)—You would use this parenthetical expression when your claims are being withdrawn in response to a restriction requirement. The proper term to use in such a case is "withdrawn" rather than "canceled."

- ✪ (new)—This indicates that the claim you are presenting is completely new. When you add new claims, you do so by simply writing the claim after this parenthetical status. You do not underline this new claim.

✪   (not entered)—You would use this parenthetical expression in reference to claims that you previously submitted after a final action but that your examiner refused to enter, which the examiner has the right to do (recall from the previous chapter that your rights are limited after a final action).

Example 1:

You receive an office action from your examiner that rejects all thirteen of your claims you have written. You decide that you are going to need to change around each of these claims to overcome rejection and gain allowance. Instead of using the "currently amended" parenthetical expression for each of your claims and having to underline added matter and strike through deleted matter, an easier method to make your amendments would be to simply cancel all of your rejected claims and then add these claims back with their modifications as "new" claims in ascending numerical order. Ascending numerical order means that your new claims must start at the next highest number that your cancelled claims stopped.

Amendments to the Claims:

This listing of the claims will replace all prior versions, and listings, of claims in the application:

Listing of Claims:

1–16 (canceled)

17 (new): A method for reducing neuronal degeneration caused by the neurodegenerative effects of disease, or for reducing secondary neuronal degeneration that follows the primary neuronal damage of an injury, in the central or peripheral nervous system of an individual in need thereof, comprising:

causing T cells activated by Copolymer 1 or a Copolymer 1-related peptide or polypeptide to accumulate at the site of neuronal degeneration in the individual in need, thereby reducing neuronal degeneration at that site.

18 (new): [You would carry on just as with Claim 17 in ascending numerical order for each of your amended claims.]

Example 2:

Suppose that things are not quite as clear cut as in Example 1. There are certain claims that you wish to cancel, claims that you originally presented in the application that you do not want to change, and claims that you have previously presented to your examiner after an amendment that you do not intend to change in this current amendment. Suppose that you have 13 claims. You would like to cancel Claims 1–6, 9, 11, 13. You would also like to make changes to Claim 8 and add a new claim. You previously made an amendment in your application in which you made changes to Claim 7. Claim 10 is in original form from the time that you filed your patent application. In your amendment, before the "Remarks" section, you should create the following entitled section heading on a separate page of your amendment.

Amendments to the Claims:

This listing of the claims will replace all prior versions and listings of claims in the application.

Listing of claims:

Claims 1–6 (canceled)

Claim 7 (previously presented): A bucket with a handle.

Claim 8 (currently amended): A bucket with a green-blue handle.

Claim 9 (canceled)

Claim 10 (original): The bucket of claim 8 with a wooden handle.

Claim 11 (canceled)

Claim 12 (previously presented): A bucket having a circumferential upper lip.

Claim 13 (canceled)

Claim 14 (new): A bucket with plastic sides and bottom.

Amendments to the Drawings

When you get a Notice of Draftsperson's Drawing Review, it is normally attached to the first office action that you receive from the PTO. If the notice requires you to correct your drawings, you can simply make such corrections and resubmit the corrected drawings either with your response or after you have received a Notice of Allowance. If you want to wait until after you receive your Notice of Allowance, you should state the following in the "Remarks" section of your response: *The objection to the drawings is noted. Formal drawings will be filed after allowance.*

If you wait to file your corrected drawings after you receive your Notice of Allowance, you will have three months from the mailing date of the Notice of Allowance to file such corrected drawings. This date is not extendable. You should try to submit your corrected drawings as soon as possible after you receive your Notice of Allowance, because if the drawings are again objected to, you will have to file another set of corrected drawings within the three-month time limit.

You can use the form contained in Appendix G to submit your corrected drawings. You should file this form with your corrected drawings and then send them as a separate mailing to the Official Draftsperson, whose address should appear on your Notice of Draftsperson's Drawing Review. You will notice in the form that you should include a copy of any relevant drawing replacement sheets that include your changes, as well as a copy of any such drawing sheets marked up (red ink is preferable), in which you show the changes you have made. The replacement sheets without the markings should be identified in the top margin as "Replacement Sheet," and the marked-up copies should be labeled as "Annotated Marked-Up Drawings."

If you want to make changes to your drawings with your response to an office action, you should include a reference to the page number of your *Amendments to the Drawing* section on your cover sheet. Next, create a separate heading on your reference page entitled "Amendments to the Drawings." This section should follow your *Amendments to the Claims* section. In this new section, you need to explain all the changes you have made to your drawings. The last thing you should do is attach replacement sheets for any amended drawing sheets. This sheet should be identified in the top margin as "Replacement Sheet." In addition to the replacement drawing sheets that include any changes, you are also allowed to submit a marked-up copy of such replacement sheet, which must be clearly labeled as "Annotated Marked-Up Drawings." Attach all of these sheets (replacement sheets and annotated, marked-up drawings) to your amendment at the back with a paper clip (do not staple them).

Remarks

Your *Remarks* section is where you submit any arguments in order to persuade your examiner that your claims are now ready for allowance. You will learn about the types of substantive arguments that you can make in response to common examiner rejections in the coming chapters. However, you must respond to every ground of objection and rejection in your office action. In other words, you cannot pick and choose your favorite rejections. A general allegation that your claims are patentable without pointing out specific instances is also not a sufficient reply.

You should start off your remarks section with a statement as to the status of your claims (e.g., which claims remain, have been canceled, or have been amended).

Example:

Your office action notifies you that your examiner has allowed Claims 1–5 and 7–10 in your application. However, Claim 6 has been rejected for a lack of enablement and Claim 7 has also been objected to because it is in improper form. After serious consideration, you decide that Claim 6 is really not an embodiment of your invention that you are interested in anymore and that Claim 7 can easily be amended to clear up the improper form issue. Since your "Remarks" section is the last section of your amendment, you will need to also add a signature box. Your "Remarks" section (which must start on a separate page of your amendment) might read as follows:

Remarks

Claims 7, 10, and 12 remain in this application. Claims 1–6 have been canceled. Claim 7 has been amended.

The examiner has acknowledged that Claim 10 is directed to allowable subject matter. Claims 1–6 have been canceled as being drawn to an embodiment no longer of interest to applicant.

Claim 7 has been amended for the following reasons:

[Inserted reasons]

Applicant respectfully requests that a timely Notice of Allowance be issued in this case.

Respectfully submitted,

By ———————— ,

Applicant

Sample Amendment

Over the next few pages is an example of an amendment. In this simplified example, the invention is directed toward a *griller*. Joe Genius has received back an office action dated October 10, 2006. The OA has allowed his main Claim 1, but has rejected both of his two dependent Claims 2–3. Joe also wants to make a change to his specification. There are no changes in the drawings.

NOTE: *The pages are condensed here, but would start as indicated in your filed amendment.*

IN THE UNITED STATES PATENT AND TRADEMARK OFFICE

Amendment

Dear Sirs:

In response to the Office Action of October 10, 2006, please amend the above-identified application as follows:

- Amendments to the Specification begin on page 2 of this paper.

- Amendments to the Claims are reflected in the listing of claims that begins on page 3 of this paper.

- Remarks/Arguments begin on page 4 of this paper.

Serial No. 09/106,043   Page 2 of 4

In the Specification:

Please replace paragraph [0071], with the following rewritten paragraph:

In this construction the electric heating elements are positioned directly beneath the iron grid bars and melted fat is carried off in grooves formed in the upper surfaces of the bars.

In the Claims:

Claim 1 (original): An electric griller comprising a seat having a side wall defining a container and a grill frame releasably mounted to the seat, the grill frame having a substantially flat top surface on which a plurality of strips are formed to define therebetween oil-leading channels, each having a plurality of through holes, electric heating means mounted to underside of the grill frame, having a socket adapted to receive and electrically connect to a plug of a power cord in connection with an external power supply, a plurality of vent holes being provided on the side wall of the seat.

Claim 2 (canceled)

Claim 3 (amended): A griller as claimed in Claim 1 wherein the power consumption of the heater means is 1600 watts and the weight of the grill is about 3.5 kg.

REMARKS

Claims 1–3 remain in this application. Claim 2 has been canceled. Claim 3 has been amended.

The examiner has acknowledged that claim 1 is directed to allowable subject matter. Claim 2 has been canceled as being drawn to an embodiment no longer of interest to applicant.

Claim 3 has been amended to correct an editorial error.

Applicant respectfully requests that a timely Notice of Allowance be issued in this case.

Respectfully submitted,

By _____

(Applicant)

EXAMINER AMENDMENTS

Small mistakes to your application, such as misspelled words, grammatical errors, or other informalities, may be corrected by your examiner in what is called an *examiner's amendment*. In an examiner's amendment, you do not need to submit a formal amendment to your application since your examiner makes the amendment. But if the examiner's amendment will occur after any response due date has passed, you must still obtain and pay for the necessary extension of time so that the examiner's amendment can be made.

Example:

You receive a final rejection on March 1, 2009, setting a three-month shortened statutory period. On June 1, 2009, you file a response by Express Mail. The PTO sends you an Advisory Action on July 21, 2009, indicating that your claims will be allowed with a few minor amendments that can be made by the examiner. In order to obtain these amendments and push your application into allowance, you must obtain a two-month extension of time.

Filing Your Amendment

If you are filing by mail, you should address your cover letter and amendment to the following address:

> Mail Stop Amendment
> Commissioner for Patents
> P.O. Box 1450
> Alexandria, VA 22313

You can also file your amendment electronically, which is strongly recommended.

Whether you file by mail or electronically, you should include a Fee Determination Record (PTO/SB/06) with your amendment. Any time that you add any extra claims to your application by amendment, you must pay for these extra claims if they take you over the twenty claim limit. However, if your amendment also cancels claims, then you can offset any extra claims you add by these canceled claims (see MPEP 608).

Example:

John electronically files an amendment that cancels claims 10–14 but adds new claims 21–25. John has effectively added five new claims but these claims will be offset for fee purposes by the five cancelled claims so no new fees will be due. However, had John withdrawn claims 10–14 (e.g., in response to a restriction requirement where one withdraws claims to nonelected inventions) rather than cancelled them, then John would owe extra fees for the five added claims since MPEP 608 provides that nonelected claims will be included in determining the dues in connection with a subsequent amendment. In either case, John should include a Fee Determination Record.

Amending Oaths or Declarations

You cannot amend an oath or declaration. If your oath or declaration is defective, you must instead execute a new one. A new oath is called a *substitute oath*. A substitute oath must identify the application that it goes along with, preferably by giving the serial number and the filing date of the application.

If, at any time after filing your oath or declaration, you add claims to your application, you should also file a new oath or declaration, called a *supplemental oath* or *declaration,* to cover such claims. (MPEP §608.01 and Rule 1.52(c).)

CORRECTING INVENTORSHIP

Correction of inventorship is not common. If you need to make a correction to the inventors that you named as inventors of your application, you should consult 37 C.F.R. §1.48 and MPEP §201.03. Some of the situations in which you may need to correct inventorship in your application are discussed in this section.

Inventorship Incorrect from the Start

If your inventorship was improperly set forth in the oath or declaration that you filed with your patent application, you need to correct inventorship in your application. In this case, you can correct your inventorship by filing an amendment, as discussed earlier, so long as you include the following in your amendment:

✪   a request to correct the inventorship and the desired change you want to make;

✪   a statement from each person that you are adding and from each person being deleted as an inventor that the error in inventorship occurred without deceptive intention on his or her part;

✪   a new oath or declaration by the actual inventors;

✪   the appropriate fee (37 C.F.R. §1.17(i)); and,

✪   if any assignment was made by any of the original named inventors, the written consent of such assignees.

Deleting Inventors

You may need to correct inventorship if your oath or declaration is set for the correct inventorship, but, during prosecution of your application through claim cancellation or other amendment, fewer than all of the currently named inventors are the actual inventors of your remaining claims. In such a case, you can submit an amendment that identifies the inventors you want to delete. It must indicate that the inventor's contribution is no longer being claimed in your application. You must also submit the required fee. (37 C.F.R. §1.17(i).)

Adding Inventors

If your application correctly sets forth the inventorship in the oath or declaration but you subsequently add claims to your application that require you to add inventors who you did not previously name, you will be required to supply the following (37 C.F.R. §1.48(c)):

✪   a request to correct the inventorship that sets forth the desired inventorship change;

✪   a statement from each inventor being added that the addition is necessitated by the amendment to your claims and that the inventorship error occurred without deceptive intent on his or her part;

✪   an oath or declaration signed by all the inventors;

✪   the appropriate fee (37 C.F.R. §1.17(i)); and,

✪   if an assignment was granted by any of the originally named inventors, the written consent of the assignee.

Other Ways to Correct Inventorship

Correction of inventorship in your regular *non-provisional application* can also be done by filing a *continuing application* (37 C.F.R. §1.53), so long as there will be at least one common inventor between the continuation and the application that you filed (yet another purpose for a continuation application). It is also possible to correct inventorship in a *provisional application,* but you should consult 37 C.F.R. §§1.48(d) and (e) for those situations.

chapter 12

Dealing with Preliminary Examination Communications

You will recall from Chapter 10 that the PTO will usually give you a shortened statutory period of three months to respond to an office action before you need to pay for extensions of time. In some cases, the PTO will give you an even shorter time to respond. These cases are usually preliminary matters that are covered in this chapter.

NOTICES THAT RELATE TO AN INCOMPLETE APPLICATION

If you submitted your patent application without a description (or one that cannot be construed as a written description), any required drawing, or at least one claim, you will receive a Notice of Incomplete Application (PTO-1123). You will not be granted a filing date for your application until you submit the necessary parts of your application. You have the following options to deal with this notice:

✪ *Assert that you submitted the required parts of your application.* To do this, you will need to file a petition under 37 C.F.R. §1.53(e), along with the appropriate fee under 37 C.F.R. §1.17(h), asserting that:

- your missing specification was submitted, or

- that your papers contained an adequate written description.

- You must also present evidence, such as a date-stamped return postcard from the PTO, that shows you did submit the required parts of your specification.

✪ *Submit your specification again.* Submit the specification with the missing parts, including a new oath or declaration that refers to your specification being submitted. If you do this, you are basically agreeing with the PTO that you forgot to add the missing part of your specification. *The filing date of your application will be the date that you provide your missing parts.* The filing date of your application will be the date that these required parts of your application are filed. (MPEP §506.)

NOTE: *Remember that you do not need to submit claims for a provisional application. A provisional application will only be incomplete if you neglect to file a description or any required drawings.*

Notice of Omitted Items

You receive a *Notice of Omitted Items* when you have filed everything that you need to in order to get a filing date (i.e., a written description, a claim, and any necessary drawing), but you have mistakenly left out one of the pages of your specification. (MPEP §601.01(d).) Your notice will state that your submitted application papers will be afforded a filing date, but are lacking some pages of the specification.

You have three options in dealing with a notice of omitted items.

1. *File a petition.* If you believe that you did, in fact, send the alleged missing pages to the PTO, you can file a petition along with the appropriate fee, proving that you did send the missing pages. (37 C.F.R. §§1.53(e) and 1.17(h).) You can prove this through the self-addressed postcard that you should have received back from the PTO identifying receipt of all the pages of your specification. You have two months from the date of your Notice of Omitted Items to pursue this option. If the PTO

determines that you are correct, the PTO should return your petition fee.

2. *Submit omitted pages.* You can submit the omitted pages in your non-provisional application within two months from the mailing date of your Notice of Omitted Items. Extensions of time are *not* permitted. If you elect this option, you must accept as the filing date for your application the date that you submit such omitted pages. This is really the equivalent to simply filing a new application (which, of course, you are also allowed to do). You must submit a petition, along with an appropriate fee, requesting the later filing date. (37 C.F.R. §§1.17(h) and 1.182.)

3. *Do nothing.* You can simply do nothing in response to your Notice of Omitted Items. This will be treated as an acceptance of your application as filed with the PTO. You must then amend your specification to clean up your application so that your omission makes no difference. The problem with this last item is that if you try to add back your omissions in an amendment, this will likely be considered as adding new matter to your application. As stated earlier, the PTO will never allow the addition of new matter to a patent application.

Notice to File Missing Parts

If you have submitted all the necessary parts of your application to obtain a filing date (claims, specification, and required drawings), but have left out other parts, such as the oath/declaration or the filing fee, you will receive the following notice:

```
An application number and Filing Date have been
assigned to this application. However, the items
indicated below are missing. The required time
and fees identified below must be timely submit-
ted ALONG WITH THE PAYMENT OF A SURCHARGE.
```

You are given two months from the filing date, or one month from the date of this notice, to submit the missing parts in order to avoid abandonment of your application. Upon timely submission of the missing parts, your application will receive as a filing date the date of your incomplete application.

You can take extensions of time up to five months under to file your missing parts, even if this will take you past the statutory deadline of six months to respond to office actions. (37 C.F.R. §1.136(a).) This is because a Notice to File Missing Parts is not identified on the notice as a statutory period subject to 35 U.S.C. §133. (MPEP §710.02(d).)

NOTICE OF INCOMPLETE REPLY

You receive the following notice from the PTO if you have made a response to an action from the PTO, but your reply is incomplete for some reason.

```
The reply filed on [date] is not fully responsive
to the prior Office Action because of the follow-
ing omission(s) or matter(s) [ ]. See 37 C.F.R.
§1.111. Since the above-mentioned reply appears
to be bona fide, applicant is given a TIME PERIOD
of ONE (1) MONTH or THIRTY (30) DAYS from the
mailing of this notice, whichever is longer,
within which to supply the omission or correction
in order to avoid abandonment. EXTENSIONS OF TIME
MAY BE GRANTED UNDER 37 C.F.R. §1.136(a).
```

This could happen if you fail to respond to each and every rejection or objection in your action. (MPEP §714.03.) The PTO will usually give you a period of one month from the date of the notice to submit a proper reply. You are also allowed to obtain automatic extensions if you need even more time to correct your response.

RESTRICTION REQUIREMENT

The PTO will not allow you to claim two or more independent or distinct inventions in a single patent application. If you try to do this, the PTO will send you a restriction requirement, which requires you to *elect* the invention that you want to pursue in your application.

Restriction is required by statute (35 U.S.C. §121). This statute states that if two or more independent and distinct inventions are claimed in one application, the PTO may require that the application to be restricted to one of the invention. Note that the statute does not provide for restriction where there are two or more inventions within a single claim. Claims by their very nature often cover multiple inventions. An example of this is a generic claim. Thus, it is not proper for your examiner to require restriction within a single claim merely because it contains multiple inventions.

For a restriction requirement to be proper, not only must the inventions be distinct, but examination of the inventions in one application must create an undue burden on the examiner. (MPEP §803.) One strategy to argue against a restriction requirement is to convince the examiner that the application will not be unreasonably burdensome to examine.

NOTE: *The issue of whether a search and examination can be made without serious burden to an examiner is not applicable to design applications when determining whether a restriction requirement should be made.*

Dealing with a Restriction Requirement

You have a few options in dealing with a restriction requirement made by the PTO. The more difficult option you have is to argue that the restriction requirement is wrong and request a reconsideration of your examiner's decision. Arguing that your examiner is wrong is referred to as *traversing* the restriction requirement. Even if you traverse your examiner's restriction requirement, you must still elect which invention you want to pursue in your application.

If you are unable to overcome the restriction requirement, your examiner will make the next action final and withdraw the claims that you have not elected to pursue.

Your second, easier option in dealing with a restriction requirement is to elect the invention you want to pursue without traversing. You can still prosecute your nonelected inventions in divisional applications. (See Chapter 8 for more information on this.) Filing a divisional application can be deferred no later than the issue date of your parent application.

Accepting a restriction requirement without traversal may be your best course of action. By traversing your restriction requirement and arguing that your claims are not distinct, there is a good chance you are going to lose the battle. Not only may you lose the battle over the restriction requirement, but by asserting that your claims are not distinct, you may be admitting that your claims are not patentable over each other later on if you ever face litigation in court. Prior art might then be presumed to invalidate your *other* claims that you previously argued were not distinct.

Author's Note: Double Patenting

Restricting your other inventions can actually be advantageous from a double-patenting perspective. This is because a later filed divisional application filed in response to a restriction requirement is immune from obviousness double patenting. We will talk about double patenting in Chapter 14.

The following is an example of wording that you can use in the *Remarks* section of your amendment/reply to a restriction requirement if you pursue the easier second option:

```
I. Response to Restriction Requirement

The Examiner has imposed a restriction require-
ment on the application. By way of this amendment,
Applicants elect the Group II Claims 6, 7, 15,
26, 27, 36, 40, 41, 44-54, and 75. The nonelected
claims have been cancelled without prejudice
for later prosecution in a divisional or other
related application. The dependencies of other
claims have been modified.

The Examiner has noted that upon canceling
claims, the inventorship of the application
must be amended if one or more inventors is no
longer an inventor of the remaining subject mat-
ter. Applicants have made a good faith review of
the remaining claims and believe that the named
inventors each contributed to the conception
```

```
of the subject matter or at least one of the
remaining claims.
```

Linking Claims

There are a number of situations in which you may claim two or more divisible inventions that are subject to a proper restriction requirement, but one or more of your claims (called *linking claims*) are part of the claims that you elect in your current application to pursue. These linking claims are related to certain other claims that you have elected not to pursue, but are separate enough that your examiner has the right to require that the claims be separated, at least at the start of prosecution of your current patent application. If such linking claims do become allowable, however, you will be given the automatic right to bring your nonelected claims, which are linked to those allowed linking claims, back into your current patent application. This will save you the expense of having to file divisional patent applications on those nonelected claims. By far the most common example of linking claims are claims to a genus and claims to a species.

Example:

Ed's first claim in his patent application claims a composition comprising a reagent. In Claim 2, Ed specifies that the agent of Claim 1 is a polypeptide. In Claim 3, Ed species that the agent is an organic phosphate. Claim 1 is referred to as a genus claim because it is a broad claim, which encompasses species claims like Claims 2 and 3. Claim 1 is also a linking claim. Although Ed's examiner can require that Ed restrict out Claims 2 and 3 from his current application should Ed elect to pursue Claim 1, Ed will have the automatic right to bring back Claims 2 and 3 should Claim 1 become allowable during prosecution.

– Caution –

Be careful about filing any divisional patent application on claims that are linked to claims in your main patent application. If you are allowed to rejoin or bring back linked claims into your current application, do so. You may be faced with double patenting issues on those linked claims should you try to place them in a separate patent application.

NOTE: *For more information about restriction practice, see Chapter 800 of the MPEP.* Specifically, Sections 806.05(a)-(j) specify what an examiner may and may not restrict with respect to a variety of related inventions.

Overcoming Novelty and Obviousness Rejections

By far the most frequent ground for rejection is unpatentability in view of the prior art. In other words, your claimed subject matter is either not novel or it is obvious based on prior art references. (35 U.S.C. §§102 and 103.)

In a proper prior art rejection, your examiner must identify and communicate to you a reason, based in law, why your claimed subject matter fails to satisfy the novelty and nonobviousness requirements. If the PTO succeeds, the burden shifts to you to rebut, or knock down, the examiner's case. You cannot achieve allowance for your rejected claims without coming forward with evidence to rebut his or her case. The only exception to this rule is when you can point to sufficient evidence of patentability in the existing prosecution record.

Your first question to ask in dealing with prior art rejections is whether each cited reference in the office action constitutes prior art against your claims under examination. The criteria for determining whether patents and publications are prior art were discussed in Chapter 3. This chapter provides a more detailed examination of each of these prior art sections in order to tackle the specific rejections raised by your examiner.

As you go through the references that your examiner is using against you, make sure that such references meet the criteria under one of the prior art sections. Your examiner will state in the rejection which one of the prior art sections he or she is relying on. Go right to the relevant prior art section and make sure that the reference your examiner is using meets the necessary criteria.

Sometimes examiners can make mistakes. For example, if your examiner cites a U.S. patent filed after your filing date, you should simply (and respectfully) respond by explaining, based on the reference and filing dates, why the reference is not prior art. In such a case you would not need to submit any additional evidence, because you have all of the evidence that you need correct in the record.

As discussed in Chapter 3, it is not enough that a reference constitutes prior art under one of the sections to follow in this chapter. That prior art reference must also anticipate your invention. Anticipation requires that a reference disclose all the elements of your claimed invention, or their equivalents. In addition, the reference must also disclose those elements arranged in your claim. Anticipation also requires that the reference teach sufficient information to enable one skilled in the art to practice your invention. (*Garrett Corp. v. United States, 422 F.2d 874, 878 (Ct. Cl. 1970).*) A reference is enabled when its disclosures are sufficient to allow one of skill in the art to make and use your claimed invention. (*Elan Pharms., Inc. v. Mayo Found.,* 346 F3d 1051, 1054 (Fed. Cir. 2003).)

It may be necessary to introduce evidence rebutting enablement of a prior art reference in the form of a 132 Affidavit, which is discussed in the following section. The affidavit must specifically identify the alleged deficiencies of the reference and must explain why those deficiencies preclude a person of ordinary skill in the art from possessing the subject matter allegedly disclosed. (*In re Lamberti,* 545 F.2d 747 (C.C.P.A. 1976).)

> ### Author's Note: Anticipation
> While anticipation requires that the prior art reference is enabled, nonenablement does not preclude a finding of obviousness.

NOVELTY

Novelty should sound familiar to you at this time since it is one of the requirements for patentability already discussed. Novelty requires two things. First, it requires that the reference your examiner is applying against your patent must constitute prior art under one of the sections specified in 35 U.S.C. §102. If this reference does constitute prior art under one of these sections, then the next requirement is that the reference must teach each and every element of your claimed invention. In other words, the prior art reference must *anticipate* your claimed invention. The sections that follow break down each of the §102 prior art sections. This tells you what is required under each one of those sections for your examiner to apply it against your claims. For an introductory setting to these sections, you may want to go back and review what was said in Chapter 3. What follows now is a more detailed examination of the sections and strategies you can use to overcome their application by your examiner.

UNITED STATES CODE, TITLE 35, SECTION 102(A)

A person shall be entitled to a patent unless (a) the invention was known or used by others in this country, or patented or described in a printed publication in this or a foreign country, before the invention thereof by the applicant for a patent.

Overcoming §102(a) Prior Art Rejections

You have the following options to choose from in overcoming a §102(a) rejection:

✪ Argue that your claims are distinguishable from the references being used by the PTO to reject your claims. This is true because even if an act or document constitutes prior art under §102, it will not bar patentability of your claims unless it anticipates your claims. If you are successful in arguing that the reference does not anticipate your claims (because it is distinguishable), you will have removed that reference as a §102(a) prior art bar to the patentability of your invention.

- ✪ Argue that the references being used are not enabling. A reference that is not enabling is not anticipating. (*Elan Pharm., Inc., v. Mayo Found. For Med. Educ. & Research,* 346 F3d 1051, 1054 (Fed. Cir. 2003).)

- ✪ Amend your claims (as discussed in Chapter 11) so that they are distinguished from the prior art references. This is really the same means to overcoming a §102(a) prior art rejection as just discussed, except that here you actually make changes to your claims to negate anticipation. Again, this can be used with any of the prior art rejections you will encounter.

- ✪ Perfect any priority claims to any earlier applications that you may have filed on your invention. You would do this by amending your specification to contain a specific reference to the prior application or by filing a new application data sheet that contains a specific reference to the prior application. If you are claiming priority to an earlier filed foreign application, you will need to provide a certified copy of that priority document as well as an English language translation if the document is not in English.

- ✪ File an affidavit or declaration that shows that your invention was made prior to the effective date of the reference being applied against you by the examiner. (37 C.F.R. §1.131.)

Rule 131 Affidavits/ Declarations

The purpose of filing a 37 C.F.R. §1.131 declaration is to overcome the effective date of a reference cited in support of your rejection. If the declaration demonstrates that your date of invention is earlier than the effective date of the reference, the reference is eliminated as support for the rejection. A *Rule 131 Affidavit/Declaration* is sometimes referred to as swearing back of reference that your examiner is using against you. In other words, a Rule 131 Affidavit/Declaration supports the proposition that your claimed invention was made before the date on which your cited reference became prior art under one of the categories previously discussed.

There are three ways that you can establish that your invention was made prior to the effective date of your prior art reference.

1. First, you can show that your invention was put to actual practice (*reduction to practice*) prior to the effective date of your reference.

2. Second, you are also allowed to show that you conceived your invention prior to the effective date (even without actual reduction to practice of your invention prior to the effective date of your cited reference). As long as you also show that you took steps with due diligence to reduce your invention to practice prior to the effective date of the cited prior art reference, it is not absolutely essential that you show you have reduced to practice your invention before the effective date of the prior art reference.

3. Third, you can show *conception* of your invention before the effective date of the reference, coupled with due diligence from before to the reference date up to the filing of your application (constructive reduction to practice). This is the same way as discussed in the second option, except here you are considered to have constructively reduced to practice your invention when you file your application.

Conception is when the inventor forms, in his or her mind, a definite and permanent idea of the complete and operative invention as it will be applied in practice. (*Coleman v. Dines,* 754 F.2d 353 (Fed. Cir. 1985).) Conception is more than a vague idea of how to solve a problem. The requisite means themselves and their interaction must also be comprehended. Conception must include every feature or limitation of your claimed invention. (*Davis v. Reddy.* 620 F.2d 885 (C.C.P.A. 1980).) Conception is made when the invention is made sufficiently clear to enable one skilled in the art to reduce your invention to practice without the exercise of extensive experimentation.

While conception is the mental part of your inventive act, it must be capable of proof, such as by demonstrative evidence or by a complete disclosure to another person. The sufficiency of corroborative evidence is determined by the *rule of reason.* Accordingly, a court must make a reasonable analysis of all of the pertinent evidence to determine whether an inventor's testimony is credible.

Reduction to practice may be either actual or constructive. *Actual reduction* requires that the invention is reduced to a physical or tangible form. Actual reduction for a process requires successful performance of the process. For a machine, actual reduction requires that the machine be assembled, adjusted, and used. For a manufacture, the article must be completely manufactured. For a composition, the matter must be completely composed. *Constructive reduction* is the filing of a patent application.

Example:

Sally conceived of an invention on June 8, 2006, but did not start to take any actions in reducing her invention to practice (no reasonable diligence) until June 7, 2007. Just after this day on June 8, 2007, Molly claimed to invent the same invention and reduced it to practice on September 1, 2007. Even if Sally reduces the invention to practice on October 1, 2007, she is awarded priority since she took reasonable diligence to reduce the invention to practice prior to Molly's conception. However, if Sally had not taken this reasonable diligence prior to Molly's conception, the results would be reversed.

– Caution –

In highly unpredictable arts like biology and chemistry, sometimes the rule that reduction to practice can follow conception later on is not always the rule. In some inventions, the level of unpredictability is so high that an inventor is unable to establish a complete conception prior to reduction to practice. In such inventions, an inventor is unable to establish a complete conception prior to his/her reduction to practice of the invention. This is known as the *doctrine of simultaneous conception and reduction to practice.*

Example:

Chiron brought an infringement action against Abbott. The claimed invention in Chiron's patent was directed to an HIV immunoassay utilizing proteins genetically engineered from the Env region of the HIV virus. Although the invention did not claim the HIV gene sequence encoding for Env protein, the gene sequence was required in order to produce the desired Env protein. Abbott alleged prior invention under §102(g). Chiron argued that the doctrine of simultaneous conception and reduction to practice should apply because the instant invention involved isolation of proteins at the genetic level. The court agreed holding that the mere idea of a recombinant immunoassay based on Env region polypeptides, without knowledge of and analysis of the nucleotide sequence of specific Env DNA fragments, is, simply a wish to know the identity of any material that would be immunoreactive with HIV, not a definite and permanent idea of the complete and operative invention. Until the inventor possesses knowledge of both the nucleotide sequence of an HIV fragment, and has an operative method for isolating that fragment, the mere idea that immunoreactive polypeptides from the Env region would be capable of serving as an immunoassay (its functional utility) is inadequate as a matter of law to constitute conception.

The essential thing is that you show priority of your invention. This may be done by any satisfactory evidence of the facts. Facts—not conclusions—must be alleged in your declaration. A general allegation that your invention was completed prior to the date of your cited reference is *not* sufficient. You need factual evidence.

The allegations of fact might be supported by submitting as evidence one or more of the following:

- attached sketches;

- attached blueprints;

- attached photographs;

- attached reproductions of notebook entries;

- ✪ an accompanying model (however, you must comply with rule 37 C.F.R. §1.91 if you want to enter a model into your application file); or,

- ✪ attached supporting statements by witnesses, in which verbal disclosures are the evidence relied upon.

Finally, you and any other coinventor(s) must sign your declaration.

Sample Rule 1.131 Declaration

IN THE UNITED STATES PATENT AND TRADEMARK OFFICE

_____

_____

Declaration under 37 C.F.R. Section 1.131

Dear Sirs:

I, Paul Jones, declare that I am the inventor for the above-identified patent application and that I conceived in the United States the invention claimed in the above-identified patent application prior to October 30, 2008, the filing date of the cited U.S. Patent No. 3,588,784 to Harris.

Attached Exhibit A is a copy of notebook records relating to this conception wherein nucleotides are attached to carbohydrates by mixing precursor DNA, water, enzyme, and magnesium chloride in the presence of ultraviolet wavelengths.

Pursuant to this conception, I actually reduced to practice in the United States, the invention claimed in the above-identified patent application prior to the filing date of the cited Harris patent. Attached Exhibit B is a copy of a memorandum relating October 30, 2008, to this reduction to practice wherein 100 parts of a 5% aqueous solution of magnesium chloride was added to precursor DNA, water, enzyme, and carbon dioxide in the presence of ultraviolet wavelengths.

Exhibits A and B, which relate to the aforementioned conception and actual reduction to practice, correspond to the invention broadly disclosed and claimed in the above-identified patent application.

I hereby declare that all statements made herein of my own knowledge are true and that all statements made on information and belief are believed to be true; and further that these statements were made with the knowledge that willful false statements and the like so made are punishable by fine or imprisonment, or both, under Section 1001 of Title 18 of the United States Code, and that such willful false statements may jeopardize the validity of the application or any patent issued thereon.

Respectfully submitted,

_____

Inventor/Applicant

Rule 132 Affidavits/ Declarations

File an affidavit or declaration under 37 C.F.R. §1.132 showing that the prior art reference is by you and not by another person. Even when published within the year preceding the filing date of your application, inventor-authored publications may constitute prior art against your claims if the authors of the publication and the inventors of your application overlap but do not completely correspond. In such a case, the publication is considered the work of another, and therefore is available as a §102(a) prior art against your claims.

Example:

You file a U.S. patent application for your invention on June 14, 2006. Your invention is described in a publication of yours dated May 2006. The publication is not prior art under §102(a) because it is your own work, and if the PTO rejects your claim(s) on the basis of the publication under this section, you should submit a §1.132 affidavit or declaration that the publication was your own.

You can use a §1.132 affidavit or declaration to remove such coauthored publications and coinvented patents that your examiner seeks to use against you. If you are one of the coauthors of a publication cited against your application, you may also remove the publication as a reference by filing a §1.132 affidavit or declaration signed by any of your coauthors that disclaims any inventive contribution to your claimed subject matter.

Rule 132 affidavits are useful in a variety of situations. A Rule 132 affidavit can also be used to overcome prior art rejections under 35 U.S.C. §102(e) by proving that the subject matter relied upon in the reference was your own invention.

Rule 132 affidavits are also very useful in dealing with obviousness rejections. How to prepare such an affidavit is discussed with the obviousness rejections material later in this chapter.

UNITED STATES CODE, TITLE 35, SECTION 102(B)

> *A person shall be entitled to a patent unless (b) the invention was patented or described in a printed publication in this or a foreign country, or in public use or on sale in this country, more than one year prior to the date of application for patent in the United States.*

If you have language like this in your office action, then your claims have been rejected under 35 U.S.C. §102(b).

The *on sale category* of §102(b) means the sale of your invention and not the sale of the rights to your invention as in an assignment. Two conditions trigger the on sale bar. First, there must be an offer for sale. Second, the invention must be *ready for patenting. (Pfaff v. Wells Electronics, Inc.,* 525 U.S. 55 (1998).)

A single sale or offer to sell is enough to bar patentability. Even distribution of no more than a prototype, and at no charge to the recipient, may trigger the bar if it is done to solicit future sales.

An invention is ready for patenting if it is reduced to practice or if the inventor prepares drawings or other descriptions of the invention that are sufficient to enable one skilled in the art to practice the invention. If someone only conceives an invention, there is effectively no invention that could be placed on sale. Therefore, the offer for sale would not be a bar to patentability. (*Micro Chemical, Inc. v. Great Plains Chemical Co.,* 103 F.3d 1538 (Fed. Cir. 1997).)

If a sale was made primarily for the purpose of experimentation rather than for commercial exploitation, then the bar does not apply. However, this is a limited exception. Courts consider a variety of factors in determining whether such an experimental exception applies, such as whether the inventor controlled the testing, whether detailed progress records were kept, and whether the testers knew that testing was occurring. Moreover, if the invention was reduced to practice, then there can be no resort to the experimental purpose exception.

The main difference between a rejection under §102(b) and §102(a) is that, whereas a §102(a) category act or publication must be made by *another,* a §102(b) act or publication can be made by another or yourself. For example, if you disclose your own work in a publication more than one year prior to filing a patent application for that work, then you will be barred from obtaining a patent for the invention under §102(b), but not under §102(a).

The rationale for barring you under §102(b) is that once you have decided to lift the *veil of secrecy* from your work, you must choose between the protection of a federal patent or the dedication of the idea to the public at large. There are penalties for revealing your invention without obtaining a patent.

The second difference between §102(a) and §102(b) is that §102(a) is keyed off of one of its categories occurring *prior to the date of your invention,* while §102(b) is keyed off of one of its categories being before *the date of your patent application.* The date of invention referred to in §102(a) is sometimes termed soft and open for debate on a case-by-case basis, whereas the §102(b) filing date of an application is certain. Prior art that arises under §102(b) is unforgiving and, hence, a bar to patentability. Section 102(b) is sometimes termed an *absolute statutory bar.*

> ### Author's Note: Section 102(b)
> Section 102(b) is very important for any of your improvement inventions. You should file applications for improvement inventions within a year of your first filed application for your original invention so as to ensure that your prior filed basic application does not become prior art under §102(b).

Overcoming Your Section 102(b) Rejection

There are three possible ways that a §102(b) rejection can be overcome.

1. You can argue that your claims are distinguishable from the prior art references being used by the PTO to reject your claims. As with §102(a), you argue that your claims are not anticipated by the references in your response.

2. You can amend your claims to distinguish your claims from the prior art.

3.   You can also overcome this rejection if you have previously filed another U.S. application for the same invention, but you have forgotten to perfect priority to that application. In such a case, you should file a new *application data sheet* that contains a specific reference to the prior application so that you can obtain the earlier priority date.

Claiming foreign priority does not help you in overcoming prior art based on a §102(b) rejection. The one-year bar dates from the U.S. filing date and has nothing to do with any foreign filing date. When the statute says "prior to the date of application for patent in the U.S.," that is really what is meant. You cannot use a prior foreign application date for your invention to overcome this.

As stated earlier, your options are more limited under §102(b) as compared with §102(a). You cannot use a §1.131 affidavit as you could in §102(a) because §102(b) is keyed off of the date of your U.S. application. On the other hand, §102(a) is keyed off of the date of your invention, which the PTO assumes to be the date you file your patent application, but can be otherwise shown by presenting a §1.131 affidavit.

You also cannot present a §1.132 declaration or affidavit showing that the prior art reference is of your own work, because §102(b) applies to acts or documents by *you,* unlike §102(a).

UNITED STATES CODE, TITLE 35, SECTION 102(C)

A person shall be entitled to a patent unless (c) he has abandoned the invention.

In order to have a rejection under this part of the prior art statute you must have abandoned your invention. The PTO must show that you have intended to abandon your invention as shown by your actions. Abandonment of an invention occurs when an inventor either does not intend to further pursue an invention or intends to suppress or conceal it. Delay in filing a patent application is not sufficient to infer the necessary intent to abandon your invention. (MPEP §2134.)

UNITED STATES CODE, TITLE 35, SECTION 102(D)

A person shall be entitled to a patent unless (d) the invention was first patented or caused to be published, or was the subject of an inventor's certificate, by the applicant or his legal representatives or assignees in a foreign country prior to the date of the application for patent in this country on an application for patent or inventor's certificate filed more than twelve months before the filing of the application in the United States.

Four conditions must apply for a proper rejection under §102(d).

1. There must be a foreign application filed more than twelve months before the effective filing date of your U.S. application.

    NOTE: *A U.S. design patent application must be filed within a shorter six months of the foreign filing.*

2. The foreign application must have been filed by the same applicants as in the United States or by his or her legal representatives and assigns.

3. The foreign patent must have been granted prior to the U.S. filing date. Normally, an inventor's foreign patent will not issue before a U.S. filing date, making §102(d) prior art rejections rare. For example, a patent may not issue in Japan for over a decade. However, issuance could occur in other countries, such as Belgium, where a patent may be granted just a month after its filing.

4. The same invention in both the foreign filing and U.S. filing must be involved. So long as the foreign patent contains the same claims as the U.S. application, there is no question as to the same invention. However, the inventions are considered

the same even where the foreign application supports the subject matter of the U.S. claims.

UNITED STATES CODE, TITLE 35, SECTION 102(E)

A person shall be entitled to a patent unless (e) the invention was described in (1) an application for patent published under U.S.C. Title 25, Sec 122(b) by another filed in the United States before the invention by the applicant for patent; or (2) a patent granted on an application for patent by another filed in the United States before the invention by the applicant for patent, except that an international application filed under the treaty defined in Section 351(a) shall have the effect under this subsection of a national application published under Section 122(b) only if the international application designating the United States was published under Article 21(2)(a) of treaty in the English language.

American Inventors Protection Act

The *American Inventors Protection Act* (AIPA) amended 35 U.S.C. §102(e). This act provides that U.S. patents, U.S. application publications, and certain international application publications can be used as prior art based on their earliest effective filing date against applications filed on or after November 29, 2000, and applications filed prior to November 29, 2000, that have been voluntarily published. Applications that were filed prior to November 29, 2000, and were not voluntarily published are subject to the older version of the statute.

Section 102(e) was a complex piece of legislation even before the new revisions. Even patent attorneys and agents have great difficulty in understanding this one, and it is easy to understand why. However, if you break down the types of references that can be used against you as §102(e) prior art, then the statute can be understood.

For §102(e) to apply, the reference must be a U.S. patent, a U.S. patent application publication, or an international application publication with a filing date earlier than the effective filing date of your application being examined.

There are really two important dates at play in the statute. First, there is the effective filing date of the §102(e) prior art reference, which your examiner is trying to use against you. Your examiner would like this effective filing date to precede your date of invention.

The second big date is the date that you *conceive* and *reduce to practice* your invention. In other words, the second big date is your date of invention. Since your examiner does not know the actual date of your invention, your examiner will take this date to be the effective filing date of your own patent application.

Therefore, §102(e) rejections for examiners really involves comparing the effective filing date of the §102(e) reference with the effective filing date of your own application to see which one came first. For §102(e) to apply, the inventive entity of your application must be different from the reference. However, all that needs to be true for §102(e) to apply is for there to be one inventor who is different even if there are some common inventors between your application and the applied reference. There are other ways §102(e) can apply to the various references that your examiner may use against you.

Published U.S. Patent Applications

You will notice that §102(e)(1) starts off by saying that you are not entitled to a patent if the invention was disclosed in a published application "filed in the United States before the invention by the applicant for patent."

Author's Note: Prior Art Date

The prior art date is different for U.S. patent publications under §102(e) in contrast to what was discussed earlier in the chapter for §102(a) or §102(b). In a §102(a) or §102(b) rejection, the prior art date is the application's publication date, whereas in a §102(e) rejection, the prior art date is the application's filing date.

Under this portion of the statute, as soon as a U.S. patent application is published, that patent application becomes eligible as §102(e) prior art. Its effective filing date, for §102(e) prior art purposes, is the U.S. filing date of that application. If this date is prior to your own application's effective filing date, your examiner has made a proper §102(e) rejection. Your only course of action in such a case will be to submit a

§1.131 affidavit proving that your date of invention was earlier than your effective filing date and that it occurred before the effective filing date of the §102(e) reference.

To determine if a reference is prior art under §102(e), you will need to know not only your date of invention, but also the effective filing date of the reference. Some examples on how to determine the effective filing date of a §102(e) reference may help.

Example 1:

Competitor A files a 111(a) patent application (a U.S. regular application) on January 1, 2005, which is published under 35 U.S.C. §122(b) on July 1, 2006, eighteen months after its filing date. Under §102(e)(1), the published application is now a prior art reference. The effective filing date for prior art purposes is the earliest effective U.S. filing date, which is January 1, 2005. If the effective filing date for your own patent application is after January 1, 2005, the examiner has made a proper rejection.

Example 2:

Competitor B files a §111(b) application (a U.S. provisional application) on January 1, 2006, and then a §111(a) application on January 1, 2007, claiming priority from the provisional application under §119(d). The 111(a) application is published on July 1, 2007. The effective filing date in this case is January 1, 2006.

Published U.S. National Stage Applications

You may recall from Chapter 9 that there are two possible routes to follow in order to file a U.S. national application. Your first option is the so-called *national stage perfection route,* and the second option is the *bypass route.* The 102(e) date is similar under either of these two routes. For all PCT applications filed on or after November 29, 2000, that designate the United States and that are published in English, the §102(e) date is the international filing date of the international application, or earlier if priority is claimed to an earlier U.S. filing under 35 U.S.C. §§119(e), 120, or 365(c).

Example 1:

Bob files a PCT application on January 1, 2006, and then files a 111(a) application in the United States on December 31, 2006, claiming priority from the PCT application. If the PCT application designated the United States and is published in English, Bob can use its filing date of January 1, 2006, as a §102(e) prior art date.

Example 2:

John files a U.S. provisional application on January 1, 2006, then a PCT application on January 1, 2007, which designated the U.S. and was published on July 13, 2007. John's application would be prior art under 35 U.S.C. §102(e)(1) as of January 1, 2006.

The difference between the national stage perfection route and the bypass route for §102(e) purposes depends on whether the PCT application is published in English. In such a circumstance under the national stage perfection route, the effective date as a prior art reference is determined in accordance with §102(a) or §102(b), which usually coincides with the eighteen-month PCT publication date. What this means if you are facing a §102(e) rejection in such a situation is that you may be able to argue the PCT reference does not constitute prior art with respect to your own application, particularly if the PCT application entered the United States as a §371 filing.

Example:

Francois, a French applicant, chooses to file his PCT application in the French language in France. He designates the United States and later chooses to enter the United States under the national stage perfection route. His examiner is trying to use the PCT filing date as a §102(e) bar to your patent. Francois should argue that his examiner is wrong. The PCT application should not obtain any §102(e) date because it is not in English. His examiner would have to resort to other §102 prior art sections to try and use the reference against his application (e.g., his examiner might still be able to apply the reference against him as a printed publication under §102(a) once the PCT application was published eighteen months from its filing date).

You may notice in the example that filing a bypass application for the French applicant would have been more beneficial to that French applicant in as far as blocking your own patent under §102(e). This is because the application would take on a §102(e) date on the date it was filed in the United States under the bypass route. This is not automatically the case for a §371 filing. Thus, foreign applicants who have not filed their PCT application in English should consider coming into the United States under the bypass route rather than a §371 filing in order to obtain an earlier §102(e) date. If the PCT application is published in English, however, entering the United States under the §371 route may give an earlier §102(e) date because in that situation, the §102(e) date would be the date the PCT application is filed.

International Application (PCT) Publications

Applicants get two published applications, one corresponding to the PCT application as it is filed and another application as it is filed in the United States (either as a §371 or bypass route filing). This section discusses the published PCT application. A PCT application is prior art under §102(e) only if:

- ✪ the international application designated the United States;

- ✪ the international application was published under PCT Article 21(2)(a) in English;

- ✪ the international application was filed on or after November 29, 2000; and,

- ✪ the international application entered the national stage as to the United States. (MPEP §§1857.01, 706.02(a), and 2136.03.)

NOTE: *For an application to enter the national stage, all the requirements for national stage entry such as a copy of the international application with any necessary translation, national fee, and oath or declaration must be filed.*

An international application publication entitled to the filing date of a provisional application will have a reference date as of the filing date of the provisional application, but only if:

- ✪ the international application designated the United States;

✪ the international application was published under PCT Article 21(2)(a) in English;

✪ the international application was filed on or after November 29, 2000; and,

✪ the international application entered the national stage as to the United States (MPEP §706.02(a)).

U.S. Patents   If the §102(e) reference being used against you is a U.S. patent, your examiner can use the earliest effective filing date of that patent just as with published patent applications previously discussed. If the U.S. patent that your examiner is using against you was based on an international application that was filed on or after November 29, 2000, which designates the United States and is published in English, the §102(e) date will be the date that the international application was filed or even an earlier filing date if that international application itself makes a proper claim of priority under §119(e), §120, or §365(c).

Example:

Jack files a PCT application in English designating the United States on January 1, 2006 and then a subsequent §111(a) application (bypass filing) on January 1, 2007, claiming priority from the PCT under §365(c). A patent maturing from the 111(a) application will have a §102(e)(2) prior art date of January 1, 2006.

Overcoming §102(e) Rejections   Rejections based on §102(e) may be overcome by the following means:

✪ Check to see if your examiner properly applied §102(e) in light of the statutory requirements for the various references.

✪ Argue that your rejected claims are distinguishable from the prior art references or amend your rejected claims to distinguish them from the prior art.

✪ File an affidavit or declaration under 37 C.F.R. §132 showing that the referenced prior art invention is your own work and not *by another,* just as you did under §102(a).

✪ File a Rule 1.131 affidavit or declaration showing that your invention date precedes the U.S. filing date of the PTO reference. To do this, you must submit an oath or declaration alleging acts that establish a completion of the invention in this country before the effective date of the prior art. (37 C.F.R. §1.131(a).)

Example:

You conceive of a new invention in California on November 10, 2004, and work diligently to reduce your invention to practice on July 27, 2005. You file a patent application in the United States on July 12, 2006. The examiner rejects both of your claims on January 18, 2007. Your first claim is rejected as being anticipated under §102(b) by a German patent filed on December 20, 2003, and issued on June 15, 2005.

Your second claim is rejected as anticipated under §102(e) by a U.S. patent filed on June 10, 2005, and issued October 4, 2006. Since the German patent issued on June 15, 2005, which is more than one year prior to your U.S. filing date of July 12, 2006, you cannot overcome the §102(b) rejection.

However, the §102(e) rejection can be overcome because your conception date, November 10, 2004, is before the U.S. patent filing date of June 10, 2005. In your response, you should file an amendment canceling Claim 1 and file an antedating affidavit proving that you conceived and diligently reduced it to practice prior to the U.S. filing date.

You should note that where the claims of the reference and your application are directed to the same invention, an affidavit or declaration under 37 C.F.R. §1.131 is not an acceptable method of overcoming your rejection. Under these circumstances, your examiner must determine whether a double patenting rejection or interference is appropriate. If there is a common assignee or inventor between your application and a patent, a double patenting rejection must be made. If there is no common assignee or inventor and the rejection under 35 U.S.C. §102(e) is the only possible rejection, your examiner must determine whether an interference should be declared. (MPEP §706.02(b).)

❂ Make any proper claim of priority back to an earlier filed application, such as a foreign or provisional application that supports the claims of your application. This will require you to either amend your specification, to contain a specific reference to your prior application, or file a new *Application Data Sheet* that contains a specific reference to your prior application. In the case of a priority claim back to an earlier foreign application, you would need to file a certified copy of the prior foreign application and if such application is not in English, provide a translation.

You are given a little bit of an advantage here. While you can reach back to a foreign priority application in order to antedate a §102(e) reference filing date, your examiner cannot use a foreign priority date in order to antedate your own effective filing date.

❂ If the §102(e) reference was commonly owned with your current patent application at the time of your invention, a §102(e)/§103 rejection (i.e., your examiner is combining a §102(e) reference in his or her obviousness rejection) can be overcome by asserting common ownership under §103(c). So if your §102(e) reference is being combined with other references in your examiner's rejection of your patent application based on the assertion that it was obviousness, but the §102(e) reference was commonly owned with your rejected application, you should file a Rule 130 declaration just as you would for a §102(a) rejection. Your oath or declaration under 37 C.F.R. §1.130 should state that your application and reference are currently owned by the same party and that the inventor named in the application is the prior inventor under 35 U.S.C. §104, together with a terminal disclaimer in accordance with 37 C.F.R. §1.321(c).

Author's Note: Special Protection

This special protection afforded by §103(c) does not apply to §102(a) or §102(b) rejections discussed earlier in the chapter. Rather, §103(c) only applies to §§102(e), (f), and/or (g). In addition, §103(c) only applies to obviousness issues, not anticipation. Nor does §103(c) eliminate what should have been an alternative rejection for double patenting.

More will be said about the use of §102(e) when I discuss obviousness rejections later on in the chapter. Remember that this handy statute only comes into play for §102(e) references, which are being used in an obviousness rejection. If your §102(e) anticipates your invention, then you can not use §103(c).

Example 1:

Suppose that you filed a prior application for your invention, and then, prior to publishing the first application (i.e., within eighteen months), you file an add-on application. Since the follow-up application has not been published yet, it will not be prior art for most countries. However, it remains §102(e) prior art in the United States. However, §103(c)(1) provides that §102(e), (f), and (g) prior art does not preclude patentability where the two applications are owned by the same person or subject to an obligation of assignment to the same person. Thus, you can remove any §102(e) art rejection under this statute.

Example 2:

Suppose that drug manufacturer A files a patent application covering a generic class of drug molecules. Prior to eighteen months, A also files an application for specific members of this generic class of drug molecules because new pharmaceutical data becomes available for these members. A does not claim priority to the first generic file application because A does not want to lose any patent term, which would run from the priority date. Any possible §102(e) rejection based on the later filing can be removed since the applications are owned by the same person.

Author's Note: The challenges of §102(e).

U.S.C., Title 35, §102(e) is a challenging statute even for a patent attorney. If you do not understand the material after an initial reading, do not despair. An excellent flowchart on applying the statute as well as several more examples can also be found at the MPEP §706.02(f)(1), Examination Guidelines for applying references under 35 U.S.C. §102(e).

**Provisional
§102(e)
Rejection**

A claim provisionally rejected under §102(e) as being anticipated by a co-pending application that has a common assignee or inventor with the instant application would constitute prior art if published or patented. This provisional rejection is based upon a presumption of future publication or patenting of the co-pending application. This provisional rejection might be overcome either by a showing under 37 C.F.R. §1.132 that any invention disclosed but not claimed in the co-pending application was derived from the inventor of this application, and is thus not the invention *by another,* or by an appropriate showing under 37 C.F.R. §1.131. This rejection may not be overcome by the filing of a terminal disclaimer.

It is possible for your examiner to make what is called a *provisional §102(e) rejection* even though the reference has not been published or issued as a patent. The examiner can do this only in the case of co-pending U.S. applications that have at least one common inventor or where the applications are commonly assigned.

This rejection is termed *provisional* because the reference that the examiner is using has not actually been published or patented to constitute 102(e) prior art under the statute. However, the examiner can still make a provisional rejection based upon a presumption of future publication or patenting of the co-pending application.

> *Author's Note: What about co-pending applications without a common inventor?*
> You may ask why the examiner cannot also make a provisional rejection for co-pending applications that do not have a common inventor or assignee. The reason has to do with the confidential status of applications filed with the PTO. If there are no common inventors or assignees, the PTO would not be able to divulge to you that there is another co-pending U.S. patent application that discloses subject matter that would anticipate your claims. The PTO would have to wait until such prior application becomes public knowledge as by publishing.

**Overcoming
Provisional
Rejections**

A provisional rejection can be overcome in any of the ways previously discussed. A provisional rejection can also be overcome by abandoning the two applications and filing a new application containing the subject matter of both applications.

UNITED STATES CODE, TITLE 35, SECTION 102(F)

A person shall be entitled to a patent unless (f) he did not himself invent the subject matter sought to be patented.

If it can be shown that you derived an invention from another person, then a rejection is made under §102(f). Derivation requires that someone *else* completely conceived the invention and communicated it to you before any date on which it can be shown that you had knowledge of the invention. The main focus of derivation is on the originality of the invention.

UNITED STATES CODE, TITLE 35, SECTION 102(G)(2)

A person shall be entitled to a patent unless (g)(2) before the applicant's invention thereof, the invention was made in this country by another who had not abandoned, suppressed, or concealed it. In determining priority of invention there shall be considered not only the respective dates of conception and reduction to practice of the invention, but also the reasonable diligence of one who was first to conceive and last to reduce to practice, from a time prior to conception by the other.

Section 102(g)(2) bars the issuance of a patent when another person made your invention in the United States before you and that other person has not abandoned, suppressed, or concealed the invention. Section 102(g)(2) is the basis of *interference practice*. Interference practice is a lengthy, expensive proceeding that is beyond the scope of this book. If your patent application becomes involved in an interference, you will need to retain the assistance of a patent attorney who has experience in interference practice.

OBVIOUSNESS

Novelty is not enough in patent law for a patentable invention. In the eyes of patent law, something more is required to ensure that inventions are truly new. *Obviousness* is a concept that was already discussed as a requirement to patentability, so you may want to go back to Chapter 3 as a prelude to the following discussion of obviousness rejections under §103(a).

UNITED STATES CODE, TITLE 35, SECTION 103(A)

A patent may not be obtained though the invention is not identically disclosed or described as set forth in Section 102 of this title, if the difference between the subject matter sought to be patented and the prior art are such that the subject matter as a whole would have been obvious at the time the invention was made to a person having ordinary sill in the art to which the subject matter pertains. Patentability shall not be negated by the manner in which the invention was made.

You will get a §103(a) rejection if your invention is thought to be an obvious one in light of the prior art. The PTO can take any reference that qualifies as prior art under §102 and reject your claims on the basis that such claims are obvious with respect to the prior art references. This is stated in §103.

The Supreme Court has stated that the controlling inquiry in determining obviousness is the case of *Graham v. John Deere Co.* According to Graham, the following factors are considered in determining whether an invention is obvious:

- ✪ the scope and the content of the prior art are determined;

- ✪ differences between the prior art and the claims at issue are then ascertained;

✪ the level of ordinary skill in the pertinent art is determined; and,

✪ objective evidence of nonobviousness.

Objective evidence of nonobviousness includes secondary considerations such as commercial success, long felt but unsolved needs, and the failure of others. Secondary considerations will be covered in greater detail below in discussing how to overcome an obviousness rejection.

Before discussing obviousness, you should understand something called *prima facie obviousness*. *Prima facie obviousness* is a procedural tool used to shift the burden of proof to the applicant. If your examiner meets his or her initial burden of establishing a prima facie case of obviousness, then the burden will shift to you as the applicant to overcome the prima facie case of obviousness.

Common Examples of Obviousness or Nonobviousness

Various fact patterns and examples have now been established through case law on the question of obviousness. The MPEP at section 2144.04 also sets out various fact patterns where obviousness may or my not exist.

✪ Product-by-process-claims. If the product in a product-by-process claim is the same as or obvious from a product of the prior art, the claim is unpatentable even though the prior product was made by a different process. (*In re Thorpe*, 227 USPQ 964, 966 (Fed. Cir. 1985).)

✪ DNA and protein sequences. For a long time, it was held that a claim to a specific DNA is not made obvious by mere knowledge of a desired protein sequence and methods for generating the DNA that encodes the protein. (*In re Deuel*, 51 F3d 1552, 1558, 34 USPQ2d 1210, 1215 (1995).) A prior art disclosure of the amino acid sequence of a protein does not necessarily render particular DNA molecules encoding the protein obvious because the redundancy of the genetic code permits one to hypothesize an enormous number of DNA sequences coding for the protein. (In re Bell, 991 F2d 781, 785, 26 USPQ2d 1529, 1532 (Fed. Cir. 1993).)

However, recently the Board of Patent Appeals and Interferences held that patent claims to a polynucleotide encoding a protein when that encoded protein is already known can reject the claims based on the known protein and standard cloning techniques. Whether this decision will withstand court scrutiny remains to be seen. In the meantime, one should argue that knowledge of a protein and ways of cloning it does not predict the actual nucleotide sequence and derived amino acid sequence of a nucleic acid molecule encoding the protein. The nucleotide and amino acid sequences are unpredictable, nonobvious results of the cloning methods.

✪ Genus and Species claims. A single, obvious species within a claimed genus renders the claimed genus unpatentable under §103.

✪ Reversing the order of process steps. One common scenario where obviousness exists (in the absence of new or unexpected results) is where an inventor merely changes the order of performing process steps. For example, a prior art reference might disclose a process of making a laminated sheet wherein a base sheet is first coated with a metallic film and thereafter impregnated with a thermosetting material. This process was held to render *prima facie* obvious claims directed to a process of making a laminated sheet by reversing the order of the prior art process steps.

✪ Differences in concentration or temperature. Differences in concentration or temperature will generally not support the patentability of subject matter encompassed by the prior art unless there is evidence indicating such concentration or temperature is critical.

___

Example:

Joe claimed a process performed at a temperature between forty and eighty degrees Celsius and an acid concentration between 25% and 70%. Joe's claims were rejected as *prima facie* obvious over a reference process, which differed from Joe's claims only in that the reference process was performed at a temperature of one hundred degrees Celsius and an acid concentration of 10%.

✪ Purified compounds from known mixtures. A purified compound derived from a mixture known in the prior art is not always obviousness over the mixture. For example, it may not be known that the purified compound is present in or an active ingredient of the mixture, or the state of the art may be such that discovering how to perform the purification of the invention is an invention of patentable weight in itself. However, the purified form of a known mixture is prima facie obviousness if a person skilled in the art would have some reason to believe that the mixture derives properties from particular components even without an explicit teaching that the ingredient should be purified.

Example:

Aventis Pharma had a blockbuster-selling inhibitor drug called Ramipril. Its patent claimed Ramipril was formulated "substantially free of other isomers." However, Merck had previously disclosed that the particular stereoisomer was the source of a mixture's therapeutic activity. By using Merck's findings, the court held that one of skill in the art had reason to seek a stereoisomer primarily responsible for Ramipril's activity and could predictably determine which stereoisomer in Aventis' mixture would be responsible for the mixture's drug activity.

✪ Structurally similar chemical compounds. One who claims a compound, per se, which is structurally similar to a prior art compound must rebut the presumed expectation that the structurally similar compounds have similar properties (e.g., by showing that the claimed compound has unexpected properties).

A prima facie case of obviousness for a chemical compound begins with reasoned identification of a lead compound. By *lead compound* one refers to a compound in the prior art that would be most promising to modify in order to improve upon.

Example:

Where the prior art disclosed a broad selection of compounds, any one of which could have been selected as a lead compound for antidiabetic treatment such that a person of ordinary skill in the art would not have selected compound B as a lead compound for antidiabetic treatment, a prima facie case of obviousness of compound B was not established (*Takeda v. Alphapharmy Pty., Ltd*).

Even after a lead compound is identified, it is necessary to identify some reason that would have led a chemist to modify a lead compound in a particular manner to establish prima facie obviousness of a new claimed compound.

Example:

Where there was no reason for a skilled artisan to begin with an ulcer treatment compound called Lansoprazole and to eliminate its fluorinated substituent that gave its advantageous property of increased lipophilicity in order to obtain another compound Rabeprazole, which had a different substituent on its pyridine ring, the record did not support a case of obviousness (see *Eisai Co.*).

Overcoming a Rejection Based on Obviousness

Use any or all of the following in order to overcome your obviousness rejection. Decisions for nonobviousness are also available at www.uspto.gov/go/dcom/bpai, and can also be searched through Google using the search string "site: www.uspto.gov/go/dcom/bpai" along with a key work or phrase. Such decisions may have language useful for you to counter any obvious rejection by the PTO.

✪   Your first course of action should always be to see whether you can argue that the examiner did not clearly articulate reasons why the claimed invention logically flows from the teachings of the cited art. The examiner seeking to establish prima facie obviousness must clearly articulate reasons with rational, factual underpinnings to support the conclusion of the obviousness.

✪   Argue that any one of the applied references do not qualify as prior art under any part of §102. If such references do not constitute prior art under one of those sections, then your examiner is wrong to use it as a reference in an obviousness rejection against you.

In determining whether a particular reference constitutes prior art under one of the sections previously discussed, you should make sure that the cited references meet all of the criteria necessary to constitute prior art under the particular relevant section.

Example:

Your examiner makes an obviousness rejection based on a publication that would be applied under §102(a) if it anticipated your claims. You can overcome such rejection by swearing behind the publication date of the reference by filing an affidavit or declaration under 37 C.F.R. §1.131.

✪   If the prior art that your examiner is using against you is prior art under §102(e), §102(f), or §102(g), then you should note the following rule:

If your invention and the referenced inventions were, at the time you made your invention, owned by the same person or subject to an obligation of assignment to the same person, then the references can not be considered as prior art under §102(e), §102(f), or §102(g) for §103 obvious use purposes.

Common ownership requires that the persons or organizations own 100% of the subject matter and 100% of the claimed invention at the time the claimed invention was made. (MPEP §706.02(l)(2).)

The requirement for common ownership *at the time your claimed invention was made* is intended to preclude you from obtaining ownership of subject matter *after* the invention was made in order to disqualify that subject matter as prior art against your claimed invention.

To disqualify a commonly owned patent or published patent application as prior art you will need to file a §1.130 affidavit. This effectively means that you will need to file (1) a terminal disclaimer (discussed under double patenting in the next chapter); and, (2) an oath or declaration stating that patent or published application are currently owned by the same party. (37 C.F.R. §1.130.)

> **NOTE:** *In situations when you file an application with joint inventors, your examiner will presume that the subject matter of your various claims was commonly owned at the time any inventions covered by such claims were made absent any evidence to the contrary. You have the duty to inform your examiner if this is not the case.*

✪ As with any §102 rejection, you can point out or amend your claims to include an element not shown in any of the cited references. This element may be a separate structural element, chemical component or step, or a novel relationship among other elements or steps of the claim.

To the extent that a rejected claim includes elements not found in the combination, your response should highlight the specific claim language that distinguishes the combination and show why the undisclosed features, in combination with the rest of the claimed features, are significant in achieving the benefits of the invention.

You can make a special heading in your amendment/response entitled something like the following:

```
The  References  Do  Not  Fully  Teach  The
Claimed Combination
```

Under this section heading, you can then state something like the following:

> Even if the references were within the proper
> field of endeavor, an assertion that is
> strenuously traversed, the combined teach-
> ing of the cited references still fail to
> fully teach the invention recited herein.

You should then continue to argue why this is so.

✪   State that the references your examiner wants to apply
    against you do not come from analogous art and, therefore,
    are not within the *scope and content of the prior art* as
    required by §103(a).

A reference is considered *analogous* and, therefore, available
for use in an obviousness rejection if it is either within the
field of the inventor's endeavor or reasonably pertinent to the
particular problem with which the inventor was involved. (*In
re Deminski*, 796 F.2d 436 (Fed. Cir. 1986).)

Example:
In your "Remarks" section, you create the following title:

> The Combination Draws Upon Nonanalogous Art
> References

You then state the following:

> It is well settled that, in order to combine
> references properly, each of the references
> must be relevant to the field of endeavor
> recited in the claimed invention or problem
> addressed by the invention. Such is clearly
> not the case with the cited references.

You then continue to explain why.

While PTO classification of your references and cross-references
are some evidence of *nonanalogy* or *analogy,* the important factors to consider are the similarities and differences in structure

and function of the inventions. (*In re Ellis,* 476 F.2d 1370, (C.C.P.A. 1978).)

Author's Note: Analogous art

Analogous art is an important factor to win. If all of the elements of your invention can be found in prior art that is reasonably pertinent to the problem your invention addresses, then this will go a long way toward demonstrating a reason to combine the two references to make your invention obvious. (See *In re Icon Health and Fitness* (Fed. Cir. 2007).)

✪ It may also be possible to attack a rejection based on a combination of references on the ground that nothing in the references themselves would suggest the combination.

There are three traditional ways this suggestion or motivation to combine can be found:

1. the prior art references themselves;

2. the knowledge of those of ordinary skill in the art; and,

3. the nature of the problem to be solved.

Any need or problem known in the field and addressed by the patent can provide a reason for combining the elements in the manner you have claimed. In other words, it is permissible for the examiner to look at interrelated teachings of multiple patents, to the effects of demands known to the design community or present in the marketplace and to the background knowledge possessed by a person of ordinary skill in the art in order to determine whether there was an apparent reason to combine the known elements in the manner you have claimed.

Example:

Close or established structural relationships between a prior art compound and a claimed compound may provide the requisite motivation or suggestion to modify the known compound to obtain a new compound. A known compound may suggest its homolog, analog, or isomer because such compounds often have similar properties and, therefore, chemists of ordinary skill would ordinarily contemplate making them to try to obtain compounds with improved properties. If you are up against a roadblock because of the close structural similarity of your claimed compound, you may need to argue other ways to negate obviousness discussed in this section such as unexpected properties of your new compound.

If a proposed modification would render the prior art invention unsatisfactory for its intended purpose, then there is no suggestion or motivation to make the proposed modification, and therefore the invention is probably not an *obvious* modification. (*In re Gordon,* 733 F.2d 900 (Fed. Cir. 1984).)

Example:

Joe claimed a new blood filter assembly device for use during medical procedures. In the device, the inlet and outlet for the blood were located at the bottom end of the filter assembly and a gas vent was present at the top of the assembly.

The examiner rejected Joe's claims based on a prior art reference that taught a liquid strainer for removing dirt and water from gasoline wherein the inlet and outlet were at the top of the device. The examiner thought it was obvious.

The court reversed, however, reasoning that if the prior art device was turned upside down it would be inoperable for its intended purpose because the gasoline to be filtered would be trapped at the top and water sought to be separated would flow out of the outlet instead of the purified gasoline.

If nothing in the references themselves would suggest your combination, you can create a heading in your remarks section, entitled something like the following:

```
The References Lack Suggestion to Combine
```

You then go on to state something like the following:

> ```
> Of course, even if the references were from
> the proper field of endeavor, and fully
> taught the invention herein, there still
> must be some affirmative teaching in the
> references to make the cited combination.
> Such suggestion is asserted to be lacking
> in the references cited against the pres-
> ent claims.
> ```

You should then continue to explain why this is so.

✪   There must also be a reasonable expectation of success to modify the reference or to combine the prior art references. Thus, a claimed invention is not obvious if the prior art suggests that it was merely obvious to try to make the invention. Instead, the prior art must also suggest that a person of ordinary skill in the art would have a reasonable expectation of success in making the invention. Whether the proposed modification or combination of the prior art has a reasonable expectation of success is determined at the time the invention was made. (See *Ex part Erlich,* 3 USPQ2d 1011 (Bd. Pat. App. & Inter. 1986).)

✪   Use any prior art disclosure that teaches away from, or discourages the making of your claimed invention. Using such a piece of prior art is a great way to undermine prima facie obviousness. A reference *teaches away* when a person of ordinary skill, upon reading the reference, would be discouraged from following the path set out in the reference, or would be led in a direction divergent from the path that was taken by the applicant. (*In re Gurley,* 27 F.3d 551, 553 (Fed. Cir. 1994).)

Example:

Medrad, Inc. described general injectors in its "Background of the Invention" section and stated that during the injection phase, a plunger is driven forward and pressure develops in the syringe, ranging from 25 psi to over 1000 psi. Without a pressure jacket, syringes that are able to withstand such high pressures are expensive, and therefore impractical where the syringes are to be disposable. This statement teaches away from a disposable syringe without a pressure jacket since it states that such syringes are "impractical."

If you are lucky, you may find that one of the applied references has an explicit teaching against the combination proposed by the examiner. A contrary teaching may be explicit or implicit in the structure or purpose of one of the references. The proposed combination, for example, might disrupt the operation of the structure of one of the references or obstruct its intended result.

✪ Submit evidence of *secondary considerations*. Evidence of factors called *secondary considerations* indicates that your invention is not obvious. You can submit evidence of secondary consideration in a §1.132 affidavit or declaration. (See the sample §1.132 affidavit below.)

As was already discussed under §102(a), your declaration should consist of facts—not conclusions. Although you are allowed to make the affidavit yourself, an affidavit or declaration as to the advantages of your claimed invention will be more persuasive if it is made by a person with no vested interest in your invention. A form for a §1.132 declaration is contained in Appendix G. (You will, of course, need to adapt this skeleton form to your own unique situation.)

The following are all secondary considerations that you should consider submitting evidence of if any one of them is present in your case:

✪ *Unexpected Results.* For example, if your claimed invention shows an additive result whereas a diminished result would have been expected based on a combination of the prior art, this is persuasive evidence that your invention is nonobvious.

Sometimes unexpected results can be shown through evidence of unobvious or unexpected advantageous properties of your claimed invention or by showing that your claimed invention lacks a property that would have been expected to possess based on the teachings of the prior art.

Example:

TZD's compound pioglitazone was held nonobviousness in light of prior art compound B given its unexpectedly superior properties over prior art compound B. Specifically, compound B was shown to be toxic to the liver, heart, and erythrocytes, whereas pioglitazone showed no statistically significant toxicity while being comparatively potent.

Author's Note: Unexpected Evidence

The evidence asserted as unexpected must actually have been obtained. (*In re Klosak*, 455 F2d 1077, 1080, 173 USPQ 14, 16 (CCPA 1973).) The evidence must also include a comparison with the closest prior art, which prior art must actually exist, although in some cases, an indirect comparison may suffice.

✪ *Commercial Success of Your Invention.* If your invention is highly sought after, then it is most likely something new and should be considered nonobvious.

In considering evidence of commercial success, be careful to develop a link between the commercial success and your invention and not extraneous factors, such as heavy promotion or advertising. In other words, you must show that your claimed features were responsible for the commercial success of your invention. Merely showing that there was commercial success of an article that embodies your invention is not sufficient. This can be especially difficult in design cases. Evidence of commercial success must be clearly attributable to the design and not to brand name recognition or some other factor.

- *Skepticism by Experts in Your Field that an Invention Like Yours Would Work.*

- *Licensing of Your Invention.*

- *Copying of Your Invention by Others.* More than the mere fact of copying is necessary to establish this factor because copying may be attributable to other factors such as someone's unconscientious or resentful attitude about patent protection. Evidence of copying is persuasive, however, when you can show an alleged infringer tried for a substantial length of time to design a product or process similar to your claimed invention, but failed and then copied your invention instead.

- *Long-Felt Need and Failure of Others.* Establishing this factor requires objective evidence that your art recognized that a problem existed in your art for a long period of time without solution. You must show three things.

    1. You must show the need was a persistent one that was recognized by those of ordinary skill in your art.

    2. You must establish that the long-felt need was not satisfied by another before your invention.

    3. Your invention must in fact satisfy the long-felt need.

Sample Rule 1.132 Affidavit

IN THE UNITED STATES PATENT AND TRADEMARK OFFICE

Applicant(s): Igor Baxter

Serial No.: 08/486,024

Filed: November 11, 2008

Title: Process of attaching nucleic acid to carbohydrate

Group Art. Unit: 1308

Examiner: Dr. Helen Smith

Docket No.: Baxter1

FILED BY EXPRESS MAIL
Commissioner for Patents
P.O. Box 1450
Alexandria, VA 22313

EXPRESS MAIL CERTIFICATE

"Express Mail" Label No. _____

Date of Deposit: _____

I hereby certify that this paper and the attachment herein are being deposited with the United States Postal Service as "Express Mail Post Office to Addressee" service under 37 C.F.R. §1.10 on the date indicated above and is addressed to Commissioner for Patents, P.O. Box 1450, Alexandria, VA 22313.

_____
[type or print name of person making deposit]

_____
[signature of person making deposit]

Declaration under 37 C.F.R. Section 1.132

Dear Sirs:

I, Dr. Igor Baxtor, declare and say:

That I am a citizen of the United States and reside at 224 West 4th Street, New York, New York.

That I was graduated in 1946 from University of Moscow located in Moscow, Russia, with a Bachelor of Science Degree in Biochemistry. I also graduated in 1964 from the Massachusetts Institute of Technology located in Boston, Massachusetts, with a Doctor's Degree in biochemistry.

That since 1983, I have been employed in the biochemistry department of New York University as Associate Professor.

That I have been granted twenty patents in the biochemistry field, and I am the author of sixty-two papers in the biochemistry field.

That I am familiar with the above-identified patent application Serial No. 08/486,024 and with the following references cited by the Examiner: Dr. Helen Smith.

That a test was performed by me on behalf of applicant described in detail hereinafter to compare the process of nucleotide attachment employed using aluminum dioxide as a catalyst in the Smith patent, U.S. No. 3,367,890 with the catalyst of magnesium dioxide employed in the invention described and claimed in the above-identified patent application.

That in the procedure using the Smith catalyst, DNA precursors where added to 20 micro liters of water. Aluminum dioxide micro powders were added totaling 2% of the aqueous solution and were then irradiated with a ray of wavelength between 400 and 800 millimicrons for 2 hours. The nucleotides were attached to the carbohydrates in 10 hours.

That the same procedure was repeated except for using the catalyst of the invention. Magnesium micro powders were added totaling 10%. The nucleotides were attached to the carbohydrates in 2.5 hours.

That the above test demonstrates the use of magnesium dioxide as a catalyst significantly speeds up the process of attaching the nucleic acid to carbohydrates.

I hereby declare that all statements made herein of my own knowledge are true and that all statements made on information and belief are believed to be true; and further that these statements were made with the knowledge that willful false statements and the like so made are punishable by fine or imprisonment, or both, under Section 1001 of Title 18 of the United States Code, and that such willful false statements may jeopardize the validity of the application or any patent issued thereon.

Respectfully submitted,

—————————————————,

Title/Name

How to Overcome Other Types of Rejections

This chapter looks at some other common substantive rejections that are encountered in the prosecution of patent applications.

REJECTIONS UNDER UNITED STATES CODE, TITLE 35, SECTION 112, SECOND PARAGRAPH

This statute contains two separate and distinct requirements that:

✪ the claims set forth the subject matter that you regard as your invention and

✪ your claims particularly point out and distinctly claim your invention.

Each of these requirements are discussed in the next two sections.

Failure to Claim Your Invention

You will receive the following rejection if you have stated somewhere other than in your application as filed that your invention is something different from what is defined in your claims. This is not a common rejection. Do not make it any more common by stating that your invention is something other than what you have claimed.

Claim [ ] rejected under 35 U.S.C. §112, second paragraph, as failing to set forth the subject matter which applicant(s) regard as their invention. Evidence that Claim [ ] fails to correspond in scope with that which applicant(s) regard as the invention can be found in Paper No. [ ] filed [ ]. In that paper, applicant has stated [ ], and this statement indicates that the invention is different from what is defined in the claim(s) because [ ].

Indefinite Claims

You will get this rejection if you have claims in your application that are not definite. Following the rejection language, the examiner will state why he or she regards your claim as indefinite. The primary purpose of the definiteness requirement is to ensure that the scope of your claims are clear so the public is informed of the boundaries of what constitutes infringement later on.

Claim [ ] is rejected under 35 U.S.C. §112, second paragraph, as being indefinite for failing to particularly point out and distinctly claim the subject matter that applicant regards as the invention.

The following are common reasons why your claims could be considered indefinite:

✪ You may have used a term in your claim that is contrary to the usual meaning of that term. Due to potential confusion, you are not allowed to use a meaning of a term that is different from the usual meaning of that term.

✪ You have included a process claim, but have not set forth any steps involved in the process. (You need to set forth positive "-ing" steps for your process claim.)

✪ You use indefinite claim language. One such phrase is "such as." This is considered indefinite because it is unclear whether the limitations following the phrase are merely exemplary of your claim or a required feature of your claim. The same is true for a phrase like "for example."

✪ You use a trademark to identify or describe a particular material or produce. (A trademark is used to identify a source of goods and cannot be used to identify the goods themselves.)

You should review Chapter 6 on drafting your claims if you have questions as to how to write definite claims. Fortunately, these types of rejections should not be a problem for you to overcome. All you need to do is to submit an amendment in which your claims are rewritten using more definite language.

NEW MATTER REJECTIONS UNDER UNITED STATES CODE, TITLE 35, SECTION 132

An objection can arise when you amend your application and add something that was not present in your original specification. A statement of the objection will read as follows:

> *The amendment filed is objected to under U.S.C., Title 35, §132 because it introduces new matter into the disclosure. U.S.C., Title 35, §132 states no amendment shall introduce new matter into the disclosure of the invention. The added material that is not supported by the original disclosure is as follows [identification where the new matter is in your specification].*

Once you submit your oath or declaration identifying the papers that you have reviewed and understand, the original disclosure of your application is said to be *defined,* and you cannot thereafter alter it.

The addition of new matter is defined very inclusively by the PTO. For example, if in your original written description you state a range 10–20%, you cannot later change your description by stating "15%," since your have altered your description by changing the broad range to a specific range. Even the later deletion of a step in a method will be considered by the PTO as new matter.

There are really two ways that the PTO objects to the addition of new matter. If the new matter does not concern your claims, then the issue is treated using the new matter objection. On the other hand, if the new matter involves your claims, the PTO rejects your claims based on the written description requirement that is covered in the next section.

If the new matter affects both your claims and other parts of your specification, then both an objection and rejection of your claims is made.

The following circumstances should not be considered new matter:

❂ *Rephrasing.* Rewording of a passage in your specification when the same meaning remains intact is permissible.

❂ *Correction of Obvious Errors.* An amendment to correct an obvious error in your specification does not constitute new matter when one skilled in the art would not only recognize the existence of the error in the specification, but also the appropriate correction.

Overcoming New Matter Rejections

The easiest way to overcome an objection or rejection based on new matter is to make an amendment deleting what the PTO considers as new matter.

The harder way to deal with the objection is to argue that you have not added new matter. To argue against the PTO, you must show how your additions already existed in some part of your application as filed.

A rejection of your claims is reviewable by the *Board of Patent Appeals and Interferences.* However, an objection and requirement to delete new matter from other parts of your specification is subject to supervisory review by petition under 37 C.F.R. §1.181. If both an objection and rejection are made, the issue is appealable and should not be decided by petition. (MPEP §§608.04 and 706.03(o).)

REJECTIONS UNDER UNITED STATES CODE, TITLE 35, SECTION 112, FIRST PARAGRAPH

Under 35 U.S.C. §112, first paragraph, there are three requirements. They are the written description, enablement, and best mode.

Written Description

The *written description requirement* is the first of three requirements under the first paragraph of §112. The written description requirement prevents you from claiming subject matter that was not described in your application as filed. In fact, it prevents you from doing anything to your claims that are not supported by your written description in your application. A rejection on account of written description will read as follows:

> *Claim [ ] rejected under U.S.C., Title 35, §112, first paragraph, as the specification does not contain a written description of the claimed invention, in that the disclosure does not reasonably convey to one skilled in the relevant art that the inventor(s) had possession of the claimed invention at the time the application was filed.*

The essential goal of the written description requirement is to clearly convey the subject matter that an applicant has invented. The requirement for an adequate disclosure ensures that the public receives something in return for the exclusionary rights that are granted to you by a patent.

To satisfy the written description requirement, a patent specification must describe the claimed invention in sufficient detail that one skilled in the art can reasonably conclude that the applicant had possession of the claimed invention. An applicant shows possession of the claimed invention by describing the invention with all of its limitations using such descriptive means as words, structures, figures, diagrams, and formulas that fully set forth the invention.

Possession can be shown by describing an actual reduction to practice of your invention. A specification may describe an actual reduction to practice by showing that the inventor constructed an embodiment or performed a process that met all the limitations of the claim and determined that the invention would work for its intended purpose.

Possession can also be shown by showing that your invention was *ready for patenting* such as by the disclosure of drawings or structural chemical formulas that show your invention was complete or by describing distinguishing identifying characteristics sufficient to show that you were in possession of your claimed invention.

Author's Note: Means-plus-function laws.
As discussed earlier, a means-plus-function claim under §112 must be interpreted to cover the corresponding structure, materials, or acts in the specification or equivalents thereof. A means-plus-function claim limitation is adequately described for written description purposes if your specification adequately links or associates adequately described particular structure, material, or acts to the function recited in your means-plus-function claim limitation. It is also adequately described if it is clear, based on the facts of your application, that one skilled in your art would have known what structure, material, or acts perform the function recited in the means-plus-function limitation.

Written description rejections are most common in the more unpredictable arts, like biology and chemistry. When an art is more unpredictable, the PTO will require a better disclosure to show that you were in possession of your invention as claimed. For inventions in emerging and unpredictable technologies, or for inventions characterized by factors not reasonably predictable that are known to one of ordinary skill in the art, more evidence is required to show possession of the invention.

Example:

A claim to a gene will usually require that you have sequenced the gene to show possession. You would not, for example, be able to claim the gene and show possession merely by stating that the gene codes for some particular protein. This is because a gene is a chemical compound and conception of a chemical compound requires that you be able to define it to distinguish it from other materials and describe how to obtain it.

Problems with the written description requirement arise in the following scenarios:

- ✪ *New or Amended Claims.* This is the most common situation. You add or amend one of your claims after you file your application, and the PTO rejects your new or amended claims on the basis that such claims are not supported by the description of your invention in the application that you filed. Newly added claim limitations must be supported in your specification through express, implicit, or inherent disclosure. If you amend a claim to include subject matter, limitations, or terminology not present in your application as filed, involving a departure from, an addition to, or a deletion from your disclosure as filed, your examiner will conclude that your claimed subject matter is not described in your application.

Sometimes an amendment to your specification can indirectly affect your claim, even though your amendment is not directly to the claim, thereby triggering a written description rejection. This could happen, for example, when you change the definition of a term in your specification, thereby affecting the old definition of the term that was used in your claim.

✪ *Original Claims.* Sometimes your original claims as filed in your original application may be rejected on the basis that persons skilled in the art would not recognize in your disclosure a description of your invention as defined in your original claims. This is somewhat less common than when you file new or amended claims, because the claims that you file in your original application are part of your disclosure. There is a also presumption that if a claim was in your patent application as filed, then the invention covered by that claim is within the *written description* provided in the application as filed. (*In re Anderson,* 471 F.2d 1237 (C.C.P.A. 1973).)

The rule that your original claims are part of your original disclosure means that if your examiner rejects any of your claims on the basis that there is no support for the claim in your written description, you should always look to see whether the written support that you need can be found in any of your original claims. If you can find the subject matter that you need in your original claims, you should be able to amend your application to include this subject matter in your written description. This is because your original claims are part of your original disclosure.

✪   *Entitlement to an Earlier Priority Date.* Written description problems can also arise when you make a claim of priority to an earlier application that you filed. This can happen when you make a claim of priority under 35 U.S.C. §120 to the filing date of an earlier filed U.S. application, to the filing date of a provisional application under 35 U.S.C. §119(e), or to the filing date of a foreign application under 35 U.S.C. §119(a). To be entitled to such an earlier priority date, your claims must be supported by the description of the invention in such earlier filed application.

✪   *Interference.* As stated before, interference practice is beyond the scope of this book. The issue is whether your specification provides support for a claim corresponding to a count in the Interference.

The following cases are also common fact patterns in which a lack of written description has been found to exist:

✪   An element that you described in your disclosure as essential or critical to your invention does not appear in your claim.

Example:

Anne's written description in her originally filed application described the location of a claim element, "the control means," as the only possible location for such control means. Anne would not be able to claim her invention with the control means in a different location. (*Gentry Gallery v. Berkline Corp.*, 134 F.3d 1473 (Fed. Cir. 1998).)

NOTE: *A claim that omits matter disclosed to be essential to the invention as described in the specification may also be subject to a rejection under the enablement requirement discussed below.*

✪   You claim a genus but do not describe enough representative species of that genus. You can think of a *genus* as a large circle and a species as a small circle within that genus. In general, a genus includes no more material elements than those that are included in the species that make up the genus.

Example:

In a chemical invention, you might obtain a specific material. You could then broaden this isolated concept to extend it as far as you envision that other materials will have the same utility and can be similarly made. The broadened concept would become the genus in a patent application. You would then fill in the genus with representative samples of compounds or substances that fall within the genus.

Overcoming Rejections Based on Written Description

Your examiner has the initial burden of presenting a preponderance of evidence why a person skilled in your art would not recognize in your disclosure a description of the invention defined by your claims.

To overcome a rejection after your examiner has met his or her initial burden, you must either point out where and how your originally filed written description supports the changes made to your claims or else make an amendment to your rejected claims so as to eliminate the material that the PTO finds objectionable. Some possible arguments you can make are included below.

- ✪ The *written description* requirement must be applied in the context of the particular invention and the state of the knowledge. What you are trying to argue with this point is that the state of your particular art is already sufficiently developed enough so that you have written support for your invention. For example, where prior art already discloses nulcleotide sequences of component DNA claimed in an invention, an examiner's rejection of a claimed invention on the sole basis that nucleotide sequences are not disclosed in the application is incorrect. (See *Capon v. Eshhar.*)

- ✪ Examples are not required. If your examiner rejects your application for lack of written description based on lack of examples, you can point out that a claim cannot be invalidated on Section 112 grounds simply because the embodiments of the specification do not contain examples explicitly covering the full scope of the claim language. This is because the patent specification is written for a person of skill in the art, and such a person comes to the patent with the knowledge of what has come before. Thus, it is unnecessary to spell out every detail of the invention; only enough must be included to convince a person of skill in the art that the inventor possessed the invention. (See *Falko-Guner v. Inglis.*)

✪ Actual Reduction to Practice is not required. If your examiner states that you failed the written description requirement because you have not made your invention (*actual reduction to practice*), you can point out that actual reduction is not required for a written description. (See *Falko-Guner v. Inglis.*)

✪ Recitation of known structure is not per se required. In inventions claiming macromolecular sequences where a lack of written description requirement frequently arises, many cases have stated that the specification must recite the gene or sequence. For example, a famous case—*Regents v. Lilly*—required a sequence for cDNA for human insulin where that sequence had never been characterized before. However, these cases do not set down a per se rule for disclosure of nucleotide sequences where one is claiming such sequences.

Enablement

If you see either of the following two paragraphs in your office action, your claims have been rejected for lack of enablement. The first paragraph will be used by your examiner when it is your examiner's position that nothing within the scope of your claims is enabled. The second paragraph form will be used when it is your examiner's position that something within the scope of your claims is enabled, but your claims are not limited in scope to what is enabled. (See Chapter 3 for additional information on enablement.)

> *Claim [ ] rejected under U.S.C., Title 35, §112, first paragraph, as containing subject matter that was not described in the specification in such a way as to enable one skilled in the art to which its pertains, or with which it is most nearly connected, to make and/or use the invention.*

or

Claims (PTO inserts one or more of your claims) rejected under U.S.C., Title 35, §112, first paragraph, because the specification, while being enabling for (PTO inserts claimed subject matter for which your specification is enabling), does not reasonably provide enablement for (PTO inserts your claims). The specification does not enable any person skilled in the art to which it pertains, or with which it is most nearly connected, to make and use the invention commensurate in scope with these claims.

As was pointed out in earlier chapters, enablement is a problem that occurs more often in unpredictable arts such as biology and chemistry rather than in mechanical or electrical inventions. This is because biological and chemical inventions often involve myriad factors that can not be predicted.

Example:

Inventor A's specification disclosed making a certain type of vector replicable in *Saccharomyces cerivisae*. However, A's claim used the broad term "yeast." The Patent Office rejected this claim for lack of enablement because the term "yeast" includes a number of diverse fungi that are quite different—morphologically and biochemically— from *Saccharomyces cerivisae*. Given the highly unpredictable factors, including the unique, delicate, and unpredictable biochemical and genetic actions involved, this rejection would probably be proper given A's limited disclosure that did not provide details for preparing vectors in yeast.

Lack of Essential Features

Your examiner may also reject any of your claims in which any feature considered critical or essential to the practice of your claim invention is missing from your claims. The rejection will appear as follows:

Claim [ ] rejected under U.S.C., Title 35, §112, first paragraph, as based on a disclosure that is not enabling. [Recited subject matter omitted from your claims] critical or essential to the practice of the invention, but not included in the claim(s) is not enabled by the disclosure.

Such essentiality will be determined by looking at your specification and looking to see if you have recited any feature as being critical to the practice of your claims. Again, you must be very careful about emphasizing the criticality of any feature of your invention.

Example:

When the only mode of operation of a process disclosed by Joe in the specification involved the use of a cooling zone at a particular location in the processing cycle, the examiner made a proper rejection of Joe's claims because he failed to specify either a cooling step or the location of the step in the process. (In re Mayhew, 527 F.2d 1229 (C.C.P.A. 1976).)

Depositing Biological Materials

MPEP §2402, paragraph 1 states that:

> *where the invention involves a biological material and words alone cannot sufficiently describe how to make and use the invention in a reproducible manner, access to the biological material may be necessary for the satisfaction of the requirement for patentability under U.S.C., Title 35, §112.*

A deposit of biological material is necessary when the material is essential for the practice of the invention, and:

- the material is not known and readily available to the public; or,

- when the material cannot be made or isolated without undue experimentation.

If an application as filed includes sequence information and references a deposit of the sequenced material made in accordance with the requirements of 37 C.F.R., beginning with Section 1.801, corrections of minor errors in the sequence may be possible based on the argument that one of skill in the art would have resequenced the deposited material and would have immediately recognized the minor error.

It may also be useful to deposit essential biological materials if the material is only referred to in a publication, but is not commercially available. MPEP §2404.01 states that:

> *those applicants that rely on evidence of accessibility other than a deposit take the risk that the patent may no longer be enforceable if the biological material necessary to satisfy the requirements of U.S.C., Title 35, §112 ceases to be accessible.*

If, at some point during the patent term, the material becomes unavailable and cannot be obtained without undue experimentation, the patent would become unenforceable.

You must also make reference to your biological deposit in your specification by indicating:

- ✪ the name and address of the depository institution with which the deposit was made;

- ✪ the date of deposit of the biological material with that institution;

- ✪ the accession number given to the deposit by that institution; and,

- ✪ to the extent possible, a taxonomic description of the biological material.

Computer Programs

While no specific universally applicable rule exists for recognizing an insufficiently disclosed application involving computer programs, the failure to include either the computer program itself or a reasonably detailed flowchart that delineates the sequence of operations the program must perform are subject to challenge by your examiner.

Moreover, as the complexity of functions and the generality of the individual components of a flowchart increase, the basis for challenging the sufficiency of such a flowchart becomes more reasonable because the likelihood of more than routine experimentation being required to generate a working program from such a flowchart also increase. (MPEP §2106.02.)

Overcoming Enablement Rejections

Once your examiner has advanced a reasonable basis to question the adequacy of your disclosure, you must show that your specification would enable one of ordinary skill in the art to make and use your claimed invention without resorting to undue experimentation. This will involve making arguments as to why your specification is enabling based on what has been previously said about enablement. You may also want to reference prior art patents or technical publications and explain how these materials show that your specification is enabling.

You should also consider submitting a *factual affidavit/declaration* under 37 C.F.R. §1.132 to show what one skilled in the art knew at the time your filed your application. (See Chapter 13 for a discussion of these affidavits.) Your §1.132 affidavit will be more convincing if it is made by someone other than yourself. It should be made by a person who has a skill level and qualifications that are routine in your art. If the level of skill is too high, your examiner may challenge the affidavit, since it would not help in determining the amount of experimentation required by a routineer in the art to implement your invention.

Your affiant should submit as many facts as possible and show how these facts support the argument that your invention is enabling. Concentrate on the factors discussed and see what evidence you can include to argue those factors in your favor. Mere conclusions by your affiant or declarant will not be persuasive.

The state of the art existing at the filing date of your application is used to determine whether a particular disclosure is enabling as of your filing date. Therefore, publications dated after your filing date providing information publicly first disclosed after your filing date generally cannot be used to show what was known at the time you filed your application. (MPEP §2164.05(a).)

Although a later dated publication cannot supplement an insufficient disclosure in a prior dated application to make it enabling, you can offer the testimony of an expert based on the publication as evidence of the level of skill in the art at the time you filed your application. (*Gould v. Quigg,* 822 F.2d 1074 (Fed. Cir. 1987).)

Although you must demonstrate that your disclosure, as filed, would have enabled your claimed invention for one skilled in the art at the time of filing, this does not preclude you from providing a declaration after your filing date that demonstrates your claimed invention works. (MPEP §2164.05(a).)

Best Mode   Rejections based on the *best mode requirement* are rare in the prosecution of your application. This is because the information that is necessary to form the basis for a rejection is rarely accessible to your examiner, but is generally uncovered during discovery procedures in litigation. The rejection will be stated as follows:

> *Claim [ ] rejected under U.S.C., Title 35, §112, first paragraph, because the best mode contemplated by the inventor has not been disclosed. Evidence of concealment of the best mode is based upon [ ].*

One case in which this rejection could arise is when the quality of your disclosure is so poor as to effectively result in concealment.

UTILITY REJECTIONS UNDER UNITED STATES CODE, TITLE 35, SECTION 101

If you have made no explicit mention in your specification of how your invention might have some practical application and none can be inferred from the nature of your invention, then a rejection based on lack of *utility* is likely. (35 U.S.C. §101.)

A rejection under 35 U.S.C. §101 for lack of utility will usually be accompanied by a rejection under 35 U.S.C. §112, first paragraph, for lack of enablement, since if a claimed invention lacks utility, the specification cannot enable one to use it. Thus, the how to use prong of Section 112 (enablement) incorporates as a matter of law the requirement of 35 U.S.C. §101 that the specification disclose as a matter of fact a practical utility for the invention (*Rasmusson v. Smithkline Beecham Corp.,* 2005).

Overcoming Rejections Based on Lack of Utility

You can overcome a rejection based on lack of utility in two main ways. First, you can argue that your invention has utility in your response. Under this option, you are arguing that the PTO is just plain wrong about their assertion that your invention lacks any practical value. The best way to argue this is to point out in your specification where you have stated some practical application of your invention, since you only need one such assertion to show utility. If you have made no mention of practicality, then you might argue that your invention has a well-established utility.

Your second option to overcome a utility rejection is to amend your application so that you state a practical application of your invention.

You can also submit an affidavit or declaration under 37 C.F.R. §1.132 to present new evidence that shows that your invention has utility. Your new evidence must be relevant to the issues raised in your rejection. For example, declarations in which conclusions are set forth without establishing a link between the conclusions and the supporting evidence, or that merely express opinions, may be of limited value in rebutting your examiner's case.

DOUBLE PATENTING REJECTIONS

Double patenting was discussed in Chapter 13 and prevents you from trying to extend patent protection on your invention by trying to file a second patent application for the same invention. A rejection on account of double patenting will read as follows:

> *Claim [your claim] rejected under U.S.C., Title 35, 101 as claiming the same invention as that of claim [relevant claim] of prior U.S. Patent No. [ ]. This is a double patenting rejection.*

Same Invention Type Rejection

Double patenting rejections seek to prevent any person from unjustly extending the patent term over a claimed invention by trying to patent the invention twice. There are two types of double patenting rejections. The first type (and the subject of this section) is called a *same invention* type double patenting rejection. Same invention type double patenting is also sometimes called *statutory double patenting* because it is based on 35 U.S.C. §101, which states that you may only obtain a patent for any new or useful invention. Basically, you have statutory double patenting if your claim is identical or nearly identical to the claim in your prior patent.

The test to determine whether a statutory basis for double patenting exists is whether the same invention is being claimed twice by either the same inventive entity or by an entity that has at least one common inventor or by an entity which has a common assignee. *Same invention* means identical subject matter.

Statutory double patenting rejections can be made in your application with respect to an issued patent or with respect to another pending patent application. In the case of double patenting rejections with two pending applications, your examiner will give provisional double patenting rejections in each of the applications.

Overcoming Statutory Rejections

You can overcome a statutory type double patenting by canceling the conflicting claims in all but one of your applications or by amending your conflicting claims in one application so that they are not the same as the other application. These are the only things that you can do to overcome a statutory double patenting rejection. You do not have the added convenience of simply filing a *terminal disclaimer,* which is something that you will shortly learn is an option for you in the case of an obvious-type double patenting rejection. (MPEP §804.02.)

Obvious-Type Rejection

The second type of double patenting rejection that you can receive will read as follows:

> *Claim [your claim] rejected under the judicially created doctrine of obvious-type double patenting as being unpatentable over claim [relevant claim] of U.S. Patent No. [ ]. Although the conflicting claims are not identical, they are not patently distinct from each other because [reasons].*

Obvious-type double patenting is a judicially created doctrine based on the rationale that the public should be able to freely use not only the invention claimed in a patent after the expiration of its term but also on modifications that would have been obvious to those of ordinary skill in the art at the time the invention was made.

The purpose of the rule against double patenting is to prevent an inventor from effectively extending the term of exclusivity by the subsequent patenting of variations that are not patently distinct from the first patented invention.

> ### *Author's Note: Obviousness-Type double patenting*
> As with an obviousness analysis, obviousness-type double patenting requires an inquiry as to whether the claimed invention in the application for the second patent would have been obvious from the subject matter of the claims in the first patent, in light of the prior art. The inquiries differ, however, in terms of what is being analyzed. Double patenting is entirely dependent on what is claimed in an issued patent, while obviousness relates to what is disclosed—whether or not claimed—in a prior art reference—whether or not a patent. A case of obviousness-type double patenting is analogous to the nonobviousness requirement of 35 U.S.C. §103, except that the patent principally underlying the double patenting rejection is not considered prior art. (*In re Braithwaite,* 379 F.2d 594, 154 USPQ 29 (CCPA 197).) Accordingly, the analysis employed in determining whether obviousness-type double patenting exists parallels the guidelines for analysis of a 35 U.S.C. §103 obviousness determination. (*In re Braat,* 937 F2d 539, 19 USPQ2d 1289 (Fed. Cir. 1991).)

There are technically two tests that you can apply to know if obviousness-type double patenting exists. These two tests are called *one-way determination of obviousness* or *two-way determination of obviousness.* Under the one-way test, the question is whether the claims of the later issued patent are obvious over the claims of the earlier issued patent. Under the two-way test, the question is whether the earlier issued patent claims are obvious over the later issued patent claims. Therefore, the two-way test favors the patentee to the extent that some claims may be allowed that would have been rejected under the one-way test.

You apply the one-way test if your application has the same or a later effective filing date than the effective filing date of your earlier issued patent. The relevant inquiry using this one-way test is whether the invention defined in a claim in your application is an obvious variation of the invention defined in a claim in the earlier patent. (*In re Berg,* 140 F.3d 1428 (Fed. Cir. 1998).) If your claimed invention in your application is obvious over a claimed invention in your earlier patent, then an obviousness-type double patenting situation exists.

The two-way test is a narrow exception to the general rule of the one-way test. You apply the two-way test only if your earlier granted patent bears a later effective filing date than your application. The test arose out of the concern to prevent rejections for obviousness-type double patenting when the applicants filed first for a basic invention and later for an improvement, but through no fault of the applicants, the PTO decided the applications in reverse order of filing, rejecting the basic application although it would have been allowed if the application had been decided in the order of their filing. In such a case, you must ask two questions to determine whether double patenting exists. First, you must ask whether the invention defined in a claim in your application is an obvious variation of the invention defined in a claim of your earlier granted patent. Second, you must ask whether the invention defined in a claim in the earlier granted patent is an obvious variation of the invention defined in a claim in your application. (MPEP §804.)

Overcoming Obvious-Type Rejection

There are three ways to overcome a double patenting rejection made against your pending application. The first way is to amend your pending application claims to patently distinguish those claims from the earlier patent claims. The second thing that you can do is to argue that your pending application claims are already patently distinguishable from the earlier patent claims.

The third and easiest way to overcome an obvious-type double patenting rejection is to file a *terminal disclaimer*. A terminal disclaimer is a statement in which you give up that portion of time on a patent to issue so that it will end at the same time as the patent being used as the reference for double patenting. The terminal disclaimer must cover all of your claims in your application.

A terminal disclaimer provision under 37 C.F.R. §1.321 must include the following provision:

any patent granted on that application shall be enforceable only for and during such period that said patent is commonly owned with the application or patent which formed the basis for the rejection.

The PTO website has two terminal disclaimer forms at its website—PTO/SB/25 and PTO/SB/26—depending on whether the rejection concerns a pending application or issued patent. A terminal disclaimer can be filed electronically using EFS-Web. When paying for terminal disclaimers, the correct fee code is "1814" under "Statutory Disclaimer" located in the post issuance and post allowance section of the "calculate fees" page in EFS-Web.

> **Author's Note: Do not let the examiner mistakenly issue you a double patenting rejection.**
> It is not appropriate for your examiner to issue a double patenting rejection against a divisional application that you later filed on an invention that your examiner required you to take out of your original filed patent application due to a restriction requirement. If you are up against such a double patenting requirement in your divisional application, you should point out to your examiner that 35 U.S.C. §121 prohibits this. This rule means that applicants should present claims in a patent application drawn to all aspects of the invention as to which divisional applications may later be desired, so that a formal restriction requirement is entered as to them.

ABANDONMENT OF YOUR APPLICATION

Abandonment is not something that you like to see happen during the course of your prosecution. Abandonment means essentially that your application has died and the PTO has taken it out of the examination process. Abandonment is not a rejection of your application for some statutory reason. However, it is included in this chapter under other types of rejections because, as with a statutory rejection, you will need to take action to deal with a Notice of Abandonment if you want a patent. The Notice of Abandonment will state as follows:

The application is abandoned in view of applicant's failure to submit a response to the office action mailed on [date] within the required period for response.

There are many reasons that you may get an abandonment notice. The most common reason, of course, is that you have failed to respond to an office action within the statutory six-month requirement. Recall that you are allowed to take extensions of time to respond to an office action, but the cut-off date is six months from the mailing date of the action. After that time, your application will go abandoned, and the PTO will notify you of this in a Notice of Abandonment.

Overcoming a Notice of Abandonment

You have several options to overcome a Notice of Abandonment of your application. If you think the PTO is wrong in its holding of abandonment, you can file a petition under 37 C.F.R. §1.181(a) to withdraw the holding of abandonment. This may occur when you disagree as to the dates used by your examiner in determining that your application became abandoned. There is no fee for this petition, but you must file it within two months from the mail date of your Notice of Abandonment. If your petition is granted, your application is considered to never have been abandoned. (MPEP §711.03(c).)

A second option that you have at your disposal is to simply file a new patent application. Such an application is referred to as a *substitute application* because it is not filed while your prior application is still alive. Thus, it is not co-pending, as with a continuation. The problem with filing a substitute application is that you lose the effective filing date of your earlier filed application, which could cause difficulties with any prior art.

A third option, and more ordinary course of action to overcome a Notice of Abandonment, is to file a petition to revive your application along with the appropriate fee.

Reviving an Abandoned Application

There are two ways to revive an abandoned application. The first way is on the basis that your delay was unavoidable. *Unavoidable* means that something occurred beyond your control. This is a less common way to revive your abandoned application because it requires you to do more.

The second way to revive your abandoned patent application is on the basis that your delay was *unintentional*. This is the more usual way that one goes about reviving an abandoned patent application. It is easier to do than on the basis that your delay was unavoidable. However, it does cost more.

Whether you choose to revive based on unavoidable or unintentional delay, you must include a petition and a petition fee. This is set forth in 37 C.F.R. §1.17(l) if you are claiming unavoidable delay or in 37 C.F.R. §1.137(b) if you are claiming unintentional delay.

NOTE: You should complete form PTO/SB/61, along with the required accompanying evidence listed on that form as your petition for revival of an application abandoned unavoidably under 37 C.F.R. §1.137(a). Use form PTO/SB/64 as your petition for revival of an application for a patent abandoned unintentionally under 37 C.F.R. §1.137(b). Both of these forms can be found in the forms section under "patent" at Patent Office website. You should include a cover letter entitled "Petition to Revive" with your petition.

A petition for revival of an application abandoned unavoidably requires the submission of the following three items:

1. the required reply you should have submitted on time but failed to;

2. the proper petition fee as set forth in 37 C.F.R. §1.17(i); and,

3. a showing that the entire delay in filing your required reply from the due date of the reply until the filing of your petition was unavoidable.

Delay resulting from things like lack of knowledge of the patent statute or the MPEP, however, cannot serve as a basis for unavoidable delay. (MPEP §711.03(c).) You will need to show not only that the delay that resulted in abandonment of your application was unavoidable, but also unavoidable delay from the time you were notified of abandonment to the time you file your petition to revive. Thus, if you failed to file your petition promptly after the PTO notified you that your application was abandoned or after otherwise becoming aware of the abandonment, you will not meet the unavoidable standard.

For the required accompanying evidence to a petition based on unavoidable delay, you should include:

1. evidence concerning the procedures in place that should have avoided the error resulting in the delay;

2. evidence concerning the training and experience of the person responsible for the error; and,

3. copies of any applicable docketing records to show that the error was in fact the cause of the delay.

The requirements pertaining to evidence needed to convince the PTO to revive your application based on unavoidable delay are quite stringent. As a result, most people will choose the unintentional delay petition, which does not require this additional evidence, despite its higher petition fee.

Obtaining a revival of your application based on unintentional delay is much easier than based on unavoidable delay. Filing your petition is also easier. If your petition for revival is based on unintentional delay, you need only state that your delay was unintentional. You should include the statement that:

❂ The required reply you should have submitted on time but failed to was unavoidable abandonment;

❂ the proper petition fee set forth in 37 C.F.R. §1.17(m);

❂ a statement that "the entire delay in filing the required reply from the due date for the reply until the filing of a grantable petition pursuant to C.F.R., Title 37, §1.137(b) was unintentional"; and,

✪   any required terminal disclaimer (which is only a concern for applications filed on or before May 29, 2000.

You may have noticed that a petition for unintentional abandonment is much less burdensome than a petition for unavoidable abandonment. This is because for unintentional abandonment, you do not need to submit evidence explaining your delay; the statement included on your petition that the delay was unintentional is sufficient.

The PTO does not generally question whether your delay is unintentional so long as you file your petition within three months of the date you are first notified that your application is abandoned. It also should be filed within one year of the date of abandonment of your application. So it is to your advantage to file your petition as soon as possible after your Notice of Abandonment.

If you file your petition to revive more than three months from the date of your Notice of Abandonment, you should include a showing as to how such delay was unintentional. If your petition is not filed within one year of the date of abandonment of your application, you will also need to submit information as to when you first became aware of the abandonment of your application and a showing as to how the delay in discovering the abandoned status of the application occurred despite the exercise of due care or diligence on your part. If you do not file within a year after abandonment, you should include evidence as to when you first became aware of abandonment and how the delay in discovering the abandonment occurred despite the exercise of due care on your part.

You must also include a complete and proper reply to the outstanding office action that you failed to respond to resulting in the abandonment of your application. This reply is usually in the form of an amendment. However, your reply can also be satisfied by filing a continuation or *Request for Continued Examination.*

If you are unhappy with a decision of the PTO to revive your application, you should make a request for reconsideration within twelve months from the date of the decision.

You should mail your petition to the following address:

Mail Stop Petition
P.O. Box 1450
Alexandria, VA 22313

For more information on revival of an abandoned application see MPEP at §711.03(c).

SECTION IV

AFTER YOUR PATENT ISSUES

Maintaining and Correcting Your New Patent

A U.S. patent gives you the right to exclude others from making, using, selling, or offering for sale, or importing within the United States, its territories, and possessions that which is covered by the claims of your patent. Section 271(g) of U.S.C., Title 35 also provides that a product imported into the United States will infringe a process patent for making the product if the patented process was implemented abroad. For a product to have been made by a process patented in the United States, it must be a physical article that was manufactured.

If you stop to think about it, the right to exclude can be a considerable right. Not everyone in the marketplace has the right to stop others from selling their product. But with a patent, this is possible. This chapter discusses how to maintain your new patent and keep it in top shape.

LABELING YOUR PRODUCTS

If you manufacture any products covered by your patent, you should label such products with the word "Patent" or the abbreviation "Pat" with the number of your patent. If you cannot directly label your product because of the character of your product, then you should label the packaging of your product the same way.

The reason that such labeling is so important is because 35 U.S.C. §287 specifically says that you can only recover damages from the time that you give an infringer notice of infringement if your goods are not labeled. This sets up the following scenario: You fail to label goods covered by your patent claims. Several years later, you discover that Infringer X is selling your product. Since you have not labeled your product, you have forgone any chance to obtain damages from Infringer X until you now actually give notice to Infringer X about the infringement. You have forgone the chance to collect damages for several years. This could all have been avoided if you had simply labeled your goods.

> ### Author's Note: Mark all components.
> If you sell a component that is not specifically covered by your patent claims but which is used in combination with other components to form a device that is covered by your patent, you should similarly mark such component. In this case, you can say For Use Under U.S. Pat. No.__. You should not specifically state that such component is covered by your patent when it is not because 35 U.S.C. §292 prohibits the marking of a product with a patent number when it is actually not patented.

CORRECTING MINOR MISTAKES

If there is a minor mistake in your issued patent due to a mistake on your part that occurred in good faith, you may obtain a *Certificate of Correction* to correct the mistake. Minor mistakes include any type of change that would not materially affect the scope and meaning of your patent.

Mistakes of a clerical or typographical nature are clear candidates for *Certificate of Corrections*. For example, you may notice after you have received your patent that you misspelled certain words or incorrectly cited a reference in your patent. You can use a *Certificate of Correction* to correct such errors.

You should submit the text of your correction on form PTO-1050 provided by the PTO. This form can be obtained online at www.uspto.gov. In the body of form PTO-1050, you will need to specifically identify where in your patent your error appears and how you want your patent to now read.

Example:

You reference on page 6, line 15 of your patent an article, but incorrectly cite the location of the journal at page 5 instead of page 10. You could make the change in your Certificate of Correction as follows:

Please replace the number "5" on page 6, line 15, with the number–10–.

You must include the appropriate fee with your *Certificate of Correction*. Go to the PTO website (www.uspto.gov) to check for the most recent fee. Fees change regularly at the PTO.

Any time that you send something to the PTO, it is also a good idea to include a cover letter telling the PTO exactly what you are submitting. A sample cover letter form is included in Appendix G.

It is also a good idea to include a postcard that lists what you are submitting. If you stamp the postcard and include it with your submission, the PTO will send it back to you. This will let you know that the PTO has received your *Certificate of Correction*.

On the front of the postcard, print your name and address, and place a stamp on it. On the back of your postcard, list each document that you are including in your package to the PTO. The back of your postcard can be organized as follows:

Patent No.: [Insert Patent Number]	The following papers have been received:
Filed: [Insert the Patent Application Date]	(1) Cover Letter
	(2) Form PTO/SB/44
Title: [Insert Title]	(3) Postcard

Mistakes on the Part of the PTO

Certificates of Correction are also available for mistakes in your patent due to the fault of the PTO. The procedure to correct such mistakes is the same as for mistakes due to your errors. The only difference is that no fee is required to obtain such a certificate.

INCORRECT INVENTORSHIP LISTED IN A PATENT

Under 35 U.S.C. §256, a Certificate of Correction can also be issued by the PTO that deletes an incorrectly named inventor or adds an inventor who should have been named as an inventor, so long as the error was not made with deceptive intent of the person being deleted or added.

> **Author's Note: 35 U.S.C. §256**
>
> Under a special statute, 35 U.S.C. §256, a court before which the matter of incorrect inventorship is called into question may order correction of the patent on notice and hearing of all parties concerned, and the director must issue a certificate accordingly.

Where to Send Your Certificate of Correction

Requests for Certificates of Correction should be addressed to the attention of the following address:

> Certificate of Correction Branch
> Commissioner for Patents
> P.O. Box 1450
> Washington, DC 20231

You can send this form by regular first-class mail.

For more information on Certificate of Correction, see MPEP §1480 and §1481. This manual is available online at the PTO website by clicking on "Site Index" at the top of the home page and then clicking "M," where you can then select the MPEP.

MAINTENANCE FEES

If you have obtained a patent, you know that obtaining one is not an inexpensive proposition. There are fees for just about anything that you submit to the PTO.

Unfortunately, the PTO gets you again for fees after you have obtained a patent. But this time the only thing that you need to submit to the PTO is the fee itself. Fees that the PTO gets are called *maintenance fees,* and you absolutely must submit these fees if you want your patent to remain in force.

You only need to make three fee payments during the lifetime of your patent. Small entities also get one-half off the regular price for maintenance fees. Despite this, maintenance fees can be considerable for the individual inventor. The cost and time frame for a small entity, at the time this book was written, is $465 at your first three-and-a-half-year interval, another $1,180 at your seven-and-a-half-year interval, and $1,955 at your eleven-and-a-half-year interval.

Maintenance fees are not required for plant or design patents.

When to Submit Your Maintenance Fee

You should pay your maintenance fees within a six-month time period prior to the last day of the intervals. If you submit your maintenance fee during this six-month period, your fee will be considered timely and you will incur no extra charge. Do not try to pay your fee early, because the PTO simply will not accept fees prior to the six-month period.

The intervals that start your six-month time period to timely submit your maintenance fee follows:

- ✪ 1st Maintenance Fee: 3 years

- ✪ 2nd Maintenance Fee: 7 years

- ✪ 3rd Maintenance Fee: 11 years

You can still pay your maintenance fee six months after each of the specified time intervals so long as you do not take more than six months to do so. Therefore, the late payment intervals are as follows:

- ✪ 1st Maintenance Fee: 3.5 years

- ✪ 2nd Maintenance Fee: 7.5 years

- ✪ 3rd Maintenance Fee: 11.5 years

Any maintenance fee paid during this additional six-month period will be considered late and you will need to submit a surcharge fee to the PTO. This means that your absolute cut-off date for paying your maintenance fees will be four, eight, and twelve years after your patent is issued. If you miss any one of these absolute cut-off dates (four years, eight years, and twelve years, respectively), then your patent will automatically expire. The PTO will send you a Notice of Patent Expiration. This is something that you obviously do not like to see unless of course you want your patent to go out of force.

If the last day due for paying your maintenance fee falls on a Saturday, Sunday, or federal holiday, you are given the next succeeding business day to pay the fee.

Example:

Your first maintenance fee is due June 1, 2007, (three-and-a-half years after your patent issues). The six-month grace period that you can pay your fee late with a surcharge happens to fall on December 1, 2007, which is a Saturday so that your payment of the fee with the surcharge on Monday, December 3, 2007, is proper. However, if you wait until Tuesday to pay your fee, you are too late; your patent will have expired as of December 1, 2007.

Submitting Payment

The easiest way to pay your maintenance fee is by going to the PTO website at www.uspto.gov and paying it electronically. At the PTO main site, hit the "Patents" icon, then hit the "Fees," then the "Online Fee Payment" icon. Now select the "Pay/Look Up Patent Maintenance Fees." You will then need to enter your application and patent number.

If you do not want to pay electronically, you will need to send your payment in by mail. Use a *Maintenance Fee Transmittal Form* PTO/SB/45 along with your patent. You can get this form from the forms section of the PTO website. Send the form to the following address:

United States Patent and Trademark Office
P.O. Box 371611
Pittsburgh, PA 15250–1611

Missing a Maintenance Fee Cut-Off Date

If you make a mistake and neglect to pay your maintenance fee, you may not be out of luck. The PTO may accept payment of the fee even after your patent expires if upon petition you show that your delay was either unavoidable or unintentional.

There are three time periods for late payment of maintenance fees (See 35 USC §41(c)):

1. within six months of due date, late payment always allowed;

2. within thirty months of due date, late payment allowed only if your delay was unintentional; and,

3. any time after this, late payment allowed if delay was unavoidable.

The petition based upon unavoidable delay will cost you less than a petition based on unintentional delay. However, to get an unavoidable petition granted, you will need to provide facts in your petition that you took steps to pay the fee but were unable due to circumstances beyond your control. Provide these facts in a *Declaration,* which you should submit behind your petition. A sample *Declaration* form that you can use is included in Appendix G.

You do not need to provide a *Declaration* with a petition based on unintentional delay, which makes these types of petition easier to get granted.

You can find forms for your petition to accept unavoidably or unintentionally delayed payment of maintenance fees in an expired patent on the PTO website (www.uspto.gov) by going to "Patents" and then "Forms."

REISSUE OF YOUR PATENT

If the correction that you want to make to your patent cannot be corrected through a *Certificate of Correction,* then your only other alternative to make changes to your patent is through a *reissue* of your patent. A common situation in which you might want to correct your patent through a reissue is if a competitor is not literally infringing on one of your patent claims, but his or her action is still causing you damage. To solve this problem, you can change your patent claims so that what your competitor is doing literally comes within the scope of protection afforded by your patent claims. If you are successful in this very sophisticated strategy, you will be able to obtain a reissue of your patent with your new amended claims.

Example:

In your claim of your patent you use the word "and" between two features of your claimed invention. You later discover that your competitor is selling a product that contains just one of your features so that the product does not infringe your claim because it does not include both features. You seek and obtain a reissue of your patent substituting the word "and" for "or," so that your claim will now cover the activity of your competitor.

Trying to enlarge coverage of your claims is not the only possible strategic use of reissue of a patent. On the reverse side, you might even be interested in narrowing the scope of your claims. This could happen, for example, when you discover prior art and determine your claims are too broad and invalid. You might seek a reissue to narrow your claims in such a case.

When You Can Seek a Reissue

If all you want to do is make changes to your patent that do not enlarge the scope of your claims, then you can seek a reissue of your patent at any time. As pointed out, however, the common purpose of a reissue will be to strengthen your claims. To strengthen your claims you will usually want to make changes that enlarge their scope in order to afford broader patent coverage.

When it comes to enlarging the scope of your patent claims, you must apply for your reissue patent within two years from the issue date of your patent. The PTO will not allow you to try to enlarge the scope of your claims beyond that two-year mark.

> ### Author's Note: What constitutes broadening of claims?
> According to a U.S. Court of Appeals for the Federal Circuit Court case, a reissue (or reexamination, which will be discussed later in the book) is *broadening* if it could be infringed by something that would not have infringed any claim of the original patent. A claim is broadening if broader in any aspect, even if narrower in other aspects. (*Tillotson, Ltd. V. Walbro Corp.*, 831 F.2d 1033, 1037, 4 USPQ2d 1450, 1453 (Fed. Cir. 1987).) The PTO seems to take even a broader view and has held that claims are *broadening* if they recite a statutory class (ie., "process, machine, manufacture, or composition of matter") that was not recited in the original patent, even if the new claims include all the limitations of the original claims. (*Ex parte Logan*, 38 USPQ2d 1852 (Bd. Pat. App. & Inter. 1994).)

This rule makes some sense if you think about it. At some point in time, the scope of patent protection afforded to you by your patent should become etched in stone so that your competitors can rely upon your claims for what they can and cannot do without worrying about a patent lawsuit for infringement. This time period is set by law at two years. Within that two-year period, the law will give some leeway for things that you did not anticipate when you originally drafted your claims. After this point, however, you will not be allowed to enlarge the scope of that patent.

> ### Author's Note: If your patent has not issued, file a continuing application.
> If your patent application has not yet issued, then you should make your changes in one of the various forms of continuing applications that you can file. A continuing application is something that you can file before your current patent

application is a patent. If your patent application has not yet issued and you want to enlarge the scope of your patent claims, you will find filing a continuing patent application the easier and less expensive way to go to make changes to your claims.

Reissue Limits   A very important limiting point about seeking a reissue patent is that you are only allowed to make changes to your patent if those changes are *supported* by your originally filed patent application. Supported means that if you want to change a claim, then the change that you make had better be discussed somewhere in your patent application as you originally filed it. In other words, you could not delete a word from your claim like "handle" if your originally filed patent application makes it clear that a handle is a necessary part of your invention.

Example:

Harry's original disclosure in his patent application described his invention as having only scanning and indexing means in synchronism. In a reissue application, Harry omitted the in synchronism limitation, thereby permitting his claimed invention to have scanning and indexing means not in synchronism. The reissue claim is properly rejected since the new broadened claim (covering scanning and indexing means not in synchronism) is no longer supported by the original patent's disclosure.

A final thing that you should remember about a reissue application is that you cannot try to claim subject matter you deliberately gave up during *prosecution* of your original patent application. Prosecution means anything that you filed during the application phase of your patent in which you specifically told the PTO that your patent claim would not cover.

Example:

You claimed a table with legs, a top, and an enamel surface during the prosecution of your patent application. You file an amendment that adds the element of enamel surface to distinguish your invention from prior disclosed tables, which, like your invention, also have a top and legs. The PTO grants you a patent. You would not be able to try and broaden the scope of your patent claim coverage by eliminating this element of enamel surface and thereby try to sue competitors who made a table without the enamel surface, because you would have been deemed to have given up that broadened coverage by your amendment. By making that amendment, you will have been considered to have told the PTO, "I agree that, if you give me a patent based on a table having an enamel surface, I will give up the right to sue anyone later on for making tables that do not include that enamel surface."

Some Cautionary Words about Reissue Patents

Seeking a reissue patent can be a great strategy to use to strengthen the scope of coverage afforded by your patent. Many patent litigation infringement actions have been won on the basis that the patent holder was strategic enough in thinking to do just this. However, a few cautionary words about reissue patents are in order here before you jump with joy and decide to go out and try to enlarge the scope of your patent claims.

When you file a reissue, the claims of your original patent will be reexamined. In short, your entire patent will return to an application phase stage and will be reexamined again by a patent examiner at the Patent and Trademark Office.

What does this mean for you? It is possible that although you were lucky in getting your patent claims of your original patent allowed the first time, you may not be so lucky the second time around. In other words, there is a possibility that some or even all of your patent claims could be rejected the second time around. You could end up in such a situation with even more restricted patent claims than when you started or, worse yet, with no patent at all. So you need to recognize that there are some risks in this respect with seeking a reissue of your patent.

The second cautionary point here has to do with the *Festo* case. In short, a change made to your patent claims through the use of a reissue will, in almost all likelihood, be considered the exact same as if you had made an amendment (a change to your claims during the application process). What this can mean for you is that you will have probably given up any chance of relying on any equivalents to your amended term when it comes time for patent infringement.

But you probably should not worry about this second point too much. If you can make a change to a patent claim that enlarges its scope through a reissue, and this enlargement now covers the activity of your competitor, the literal patent protection you now have with your broadened patent is much better than if you go into court without the enlarged scope and try to rely upon the doctrine of equivalents. The only possible problem here is where your enlarged scope still does not literally cover the activity of your competitor. In that case, you will in all likelihood not be able to rely upon the doctrine of equivalents to capture the activity of your competitor because you have in essence made an amendment to your claim.

Now for a final point about reissue patents. You should be aware that anyone who engages in infringing activity (by making, using, selling, or offering to sell a product) that infringes the claims of your new reissue patent, but which does not infringe the scope of coverage of your original patent, has defense to patent infringement with respect to that time period up until your new reissue patent issues. This defense is referred to as *intervening rights* and is based on 35 U.S.C. §251 and §252.

This rule probably makes sense to you on the basis that someone should not be liable for damages for infringing activity until a patent is issued that actually covers that infringing activity. A reissue patent is not a measure to collect damages against a competitor who has legitimately been making a noninfringing product before you are able to obtain a reissue patent, which covers such activity. You will only be able to sue for damages based on the infringing activity that occurs after your reissue patent is issued.

Filing a Reissue Patent Application

An application for reissue must contain the same parts as your originally filed application and comply with all of the rules relating to the filing of a patent application.

In addition to everything you need to know about filing a patent application, there are some special rules that pertain to filing a reissue patent application. These special rules can be found at 37 C.F.R. §§1.171–1.179. Some examples of these special rules are the following:

- ✪ Your patent application should consist of an exact copy of your patent. Each page of your application should correspond exactly to each page of your patent. In other words, page one of your patent should appear as page one of your application. You are not allowed to combine more than one page of material of your patent onto more than one page of your application.

✪   You will need to show the changes you want to make. You can do this in one of two ways. You can either make the changes on the application that you are submitting or you can submit a separate paper filing, called an *amendment,* which shows these changes. In either case, you will need to show any deletions you want to make by bracketing the deleted material and show any additions by underlining the added material.

✪   You will need to provide an oath or declaration just as you did when you filed your original patent application. This declaration must also contain some special statements, which you can find listed in 37 C.F.R. §1.175. A form that you can use for your declaration is provided at the PTO website. Simply click on "Patents" at the home page and then "Forms," and look the form listed as "PTO/SB/51."

✪   You should include a special transmittal form with your reissue, which you can again find at the PTO site. Look for the form labeled "PTO/SB/50." You should also include a *Reissue Application Fee Determination Fee Record* (PTO/SB/56) with your application. Again, this form can be found on the PTO website.

Given the highly strategic and detailed claim drafting points that can be associated with the filing of a reissue patent, it is highly recommended that you consult a patent attorney in seeking a reissue patent.

After You File Your Reissue   Your reissue patent application will be examined in the same manner as your originally filed patent application. If you are successful, you will be issued a reissue patent having any brackets or underlining you have inserted.

Monitor Your Competitors

This chapter covers what has come to be known as *competitive intelligence*. Competitive intelligence is a batch of subjects and ideas. It really boils down to knowledge, which improves the chance that you will know what your competitors are doing. Knowing what your competitors are doing is essential to protecting your patent. Think of it this way—how are you going to protect your patent invention if you take a blind eye to what competitors are doing? To maximize the value of your intellectual property portfolio you need to be vigilant in identifying infringers. This chapter gives you the tools you can use to help you identify potential infringers. Patent protection is a self-policing right. No government agency will do this for you.

Competitive intelligence can be used for much more than determining potential infringers of your patent even though a great deal of time will be spent on this subject. It can also be very useful for you to discover potential licensees as you embark upon commercializing your invention, something that is discussed in Chapter 27. In the end, you will be in a better position to make more informed business decisions by utilizing the tools discussed in this chapter.

PEOPLE YOU SHOULD RELY ON

Different professionals will bring different insights into competitive intelligence. For example, the ideas of an attorney, invention promoter, and a private investigator will stress different techniques. This is natural because one's expertise in a particular field will influence the approach to any particular problem.

Professionals from all different backgrounds can be invaluable as you approach the very broad subject of competitive intelligence. You should not discount anyone in your company for assistance in approaching this problem. Everyone from the scientist or inventor to the salesperson can be helpful in your quest for competitive intelligence.

WHAT COMPETITIVE INTELLIGENCE UNCOVERS

Competitive intelligence can provide a whole range of information you can use to protect and strengthen your patent. The following are some of the types of information that you will gain through the use of competitive intelligence:

✪ *Patent Infringement.* You should be using competitive intelligence to help you uncover possible infringement of your patents as well as using the information to help you avoid infringement of the patents of others. This is a double-edged sword. You can use your competitive intelligence to uncover potential infringers so that you can take steps to make such infringers financially accountable for your patented technology. On the reverse side, you can use competitive intelligence to learn about the patents of others so that before you engage in expensive product development, you will have a good idea as to any obstacles that you might face from patent holders. For example, if you uncover through your competitive intelligence that a competitor already has patents covering products you want to develop, you would probably be wise to research your strategies with respect to such product development before you spend the time and money with the development. This is a *defensive* use of competitive intelligence.

Author's Note: Offensive and defensive uses with respect to patents

When people talk about offensive use of patents, they are usually talking about using a patent to block competitors from a particular market space or to generate licensing revenue. When they talk about defensive use of patents they usually mean that patents can be used to ensure your freedom to operate in a particular field. In particular, if someone comes after you alleging that you have infringed some patent, you may be able to use your own patents to allege that the party is also infringing your patent. This way you might be able to use your patent as a bargaining chip with the patent holder. You could, for example, offer the patent holder permission to use your patented technology in exchange for permission to use their patent. Offensive strategies in this book refer to what a patent holder should be doing to enforce patent rights against competitors. Defensive strategies refer to what you should be doing to reduce or eliminate your chances of being held a patent infringer.

✪ *Potential Licensees.* Competitive intelligence will help you uncover potential licensees for your patented technology. This will apply equally as well if you are searching for potential purchasers of your patents or with respect to consumers of products covered by your patents.

✪ *Be Proactive in Your Business Decisions.* Competitive intelligence will allow you to be proactive in your business strategies rather than reactive. You can use competitive intelligence to plan and make decisions rather than wait for things to happen. In other words, competitive intelligence allows you to take charge of your future. You can be revolutionary rather than evolutionary. For example, you might use competitive intelligence to help guide you in what areas that you want to conduct research and development based on such business objectives as where you think the market is headed.

✪ *Stop the Patents of Others.* Use of competitive intelligence will also assist you with stopping competitors from seeking patents that you believe they should not be allowed to obtain. This is a preemptive use that you can employ in a variety of ways. Two examples of such preemptive uses include the following:

- *Interference Context.* If you have early notice about a competitor who has filed for patent for an invention that you were in fact the first to invent, this knowledge should provide you time to start an interference with respect to that patent application so that you can stop your competitor's patent and obtain your own patent for the invention.

- *Foreign Opposition Context.* These days most companies do not just file patents on inventions in the United States. Increasingly, patents are filed globally. Most countries outside the United States have a period of time in which you can seek to oppose the patent grant of another so long as you act within that period of time. Competitive intelligence about what your competitors are doing abroad will help you in meeting this deadline.

Author's Note: European oppositions

You should be aware about what your competitors are doing in Europe since this has become a very large potential market for your patented technology. You can file an opposition to the grant of a European patent on various grounds such as lack of novelty and obviousness. Many of these grounds are very similar to the defenses to patent infringement covered in Chapter 17.

TOOLS FOR COMPETITIVE INTELLIGENCE

There are going to be many ways that you can gain competitive intelligence. This list is not meant to be exhaustive of such tools that you can employ. You may notice that many of the tools discussed here were also discussed with reference to conducting a patent search before writing your patent application. The reason for this is that both the patent search and now the monitoring of your competitors have the common goal of discovering information pertaining to your invention.

The good news is that most of the tools are absolutely free to you. So there is really no reason not to use them to give you a competitive edge.

Internet Searches

One of the best ways to gain competitive intelligence is right through the Internet. Just about every business has a website. You can do searches on some of the search engines to search for websites that relate to your technology. Once you find such websites, look into what that business is doing.

You can find various search engines listed in Appendix B. One highly recommended site, which tells you everything you want to know about the types of search engines, is called Search Engine Watch. It can be found at http://searchenginewatch.com. This site offers very good tutorials on how to perform good searches on the Internet.

The PTO Website

The PTO website is discussed in detail in Chapter 4. Go to the PTO site at (www.uspto.gov), hit the "Patents" icon, and then hit "Search existing patents and published applications." This will bring you up to a page that has "Issued Patents" on the left-hand side of the page and "Published Applications" on the right-hand side of the page. You are also given several types of searches that you can perform. For example, if you know a patent number, you can click the icon labeled "Patent Number Search" and bring up that patent using the number that you input.

One particularly useful type of search that you can select at this page is called the *advanced search*. This type of search requires a little more time to learn but the results can be much more fruitful. For example, if you know the name of your competitor, you could do a search for all patents that competitor owns as an assignee. To do this, you type the listed field code *AN* followed by a forward slash followed by the name of your competitor. There are other field codes listed on the page you can use to conduct your search. One such useful field code is *REF,* which will bring up all patents that reference the patent number you input. This type of forward searching is something that you could employ with your own patent. Simply bring your own patent up on the PTO website and click on the "REF" link. You will thereby obtain a listing of any patents (and hence possible competitors) who are citing your own patent as prior art.

Searching for published applications will give you an even earlier understanding of what your competitors may be up to since patent applications are typically published eighteen months after they are filed. This means that within eighteen months from the date that your competitor files a patent application, you will be able to retrieve that application from the PTO website.

In addition to patent searches, you can use the PTO site to search for owners of patents by searching through the assignment database. Assignments of patents are discussed in Chapter 28. One thing to remember when searching for assignments, however, is that any paper filed assignments will not show up in the database for about six months.

European Patent Office (EPO) Website

The *European Patent Office* (EPO) puts out a very good website at www.european-patentoffice.org. If you hit "Search engines and site index" at this page, you will find several databases. One of the databases you can choose is "esp@cenet—free patent searching," which will bring you to a page where you can search patents worldwide. There are also options for searching specific countries abroad.

The EPO site also offers a way to obtain documents that were field during the prosecution of a European patent application, much like with the PAIR system at the PTO. What you need to do is to visit the EPO's site at http://my.epoline.org/portal/public and then hit "File Inspection." All you will need now is the European patent application number that you want information on which you can type in the provided box. The nice thing about this site is that you can immediately display each document for printing without even having to order the document to be sent to you.

Patent Application Information Retrieval System

In an earlier chapter, the Patent Application Information Retrieval System (PAIR) was discussed. It can be used to access a lot of information about a patent and, in some cases, even patent applications. You can access the PAIR system by going to the *electronic business center* (EBC) page at the PTO website. This page can be found at www.uspto.gov/ebc.

There is a public and a private side to PAIR. The public side is something that everyone in the world can see about issued patents and published patent applications. The private side of PAIR is what only applicants and their attorneys can see about their own prepublished patent applications. What does this mean for you? Well, if you want to check PAIR for information about an application that you know a competitor has filed, you will need to wait until that application has been published before you can see the information by using PAIR. However, if you were the applicant who filed that application, you will be able to see this confidential information even before the application is published if you set yourself up for the private side of PAIR.

Author's Note: Accessing the prepublished patent applications of others

Under a few limited circumstances, you can request that the PTO provide you access to the prepublished patent application of others. Some of those situations include the following:

❂ *If a U.S. patent or published application incorporates by reference or makes a claim of priority back to an application you want to obtain, then you are allowed to obtain that desired application upon written request to the PTO and payment of a fee specified in 37 C.F.R. §1.19(b)(1).*

❂ *If an abandoned application is referred to in another U.S. patent or published patent application, you can gain access to that abandoned patent application. (See form PTO/SB/68.)*

❂ *Very limited special circumstances under 37 C.F.R. §1.14.*

One of the most useful things that you will be able to find out from PAIR is everything that occurred between the applicant for that patent and the PTO during the *prosecution* stage of the patent application. All of the documents that are filed relating to that patent application are accumulated together by the PTO into something called a *file wrapper*. By using PAIR, not only will you be able to see the dates and names of each document filed in the file wrapper, but you will be able to order that file wrapper so you can analyze any of those documents.

How does all of this help you? File wrappers can be very useful to understanding how to construe the meaning of patent claims. This, in turn, is essential to recognizing patent infringement. By seeing, for example, through the use of PAIR that a patent applicant filed an amendment, you will be able to order that amendment to see if you can uncover any useful information with respect to your infringement analysis.

To do all this, go to the EBC page at the PTO site (www.uspto.gov/ebc) and click on the "Patent Application Information Retrieval" icon on that page. You will now have three methods to search. You can enter:

1.   a patent application number;

2.   a patent number; or,

3.   a patent application publication number.

Try entering a patent number for a patent that you want to search. What you will find if you do this is a page with a lot of biographical information about the patent. In addition, you will see the entire file history contents for that patent.

Another useful icon on that same page is something called *continuity data*. If you click on this icon you will come to a page that will give you both *parent* as well as *child* continuity data for that patent. Knowing continuity data just adds to your information about the patent or patent application you are searching. It gives you a more complete picture of the patent or application because you will learn also about related applications that the applicant has filed concerning that same invention.

Author's Note: What is continuity data?
Sometimes a patent applicant will file a single patent application that issues into a patent and that is the end of the story. What you will see on the PTO continuity data sheet is no continuity data for that issued patent. However, patent applicants often file a patent application as either a child or a parent, or both of other patent applications. For example, if an applicant files application A for invention X and then files what is

called a continuation application of application A for invention X several years later, that continuation application would be considered a child of application A. Application A itself would be considered a parent application of that continuation application. The child application would make a specific reference (claim of priority) back to its parent application.

The PAIR system is an extremely useful tool you can use to your advantage with competitive intelligence.

Fee-Based Databases

There are various databases that you can use. Some of these may offer a trial period, but they all require you to eventually pay for the service. However, their in-depth, worldwide coverage may be worth the fee.

One such database is Delphion, which you can find at www.delphion.com. Delphion allows you to search the world's top patent databases as well as search for various nonpatent information such as science abstracts. It also offers a lot of enhanced tools that you cannot do at the PTO site, such as graphical maps of references that cite a particular patent.

Another database is Dialog (www.dialog.com). It is also very comprehensive, covering worldwide patents as well as other information about competitors. Yet another fee-based database you might want to check out is Micropatent (www.micropat.com).

Two other useful fee-based databases are Westlaw (www.westlaw.com) and Lexis (www.lexis.com). Both allow you to search for patents. In addition, they both have very good public information databases in which you can gather a lot of information about your competitors. You will need to sift through all of the legal searching options since these two databases started as tools for only attorneys. They have now become, however, very useful tools for anyone looking for competitive intelligence.

Journals

Journals, such as those that people in your field typically publish articles, can be very helpful. Many of these journals can now be accessed online in addition to going to the library. For example, if you are interested in journals relating to the medical field, a good site to go to is the NCBI site at www.ncbi.nlm.nih.gov/entrez/query.fcgi. This site has a list of journals with links to full text websites for the journals. The site also has a database called *Pub Med,* which allows you to search for articles in all the journals according to your inputted search terms. You can always obtain an abstract about any article on Pub Med, although many of the full text articles will require a subscription fee.

Product Catalogs

All companies have catalogs that list what they sell. Many of these catalogs can be read directly online by visiting the company's website. If they cannot be read directly online, you can go to the website of the company and request that a catalog be sent to you.

You should regularly monitor the current catalog of all your competitors. This is where you are most likely going to find your infringement.

Security and Exchange Commission Filings

All companies are required to make certain filings with the *Security and Exchange Commission* (SEC). These filings are public and can greatly assist you in learning more about your competitor. The SEC website is at www.sec.gov.

At the SEC home page you will see an icon called "Filings and Forms." Under this icon you can "Search for Company Filings" by simply entering the name of your competitor. Type of forms filed here include some of the following:

- *Annual Report to Shareholders.* This is also known as a 10-K form. It is filed by public companies to disclose corporation information to shareholders. The report includes a wealth of data including things such as the finances of the company, market segment information, and new product plans.

- *Quarterly Report to Shareholders.* This is also known as a 10-Q form. It contains data similar to the 10-K form but is filed on a quarterly rather than an annual basis.

- *Prospectus.* This form contains business and financial information on an issuer with respect to a particular securities offering. The investors use the information to judge the merits of the offering and to make educated investment decisions. You can use the prospectus to increase your knowledge about your competitor.

FDA Filings   With respect to the pharmaceutical industry, various FDA filings must be made before a drug can be marketed. You can also obtain a lot of useful information from such filings.

The FDA maintains a reference referred to as the *Orange Book*. This publication will identify a company's pharmaceutical products approved for marketing as well as patents that can be infringed by such marketing.

ORGANIZE AND ANALYZE YOUR INTELLIGENCE

To make the most out of the intelligence that you gather using the tools discussed, it is often helpful to organize your data in some meaningful way. One technique that is being increasingly used to organize competitive intelligence is called mapping. Here are a couple of types of mapping that you might consider doing.

- *Technology Mapping.* One thing you could do is to take all of the patents of your competitor and organize them into various technology groups in which they are associated. This type of technology mapping can provide valuable insight into the strengths and weaknesses of your competitor with respect to the respective technologies. You could even do this type of technology mapping with respect to your own patent portfolio to size up your own strengths and weaknesses and then compare your position with that of a competitor. You could also set up a graph that shows your mapping results. Graphs are a great way to quickly analyze data. For example, using the map below you can quickly see that the company represented by the first bar has a leading number of patents issued with respect to Technology C.

- *Patent Mapping.* This type of mapping refers to looking at patents that are referred to by your own patent (forward citing) and those patents that refer to your own patent (backward citing). One thing that you can glean from such an analysis is the importance of various technologies. If a particular patent has been referenced a large number of times, chances are that it is an important patented technology.

✪ *Market Activity Mapping.* This type of mapping refers to comparing the claims of your patent with the market activity of your competitor.

STRATEGIC PLANNING

Once you have gathered all your competitive intelligence data, organized it into a meaningful way, and have made an analysis, you are now ready for your last step, which is to plan your strategy. There are many ways that your analysis may help guide your patent strategy. The following are just a few:

✪ *Find Licensing Partners.* After you have done a technology map, you may notice that a company is directing a lot of marketing activity with a high correlation to your patenting technology. This could be an indicator that your technology could be very useful to that company and that it could be a great partner for you to try and license your patent.

✪ *Pursue Certain Technologies.* Through your technology mapping, you may notice that one technical area is being pursued by your competitors. Perhaps this is a signal that the technology is valuable, and perhaps you should be devoting more effort to try and obtain more patents in this area also. Looking at this in the reverse, perhaps you may decide that the technical field is an overcrowded field and that you would be better off pursuing other technical areas.

✪ *Protect Important Patents.* If you find that one of your patented technologies is being referred to by a lot of other patents of your competitors, then you probably have an important patented technology. If so, you should consider ways to strengthen this patent. One thing you could do is to file patent applications on improvements for this technology. This will help ensure that you are at the forefront with this important patented technology.

SECTION V

PROTECTING YOUR PATENT

Patent Infringement

This chapter will introduce you to types of activities that constitute patent infringement. The most common types of activities constituting patent infringement fall under a type of patent infringement called *"direct patent infringement."* Direct patent infringement occurs when someone makes, uses, sells, or offers for sale, your patented invention. Direct infringement requires a party to perform or use each and every step or element of a claimed method or patent.

But what if someone decides that, rather than sell your invention, he or she will only sell components of your patented invention? Once those components are sold, the consumer can then easily assemble them together to make your product. Is the manufacturer of the components an infringer?

Certainly, the consumer who is assembling the components to make your invention will be liable to you for direct patent infringement. However, the individual consumer is probably not going to have a lot of money to satisfy any judgment that you obtain. Further, perhaps this consumer is also your customer, or perhaps there are thousands of such consumers and you would have to go after each one. So the real person that you want to sue is the big manufacturer who is selling the components to the consumers.

You will need to rely upon another type of patent infringement called *"contributory infringement"* to get at this big manufacturer. Since the manufacturer is not actually selling your invention, the manufacturer is not liable for direct patent infringement, but that manufacturer is liable for *contributory infringement.* This chapter will discuss contributory as well as other types of activities that can constitute infringement of a patent.

It will be important for you to note too that even if you believe a competitor is engaging in one of the prohibited types of activities covered in this chapter, you still must make sure that the product subject to such activity is within the scope of one of your patent claims. Construing the scope of patent claims and whether a product is covered by such claims will be the subject of the following chapter.

THE IMPORTANCE OF LEARNING WHAT CONSTITUTES INFRINGEMENT

Before starting with a discussion about patent infringement, it is important to discuss the reasons why this chapter is important.

As a *patent holder,* you will not be able to take steps against competitors if you are unable to have a good idea about whether their actions infringe your patent. If you cannot recognize infringement in the first place, you will have a hard time taking steps to stop infringement. If you do not take steps to counteract patent infringement, you will be inviting even more people to infringe your patent. This will of course defeat the whole purpose of your patent, which is to define an exclusive niche in the marketplace. Ultimately your profits will be eroded.

The flip side is also true, in that if you have been accused by a third part of patent infringement, you will be in a much better position to defend yourself. In fact, the argument that your actions do not constitute infringement is a number one defense that you can make in response to allegations of patent infringement. Having a good hunch that you may or may not be infringing a patent will also enable you to decide whether it is better to try and negotiate a quick settlement to the problem, or whether you should continue with your activity despite infringement allegations. If you do not understand whether or not your activities constitute infringement, you will be making important decisions based on no knowledge.

NOTE: *Obtain the opinion of outside counsel if you are charged with infringement. While you should still engage in your own opinion analysis if you are charged with patent infringement, you should also obtain a written opinion from competent outside counsel. You can use this to insulate yourself against liability for willful patent infringement. Willful patent infringement subjects the infringer to greater damages than would normally be granted for infringement alone.*

It is also important to understand what constitutes infringement *before* you spend money on research and development. If you are just about to embark on a highly expensive market launch, you will want to know if your actions may infringe the rights of others. If your actions do infringe later on, you may be stopped from selling your product after having invested a lot of time and money in the manufacture, marketing, and distribution of it. What you learn here about forming your own opinion as to patent infringement can be used to allow you to make more informed decisions with respect to your future product development.

Another reason for this understanding is that Intellectual Property (IP) litigation is expensive. It is probably the most expensive type of litigation. The cost of an average patent lawsuit is around one million dollars. Whether you are the plaintiff or the defendant, you need to have a good idea as to whether you can win the lawsuit before you spend huge amounts of money in litigation. If you think that you cannot win because you think there either exists or does not exist patent infringement, you will probably be better off opting for a non-litigation strategy such as a *license* or a *settlement*.

Further, if you are considering the *license* of patent technology, you will want to know the strength of the patented technology that you are considering to license. This is what is referred to as a *due diligence* inquiry. If you think that by practicing such technology you might thereby infringe the patent rights of others, then you will want to seriously consider your options. Perhaps it will make more sense to not license such technology and seek some alternative technology.

Perhaps you still decide to license the technology, but can negotiate a stronger position for a lower *royalty rate* on the premise that you will need to obtain licenses from additional patent holders in order to securely practice the technology. Under either scenario, knowing about the strength of the patents you seek to license will make you a wiser party.

And finally, perhaps you are considering buying a business or the patent owned by another person. If patents are part of the sale, you will want to ensure the strength of those patents. To ensure the strength of those patents, you will want to know if you can practice the patented invention without infringing the rights of other patent holders. Again, this type of analysis is part of a *due diligence* inquiry into the nature of the seller's business to determine its real value.

It may be the biggest myth around, that by having a patent, you have the right to make, use, offer for sale or sell your patented invention. This is incorrect. A patent only gives you the right to *exclude* others from practicing your claimed invention. It does not give you the right to practice your invention. Even if you obtain a patent, you may still infringe the claims of another patent if you start to make or sell your invention. If you buy a patent and become a patent holder, keep this in mind—make sure that your actions do not infringe upon the rights of other patent holders.

DIRECT PATENT INFRINGEMENT

Direct patent infringement is defined at United States Code Title 37, Section 271(a). This statute provides that "except as otherwise provided in this title, whoever without authority makes, uses, offers to sell, or sells any patented invention, within the United States or imports into the United States any patented invention during the term of the patent therefore, infringes the patent."

Section 271(a) clearly specifies the type of activities that can constitute infringement. These activities are the following:

- ✪ *Making.* If someone manufactures or otherwise produces your invention, this will constitute direct patent infringement.

The reverse is true if you do this with respect to someone else's invention.

- ✪ *Using.* If someone uses your patented invention, then that will also constitute infringement under the statute. For example, if you develop a new battery and someone uses that battery to power their own machine, that use can constitute infringement.

- ✪ *Offering for sale or selling.* The mere offering for sale of your infringement constitutes direct infringement even if nothing is ever sold. This allows a patentee to sue, and potentially secure an injunction, before a product actually hits the market. This part of the statute could cause problems for an offer to sell in the United States even though the sale is contemplated abroad.

In essence, all you need to do to determine patent infringement is to determine if the activity you are interested in falls into one of the specified categories. However, determining patent infringement seldom is as easy as that. First, it can be difficult discovering whether someone is engaging in one of the prohibited activities. Discovering such activity often takes a lot of work using all of your competitive intelligence tools.

Second, even if you find someone who you think is doing one of the prohibited activities, you will still need to determine whether that activity concerns your patented invention. This second part of your job can actually be the more difficult one. Determining whether any such activity is subject to the scope of your claimed invention will be discussed in the following chapter.

CONTRIBUTORY INFRINGEMENT

A *contributory infringer* is defined as a person who, with knowledge of the infringing activity, induces, causes, or materially contributes to the infringing conduct of another. (*Gershwin Publ'g Corp. v. Columbia Artists Mgmt., Inc.,* 443 F.2d 1159 (2nd Cir. 1971).)

In patent law, there are two types of contributory infringement. The first type is referred to as *active inducement* or simply *induced infringement.* The second type is simply referred to as *contributory infringement.*

The basis for suit against someone who *actively induces infringement* is United States Code, Title 35, Section 271(b). This statute provides that "Whoever actively induces infringement of a patent shall be liable as an infringer."

Induced infringement arises if a seller actively aids or abets direct infringement by a purchaser, such as by instructing the purchaser on how to use the item in a patented combination. Induced infringement does not require that someone's inducement take place in the United States. Thus, the fact that someone's inducing activity occurs from somewhere in Asia does not insulate this person from liability.

The basis for *contributory infringement* is United States Code, Title 35, Section 271(c). This statute provides that "Whoever offers to sell or sells within the United States or imports into the United States a component of a patented machine, manufacture, combination or composition, or a material or apparatus for use in practicing a patented process, constituting a material part of the invention, knowing the same to be especially made or especially adapted for use in an infringement of such patent, and not a staple article or commodity of commerce suitable for substantial noninfringing use, shall be liable as a contributory infringer."

Contributory liability requires that the secondary infringer know or have reason to know of the direct infringement. (*Religious Tech. Ctr. V Netcom On-line Comm. Servs., Inc.*, 907 F. Supp. 1361 (N.D. Cal. 1995).)

Defenses to Contributory Infringement

Defenses that can be used against direct patent infringement are discussed later, in Chapter 23. However, there are some special defenses to contributory infringement, which I will discuss here.

Lack of Direct Infringement. One such defense to contributory infringement is the lack somewhere of *direct infringement.* In other words, if no person has directly infringed a patent, then one cannot argue that anyone else (such as a big manufacturer) has made some contribution to the infringement of the patent. This is because there is simply no infringement to contribute to.

The requirement that there be direct infringement of the patent is a particularly useful defense to a lawsuit for contributory infringement. If you can think of anyway to negate direct infringement of the patent, then you will succeed in negating contributory infringement at the same time. This strategy is illustrated in the following case example.

Example:

Convertible Manufacturing Company obtained its long-awaited patent that covered a specially designed top for use in convertible automobiles. The patent had several claims that were all directed to the top as a combination of a flexible top fabric, supporting structures, and a mechanism for sealing the fabric, against the side of the convertible in order to keep the rain out. All of the components of the top would last for the lifetime of the car except for the fabric, which would normally need to be replaced within three years.

The Company had been selling its top well before the patent came out with huge success. At least three major car manufacturers were purchasing the top sold by the Company. The fact that the fabric wore out in three years also led to a great need for suppliers of the fabric that could be used to replace the worn fabric in the tops.

Aro Manufacturing saw this great need and had been selling fabric that could be used as a replacement. In fact, Aro had been making millions of dollars off of its sale. To the dismay of the Company, it was also making millions of the sale of replacement fabric, but could be making many more millions if it were not for Aro.

At last, the issue of the patent gave the Company hope. As soon as the patent issued, the Company sued Aro Manufacturing for contributory patent infringement. The Company claimed that Aro was selling a material component of the patented invention and thus was liable for patent infringement as a contributory infringer. The court disagreed with this reasoning, however, finding instead that the consumer's use of the fabric did not constitute direct patent infringement. Since there was no direct patent infringement, there could be no contributory infringement. (*Aro Mfg. Co. v. Convertible Tob Replacement Co.,* 365 U.S. 336 (1981).)

In this case example, the company argued that the consumer's use of the fabric to replace the worn out fabric constitute direct infringement. The consumer, arguably, was making the patented combination, which if true, would thereby constitute patent infringement. However, buyers of a patented invention (here the consumer who bought the original top) are allowed to make certain *repairs* to the invention in order to keep it in working condition. (This defense to patent infringement is called *permissible repair*. It will be discussed in Chapter 24.)

Staple Article defense. A second defense to contributory infringement is the *Staple Article defense. Staple Article defense* is based on the statute for contributory infringement. (U.S.C., Title 35, Sec. 271(c).) If you review the statute for contributory infringement, you will see that it includes the phrase "not a staple article or commodity of commerce suitable for substantial noninfringing use." Therefore, if you can successfully argue that the component is a *staple article suitable for substantial noninfringing use,* you will have a valid defense to contributory infringement.

A *staple article* is some product that is considered to have a broad range of uses besides the use in your patented invention. Some courts have held that for a component to lack substantial noninfringing uses, the component must almost be uniquely suited for use in practicing the patented invention.

If you think about it, this defense makes a lot of sense. It would be unreasonable, for example, to hold that a patent holder of, say a fountain pen, could hold as a contributory infringer, someone who supplies ink for the pen, even if the patent holder has a claim for the pen with its ink. To take this to an extreme, if the rule were otherwise, a court might have to find the supplier of ice to be a contributory infringer of the patentee of a refrigerator. That would be absurd, and such a supplier can raise the defense that the ice is a staple article, as it has many other non-infringing uses.

IMPORTED PRODUCTS MADE WITH A U.S.-PATENTED PROCESS

A special statute (35 U.S.C. §271(g)) also provides that a product imported into the United States will infringe a process patent for making the product if the patented process was implemented abroad. For a product to have been made by a process patented in the United States, it must have be a physical article that was manufactured. Excluded from protection are products that are materially changed by subsequent processes or that become a trivial or nonessential component of another product.

The process covered by this statute must also be used directly in the manufacture of the product, and not merely as a predicate process to identify the product to be manufactured.

Example:

Housey Pharmaceuticals owned patents directed to a method of screening for substances that specifically inhibit or activate a particular protein. Bayer used the patented process outside the United States, and as a result, identified candidate drug compounds that could be patented and used within the United States. Housey alleged that the importation of the products identified by the claimed process was an act of infringement. The Federal Circuit Court held against Housey on the basis that the characteristics of that were studied using the claimed research processes were not a product "made by" those claimed processes. Knowledge is not the subject of patent protection, only its application.

There are a couple of exceptions to the statute. For example, you will not be able to sue retailers or personal consumers of the products being imported unless you have no other adequate remedy at law. This means that if you can sue the manufacturer, you cannot go after the retailer or consumer of the products. An example of this might be a manufacturer who sells a pesticide that is made using your patented process. If you can sue that manufacturer, you cannot go after the nursery that sells the pesticide, or the consumer who buys the pesticide, using this special statute.

The statute also exempts from its coverage, products that become a trivial component of another product, as well as those products that have been materially changed by a subsequent process. In other words, if there is a real difference between the products that are being imported, offered for sale, sold, or used in the United States, then you will not be able to use this statute to your advantage.

Section 337 of the Tariff Act of 1930, otherwise known as *Section 337,* does the same thing and prohibits the importation in the United States, the sale for importation, or the sale within the United States after importation, of a patented product or a product made by a patented process.

UNASSEMBLED COMPONENTS SHIPPED OUTSIDE THE UNITED STATES FOR ASSEMBLY

Back in the 1970s, many unauthorized manufacturers of patented products were able to avoid liability for infringement by manufacturing unassembled components of those patented products in the United States and then shipping them outside the United States for assembly. In response to this, Congress enacted 35 U.S.C. §271(f).

The first part of 35 U.S.C. §271(f) provides that any person who, without authority, supplies in or from the United States all or a substantial portion of the components of a patented invention, where such components are uncombined in whole or in part, in such manner as to actively induce the combination of such components outside the United States in a manner that would infringe the patent if such combination occurred within the United States is liable as an infringer.

The rest of 35 U.S.C. §271(f)(2) further provides that any person who supplies in or from the United States any component of a patented invention that is especially made or especially adapted for use in the invention and not a staple article or commodity of commerce suitable for substantial noninfringing use, where such component is uncombined in whole or in part, knowing that such component is so made or adapted and intending that such component will be combined outside of the United States in a manner that would infringe the patent if such combination occurred in the United States is liable as an infringer.

Example:

Company S exports a noninfringing catalyst from the United States. The catalyst is used abroad in a process patented by company A in the United States. Company S can be liable as an infringer under §271(f).

Although the above statutes are a big boost to U.S. patentees and were enacted for this reason, some of their effect has actually been counterproductive, creating incentive for companies to make products outside the United States. This is because the statute simply does not apply if the infringing components are made and assembled outside the United States.

Example:

NTP sued RIM claiming that its system process claims were infringed by RIM, the maker of the BlackBerry device. However, in this case RIM's process occurred in Canada. Since the process was not within the United States, there was no direct infringement under §271(a) since each of the steps was not performed within this country. But NTP sought to use §271(f). Unfortunately, in this particular case §271(f) was to no avail because RIM was not supplying or causing to be supplied in the United States any steps of the patented process invention for combination outside the United States.

DESIGN PATENTS

Design patents are treated differently for infringement purposes. The basis for most design infringement cases is given by a case called *Gorham v. White*. The test stated in *White* is that if, in the eye of an ordinary observer, two designs are substantially the same, if the resemblance is such as to deceive such an observer, inducing him to purchase one supposing it to be the other, the first one patented is infringed by the other. Recently, the Federal Circuit Court has added to this test of infringement by requiring that the accused design must also contain substantially the same points of novelty that distinguished the patented design from the prior art. This *point of novelty test* requires that no matter how similar two items look, the accused device must appropriate the novelty in the patented device that distinguishes it from the prior art. The test thus requires an identification of the point of novelty and then a determination as to whether the accused design has appropriated that point of novelty.

How to Form Your Own Patent Infringement Opinion

Even if you do uncover one of the enumerated prohibited activities that constitutes direct patent infringement discussed in chapter 17, your next job will be to determine whether that prohibited activity relates to your patented invention. This, in fact, is the major task of coming up with a patent infringement opinion. It is a two task process.

Your first task will be to interpret the scope and meaning of the claims of the patents that are possibly infringed. After you have construed the claims, your next task is to determine whether what is being used, made, offered for sale, or sold is covered by those construed claims. If covered by the construed claims, the claims will be said to *read* upon the accused device or process that is being made, used, offered for sale, or sold.

The two step task process is broken down into a series of steps in the next section. These steps will show you how to construe patent claims and will also show you how to determine if those construed claims *read* upon the accused device or process that relates to your situation. If the construed claims do read upon the accused product or device, your opinion as to patent infringement will be in the affirmative. If the construed claims do not read upon the accused product or device, then your opinion as to patent infringement will be in the negative. This occurs unless the construed claims cover the accused device or process under the *doctrine of equivalents*. (The doctrine of equivalents is discussed as the last step in coming up with a patent infringement opinion in the next section.)

Before proceeding further, notice that *opinions* are given in relation to infringement claims. The word *opinion* is used because no one can know for sure whether an alleged activity really does constitute patent infringement. Law is not an exact science, and one can know whether a patent infringement has occurred only after a court issues an opinion. However, by following these next steps, you can come up with a pretty good idea as to whether an activity constitutes direct patent infringement.

FORMING A PATENT INFRINGEMENT OPINION

Determining a patent infringement opinion of your own really only involves two steps. First, you need to construe the claim of the patent at issues. Second, you need to look at the product at the issue and ask whether or not that product comes within the scope of your construed patent claim.

To help you complete this two step process, a series of steps are outlined in the next few sections. If you follow these steps in order, you can determine your own patent infringement opinion.

Step One: Gather Information

The first thing that you need to do to determine patent infringement is to gather the patent or patents that are the subject of the infringement. If you are the patent holder, you only need to bring out the patents that you believe are being infringed.

If you are the person against whom an infringement claim is being asserted, or perhaps you want to know if your future actions could infringe a patent of another person, then you will need to obtain the patents that you may infringe. This should also be a fairly easy task since you can go right to the PTO website and print out patents. (See Chapter 4 for additional information.)

The reason that you will need the patents that are the subject of interest is that the task of determining patent infringement involves interpreting or construing the claims of the relevant patents. The claims of a patent are what define the invention and are what are infringed in patent law. As mentioned already, construing the claims of the patents is your first task in forming an opinion about patent infringement.

In addition to the patents of interest, you should try to get a hold of what is called the *file wrapper* for each of the patents of interest. File wrappers are the folders at the PTO that contain everything that occurred between the patent holder and the PTO right through to the issuance of the patent. In other words, if an amendment or change to the patent application was made at some point during the patent application process, you will find that amendment in the file wrapper. The file wrapper also provides the rest of the parts of the patent, as well as statements made during prosecution of the patent to construe those claims.

File wrappers, unlike the patent itself, are not available for free at the PTO website. However, you can pull up the file history for a patent using the PAIR system at the PTO website. You can also order from the PTO any file history that you pull up. Simply go to www.uspto.gov, click on "patents," then click on "PAIR," and then click on "order copies and publications." You will then need to request a new user ID to use the system.

There are also many firms that will obtain the file wrapper for you. These firms charge a fee for their services. You can easily find such services by doing an online search for "patent file retrieval" on the Internet.

Step Two: Independent Claims

You already understand what an independent claim is if you have drafted a patent application. However, a bit of review is in order.

An *independent claim* is a claim in a patent that does not refer back to any other claim in the patent. In other words, an independent claim stands alone. It does not incorporate any features of any other claim in the patent because it will make no reference to any other claims in the patent.

An *independent claim* should be contrasted to what is called a *dependent claim* in the patent. A dependent claim *does* make reference to other claims in the patent. In other words, a dependent claim will incorporate features or elements of prior claims by making reference to those prior claims. See if you can find the dependent claim in the following example.

Example:

Claim 1: A table comprising: a top, said top being attached to three (3) legs.

Claim 2: A table as in Claim 1, further comprising nine (9) rivets that attach said three (3) legs to said top.

Claim 2 is the dependent claim because it refers back to a prior claim (Claim 1 in this case) and incorporates the features or elements of the prior claim (the top and three legs). As you can see, a dependent claim will also add some new features or elements—in this example, the rivets.

Claim 1 in the example above is an independent claim. It does not make reference to any other previous claims. It contains all of its elements right in its claim.

It is best to start your infringement analysis with the independent claims from your patents of interest and spend time construing only those claims, first. This is because patents typically have dozens of claims. If you are lucky in that the patent only has a handful of claims, then you can tackle all of the claims at once. However, this task becomes more involved with each additional claim.

Another reason to construe only the independent claims of your patent at first is that it will typically be unnecessary for you to construe the dependent claims of the patent to form an infringement opinion. The reason for this is that a dependent claim, by definition, must further define an independent or main claim to which it refers. In patent law, when you add additional elements you necessarily narrow the scope of coverage of your claim. Thus, dependent claims are narrower in scope than the main claim to which they refer.

The logic of this is the following: Since independent claims are broader in coverage than dependent claims, if you infringe an independent claim you will necessarily infringe a dependent claim. It is impossible to infringe something that is broader in scope (an independent claim) and not infringe something that is narrower in scope (a dependent claim). Thus, if you find that there is no infringement of the broader independent claim, you have by implication, found that none of the more narrow dependent claims that refer back to that broader claim are infringed. You can stop right there. Finding no infringement of that independent claim *necessarily* means that you will find no infringement of the claims that depend on that independent claim.

The only time that you will need to be concerned with dependent claims is when you find infringement of the broader independent claim. In that case, you may want to construe the dependent claims that refer back to the independent claim in order to see if those dependent claims are also infringed.

Infringement of *any* claim constitutes patent infringement. By coming into court with more claims that you think are infringed, you will have a better chance of finding at least one of those claims infringed. Moreover, if the independent claim is held invalid due to some particular patent defense (discussed in Chapter 10), infringement can still occur, if any other valid claim (even a dependent claim) is infringed. All you need to show patent infringement is infringement of one claim, even if that patent has hundreds of claims to choose from.

Step Three:
Construe Your
Claim

Look at the ordinary language of the claim
You will need to construe each claim one at a time. Pick one of the claims that you are going to analyze (start with an independent claim) and conduct an infringement analysis of it by following the steps in this section. If you do not find infringement of that independent claim, then you will not find infringement of any of the dependent claims that refer back to it. In such a case, you can move on to repeat your analysis with your next independent claim of the patent.

To start your analysis of a claim, list what you believe to be each of the required elements or features that the claim recites. In the earlier example, the elements of independent Claim 1 are a top and legs. These are the only two elements or features of this claim.

To construe the claim, first ask yourself what is the *ordinary* and *customary* meaning of each term that you have listed out.

If you were to look at a word or term and just know offhand what people meant when they used that term, you would be pretty close to the ordinary and customary meaning of the term. In patent law, however, the *ordinary* or *plain meaning* of a term is not looked at from the point of view of the general public, but rather from the point of view of someone who is skilled in the art of the type to which the invention pertains. (MPEP 2111.01.)

You could look in the dictionary to determine *ordinary meaning* of an element in the claim. If the element is not a specialized term in the art of the invention, but rather something that people use every day, it is completely permissible to define the term according to its everyday usage. However, if the term is a specialized term in the art of invention, then you will have to try to figure out how a person who is skilled in the art to which the invention pertains would define the term.

There are several common circumstances where you cannot just rely upon the ordinary or plain meaning of a term in the claim. If the patent applicant has given the term a different meaning than its ordinary and customary meaning, then you should rely upon the meaning given by the *drafter* (applicant).

The applicant can give a term a different meaning in a number of ways. First, the applicant may specifically define the term somewhere in the patent outside of the claim such as in the detailed written description of the patent. (Reviewing the disclosure of the patent outside the claim is covered later in this section.)

The applicant may also define the term in less obvious ways. The applicant might describe a particular embodiment of the invention in a particular manner, so that the term can only have a specified meaning. The applicant might also comment on what people have done previously in the art, in an effort to show how the applicant's way of doing things is new and different. In such a case, the applicant will probably limit the term to the different way of doing things.

Example:

In construing the meaning of Alice's claim, the court relied heavily on a paragraph in her disclosure that stated that "passages" of the prior art were generally smooth. The court took this statement and concluded that "passages" of Alice's claim must exclude smooth passages. Since the infringer was using smooth passages, the court found that there was no infringement of Alice's claim.

A less obvious way that the applicant may give meaning to a term, other than its ordinary meaning, is when the applicant has made some statement in the course of prosecution of the patent that gives the term some other meaning. For example, the applicant may state in an amendment to the claim during prosecution that the term has some specific meaning. Determining this exception involves reviewing the file wrapper.

If the applicant uses a term that makes it impossible to understand the scope of the claim by one of ordinary skill in the field of the invention, then you can look outside the claim to other parts of the patent and the file history to ascertain the meaning of the term. In other words, when the term is ambiguous, you can look elsewhere, either in the *disclosure* or in the *file history*. (Both points are addressed later in this section.)

Sometimes you will encounter a claim language that starts with the clause "means for" followed by some specified function. When you see this language, you are dealing with what is termed in patent law as a *means-plus-function* clause. This type of clause is illustrated in the claim below where you will see the clause "means for" followed by the function "coupling."

"A DECORATIVE FIGURE ASSEMBLY, COMPRISING: A PLURALITY OF COUPLING MEANS FOR COUPLING A TORSO BAG TO A HEAD BAG, TO ARM BAGS, AND TO

LEGS BAGS, WHEREIN SAID HEAD BAG, SAID ARM BAGS, AND SAID LEG BAGS ARE COUPLED BY SAID PLURALITY OF COUPLING MEANS TO SAID TORSO BAG AND FORM A FIGURE PROPORTIONED TO A COSTUMED HUMAN."

The term *means for* is handled in a particular way in patent law due to a specific statute. To construe the clause, you must go to other parts of the patent outside the claim (the *disclosure*) and look for materials the applicant has specified for performing that coupling function. For example, if the applicant only specifies that rope is to be used for coupling, then the applicant would be limited only to rope or its equivalent for the coupling of the torso bag to the head, arm, and leg bags. The term *equivalent* for purposes of a means-plus-function clause includes those structures, materials or acts which:

1. perform substantially identical functions in substantially the same way to produce substantially the same result (*Odetics Inc. v. Storage Tech. Corp.,* 185 F3d 1259, 1267, 51 USPQ2d 125, 1229 (Fed. Cir. 1999));

2. have insubstantial differences (*Valmount Indus. Inc. v. Reinke Mfg. Co.,* 983 F2d 1039, 1042–44, 25 USPQ2d 1451, 1453–56 (Fed. Cir. 1993));

3. are structurally equivalent (*In re Bond,* 910 F2d 831, 833, 15 USPQ2d 1566, 1568 (Fed. Cir. 1990)); or,

4. a person having ordinary skill in the art would have recognized as interchangeable. (*Al-site Corp. v. VSI International Inc.,* 174 F3d 1308, 1316, 50 USPQ2d 1161, 1165 (Fed. Cir. 1999).)

Such equivalent structures, materials and acts must have been available at the time of the issuance of the claims.

Product-by-process claims are also handled a little differently when it comes to claim construction. As you might recall, a product-by-process claim is defined by Section 2173.05(p) of the Manual of Patent Examining Procedure (MPEP) as "a product claim that defines the claimed product in terms of the process by which it is made." The patentability of a product-by-process claim as determined by the

PTO is based solely upon the product claimed, not the method used to make the product. (See Section 2113 of the MPEP.) However, for purposes of patent litigation and patent infringement things are not so clear. Some federal courts ignore process limitations, whereas other federal courts consider process limitations. Probably the best way to handle the construction of such claims is in light of the specification. If the patentee from the specification intended the process limitations in a product-by-process claim to limit the scope of the claim to a product made by that process, then the claim should also probably be limited by the process limitations. Certainly if the patentee somewhere in the prosecution history of the patent includes such process limitations to overcome prior art rejections, then they should be part of the claims limitations.

Review the disclosure outside the claims

Because an applicant may give a claim term a meaning other than its customary and ordinary one, you must review the entire patent to see if the applicant has given the term any *special meaning*. In other words, you have a paradox. On one hand, courts say that you should construe a claim term using its ordinary and customary meaning and look no further than that. On the other hand, courts say that the applicant can define that term in a different way somewhere outside the claim. The end result is that you must always review the disclosure of the patent to come up with an accurate construction of a claim term. It is simply not possible to construe a claim term without having read the entire disclosure outside the claim.

As you review the disclosure of the patent outside the claim, be aware that an applicant may not only specifically define a term somewhere in the disclosure, but also give it a meaning in other less obvious ways.

Example:

Justin obtained a patent on an improved dual-lumen balloon catheter. The lumens could occur in two configurations—side-by-side and coaxial. While the claim language did not specify a particular configuration, the court limited the claim to cover only the coaxial configuration because of explicit statements made in the patent specification. The court found, for example, that Justin had distinguished his invention over side-by-side configurations by stating its advantages over those configurations. In addition, the court noted many times where Justin referred to his catheters as being coaxial or annular. (*SciMed Life Systems v. Advanced Cardiovascular Systems*, 58 U.S.P.Q.2d 1059 (Fed. Cir. 2001).)

Look at the file wrapper

The disclosure of a patent is not the only place that an applicant can give a term in a claim a meaning that is different from its ordinary or plain meaning. The other place is in a document that the applicant filed with the Patent and Trademark Office during prosecution of the patent. Therefore, to do a thorough job at construing terms in a claim, you need to review the *prosecution* for the patent that contains that claim. Prosecution papers are contained in the *file wrapper* for the patent.

As you conduct your review of the file wrapper, look for any statements made by the applicant that relate to the claim terms. Ask yourself whether those statements define or limit the terms in any particular way. You can use such limitations or characterizations in coming up with the meaning of the terms for patent infringement purposes. If an applicant states that a term must mean something somewhere in the file history, you can rely upon that characterization. You should also check for statements made by the applicant that would lead a competitor to believe that the applicant had disavowed coverage of the relevant subject matter. If the applicant does disavow such coverage, then a patent claim cannot be construed to cover such disavowed coverage. In court, the judge construes patent claims because such construction is considered a matter of law and not of fact.

If the patent application which you are reviewing is a continuation of an earlier filed patent, you should also be alert for statements made by the patentee during the prosecution of the earlier patent. The general rule is that an applicant cannot recapture claim scope that is surrendered or disclaimed even when a continuation is filed.

Example:

In his original application, Hakin argued over prior art by stating that his claim element "a flexible-member opening" was a "slit." Due to this disclaimer the court found no infringement as against Cannon-Avent. This was true even though Hakim notified the examiner that new claims in his continuation were broader than those previously filed (the court finding that simply informing the examiner of new broader claims was not enough to rescind the prior disclaimer scope).

Also be on the lookout for special words used by patent drafters. For example, Drafters often use the word "about." Use of "about" is particularly frequent when it comes to percentages or other numerical limits. Thus a drafter might say "about 1:5" rather than simply "1:5" The word "about" does not have a universal meaning in patent claims. Instead, its meaning depends upon the facts of each particular case. Thus you will need to try to come to the numerical limits of this word given the patent specification, the prosecution history and even other claims in the patent.

Example:

Ortho-McNeil Pharmaceutical, Inc. sued Caraco Pharmaceutical Laboratories for patent infringement of its claim 6, a dependent claim that stated "a pharmaceutical composition comprising a tramadol material and acetaminophen wherein the ratio of the tramadol material to acetaminophen is a weight ratio of about 1:5." Caraco's new drug application showed that it intended to make and sell a pharmaceutical composition containing tramadol and acetaminophen with an average weight ratio of tramadol to acetaminophen of 1:8.67. The court held no literal infringement by finding the term "about 1:5" to mean "approximately 1:5, encompassing a range of ratios no greater than 1:3.6 to 1:7.1." The court also found no infringement under the doctrine of equivalents (discussed below). In arriving at its decision, the court focused on the intrinsic evidence of the case (the patent specification itself in the form of experiments cited) disclosed data points for ratios in the lower ratio quadrant of 1:1, 1:3, 1:5, 1:5.7 and 1:15. The court also noted that the term "about 1:5" is narrow because this ratio is distinctly claimed and distinguished from other broader weight ratio ranges found in the patent. The court also focused on prosecution history of a reissue of the patent that cancelled broader "comprising" claims except for claim 6. This was particularly important with respect for the doctrine of equivalents where the court stated that having so distinctly claimed the "about 1:5" ratio. Ortho could not now argue that the parameter was broad enough to encompass, through DOE, ratios outside of the intervals expressly identified in the patent.

At this point you have finished construing each and every element of feature in your claim. You are ready for step four of your analysis which will be to compare your construed claim with the infringing product in question. But first examine the simple flowchart on the next page to review how to construe an element or feature in the claim.

Claim Construction Flowchart

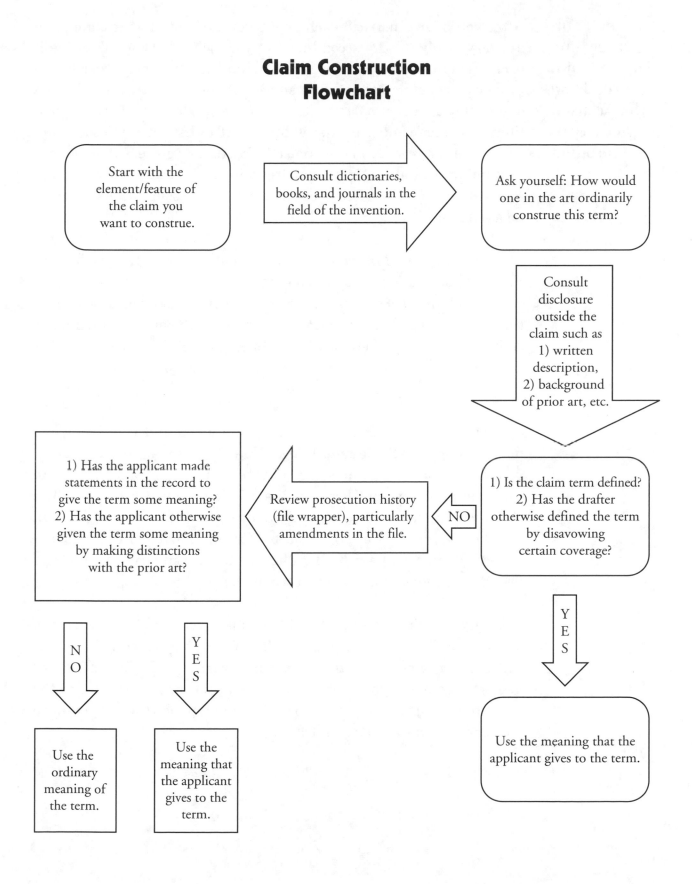

Step Four: Determine if the Claim Reads on the Accused Activity or Product

After you have construed each feature or element of your claim, you are now ready for the second part of your job. This task is to see if each one of those elements that make up the claim also exist in the product (or method) that is the subject of your investigation. If each one of those elements can be found in the product (or method) then literal infringement will exist with respect to that claim. Your claim will be said to *read* upon the accused structure or process that you are examining. In court, a jury compares your construed claims with the accused product or process because such a question is considered to be a question of fact.

The best way to compare your claimed features with the product (or process) you think may be infringing your claim, is to set up what is called a *claim chart*. This will systematically allow you to compare the features of your claim with the features of the accused product. A claim chart is simply a table or some other type of chart where you list the features of your claim so that you can readily visualize whether they exist in the accused products.

Suppose your invention is a table having a top and legs. Your elements would be: 1) top and 2) legs. Now see if the accused products you are examining contains each of these features. Product A does in the example below, but Product B is missing the feature of legs. The claim would therefore *read* on Product A, but *not read* on claim B. In other words, Product A would be literally infringed by the claim (direct infringement exists). Product B, on the contrary would escape literal infringement (no direct infringement).

The only way that Product B could be considered to infringe the claim is if the claim to the table captures the product by something that is called the *doctrine of equivalence*. This doctrine is the last thing you need to consider in your infringement analysis and is discussed in the next step. (You will only need to go to that step, however, if you have not found literal infringement.)

	Top	Legs
Product A	X	X
Product B	X	

Reverse doctrine of equivalence

There is one special exception to the rule that a product that falls within the literal scope of a claim as above constitutes direct infringement. This exception is sometimes referred to as the *reverse doctrine of equivalence*. This exception does not come up very often, but you should be aware that it exists.

Under this doctrine, even if you can show that the accused device contains each and every feature of your claim, your accused infringer can escape infringement liability if he or she can show that the accused device is so far changed from your claimed invention, so as to function in an entirely different manner.

For example, even if Product A in the earlier example contained a top and legs, it could possibly escape literal infringement under this doctrine if it functioned in an entirely different manner. One example of this might be if the top of Product A functions as a propeller, rather than something to place things on. In such a case, the law would treat the two inventions as different, even though they both contain a top and legs. (*SRI International v. Matsushita Electric,* 775 F.2d 1107, 227 U.S.P.Q. 577 (1985).)

Step Five: Look for Equivalence, if Necessary

This is the final step of your infringement analysis. As stated, you will not need to complete this step if you have found literal infringement of your claim under steps 1–4 above. If you have literal infringement, you job is done. Infringement exists, and there is no need to determine if infringement exists under the *doctrine of equivalence.*

If you do not find literal infringement because your claim does not *read* on the accused product or device, then you should look to see whether the accused product or device is captured under the *doctrine of equivalence.*

The *doctrine of equivalence* has probably become the most discussed topic among patent attorneys. In fact, you might say that patent attorneys have a love-hate relationship with this doctrine. This has become increasingly true with the recent case of *Festo Corporation v. Shoketsu Kinzoku Kogyo Kabushiki Co. Ltd.,* 535 U.S. 722 (2002).

However, let us begin with an explanation of how to initially conduct your doctrine of equivalence analysis. A simple example will assist in this analysis.

Suppose that you draft a claim directed toward a table having a top, a group of legs, and the legs are attached to the top using rivets. Suppose further, that an accused infringer comes along years later and starts to make the table, but uses screws instead of rivets to attach the legs to the top.

Now, using the steps above for literal infringement, you would see that "rivets" are missing in the accused product so you do not have literal infringement. Would you be out of luck in stopping this infringer? The answer is no. Even though the claimed feature "rivets" is not contained in the accused device, the "screws" of the accused product would, in all likelihood, be considered an equivalent to the rivets of the claimed table. The reason for this result is that substituting "screws" for the "rivets" would probably be considered to be an *insubstantial modification*. The accused product would therefore infringe the claimed table under the doctrine of equivalence, even though each feature of the claimed invention is not literally contained in the accused product.

Two tests can be used to determine whether or not one element is an equivalent of another element. One of the more popular tests is what is called the *function-way-result* test. Under this test, if the accused device includes a feature that performs substantially the same function, in substantially the same way to yield substantially the same result as the claimed feature, then the accused feature will be an equivalent. (*Schoell v. Regal Marine Indus., Inc.*, 247 F.3d 1201, 1209–10 (Fed. Cir. 2001).) The second test is called the *insubstantial differences test*. Under this test, an element in the accused device is equivalent to a claim limitation if the only differences between the two are insubstantial. (*Honeywell International, Inc. v. Hamilton Sundstrand Corp.*, 370 F.3d 1131, 1139 (Fed. Cir. 2004).)

Limitations on the Doctrine of Equivalence
Although the *doctrine of equivalence* can be a potent litigation tool that can expand the scope of coverage of your claims beyond their literal meaning, courts are increasingly limiting the application of this

doctrine. This is particularly true any time a patent applicant amends a claimed feature during the *prosecution* of the patent application. Under the *Festo* case, cited earlier, any time a claimed feature or term is amended so as to narrow that term during prosecution of the patent to satisfy statutory requirements of patentability, there is a presumption that any equivalents to that term have been given up. Any time the applicant adds additional limitations about the meaning of that term, it will be considered narrowed.

The *Festo* case means that as you conduct your analysis of equivalence of your claimed terms, you must go back to the *file wrapper* of the patent to see whether any of the claim terms have been narrowed through amendment during prosecution of the patent. If the terms have been narrowed, there is a presumption that the applicant has given up any equivalents to the narrowed claim term.

Example:

You do not find literal infringement of your patent as previously discussed because the accused product (table) uses screws instead of rivets provided by your claim. To your delight, you think you can use the doctrine of equivalents to capture the infringing product because screws, after all, function much like rivets. Unfortunately, you recall that during the prosecution of your patent you made an amendment to your originally written claim by adding the word "screws." By adding this new element you will in all likelihood be barred from now claiming equivalent attachment mechanisms such as rivets. You will be stuck with tables having screws.

Festo applies equally to all claims in the patent containing the same limitation that was narrowed through amendment by a patentee during prosecution of the patent. Thus, if you discover during examination of the file wrapper that a narrowing amendment was made with respect to a claim, Festo will apply equally to any other claim in the patent with respect to the scope of that other claim containing the same limitation.

The rationale for the *doctrine of equivalence* is if you amend any claim term so as to narrow the scope of coverage of that claim, you should not thereafter be able to argue in court that you are entitled to have the broader coverage that you relinquished.

Amendments are not the only thing that you will need to look for in determining whether equivalents have been given up. You should also review the *file wrapper* (and even the *patent disclosure*) for any statements that the applicant has made regarding the *term of interest* under your equivalence analysis. This type of analysis is the same as discussed in Step 3.

If the applicant makes statements or takes positions that seem to limit the term to a particular meaning, the applicant is going to be limited to that meaning, and will probably have given up any range of equivalents to that term. In this equivalence context, such statements or positions are known as *prosecution history estoppel*. By making such statements, the applicant is thereby estopped from being able to enlarge the scope of the term. Again, the rationale for this is the same as when you give up coverage through a narrowing amendment. If you give up coverage, you should not be able to recapture that broader coverage later.

If all of this is not enough for you, there is also another recent case *Johnson & Johnston Associates, Inc. v. R.E. Service Co., Inc.,* 285 F. 3d 1046, (Fed. Cir. 2002), which can limit the doctrine of equivalence. The *Johnson* case basically says that when an applicant has disclosed something in the patent, outside the claim, but has failed to claim it, that unclaimed material cannot be recaptured through the *doctrine of equivalence*.

Example:

In claim 4 of her patent, Anne specifically limited her substrate term in her claim to a "sheet of aluminum." Anne's specification, however, stated that "while aluminum is currently the preferred material for the substrate, other metals, such as stainless steel or nickel alloys may be used." Years later after the patent was issued, Paul started to make a product very similar to Anne's except that the substrate used was not a sheet of aluminum, but was rather stainless steel. Since Anne could not show literal infringement of her claim, Anne argued that Paul's stainless steel substrate was an insubstantial modification of her aluminum sheet substrate. The court held that even if this were true, Anne had given up her right to capture the use of any substrates other than a "sheet of aluminum" since Anne had specifically disclosed other substrates such as stainless steel in her disclosure, but had failed to claim it. Therefore, Anne was out of luck as far as the doctrine of equivalents. Paul was not an infringer of the patent.

If you have failed to claim subject matter disclosed in your patent, and you find that this has become a problem now because an infringer is using something that you disclosed but did not claim, you may still not be out of luck. If you act within two years from your patent grant, you could seek to enlarge the scope of your claim to include that unclaimed subject matter by seeking a *reissue* of your patent. A reissue would mitigate the effect of the *Johnson* case. This is a prime example of a time that you would definitely want to consider obtaining a reissue of your patent. (See Chapter 15.)

Invalid Claims   If your analysis finds that a claim of a patent has been infringed, there is another task that can be performed; namely, an analysis of whether that claim is invalid. Even if a product or process infringes a claim, there is always the chance that the claim is invalid for a host of reasons.

SAMPLE INFRINGEMENT ANALYSIS

Following is a sample infringement analysis using our simplified table claim. The facts of this example are as follows: Assume you draft your patent having one independent claim directed toward a table having: 1) a top, 2) legs, and 3) a plurality of screws that attach the top to the legs. Suppose further that you come across the web page of a competitor who is selling Product A. Product A is a table having all of the elements of your claim, except that rivets are substituted for your screws to attach the top to the legs of the table. You report your findings to a patent attorney, who conducts an infringement analysis using the steps outlined above. The findings are reported in the memorandum.

The points in the memorandum are explained so that you can better understand the thinking process of determining infringement using the steps outlined earlier.

Note the heading stating that the memorandum is privileged and confidential and constitutes attorney *work product*. This is important, because if an attorney gives you an opinion that says that you are infringing, you probably will not want to reveal that to anyone else. If your case goes to court, you should not have to reveal it because it will be privileged under the *attorney-client privilege*. This is one advantage of having attorneys determine infringement opinions for you.

A brief introduction lets the reader know the memorandum is infringement analysis of Product A with the '243 Patent. It tells the reader what materials were relied upon. In this case, the attorney relies not only upon the '243 Patent, but also the file history that goes with that patent. This completes *step one* of the analysis of obtaining any necessary patents and file histories. *Step two* is also completed, because there is only one independent claim in this example.

In the opinion, a brief synopsis of what the applicable law is for patent infringement is also given. This leads immediately into *step three,* which involves construing the only claim in issue of the '243 Patent. This begins with an accurate description of Product A, since an accurate description of the product or process in issue is needed to determine infringement. To complete *step four,* a claim chart is included in the opinion so that the reader can easily visualize that the third element (the screws) are missing from Product A. In this case, Product A uses rivets rather than screws to attach the legs. The necessary conclusion is that there is no literal infringement of Claim 1 of the patent.

Since there is no literal infringement of Claim 1, the analysis must continue to determine if there is infringement under the doctrine of equivalence. In making the case for equivalence of the "rivets" for the "screws," the 3-part test is used to determine if the table of Product A performs substantially the same function, in substantially the same way, to obtain the same result, as the table of Claim 1. An argument that "rivets" are interchangeable for "screws" is made since persons skilled in the art knew that both rivets and screws could be used to attach two articles

The memorandum continues to discuss the fact that a review of the file history for the '243 Patent was made and nothing in that history was found that would limit application of the doctrine of equivalence with respect to the claim term ("screws").

The job is done when analysis for Claim 1 is finished. In this patent, there are no other claims to examine. (If your patent has other claims, you will need to analyze each of those other claims in the same manner.)

Although this is an oversimplified example and real-world examples will be more complex, the thought process that you go through for an infringement analysis is really this simple.

SAMPLE

MEMORANDUM

To	:	
CC	:	
From	:	James Rogers
Date	:	
Subject:		Infringement Opinion Memorandum

> **PRIVILEGED AND CONFIDENTIAL**
> Attorney-Client Communication
> Attorney Work Product

As requested, I conducted a study to determine whether Product A would infringe the following patents:

(1)   U.S. Patent No. 6,114,243 (the '243 Patent), assigned to Global Crossing, Inc.

My study included a review of each of the above patents as well as the prosecution history of the patents.

I. Conclusion

For the reasons set forth below and based solely on my examination of the above patents, in my opinion, one can make the following arguments:

A well-informed court should find that Product A would infringe the claims of the '243 Patent.

Applicable Legal Principles:

A determination of whether or not a patent is infringed involves a two-step process. Markman v. Westview Instruments, Inc., 52 F.3d 967 (Fed. Cir. 1995), aff'd 517 U.S. 370 (1996). The first step in claim construction involves ascertaining the scope and meaning of the claims at issue, while the second step involves determining whether the claims as construed read on the accused device. Steamfeeder, LLC v. Sure-Feed Sys., Inc., 175 F.3d 974, 981, 50 U.S.P.Q.2d 1515, 1519 (Fed. Cir. 1999). See also, Bai v. L&L Wings, Inc., 160 F.3d 1350, 1353, 480 U.S.P.Q.2d 1674, 1676 (Fed. Cir. 1998).

Description of Product A

The significant elements of Product A are as follows:
a) top;
b) legs; and,
c) rivets that attach the top to the legs.

Claims of the '243 Patent

The '243 Patent has six claims. Claim 1 is the only independent claim. It is a product claim comprising the following significant elements:
- top;
- legs; and,
- screws that are used to attach the top to the legs.

Product A Does Not Literally Infringe Claim 1

	Top	Legs	Screws
Product A	X	X	No (uses rivets)

The elements of Claim 1 of the '243 Patent are contained at the top of the claim chart. The third element (screws) is clearly missing from Product A. Product A uses rivets instead of screws. Since each and every element of Claim 1 is not contained in Product A, Claim 1 does not read upon Product A. There is no literal infringement of claim 1.

Product A Infringes Claim 1 Under the Doctrine of Equivalence

Although Product A does not literally infringe Claim 1 of the '243 Patent because the third element of Claim 1 (the screws) does not literally exist in Product A, a jury should find that the rivets used by Product A are an equivalent to the missing limitation (screws) used in the '243 Patent.

First, whether rivets or screws are used to attach the top to the legs does not alter the fact that Product A performs substantially the same function (it is used to place objects on) in substantially the same way, to yield substantially the same result, as the table of Claim 1. Moreover, the use of "rivets" instead of "screws" should be characterized as a mere insubstantial modification. Persons skilled in the art would recognize the interchangeability of "rivets" for "screws," since both rivets and screws were well known in the art as means for attachment.

In my review of the prosecution history of the '243 Patent, I found no amendments or statements made by the applicant that would otherwise limit the application of the doctrine of equivalence.

How to Design around a Competitor's Patent

Every business involved in the making, using, or selling of products needs to be concerned with patent infringement. As a business owner, you need to be keenly aware of your competition, their products, as well as their patents. We have already discussed how to construe patent claims. If, after going through that analysis from the prior chapter, you determine that one or more patents will block the launch of your product either through literal infringement or under the doctrine of equivalence and such patent claims can not be invalidated, you have several alternative courses of action.

- ✪ The first option is to give up your new product launch. Along these same lines, if you are currently infringing, cease and desist from your infringement.

- ✪ A second option includes buying or licensing the patents.

- ✪ If you really do not want to give up your product, you can try to design around the patent claims in question.

In this chapter I will teach you how to design around any competitor's patent using tools you already know.

FESTO AND PROSECUTION HISTORY ESTOPPEL

As discussed in the preceding chapter, the *Festo* decision held that a patent applicant who narrows a claim as a condition for obtaining a patent may invoke prosecution history estoppel and thereby relinquish the ability to extend the narrowed claim under the doctrine of equivalents to cover any broader subject matter. In other words, all subject matter between the broader and narrower claim language is surrendered if *Festo* applies.

Prosecution history estoppel can arise not only from narrowing amendments to a claim that you are interested in, but also from any claim narrowing activity made for reasons relating to patentability including the following types of activity:

- Narrowing amendment in a different claim

- Narrowing arguments or remarks made by the patentee during prosecution

- Concessions or acquiescence made by the patentee during prosecution

- Addition of a new claim

- Disclaimer in the specification or statements detailing shortcomings of the prior art

- Statements made in an information Disclosure Statement or Petition to Make Special

- Narrowing postissuance activity

In short, keep you eyes open for anything done or said by your patent owner during prosecution about his or her patent application. If you see some type of activity that could be construed as giving up claim scope coverage, then use such claim narrowing activity to your advantage.

Exceptions to
Festo

As stated previously, *Festo* creates a presumption that any narrowing amendment made during prosecution relates to patentability. However, there are three ways this presumption can be rebutted.

1. Show that an equivalent was unforeseeable. If an alleged equivalent was known in the prior art in the field of the invention, it is foreseeable at the time of the amendment. However, if the alleged equivalent represents later developed technology or technology that was not known in the relevant art, then it would not have been foreseeable.

Example:

Festo sued SMC for infringement of its magnetized pistons. In its patent, Festo had claimed a "magnetizable" sleeve, whereas SMC's accused product used an "aluminum" sleeve. During prosecution of its patent, Festo amended its claim in issue, which raised the presumption that it had given up any equivalents to the element in issue. However, Festo argued that this presumption should be rebutted because aluminum sleeves were unforeseeable to one of ordinary skill at the time of the amendment. The court in this case held that the rebuttal could not apply since aluminum sleeves were already well known in the art as defined by the original claim scope. Therefore, there could be no infringement.

---

2. Demonstrate that the purpose for any amendment was merely tangential to the alleged equivalent. An amendment made to avoid prior art that contains the equivalent in question is not tangential but rather central to allowance of the claim. Moreover, the reason for any amendment has to be discernible from the prosecution history record and understandable from the context in which the amendment was made in order for this exception to apply. Thus, silence in the record will generally be construed against the patentee. Despite these rules, accused infringers have been creative in applying this tangential exception to *Festo*.

Example:

Primos, Inc. was the assignee of a patent entitled "Game Call Apparatus" (the '578 patent). The '578 patent disclosed a diaphragm mouth call that hunters use to simulate animal sounds. The diaphragm mouth call consisted of a frame, a membrane that vibrates to produce sound, and a plate extending above the membrane. Competitor, Hunter, manufactured a similar device in which the diaphragm contained a dome extending above the membrane instead of the plate as in the '578 patent, but the device also contained a space between the vibrating membrane and the dome. The '578 patent also contained a space. During prosecution of the '578 patent, Primos amended the "plate" limitation to "having a length" and to be "differentially spaced." Hunter alleged that Primos was therefore estopped from claiming that the dome was the equivalent of "plate." However, the court disagreed, finding Primos had rebutted the *Festo* presumption of surrender of the equivalent at issue. First, in as far as the addition of "length," the court noted that it was not narrowing because length is an inherent characteristic of all physical objects.

Concerning, the term "differentially spaced" added to the plate limitation, the court found it to be narrowing but found that Primos had only surrendered those apparatus that "lack a space" between the platelike structure and the vibrating membrane since the record showed (is good to create a record) that the amendment was made with the sole purpose to confirm that the invention did not invade the prior art, which contained a platelike structure positioned directly on top with no spacing. Thus, Primos surrendered only those apparatus in which the platelike structure did not have a space. Thus the accused element (dome) did not fall within the territory surrendered because the dome had such a space. Thus the amendment "differentially spaced" was merely tangential to the allegedly equivalent dome, which contained a similar space.

3.   Establish "some other reason" that the patentee could not have reasonably been expected to have described the alleged equivalent, such as a shortcoming of language, which the patentee was prevented from describing the alleged equivalent

when it narrowed the claim. This category is a narrow one and available in order to not completely foreclose a patentee from relying on reasons, other than unforeseeability and tangentialness, to show that it did not surrender the alleged equivalent.

THE *FESTO* ANALYSIS IN CONCLUSION

Under a *Festo* analysis, your first question should be whether or not an amendment has narrowed the literal scope of a claim. If the amendment was not narrowing, then prosecution history estoppel does not apply. A second issue here is that even if the amendment was narrowing, the amendment must still be made for a substantial one relating to patentability.

When the prosecution history record reveals no reason for the amendment, then this question is easy; there is a presumption that the patentee had a substantial reason relating to patentability. The patentee is then in the position to rebut this presumption. If the court determines that a narrowing amendment has been made for a substantial reason relating to patentability, then there is a presumption that the patentee has surrendered all territory between the original claim limitation and the amended claim limitation. However, the patentee can rebut this presumption of total surrender by demonstrating that it did not surrender the particular equivalent in question under one of the three ways above: (1) foreseeability, (2) tangentialness, or (3) some other reason.

HOW TO USE *FESTO* AND PROSECUTION HISTORY ESTOPPEL TO DESIGN AROUND A COMPETITOR

In the *Festo* case, there was a judge who disagreed with the decision. In Judge Michel's dissenting opinion in that Federal Circuit Court decision, Judge Michel said the following:

> *Anyone who wants to steal a patentee's technology need only review the prosecution history to identify patentability-related amendments, and then make a trivial modification to that part*

of its product (or process) corresponding to an amended claim limitation. All other limitations may be copied precisely. The competitor will then be free to make, sue, or sell an insubstantial variant of the patentee's invention.

Whether you agree that allowing potential infringers to simply design around a patent by using the *Festo* decision is correct policy or not, you should not ignore the practical implications of this decision. Judge Michel is indeed correct that *Festo* now creates a way for any business to read the patents of a competitor and design around such claims to avoid potential patent infringement.

How can you use this ruling to your advantage?

1. First, determine claims of interest in a target patent (and possibly related applications or patents since there is case precedent for extending *Festo* to these related applications also).

2. Obtain a copy of the relevant prosecution history of those patents. This is easy to do as explained in the prior chapter (prosecution histories of patents can now be obtained online at www.uspto.gov).

3. Next, identify at least one claim element that was either narrowed or partially disclaimed during the prosecution history. You will also need to keep in mind that such disclaimer has to relate to reasons of patentability as discussed above.

4. Determine a reasonably foreseeable equivalent to the narrowed element of the claim of interest. This equivalent should be acceptable to you from a business perspective.

5. Now, proceed at will to legally make, use, or sell the product or process that includes that identified equivalent, preferably after obtaining a thorough and written noninfringement opinion form competent outside patent counsel (obtaining patent counsel opinions are discussed in Chapter 21).

Festo **Flowchart**

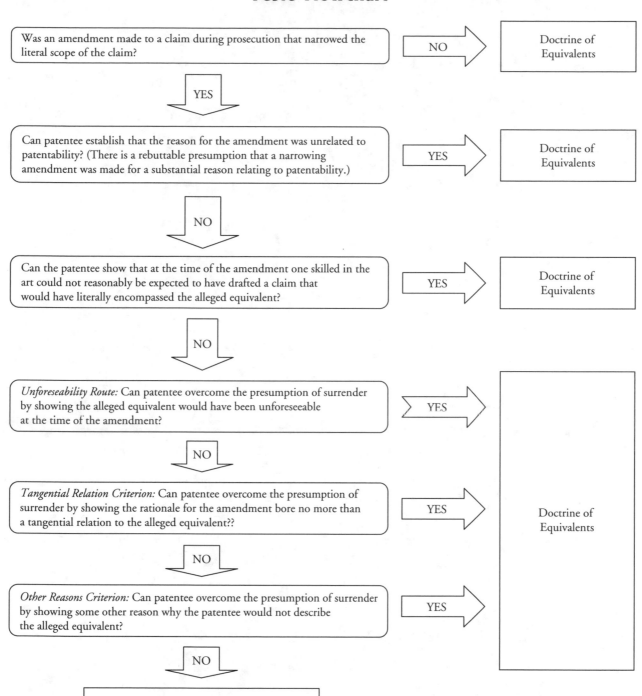

If Someone Infringes Your Patent

This chapter discusses the strategy if you have come to the opinion that a party is infringing your claimed invention. Unfortunately, patent litigation is a complex and expensive proposition. This is not something that you will be able to do alone (as you can with drafting and filing a patent application). You need to find a law firm that has experience in patent litigation. However, the information in this chapter will assist you in understanding this process and what decisions you will have to make.

CONSIDER NONLITIGATION STRATEGIES

A natural reaction when you see someone infringing on your patent rights will be the desire to bring a lawsuit. However, if you look at the situation in a different light, someone thinks your invention is so valuable that they are using it. You might look at the infringer as a potential future partner. If that party considers your invention that valuable, then you will probably be able to obtain a good license from that person for your technology. Licensing is an excellent way to market your invention and make money from it. (See Chapter 27.)

Knowing whether or not to bring a patent infringement lawsuit is a business decision unique to your own particular facts and circumstances. You can pursue various nonlitigation options on their own or in addition to a patent lawsuit. (See Chapter 20.)

Some factors that you should consider in weighing against suing for patent infringement are validity problems and costs.

Validity Problems   If you or your attorney believe that there are serious questions as to the validity of your patent, then you may be better off not pursuing the infringer. If you sue an infringer for patent infringement, and your patent is subsequently declared invalid, you will be *collaterally estopped* from suing any other infringers of your patent. (Validity defenses, such as collateral estoppel are discussed later, in Chapter 23.)

Cost   Patent infringement lawsuits are extremely expensive. There is a trial part of a case, as well as a year or two of the discovery phase. This *discovery phase* is when lawyers on each side exchange written requests for information and hold *depositions* to learn more about the issues in the case. It is not uncommon to have teams of lawyers doing this; each lawyer charging their typical hourly fee of $200 per hour and up. The average cost of patent litigation ranges between $500,000 and $3,995,000 per party. This expense may be something that you simply cannot afford at the early stage of your company. If paying a good plaintiff's team of lawyers will put you out of business before the lawsuit is even over, you may be better off either negotiating a license with the infringer, or settling your dispute out of court.

> NOTE: *The expense of a patent lawsuit is just one factor that you should consider in your overall decision, however. You need to weigh all factors, including whether you think you can be successful in your action. Also, to a potential infringer, the fact that you offered your invention for license can be used against you.*

Doing Nothing   Do not be lulled into believing that your best course of action may be to ignore the infringement since you will always be able to go to court and sue your infringer. In fact, you cannot go to court and sue for past infringements that are more than six years old. This is because there is a special statute that says that infringements occurring more than six years ago are too old to be the subject of a lawsuit. (See Chapter 10.)

Moreover, if you delay, there are other defenses that your potential infringers will surely raise such as *estoppel* and *laches*. They, in essence, bar or lessen the damages you can recover due to your inaction. These defenses are also discussed in Chapter 10.

HIRING A PLAINTIFF'S TEAM

While no firm will be able to guarantee the outcome of your case, you can stack the odds in your favor by making an informed choice for your counsel. Your first step is to locate some potential candidates to represent you. Consider the following factors as you identify some possible candidates:

Technical Expertise

If no one on your legal team can understand your technology, then they are not going to be able to do a good job explaining things about the case to a judge or jury. The technical qualifications that you should look for are education or experience in the technical field. For example, the highest educational level that can be obtained in a technical area is the PhD. However, you should look even further than this. What is the experience of the PhD in your field? A PhD with industrial experience would probably be better than one with no post-degree experience. In other words, make sure to look at the whole picture.

Specific Experience

You will want to ensure that the firm you hire has specific experience with patent litigation. If the firm has never represented anyone with a similar case to yours, then you will probably be better off not serving as a test client for that firm.

Cost

Do not be afraid to get a ballpark figure of how much the patent infringement action is going to cost you. At a minimum, you should know the hourly rates of your team of lawyers. Some firms will go as far as giving you a projection of the costs for the various stages of litigation in writing.

Who Will Handle Your Case

Make sure that you know which attorneys of the firm will be handling your case. Too often what occurs is that you are impressed by the résumés of one or two of the partners of the law firm you intend to hire, only to find out that those attorneys will not actually be doing the work on your case.

Locating Possible Candidates

Most, if not all, attorneys and their firms, have websites. One of the easiest ways to locate attorneys who are in the business of patent litigation is to do an Internet search for firms that practice in this area. You might limit your results by geography and technology. Beyond using search engines on the Internet to find firms, you can also go to www.martindale.com, which conveniently lists most of the firms in the United States and allows you to conduct searches based on criteria that you select.

After you have come up with some possible choices for representation, your next step will be to contact these firms. The best person to contact will be one of the senior partners at the firm. These persons are usually listed near the top of the firm's biographies, and their names will usually be incorporated into the name of the firm. For example, if your potential law firm is named Jones & Williams, it will be a safe bet that either Jones or Williams will be senior partners.

There are a number of ways to contact the partners. One easy method of initial contact may be an email, explaining that you are seeking potential counsel and would like to learn more about the firm. Another way is a personal telephone call. Many clients also use a *Request for Proposal*. This is simply a form or letter that asks the firm certain questions about representation.

Whatever method of contact you use, you must also have a face-to-face interview with the partners of the firm, as well as the people who will be working on your case. You should ensure at this interview that all of your questions regarding any of the factors listed above have been answered. After the interview, tell the firm that you will take some time to think things over, and that you will be in touch.

WHO TO SUE

The answer to this may seem obvious—sue anyone who is infringing your patent. In an ideal world, it probably is going to be best for you to go after anyone who you believe is infringing your patent. However we do not live in an ideal world, and often answers to seemingly simple questions are not all that simple. Just as in the case of considering your noninfringement options altogether, you may want to consider who you should sue at the outset.

Leave an infringer out of your lawsuit when your resources are limited. Big companies have a lot more resources to defend against patent infringement lawsuits. It could be that by pursuing a smaller and weaker company first, you may obtain quicker success.

Perhaps your decision may result very quickly in a settlement or license with the smaller company. By obtaining such a license, you might obtain enough resources to better prepare for an action later on against the larger company that you think is also infringing your patent. In either case, it is worth discussing with your plaintiff's team.

It will also make sense to go after the person who has the largest profits from infringement of your patent. This will be important when it comes time to determine your damages if you are successful. It will probably not make much sense to go after a customer who is purchasing the infringing product. The purchaser will probably have smaller pockets, and will probably be your own potential customer. Instead, you will want to go after the manufacturer or supplier of the infringing product or both.

NOTE: *As already alluded to, be careful though, when you pick and choose. You have six years to sue for infringing activity before that activity becomes too old. You will learn about another defense in Chapter 23, called* laches *where your delay in filing your lawsuit may preclude you from recovery from any damages that occur prior to your filing.*

A potential defendant, who you elect not to sue, will surely raise this defense in order to lessen the impact of any subsequent lawsuit that you try to pursue with that later defendant. In such instances, you might be wise to send the non-elected defendant

a letter stating that your election to pursue your other defen-
dant first, in no way should be construed as your giving up any
of your rights with respect to that non-elected defendant.

ASSERTION LETTERS

After you have considered all your options (litigation and nonlitigation options alike), you should consider drafting an *assertion letter* to be sent to your competitor. In this letter you can alert your competitor to your patent rights, and also include any proposals for resolution of the situation. The most common type of resolution is an offer to license your patent rights for future royalties on sale of the products being sold. (Licensing is discussed later, in Chapter 27.) You also have the option, however, of simply telling your competitor to stop the infringement. In other words, it is up to you whether you want to offer a license to your competitor. If you offer a license or not, you should also consider asking your competitor to pay you some compensation for the past infringement.

This letter is sometimes referred to as a *cease and desist letter* because it sometimes contains strong language that your competitor must cease and desist from any further infringing activity. The strong terminology of *cease and desist* may not be your best strategy for writing an effective assertion letter. The point of an assertion letter is often not to tell your alleged infringer to cease and desist activity immediately or else, but to start commercialization. You want to inform the potential infringer that you uncovered what you feel to be a clear violation of your patent rights, and you want to let that infringer know you mean business. However, you also may want or need certain doors to negotiation and settlement to remain open.

– Caution –

Your best course of action may actually be to alert your accused infringer about your patent rights, rather than make any specific charges of infringement and demand a cessation of activity. Plus, your hard choice of words may allow your infringer to actually sue you first for something that is called a *declaratory judgment*. In some recent cases, assertion letters have recently been construed to raise the necessary basis for a declaratory judgment.

The only case where you may want to make a specific charge of infringement is if you need to give your competitor actual notice of your patent rights. This may happen if you have failed to give the world constructive notice of your patent rights by marking your products with your patent number.

You may recall from the first chapter that, if you have commercialized products under your patent, but have failed to mark your products with your patent number so as to provide constructive notice, you are precluded from recovering damages for infringing activity until your infringer is provided actual notice. If you have marked your products, then this is not a concern. But if you have failed to mark your products, then you will need to make sure that your assertion letter is assertive enough to give your alleged infringer actual notice. Even here, however, you can word your assertion letter so as not to trigger a declaratory judgment.

To provide actual notice, you need to inform your competitor about your patent, and infringement of it. (U.S.C., Title 35, Sec. 287(a).) You should also provide your patentee's identity. You do not need to threaten a lawsuit or demand cessation of activities. You should simply alert your competitor to your patent number, that you believe your competitor's activity constitutes infringement, and include a proposal to abate or stop the infringement.

Example:

Anne finds out that a competitor in the film industry was using one of her new improved batteries to power its video cameras. Anne wrote the following letter to the competitor: "We have noted from your advertising literature that products Models Ultramark 4 and 8 may infringe one or more claims of U.S. Patent No. 4,016,750, Philip S. Green, NEW IMPROVED BATTERY DEVICE. A copy of the patent is enclosed. We would be pleased to provide you with a nonexclusive license under the patent."

The case ultimately went to court where Anne won her patent infringement action. The competitor argued that Anne could not collect damages for infringement prior to her lawsuit because she had failed to mark her products and provide the competitor with actual notice.

The court disagreed, holding that Anne had informed the competitor of the identity of her patent, the activity believed to be an infringement, and had also given a proposal to remedy the infringement.

Another reason that you may not want to make strong accusations of infringement is that if you make such accusations now, but never take any actions against the potential infringer, that infringer will have a good argument for the defense of *estoppel*. Basically, the defendant will argue that your actions (strong accusations), followed by silence on the matter, amounts to conduct that implies you really did not intend to press your infringement action since you failed to take immediate action.

If you do make strong accusations, be prepared to follow up with a lawsuit within a reasonable period of time. If you do otherwise, you may be leading your defendant into believing that you actually are not going to enforce your patent rights. Such actions on your part can bar you from recovery in an infringement action, if and when you finally do get around to bringing your action.

Your notice that your competitor's activity constitutes infringement does not have to be in the form of a specific unqualified charge of infringement. An offer to license may provide the necessary notice of infringement.

Example:

Tom included a specific reference to the claims in his patent as well as the following statement: "You may wish to have your patent counsel examine the patent to determine whether a non-exclusive license under the patent is needed." The court held that this was enough to satisfy Tom's notice requirements with respect to the patent. The court held that a reasonable person would understand that an offer to license was in effect a notice that the defendant was currently infringing the patent since the whole point of a license is to insulate a licensee from infringement charges by a licensor. *(Gart v. Logitech, 254 F.3d 1334 (Fed. Cir. 2001).)*

Declaratory Judgments

If you threaten your competitor with a lawsuit, your competitor may actually be able to bring you to court first for a *declaratory judgment*. In a declaratory judgment, your competitor might ask the court to declare that your competitor's actions are noninfringing, or that your patent is invalid or unenforceable.

While this may not sound like a big deal, a declaratory judgment can be a procedural advantage to your competitor. To illustrate, suppose your competitor is located in Texas, while you are located in New York. Your competitor may be able to gain an advantage by actually suing you first in his or her home state of Texas, where juries might be slightly more sympathetic to their hometown corporations. If you take control of the action, and sue first in New York, then you may get the advantage. Studies have also been done that have shown that a competitor or alleged infringer is much more likely to win a court case when it selects the forum. (See K.A. Moore, "Forum Shopping in Patent Cases: Does Geographic Choice Affect Innovation?, 79 N.C.L. Rev. 889, 898 (2001).)

One of the prerequisites for a declaratory judgment is that there must be something that is referred to as an *actual controversy*. If you use harsh words and threaten your competitor with a patent lawsuit, you will have created this actual controversy, which then allows your competitor to seek a declaratory judgment.

– Caution –

A new Federal Circuit Court decision—*SanDisk*—has greatly lowered the bar as to what activity of a potential plaintiff satisfies an actual controversy standard. According to this decision, as soon as a patent owner asserts its patent rights against certain ongoing or planned activity of another party and that party asserts its own right to engage in the accused activity, the "actual case and controversy" exists. Thus, not only assertion letters, but virtually any invitation to take a paid license relating to the prospective licensee's activities can potentially give rise to a case or controversy if the licensee contends it is permitted to act without a license. Not only might you have a lawsuit on your hands that you can not afford, but a declaratory judgment will give your potential infringer a strategic advantage. In light of this decision, you have two options.

1. You could file an infringement action first, and then pursue licensing negotiations. The problem with this option is that it is an expensive one. You will need to hire an attorney to file the action. This is true even if all you intend to do is to file the complaint but withhold service of the summons and complaint until licensing discussions play out.

2. Execute an agreement to negotiate with the potential infringer, which not only contains a confidentiality clause that prevents either party from divulging the contents of any discussion to third parties but also contains *non-use* and *non-litigation clauses*. A *non-use clause* contractually bars any party from using information obtained through negotiation for purposes other than settlement, such as for litigation, as a basis of establishing a case or controversy, or for developing competitive products. A *non-litigation clause* prohibits a party from initiating litigation for a determined period. A non-litigation clause can be mutual (both parties can agree not to file any lawsuit for a specified period of time) or it can be one-sided (i.e., require the potential licensee to agree not to file any declaratory judgment action within a certain period).

BEFORE FILING A LAWSUIT

You should insist that your attorney conduct his or her own investigation as to whether infringement exists and submit to you a written opinion before starting a lawsuit. Your attorney may also suggest the help of outside scientific consultants who may be able to make scientific comparisons between the product and your own invention. You should allow your attorney to hire such outside consultants.

The reason that you should insist on a written opinion now is that patent lawsuits are very expensive and you might lose the case. The opinion should give you some idea as to the prospects that you can succeed in court. Also, remember that if you go to court and your patent is determined to be invalid or unenforceable, you will not only be prevented from asserting your rights against this one company, but any other people who make, use, or sell your invention. In other words, it might make more sense to keep the whole thing quiet, and perhaps enter into a licensing arrangement with the company you think is infringing your patent, rather than risk the possibility that your patent will be held invalid or unenforceable in a court.

Another reason for obtaining a written opinion from your attorney is that you could subject yourself to expensive sanctions if it is determined that your patent lawsuit is without merit. Having a written opinion from your attorney will help you avoid such sanctions.

If after the written opinion you truly believe you have a strong case, and you cannot work things out with your alleged infringer, then by all means a patent lawsuit may be your best course of action.

WHERE TO FILE YOUR LAWSUIT

Patent law involves federal questions of law, which means that you will need to bring your action in federal court. At the outset, your case will start in federal district court. Appeals from that court will go to a special federal court that hears patent law cases, namely, the Federal Circuit Court of Appeals, which is located in Washington, D.C.

You will not always have the ability to pick and choose the district court where you want to sue your defendant. The reason for this is that lawsuits may only be filed in a court that has jurisdiction and proper venue over your defendant. The primary patent venue statute is 28 U.S.C. 1400(b), which states that a patent infringement lawsuit may be filed in a jurisdiction (a) where the defendant resides; or, (b) where the infringement occurred so long as the defendant has a regular and established place of business in that jurisdiction. However, Congress considerably broadened the definition of a defendant's *residence* in the above statute to include any jurisdiction where the court has personal jurisdiction. A defendant that is a corporation is deemed to reside in any judicial district in which it is subject to personal jurisdiction at the time the action is commenced. (28 U.S.C. 1391).

If you do have a choice, most plaintiffs will want to file in the federal court near their hometown. The reason for this is that you are more likely to obtain a favorable jury verdict in your hometown. But there are some other factors that you may want to consider. For example, some federal courts are much quicker than other courts. These quicker federal courts, often referred to as *rocket dockets* can have an average filing-to-trial length of just twelve months, which is astonishingly quicker than other federal district courts where litigation can languish on for years. Some courts are also statistically more favorable than other courts with respect to the number of judgments awarded in favor of the plaintiff versus the defendant. These are all factors that you should discuss with your attorney.

Once it is established that the forum is one in which the action can be brought, parties invariably will seek to have cases transferred to other districts for a variety of reasons. A district court is allowed to transfer a case to any other district where the lawsuit could initially have been brought for the convenience of the parties and witnesses. Courts actually use a number of factors in deciding a transfer motion, including:

1. the convenience of the parties and the witnesses;

2. the location where the alleged events took place;

3. the relative ease of access to the sources of proof;

4. the plaintiff's choice of form (with weight given to the plaintiff's choice unless it is the result of forum-shopping);

5. the pendency of related litigation in the transfer forum;

6. the relative congestion in the two courts;

7. the public interest in the local adjudication of local controversies; and,

8. the relative familiarity of the courts with applicable.

Imported Products If you think that your patent is being infringed by products being imported from abroad, you should also consider filing a complaint with the U.S. International Trade Commission (USITC). The USITC is a quasi-judicial agency created by Congress to monitor and stop unfair international trade practices. If the Commission finds a violation of the law, it may order the exclusion of the product from the United States.

Although Section 377 empowers the ITC to handle all types of infringement cases, the vast majority of Section 337 cases concern patent infringement because owners of federally registered trademarks or copyrights can exclude infringing imports by simply registering online with the customs service. Owners of patents, however, must first get an exclusion order from the ITC, which the customs service then enforces.

To get an exclusion order, a patent owner needs to prove three things:

1. that it has a valid U.S. patent;

2. the patent is infringed by an imported good; and,

3. the patent holder is using the patent in the United States (which is interpreted broadly and encompasses R&D efforts involving the patent as well as attempts to license the patent).

Advantages to initiating an ITC action include the following:

- *Time.* Unlike district court cases, which typically take three to four years, the ITC decides cases within one year.

- *Broad Jurisdiction.* The ITC holds broad jurisdiction including *in rem jurisdiction* (jurisdiction over property) and nationwide subpoena and enforcement powers.

- *Exclusion Orders.* In addition, the ITC can issue general exclusion orders, regardless of personal jurisdiction that prevent infringing articles from entering the country. Pursuant to Section 337 of the Tariff Act of 1930, the ITC can bar all imports that infringe a U.S. company's IP rights.

Example:

A Chinese company, C, makes infringing computer chips. The company may be beyond the jurisdiction of U.S. courts if the company does not sell directly to the United States, but rather sells its chips to a Malaysian circuit board manufacturer, which then sells to a Taiwanese computer maker that then exports its products to the United States. The ITC still has in rem jurisdiction over all imports. Moreover, the ITC does not even name an infringer to ban its imports; it can issue a general exclusion order that bars all imports that infringe a complainant's IP rights.

As a result of these advantages, the number of infringement cases brought to the ITC has tripled in the last decade. Given a recent 2006 Supreme Court decision (*eBay v. MerExchange*), which has toughened the requirements for issuing injunctions in patent cases, the ITC will likely become even more popular.

However, keep these points in mind about the ITC. The ITC only provides *injunctive relief* (ie., the exclusion of infringing products form the U.S. territories or prohibition of after-import sales). It does not provide monetary damages. For monetary damages, you will need to commence a court action.

There is also no jury available for an ITC proceeding. The ITC staff attorney participates in the action and the request for a temporary restraining order is heard before an administrative law judge with no interlocutory appeal or review during pendency by the commissioner.

Another thing to keep in mind is that because ITC proceedings are so quick, you must spend a lot of time, money, and effort preparing for an administrative trial up front. These costs may be too great for smaller companies to bear. This is why larger companies often initiate §337 proceedings.

> ### Author's Note: Other infringement statutes
> Do not forget your other possible infringement statutes, which may help you enforce your patent rights against infringers who import products from above, as discussed in Chapter 17. For example, there is a special infringement statute that you can use for products that are being imported into the United States if those products are being made using your U.S. patented process. (U.S.C, Title 35, Sec.271(g).) The statute provides that "whoever without authority imports into the U.S. or offers to

sell, sells or uses within the U.S. a product which is made by a process patented in the U.S. shall be liable as an infringer, if the importation, offer to sell, sale, or use of the product occurs during the term of such process patent." One strategy that you might think about is to pursue both an action with the ITC and also commence a district court action. This way you can try to obtain a quick injunction in the ITC proceeding before litigating damages in the district court.

For more information about complaints to the USITC, you can consult 19 U.S.C. 1337. You can also find more information about the USITC at their home page www.usitc.gov.

Author's Note: Intellectual property and U.S. Customs

For your other intellectual property (i.e., copyrights and trademarks), you should consider the U.S. Customs and Border Protection. U.S. Customs is divided into two separate agencies—U.S. Customs and Border Protection (CBP), and U.S. Immigration and Customs Enforcement (ICE). CBP has three main enforcement arms. Its IPR branch, based in Washington, D.C., provides pre-seizure advice, maintains an IPR database of recorded trademarks and copyrights, and provides IPR training to the field. Another CBP arm, its Office of Field Operations (OFO) has agents at every port of entry. The third arm, the Los Angeles Strategic Trade Center, coordinates overall enforcement plans in partnership with U.S. industries and operates an IPR help desk.

If a business has protectable trademarks or copyrights, which could be monetarily or reputationally harmed if infringing products gain entry into the U.S. market, it should consider registering with U.S. Customs. The recordation process requires submitting samples or photos and information regarding legitimate users and suspected infringers. The price at the time this book was published was $190 and recordation is good for ten years.

For trademarks, Customs will take action at the border if products coming in are confusingly similar to your trademark. If a product is determined to be confusingly similar by Customs, the product is detained and the importer is given a thirty-day opportunity to obtain release of the goods by either securing the trademark owner's written permission to import the goods or obliterate the offending trademarks. If this is not done, the goods are typically seized. For copyrights, Customs agents generally determine whether an ordinary observer would be disposed to overlook minor differences between two works and consider their overall aesthetic appeal to be the same.

More information about recordation can be found at the U.S. Customs website at www.cbp.gov/xp/cgov/import/commercial_enforcement/ipr/.

INTERNATIONAL LITIGATION STRATEGIES

International patent holders should consider commencing litigation against infringers abroad in the countries where patent protection has been obtained. This is an expensive proposition and will typically not apply to the individual inventor. But large corporations are constantly involved in litigation abroad with their global patents. One place to start such litigation is in Germany. Germany is well known for its expedited rulings and once these rulings are obtained, they may persuade potential defendants to stop infringing activities in other European countries.

Relief Available in Patent Infringement Cases

Patent holders obtain some of the largest damage awards reported. The amount of damages awarded will depend on the particular circumstances of your own case. It is not uncommon, however, to see awards in the multimillions of dollars. These large monetary awards, in addition to the high costs of litigation itself, make patent infringement actions something that should be seriously considered by any individual or company.

In addition to monetary awards for things like lost profits, patent holders can also be awarded an enhancement of damages where patent infringement is found to be willful. Attorney fees are also recoverable in certain circumstances.

The large possible financial exposure that patent infringers face should serve as a warning to people who blindly commence activities that can infringe upon the patent rights of others. As stated before, knowing something about what does and does not constitute infringement is not something just for the patent holder to know. Every individual or company who engages in activities that could potentially infringe upon the patent rights of others should have a good understanding of patent infringement so that financial exposure is minimized. The upcoming chapters discuss exactly what you should do if you have been threatened with patent infringement.

In addition to monetary awards, patent holders can also obtain other forms of relief that may be equally or more detrimental to competitors. This chapter will start out with the most important non-monetary relief, the *injunction*.

After this chapter you will have a solid understanding of the types of relief that you may be able to recover as a patent holder in an infringement action. Perhaps even more important, you will be aware of the type of exposure that your organization could be exposed to if your actions are found to infringe upon the rights of patent holders.

INJUNCTIVE RELIEF

One very potent weapon in patent lawsuits is the *injunction*. Injunctions are orders by a court that may, for example, require that a party stop selling a product that is alleged to be infringing a patent. Injunctions are so powerful because they can be used to squeeze out the life of your competitor. If your competitor is making most of its money through the sale of a product, and you believe this constitutes infringement of your patent, you can stop the money flow with an injunction.

There are two types of injunctions: *preliminary* and *permanent*. If you win a patent infringement lawsuit against an infringer, part of your relief, in addition to damages, will likely be a *permanent injunction,* which prevents the defendant from making, using, offering to sell, or selling products that are covered by your patent claims. (Such an injunction is something that will come with your victory.)

But, you should also consider obtaining an injunction of your defendant's activities right at the start of your lawsuit by seeking a *preliminary injunction.* By moving quickly and obtaining an injunction this way, you will more quickly damage your competitor. If you wait until you have won the case, your competitor may, in fact, have used the proceeds from its infringement sales to build up its company.

For injunction relief, a patentee must demonstrate four factors:

1. reasonable likelihood of success;

2. balance of hardships favor the movant;

3. irreparable harm; and,

4. public interest.

Reasonable Likelihood of Success

The movant (such as a patent holder) will need to make a showing that it has a reasonable likelihood of winning the lawsuit. To do this as a patent holder, you will need to make some type of showing that your patent is valid, enforceable, and infringed by the defendant. With respect to validity, you should rely on United States Code, Title 35, Section 282, which states that all patents are presumed to be valid. Therefore, if your defendant raises no issues of invalidity, then you should not have to do anything to establish your rights with respect to validity. (*New England Braiding Co. v. A.W. Chesterton Co.,* 970 F.2d 878 (Fed. Cir. 1992).)

Balance of Hardships Favor Movant

The movant must show that the harm it will incur outweighs the harm that will be inflicted upon the alleged infringer. One way to do this is to add up the economic injury that the patent holder will suffer between the date of the injunction and the conclusion of the trial, and then compare this amount with the alleged infringer's gain. If the economic injury is greater, this element should exist in favor of the movant.

Irreparable Harm

The movant must show that if the preliminary injunction is not granted, that the movant will suffer irreparable harm. If the movant can show that it will likely succeed in the lawsuit and that there is continuing infringement of the patents, a presumption of irreparable harm will exist.

NOTE: *In several cases, courts have held that a patentee's offer to license the patented technology meant that no irreparable harm could exist since it showed that the patentee was willing to forgo its patent rights for compensation in the form of a license. (T.J. Smith and Nephew Limited v. Consol. Med. Equip. Inc., 802 F.2d 646 (Fed. Cir. 1987).)*

Public Interest   This factor requires that the movant demonstrate that the public interest would not be disserved by the injunction.

LOST PROFITS

A patent owner is entitled to recover lost profits if it can be shown that he or she would have received the additional profit but for the infringement of the defendant. (*Rite-Hite Corp. v. Kelley Co., Inc.,* 56 F.3d 1538, 35 U.S.P.Q.2d 1065 (Fed. Cir. 1995).) One thing that you will be required to prove in order to recover your lost profits is the absence of what are called *noninfringing alternatives.* The existence of a noninfringing product will bar you from recovering lost profits. (*Grain Processing Corp. v. American Maize-Products O.,* 185 F.3d 1341, 51 U.S.P.Q.2d 1556 (Fed. Cir. 1999).)

You will want to claim that without the infringement, the defendant's product could not exist. In other words, you will want all the money of the defendant. Your argument is that every sale your defendant made was lost by you, and contributed to your lost profits.

In a two brand market, your argument may prevail. But the case will usually not be this clear cut. Also, the defendant may argue that the infringement relates to a specific feature of a product, and that your claim should not be based on all of the sales of the infringing party.

One way to prove lost profits is through surveys of customers. For example, you might be able to determine through such surveys what the price of the product would have had to have dropped in order to compensate for the lack of the infringing feature. This type of analysis is sometimes called *conjoint analysis,* and it used to describe a broad range of market research techniques for measuring the value people place on the features that define products. If you could show through such techniques that the infringing feature was a major part of the consumer's purchase decision, you would have a case that you lost many sales due to the infringement.

Much of the evidence required for lost profits is also evidence needed to show irreparable harm if you seek a permanent injunction. Thus putting in evidence for lost profits can help in this regard.

REASONABLE ROYALTY

A *reasonable royalty* is often regarded as the floor below which your damages for patent infringement cannot go. This is because there is a specific statute that specifically states that a patentee is entitled to no less than a reasonable royalty for patent infringement. (U.S.C., Title 35, Sec. 284.)

You can employ techniques, such as customer surveys, to determine a reasonable royalty. You might also look at what are typical royalty rates that would result from *arms-length negotiations* between a willing licensor of your invention and a licensee. Under this method, a reasonable royalty is calculated by envisioning the result of the parties' hypothetical negotiation for a license to the claimed invention at the time infringement began. This determination is made by either a judge or a jury and is guided by application of a fifteen-factor test specified in a court case called *Georgia Pacific v. United States Plywood Corp.,* 318 F.Supp. 116 (S.D.N.Y. 1970), modified and aff'd, 446 F.2d 295 (2d Cir) (1971).

Author's Note: Royalty Calculations

Current patent law permits a reasonable royalty calculation based on the invention that corresponds to the infringed claim. However, a new pending bill may change this and limit reasonable royalty recovery to the "economic value properly attributable to the patent's specific contributions over the prior art" or the inventive portion of the claim. For example, damages for a claim directed to an improved windshield wiper would be calculated based on the value of the infringing wiper rather than the sales price of the entire care into which the wiper is installed if this new law is passed. The only exception would be where the patentee can show that its claim's contribution is the predominant basis for market demand of an entire product or process.

– Caution –

A patentee can only collect damages beginning when it first began to continuously mark its products with its patent number or when the defendant was first notified of the infringement, whichever occurred first.

Provisional Rights

You might be asking from what date you are entitled to damage awards for the infringing activity of your defendant. The answer typically is from when your patent is issued. However, there is a special statute that allows you to seek a *reasonable royalty* for infringing activities of your defendant between the date your patent application was published through the date your patent was issued, so long as a few conditions are met. (U.S.C., Title 35, Sec. 154(d).)

One condition is that your claimed invention in your patent must be substantially identical to your claimed invention in your published application. You must have also given actual notice of your published application to your alleged infringer. You could provide such notice if, for example, you sent your defendant a notice that they were infringing the claims of your published application.

INTEREST, COSTS, AND FEES

A court has the power to award the prevailing plaintiff both interest on the judgment, as well as costs. (U.S.C., Title 35, Sec. 284.) The prevailing party in a patent infringement case is entitled to their own reasonable attorney fees in what are referred to as *exceptional cases*. (U.S.C., Title 35, Sec. 285.)

You should note that a prevailing party can be either the patent holder or the alleged infringer. For example, if you have succeeded on your patent infringement suit against a competitor and are awarded damages, you would be considered the prevailing party. However, if your competitor were to win the suit by having the court declare your patent invalid, your competitor would be the prevailing party, and at least qualify for attorney fees under this statute.

The award of attorney fees is not easy. The case must be ruled exceptional as the statute above states. For example, a finding of willful infringement, which can subject a patent defendant to *treble damages,* does not necessarily require a finding that a case is exceptional. (*Modine Mfg. Co. v. The Allen Group, Inc.,* 917 F.2d 538, 16 U.S.P.Q.2d 1622 (Fed. Cir. 1990).)

The court has discretion in what it thinks may or may not be exceptional. *Inequitable conduct,* a defense to patent infringement, is one type of circumstance where a court may find that a case is exceptional. (See Chapter 23.) Another example of where a court may declare a case exceptional is illustrated below.

Example:

A patent application on a surgical blade was declared invalid because the blade had been sold more than one year prior to the filing of the application. The attorney filing the patent application conducted no investigation into the facts surrounding the prior sale and the court ruled that the case was exceptional since the attorney breached its duty of candor by failing to disclose the prior sale to the PTO. The court found, in this case, that the attorney had notice that a potentially invalidating sale took place, but willfully chose to ignore such notice, making the case exceptional. The defendant was awarded attorneys fees. (*Brasseler U.S.A., I, L.P. v. Stryker Sales Corp.,* 267 F.3d 1370 (Fed. Cir. 2001).)

ENHANCEMENT OF DAMAGES

A court has the power to increase the amount of damages up to three times the amount found. (U.S.C., Title 35, Sec. 284.) Enhancement of damages does not exist to compensate a patent holder for things like lost profits. The purpose of enhancement of damages is to punish culpable conduct on the part of the infringer.

While you may think that the infringement itself is culpable conduct, what is meant here is something more than infringement. The defendant must have done something more than unknowingly infringed on your rights. You will need to show that your infringer blatantly disregarded your patent rights. This type of disregard is referred to in patent law as *willfulness.* It is probably the most important factor used to enhance damages against a defendant.

Willfulness is determined by considering the totality of the circumstances. *Gustafson, Inc. v. Intersystems Indus. Prods., Inc., 897 F2d 508, 510 (Fed. Cir. 1990).* The circumstances considered include the following:

- ✪ whether the infringer deliberately copied the ideas of design;

- ✪ whether the infringer, when he or she knew of the patent protection, investigated its scope and formed a good-faith belief of non-infringement or invalidity;

- ✪ the infringer's behavior in the litigation;

- ✪ the defendant's size and financial condition;

- ✪ the closeness of the case (e.g., whether infringement was literal or under the doctrine of equivalents);

- ✪ the duration of the defendant's infringement, including whether there was any continued infringement after judgment or affirmance of the infringement suit;

- ✪ any remedial action by the defendant;

- ✪ the defendant's motivation for harm; and,

- ✪ whether defendant attempted to conceal its misconduct.

Author's Note: Seagate

The most recent case concerning willful infringement is the *Seagate* case, which held that in order to find willful infringement a patentee must show by clear and convincing evidence that the infringer acted despite an objectively high likelihood that its actions constituted infringement of a valid patent. If this threshold objective standard is satisfied, the patentee must also demonstrate that this objectively defined risk—determined by the record developed in the infringement proceeding—was either known or so obvious that it should have been known to the accused infringer. (*In re Seagate*, 497 F.3d 1360 (Fed. Cir. 2007).) The *Seagate* decision also clarified that there is no affirmative obligation to obtain opinion of counsel in order to avoid liability for willful infringement.

While there are no hard and fast rules for determining whether infringement is willful, there are certain things that either mitigate against finding willful infringement or weigh in favor of a finding of willful infringement.

Although the *Seagate* decision stated that there is no affirmative obligation to obtain opinion of counsel in order to avoid liability for willful infringement, I would recommend that you obtain an opinion from patent counsel anyway. Patent counsel is probably the most important thing that can be used to negate a finding of willful infringement when the defendant has obtained the opinion of counsel advising the defendant that it is OK to keep doing what he or she is doing. Counsel may base such advice on its opinion that the defendant's activities do not constitute patent infringement. Alternatively, counsel may base the decision that even if the defendant's activity could constitute patent infringement, the patents are either invalid or unenforceable. There are many arguments that can be made to support the invalidity or unenforceability of a patent. (See Chapter 23.)

NOTE: *Obtaining an opinion from counsel before engaging in or continuing in conduct that could be patent infringement is so important later on in a court's decision to grant or deny enhancement of damages. It is so important that an opinion is one of the first things that anyone should do when accused of patent infringement.*

Another factor that can mitigate either for or against a finding of infringement is *good faith licensing negotiations*. For example, if you offer a defendant a license for your patented technology, and the defendant dismisses such an offer, you should be able to use the defendant's dismissal as evidence for a finding of willful infringement.

What to Do if You Are Sued for Patent Infringement

If you receive a letter from someone who alleges that you are infringing a patent, you need to take the allegations very seriously. You should not simply ignore the letter. Obtain the advice of a patent attorney right at the start. Again, select a patent attorney who has experience in patent litigation.

The reason that you need to take any such allegations seriously is that if you simply ignore the letter, and continue what you are doing, you can be liable for *willful infringement* later on if the patent holder wins his or her case in court. Willful infringement will subject you to three times the amount of damages against you, and patent awards are already some of the largest in court cases.

Remember that any potential infringer who has actual notice of another's patent rights has an affirmative duty to exercise due care to determine whether or not she is infringing. (*Underwater Devices, Inc. V. Morrison Knudsen Co.*, 717 F.2d 1380, 1390 (Fed. Cir. 1983).) This duty of due care usually includes the duty to seek and obtain competent legal advice from counsel before the initiation of possible infringing activity.

The opinion from your counsel should discuss whether the patents that are the subject of the infringement allegations are valid and enforceable. (Arguments that can be made to attack the validity and enforceability of a patent will be discussed in the next chapter. If you are accused of patent infringement you should become familiar with these arguments since you can help your attorney form a defense strategy.)

The patent holder should actively participate in the defense. This is because your attorney will need to gather the necessary facts and evidence to support your position. You can be invaluable in assisting your attorney.

Patent lawsuits are very complex. There is always the possibility that your attorney will leave something out that can assist in your defense. One reason for this is your attorney may not be fully aware of the facts in your case. By actively assisting your attorney in gathering evidence and formulating defense strategies, you will better ensure that something is not omitted.

HIRING A DEFENSE TEAM

Everything stated in Chapter 7 with respect to hiring a plaintiff's team equally applies here. You should ensure that your team of lawyers include members who have not only patent litigation expertise, but also the necessary technical expertise to understand the technology of your case.

Even if you are a corporation with inside counsel, you will want to hire the services of competent outside counsel. The reason for this is that one of the first things you should do is to obtain an opinion letter. An opinion letter that is written by counsel is seen as more credible if a charge of willful infringement is brought against you.

In making your choice of counsel, insist on seeing biographies of the people who will be working on your case. Discuss concerns with the managing partners of the firm you are considering. If you wait until the case is under way to do this, you will probably be stuck with the firm you originally chose because it will be too costly for you to switch firms during the litigation. You simply will not have the luxury once litigation is under way to hire a new law firm, which would have to play catch-up with everything that has occurred in your case.

RESPONSE TO AN ASSERTION LETTER

You may also recall from Chapter 7 that an *assertion letter* is the letter that a patent holder sends to an alleged infringer. If you receive an *assertion letter* notifying you of the patent rights of another, you should have your defense team (or you should yourself) send out a quick reply to the letter.

All your response needs to do here is to tell the patent holder that you have received the letter, and that you are currently examining the patents that are in issue. The purpose of your initial response is simply to document that you are not simply ignoring the allegations of infringement. As stated earlier, this could come in handy later on if you were to lose a patent lawsuit in court, and the plaintiff claims willful infringement against you.

Let the patent holder know in your response that you will get back to him or her in *due course* with the results of your analysis.

OBTAIN A WRITTEN OPINION

One of the first things you should get from your attorney is a *written opinion letter*. This letter should provide you with an opinion as to whether your actions constitute infringement. In addition, the letter should provide an opinion as to whether the patents being asserted against you are enforceable and valid. There are many different arguments that your attorney should look into in coming up with an opinion as to the enforceability and validity of the patents. These arguments will be discussed in the next chapter.

The most important reason for you to obtain an opinion letter is that this opinion can be used to insulate you against a charge of willful infringement if the plaintiff wins in court. As stated in the last chapter, willful infringement can subject you to treble damages. Having an opinion by your counsel that the actions do not constitute infringement or that the patents being asserted against you are invalid are significant factors a court will take into consideration in determining whether your actions were willful. The rationale for this is that even if a judgment is rendered against you for patent infringement, you should not be punished for your conduct if you relied, in good faith, upon the opinion of your counsel.

If you haphazardly engage in activities that constitute patent infringement without having first obtained an opinion by competent counsel, there is a much greater chance that you can be found liable as a willful infringer if the patent holder wins the patent infringement case against you.

Obtain the opinion letter from your attorney as soon as possible. Do not wait until your competitor has filed a lawsuit. Timeliness of your attorney's opinion letter is also a factor that is considered later on in a determination of willful infringement. As soon as you receive a letter from your competitor alerting you that you may be infringing upon their patent rights, obtain a written opinion from your patent attorney. You can, of course, engage in your own infringement opinion analysis (see Chapter 18), but it is highly recommended that you also get a professional opinion from a patent attorney.

Types of Patent Opinions

Patent infringement opinions come in two types.

1. One type of opinion is the *non-infringement opinion letter*. This letter is often used for product clearance where you desire to start selling a product and wish to proactively reduce the risk of infringing some patent. In such a circumstance, the opinion may also be referred to as a *freedom-to-operate opinion letter*. What this type of opinion involves is the construction of patent claims with a patent or service and then the reading of the claim on your product or service to determine whether or not infringement exists.

2. A second type of opinion letter is known as an *invalidity opinion letter*. This type of letter seeks to render patent claims invalid under one of the defenses, which will be discussed in Chapter 22. If you cannot avoid patent claims under a non-infringement opinion, then your only alternative will be to try

and get around those claims based on the premise that they are invalid. Alternatives after this are to try to design around the patent claims by changing your product.

What Makes a Good Written Opinion

The opinion by your attorney should be thorough enough to convey a reasonable belief that a court might reasonably hold that the patent at issue is not infringed, invalid, or not enforceable. Look for the following things in your attorney's opinion:

- ✪ The opinion should be in writing and signed by your attorney.

- ✪ The opinion should discuss the file history of the patent.

- ✪ The opinion should interpret the claims.

- ✪ The opinion should consider all relevant prior art and not just art considered by the PTO. In addition, it should link the disclosures of the prior art to the claim limitations of the patent in issue.

- ✪ If obviousness is an issue, the opinion should assess secondary indicial of nonobviousness.

- ✪ The opinion should address the doctrine of equivalents.

- ✪ The opinion should explain the heavy burden of proof on accused infringers regarding invalidity and unenforceability of patents.

It is important to note that no patent opinion letter can guarantee any outcome. This is why such a letter is called an *opinion*. Rendering an opinion in the legal system is not an exact science. Moreover, there are factors that are beyond anyone's control. For example, the effectiveness of any freedom-to-operate opinion is limited by the effectiveness of the product clearance search. Since U.S. patent applications enjoy at least an eighteen-month period of secret pendency at the USPTO, a search may not uncover patents that—at the time the search is conducted—is pending in secret at the U.S. Patent & Trademark Office. The freedom-to-operate opinion letter is also limited by its geographic scope. If foreign patents have not been searched, they will be missed. The body of knowledge these days is increasing exponentially, so it is becoming increasingly difficult to track all prior art that could cause problems down the line for a product launch. The good news is that if you are an inventor, you most likely have a good technical understanding of your new product, which will help you in identifying possible patents that could cause problems down the line for your product launch.

> ***Author's Note: Inherent inaccuracy in patent opinions***
> As another example of the inherent inaccuracy in any patent opinion, it is important to note that even if patent claims do not appear to capture your product, there is a two-year window where a patent holder can seek broader claims through a reissue patent, as discussed in Chapter 15. So if two years has not yet elapsed from the time the patent was issued, you need to keep this in mind also.

DECIDING WHAT TO DO

After your attorney writes an opinion letter, you have several options.

Continue with Your Activity

One option that you have is to simply continue with what you are doing. This is an option that you should consider if your attorney is of the opinion that your actions do not constitute patent infringement, or that the patents being asserted against you are either invalid or unenforceable. If one or more of these circumstances exist, you (or your attorney) should write back to the patent holder and state your position.

File a Declaratory Judgment Action

If you have decided to continue with your alleged infringing activity, you will also want to consider whether to gain an upper hand by filing a *declaratory judgment* action in a court of your choice. In the declaratory action you would be seeking a judgment from the court that the patents being asserted against you are invalid or unenforceable.

Stop Your Actions or Enter into a License Arrangement

If your attorney's position is unfavorable with respect to your position, then you will want to consider either stopping what you are doing now or entering into a licensing arrangement with the patent holder. Your attorney's opinion should prove useful in helping you to bargain for such a licensing arrangement. For example, if your attorney's position suggests that there is some possibility that your patent holder's patent could be invalid, but you do not believe this ground is strong enough to go to court, you can use your attorney's position to bargain for a more favorable license.

As part of the license arrangement, the patent holder may also request that you pay a stipulated sum as compensation for your past infringement. You will then also be responsible for *royalties* on any products that you sell in the future using the patented technology. (Licenses are discussed in detail in Chapter 27.)

NOTE: *The worst thing you can do when being accused of patent infringement is to do nothing. You may be held to be a willful infringer if you simply ignore charges of patent infringement and later lose in court. Strive to document that you have taken such accusations seriously. Having an opinion letter is one way to do this. Negotiating in good faith for a license is another.*

chapter 23

Defenses to Patent Infringement

This chapter discusses defenses against patent infringement. You can use these arguments in your letter in response to a charge of patent infringement, as well in your court papers (*pleadings*), if your case goes to court. Most of the defenses discussed in this chapter are simply the litigation side of reasons why a patent examiner can reject one's patent application during prosecution of the patent.

This chapter approaches the defenses from the perspective of a defendant, who is alleged to be a patent infringer. However, keep in mind that knowing about these defenses will also be very useful if you are the patent holder, who seeks to enforce patent rights.

You will probably see some of these defenses covered in your attorney's opinion letter. If you think your attorney has missed a defense, have your attorney research the issue. There is no limit to the number of defenses that you can use to attack the validity of a claim. In fact, you will want to use as many defenses as possible because if you find that you cannot rely on any one particular defense later, you may still have a chance to rely upon the other defenses that you raised. Remember, too, that attorneys will be less aware of the facts of your particular case than you. Take a proactive stance in your defense.

PATENT AND CLAIM INVALIDITY

A patent is defined by the claims it contains. If all of the claims of your patent are invalid, then your patent will similarly be invalid because there will be nothing for you to enforce against anyone since your claims define your invention. A few of the defenses below can be used to invalidate the entire patent all at once. For example, if you commit fraud in order to get a patent granted, the entire patent can be held invalid.

However, each claim of your patent stands on its own. In essence, each claim defines a *sphere of protection*. The fact that one claim may be held invalid will not alone mean that another claim is invalid. You must look at each claim independently when applying invalidity defenses. For instance, the fact that you find one claim of the patent to be invalid on the grounds of novelty, does not mean that you have an invalid patent because there may be one or more claims that are not invalid based on that same defense.

NON-INFRINGEMENT

If you have been sued for patent infringement, one of the best arguments you can make in your defense is that your activities do not constitute patent infringement. In fact, this is an important defense and your attorneys should automatically raise it. To determine non-infringement you will need to determine the scope of claim coverage of the patents in issue.

NOVELTY

Novelty is a concept that was discussed in Chapter 3. In addition to being a primary reason for rejection of many patents, it can be a great defense to patent infringement. In light of this, you should perform a complete and thorough search for any publications that describe the invention. *Printed publications* include patents, as well as any other references that are published. This can include references like science abstracts, company catalogs, and even material published on the Internet.

If you can find a reference that describes the plaintiff's invention and this reference has a publication date that precedes the date of the claimed invention, you should be able to invalidate the claim under a special statute. (U.S.C., Title 35, Sec. 102(a).)

There is another novelty statute that can make your job even easier. (U.S.C., Title 35, Sec. 102(b).) But there is a catch if you rely upon the statute. The catch is that the printed publication must have a publication date that is more than one (1) year earlier in time than the filing date of plaintiff's patent application. You will, of course, also need to show that the publication anticipates the invention.

If you can find a printed publication that is more than one year earlier in time, then that statute is your best approach for using the publication to invalidate the claimed invention. The statute does not talk about invention dates. It is a hard rule that simply says, if you have a publication more than one year before the effective filing date of your patent holder's patent application, which anticipates that claimed invention, you win. The invention is not considered *novel* and is invalid. You do not have to get into all of the questions about when your plaintiff came up with the invention. All you need to do is to compare the publication date with the filing date of the patent application.

Under this statute, also keep a look out for anything that might tend to show that the invention was either sold or was in public use in this country more than one year prior to the date the patent application was filed. You can allege public use or sale of the invention as a defense. (U.S.C., Title 35, Sec. 102(b).)

Author's Note: Sale or Public Use of Plaintiff's Claimed Invention

The sale or public use of the plaintiff's claimed invention is not going to be easy to find. This is because you will not likely be privy to whether the plaintiff placed the invention into public use or made a sale of the invention more than one year before the patent application was filed. Such information will usually reside somewhere in the plaintiff's own files, which you hopefully will obtain access to during the discovery phase of the patent lawsuit.

Also keep an eye out for any evidence that shows that the patented invention was in public use. *Public use* as a defense can exist in a number of ways. If you are lucky, you might somehow find information that someone in this country has been using the plaintiff's invention more than a year prior to the filing date of the application. This is great evidence of public use.

You might also be lucky enough to discover that the plaintiff demonstrated the claimed invention to some third party in the United States. However, such demonstration must indeed be public. If the demonstration was made under the constraints of a confidentiality agreement, then the plaintiff can argue that the use was not public. (This is one of the key uses of confidentiality agreements mentioned in Chapter 2.)

Use can also occur prior to the date of the invention. If the use of the invention falls within that one year period, your only alternative is to try and prove that the use occurred before the *date of invention*. This is alleging a defense based on United States Code, Title 35, Section 102(a), and not Title 35, Sec. 102(b).

Proving invention dates requires testimony and usually access to the plaintiff's own books and records (something you can only obtain during discovery in a lawsuit). If the use you uncover did not occur more than one year before the patent holder filed the patent application, you will need to go the harder route and try to prove that the *use* occurred before the date of invention.

PRIOR INVENTION

The question of whether the patent holder was the first person to come up with the claimed invention is the question you should be asking to see if you can apply this frequently used defense to invalidate patents. (U.S.C., Title 35, Sec. 102(g).) Look for any evidence that might suggest that you or someone else came up with the invention before the plaintiff. As with novelty, prior invention is also a reason an examiner can reject a patent application and is discussed in Chapter 3.

A tremendous amount of time can go into determining who was the first person to come up with an invention. Discovery of all the lab notebooks and just about anything else that could have some bearing on an invention date is necessary. A large amount of time spent on litigation concerning this defense revolves around just what date constitutes the invention date for all the parties involved. In order to constitute an invention date, there must be a reduction to practice of the invention.

When you file a patent application on the invention, you are generally considered to have reduced the invention to practice. But a patent applicant can show an earlier reduction to practice by showing, through laboratory notebooks and similar evidence, that he or she actually reduced the invention to a tangible form. Moreover, the applicant can even obtain an earlier conception date as the date of invention, if the applicant can show that he or she took steps in actually reducing the invention to practice from that conception date.

Since you are probably not going to have access to the plaintiff's notebooks to figure out *conception,* and earlier *reduction to practice* dates until discovery is conducted in your case, you can assume that the plaintiff's invention date is the date that the plaintiff filed his or her patent application for the invention. This information is readily available to you. Just look on the patent and it will tell you when the earliest patent application was filed for the invention. You should use the earliest patent filing date. In other words, if there are a string of *continuation applications* leading up to the patent, the plaintiff is entitled to the date that the first application was filed in that string of applications.

Once you have that application date, see if you can find any information that might support the fact that someone else came up with the invention prior to that date. The person could be you or anyone else in the world. However, the invention must have been made in this country.

OBVIOUSNESS

This defense is also a favorite reason patent examiners reject patent applications and is discussed in Chapter 3.

INADEQUATE DISCLOSURE

As with obviousness, a defense of inadequate disclosure is a favorite defense to patent infringement. The defense is based on a statute known as U.S.C., Title 35, Sec. 12. There are three main requirements that every patent applicant must fulfill under this statute. These requirements are:

1. the written description;

2. enablement; and,

3. the best mode.

Another requirement that falls under the second paragraph of the statute is the requirement that a patent claim must set forth what the applicant regards as the invention with *particularity* and *distinctiveness*, which was also discussed in Chapter 3.

LACK OF UTILITY

This defense can be a hard one to prove because most inventions have some type of *utility,* or use, in this world. However, the defense has been applied quite successfully in the less predictable arts, like pharmacology. The typical situation is this: The claimed invention is to a compound and the alleged utility specified in the disclosure for the compound is that it helps cure a disease. Yet, when you look at the disclosure, there is not much there, indicates that the compound is actually effective in combating the disease.

You might be asking how is this defense any different from the *enablement requirement*? There is a distinction in patent law. The *utility* requirement asks, whether a specific, substantial, and credible use for the invention is set out in the disclosure. Even if such a use is found to exist, you must next ask whether the disclosure shows how to carry out that use.

Example:

You claim a process of treating a certain disease condition with a certain compound and provide a credible basis for asserting that the compound is useful in that regard. However, to actually practice your invention as claimed, a person skilled in the relevant art would have to engage in an undue amount of experimentation. Your claim may be defective under the enablement requirement, but not under the utility requirement.

Utility is discussed more fully in Chapter 3.

INEQUITABLE CONDUCT

This is one of the best defenses that you can use if you can get a hold of information to support it. The reason that *inequitable conduct* is such a potent defense is that if you can prove inequitable conduct, you will render your competitor's entire patent unenforceable. In other words, inequitable conduct is not applied in respect to each claim individually. This defense can be used against all of the claims of the patent, all at one time.

Inequitable conduct consists of affirmative misrepresentations of material facts or the submission of false material information during the prosecution of a patent, both coupled with an intent to deceive the PTO.

Duty of Candor The most common type of inequitable conduct defense raised in patent litigation is when the patentee has breached the *duty of candor* by failing to disclose *material information* to the PTO during the prosecution of its patent application.

Under a special rule, applicants and other individuals, such as their attorneys, have a duty to bring to the attention of the PTO any information that is material to the prosecution of that patent application. (C.F.R, Title 37, Sec. 1.56.) Matter is considered *material* if it:

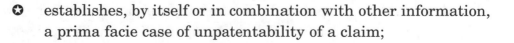   establishes, by itself or in combination with other information, a prima facie case of unpatentability of a claim;

✪   refutes, or is inconsistent with, a position the applicant takes in:

- opposes an argument of unpatentability relied on by the PTO; or,

- asserts an argument of patentability.

Applicants comply with this duty of candor by submitting what is called an *Information Disclosure Statement* (IDS), listing all references they believe to be material to the patentability of their claims to the PTO. An IDS is filed either with, or shortly after, the filing of the patent application.

The *file wrapper* will tell you what went on during the prosecution stage between the PTO and the patent holder. The file wrapper will also contain one or more Information Disclosure Statements filed by the applicant.

Review the file wrapper carefully, particularly the IDS. Look for any references that you believe are material to the patentability of the applicant's claims, but that the applicant failed to disclose in the IDS to the PTO. You will, of course, also need to uncover evidence that shows that the applicant or other party involved in the prosecution of the application knew about the materiality of the reference, but failed to bring it to the attention of the PTO.

The ways that you might be able to do this are only limited by your imagination. As stated, you will need to become an investigator. One common situation that has been used to show this is where a related foreign application filed by the same applicant used references cited as prior art in rejecting the same or similar claims as in the U.S. application that concerns you. By uncovering such information, you might be able to prove that the reference is material (since the foreign jurisdiction believed it to be), as well as intent on the part of the applicant to deceive (the applicant must have known about the materiality of the reference if it was cited to the applicant in a foreign correspondence).

False Statements   Another common situation where inequitable conduct is found is if the patent holder (usually through the attorney who is handling prosecution of the patent application) makes false statements to the PTO during the prosecution of the patent application. This can happen in any number of ways. Put on that investigative thinking cap again and look for any false or deceiving statements made to get a patent issued.

In one case, a patent was held unenforceable on the basis that the applicant (through the attorney) made a false statement that its abandonment of its patent application was unintentional, when it clearly was not unintentional. By doing this, the applicant was able to get its abandoned patent application revived so that a patent could issue. To the patent holder's amazement, however, the patent was later deemed unenforceable for inequitable conduct because it was uncovered that the applicant's statement about unintentional abandonment was false.

Be alert for inequitable conduct, which occurs even during the prosecution of the patent application in question. In such a case, you can argue that the current patent is invalid because it is infected by inequitable conduct under a doctrine called *infectious unenforceability*.

Example:

A divisional patent was held unenforceable based on inequitable conduct resulting from the intentional withholding of a prior art reference that occurred during the prosecution of the parent patent, even though the reference was submitted during the prosecution of the divisional. (See *Molines PLC v. Textron, Inc.*, 48 F3d 1172 (Fed. Cir. 1995).)

There have been many very imaginative defenses on the basis of inequitable conduct. For some idea of the range of the defenses, it was even alleged in one case that the patent attorney incorrectly cited a case in his arguments to the PTO. Keep your eyes open and try to do your best to uncover suspicious conduct. This is a very potent defense if you can prove it.

NOT IN FORCE

This is the most obvious defense, but often the most overlooked one. It is a defense that you should always consider right off the bat. If the patent that is being asserted against you is no longer in force, then it will not prevent you from making or selling the claimed invention, at least with respect to your activities that occurred while the patent was not in force.

There are two things to check for here. First, check to see when the patent *expires*. The PTO determines patent expiration dates and then prints those dates right on the front of the patent.

Utility patents, which are the most typical kinds of patents in the IP world, expire twenty (20) years from their earliest effective filing date. The PTO will determine the earliest effective filing date of a patent by looking for the first regular U.S. patent application that your patentee filed for the claimed invention. *Regular* means that provisional applications are excluded from the calculation.

Example:

Suppose your patentee filed a provisional application for the invention on June 1, 1998, then files a regular utility application on June 1, 1999, and then later files a continuation application (a type of application that can be filed off of a regular application) for the same invention on June 1, 2001. The patent term in such a case would commence from June 1, 1999, since this is the first regular U.S. application for the invention in the chain of applications.

But things are not so simple in patent law. Patent terms can also be extended for various reasons. (U.S.C., Title 35, Sec. 154(b).) So what may look to be a simple task, may not be as simple as you think. The PTO uses a computer system to figure out patent terms. But this does not mean that what was entered into that system is always correct. It is a good idea to double check the work of the PTO in calculating the patent term if it appears to be a close call.

For patents issued before June 8, 1995, the rules are a little easier. The patent is enforceable for seventeen years from the date the patent issued. So if the patent being asserted against you has a date earlier than June 8, 1995, you will only need to figure out the issue date that is printed at the top of the patent. You then calculate seventeen years from that date to figure out the date that the patent expires.

Second, make sure that the maintenance fees on the patent have been paid. *Maintenance fees* are due at regular intervals to maintain a patent. (See Chapter 2.) If your patentee has failed to pay any one of these fees, the patent will have lapsed.

You can use the PAIR system discussed in Chapter 4 to check whether maintenance fees have been paid on a patent. Simply go to the PAIR site at the PTO website, www.uspto.gov. It will list several options to obtain maintenance fee dates for a patent and whether the fees have been paid.

Even if your patentee was able to revive his or her patent, you will have *intervening rights*. (U.S.C., Title 35, Sec. 41(c).) This means that your patentee will be unable to sue you for any infringing activity that is alleged to have occurred while the patent was in the lapsed state. (Intervening rights are discussed in greater detail later in this chapter.)

FIRST SALE DOCTRINE AND EXHAUSTION

This doctrine protects you from patent infringement as to goods you have lawfully purchased from the patent holder. Once you purchase a product, you are free to use that product as you want. You can even resell the product.

The *first sale doctrine* states that once the patent holder makes a first sale of a patented product, that patent holder has exhausted his or her rights with respect to those specific goods sold. You can now do what you want with that product. But you would, of course, not be able to make more of that product. Even reconstructing the product sold could constitute infringement. However, repair of your purchased product is considered permissible.

Even method patents can be exhausted by the sale of an item that embodies the method. If this were not the case, then patentees could avoid patent exhaustion by simply drafting their patent claims to describe a method rather than an apparatus.

Example:

The sale of motor fuel produced under one patent also exhausted the patent for a method of using the fuel in combustion motors.

The first sale doctrine has often been the subject of criticism of patent holders because it has created what is sometimes called a *gray market*. This is where people buy patented products in a market where they are sold at low prices (say overseas), and then resell those same products in places that can command higher prices (say the United States). Such sellers have a defense to patent infringement because of this doctrine.

ESTOPPEL

Estoppel is a term that is used for situations where something prevents the assertion of an otherwise legal right. Four types of estoppel will be discussed as defenses to patent infringement. They are:

- equitable;

- assignor;

- judicial; and,

- collateral.

Equitable Estoppel   When estoppel arises out of the unfair activities of the party asserting its rights, then it is referred to as *equitable estoppel*. An equitable estoppel typically arises when a patent owner makes a misleading communication that it will not enforce its patent and you reasonably rely upon that communication to continue or expand your business. The communication can take almost any form, including conduct or silence, as long as it supports a reasonable inference that the patent will not be enforced.

You have the burden of proof with respect to three factors to make out of a case of equitable estoppel. First, you must show that the patentee, through misleading conduct, led you to reasonably infer that the patentee did not intend to enforce its patent against you. Second, you must show you relied on this misleading conduct. And third, due to that reliance, you would be materially prejudiced if the patentee were allowed to proceed on its claim.

Equitable estoppel can be a very potent defense because if you succeed, it is a complete bar to recovery by the patentee, including the denial of an injunction. This defense will actually be more useful to the plaintiff who wants a holding that the patent is valid, rather than a defendant who seeks to invalidate a patent.

Assignor Estoppel

Assignor estoppel is an equitable doctrine that prevents a patentee who has assigned the rights to a patent from later contending that what was assigned is a nullity. Assignments are discussed in Chapter 28, but know that it is basically the transfer of all ownership rights to a patent. The rationale for this estoppel is that an assignor implicitly attests to the value of the patent by making the assignment.

Judicial Estoppel

Judicial estoppel is a not-too-often used defense that can be raised in the case where there has already been a prior suit on the merits that involves the same cause of action in the suit against you, and both cases involve the same parties or their privies. The key word here is *privies,* because you typically do not find the patentee suing once again the same party that he or she sued in a prior suit. *Privity* exists when parties of both lawsuits are closely related with identical interests so that it is fair to treat them as the same parties for the purpose of invoking this defense. Judicial estoppel, although rare, has arisen in the context of where the patentee has sued a manufacturer of an infringing party and then later seeks to sue the end user.

Example:

Transclean, an exclusive licensee to a patent covering a machine for changing transmission fluid, filed suit against Bridgewood, who sold infringing machines, and won the suit. Later, Transclean sued an end user of the infringing machines, Jiffy Lube. However, the court held that the suit was barred by judicial estoppel since Transclean had made the choice to concede privity between Bridgewood and its customers in the earlier suit by choosing not to join the customers in the first litigation.

Collateral Estoppel

This defense relates to the principal that once a party has had his or her day in court, that party cannot go into court again to relitigate what was already decided. The easiest example of this defense is when a plaintiff's patent has been held invalid in a suit against a defendant. If that same plaintiff tries to sue a second defendant for infringement of that same patent, the second defendant can raise the defense of *collateral estoppel*. Since the issue of invalidity of the patent was already decided, the plaintiff should not have the right to relitigate that issue again in a second lawsuit.

If you lose the case against the infringer and your patent is held invalid, you will be estopped from asserting your patent against anyone else. Your patent will lose all its deterrent effect against the world. You are, in effect, better off not having sued in the first place under such a situation.

Sometimes collateral estoppel can be raised as a defense in less clear cut ways. For example, if a court has already construed the meaning of terms of patent claims in one patent infringement suit, the reconstruction of those same claims in a second patent infringement lawsuit would probably be collaterally estopped. (*Molinaro v. Fannon/Courier Corp.*, 745 F.2d 641 (Fed. Cir. 1984).)

NOTE: *Collateral estoppel applies to different lawsuits, but not the same lawsuit being heard on appeal.*

PROSECUTION HISTORY LACHES

A similar, but also rarely employed defense in the patent prosecution context, is the concept of *prosecution history laches*. This possible defense relates to unreasonable and unexplained delays in the prosecution of a patent application. Prosecution history laches is when an applicant takes an unreasonable amount of time to further prosecution of a patent application. Although it is probably more suited as a tool the PTO could use in denying the issuance of a patent, it is conceivable that it could serve as a defense to hold an issued patent unenforceable.

Such unreasonable delay might be found to exist where there is a large chain of applications leading up to the issuance of a patent. One could argue that by unreasonably delaying the issuance of the patent by filing so many continuing applications, the patent is unenforceable. Since a patent's term now runs from an application's earliest filing date, this defense will become even more rare. However, the rules for patents filed before June 8, 1995, were different—the patent term was measured from the date of patent issue—so you might have a shot with this defense for some of the older patents where there was greater incentive for patentees to delay prosecution of patents until the time was ripe for the invention.

DOUBLE PATENTING

Congress limits the duration that a patent holder can exclude others from practicing the claimed invention by prescribing a patent term of twenty years. This limited duration would be easily circumvented if a patent holder could obtain a second patent on the same claimed invention for another twenty-year period. This is where the defense of *double patenting* comes to play.

There are two types of double patenting. The first is called *statutory,* and the second is called *obviousness-type double patenting.* Both of these were discussed earlier.

> ### Author's Note: Invalidity and Double Patenting
> If double patenting—either statutory or obviousness-type—is proven, the affected claim is invalid. Invalidity of that claim for double patenting does not affect the validity of any other claim in the patent (*Ortho Pharm Corp v. Smith,* 959 F2d 936, 942 (Fed. Cir. 1992).)

One situation where statutory double patenting could occur is when the patent holder files a patent application for an invention, and before that patent issues, files a *continuation application* for the same invention.

A continuation is a second application that will typically claim priority to its *parent application*. Patent applicants file continuations for a variety of reasons. Usually it is because they want to keep patent prosecution alive in a second patent application so that they can change the scope of their claims if the need arises. Their use is similar to using a reissue to change the scope of your claims after your patent has issued. The difference between a reissue and a continuation is that a continuation must be filed *before* the prior application has issued into a patent. Reissue applications are filed *after* a prior patent application has issued into a patent.

Continuations also differ from reissue patents in that a *reissue patent* is granted as a substitute for the patent it replaces. A continuation, on the other hand, can issue into a totally separate patent from the previously filed patent application that also issues into a patent. Thus the patent holder will end up with two separate patents in the case of continuation. This is where you should consider double patenting. You will need to show that a claim being asserted against you from that second patent is the same as, or not patently distinct from, a claim of the prior patent. If so, that claim of the second patent is invalid on the basis of double patenting.

Another type of continuing application that a patent applicant may file is a *divisional application*. In short, an applicant files a divisional application if the examiner at the PTO thinks the first patent application contains more than one separate invention. The applicant will keep one invention in the originally filed patent application and later file divisional applications for the other inventions that the examiner thinks are distinct. If the applicant obtains patents on each of the applications, the applicant (now patent holder) can use a special statute if anyone claims that those later obtained patents are invalid due to double patenting. (U.S.C., Title 35, Sec. 121.) If the examiner required the applicant to file separate applications, it is believed to be unfair, to now tell the patent holder that the inventions were not distinct after all.

Another situation where you might see double patenting is the situation where you have species claims and later-issued genus claims. In this situation, an application contains claims to a genus and a commonly owned, earlier-issued patent contains claims to a species of the genus. Since a genus is anticipated by the species, this is a violation of the rule against obviousness-type double patenting.

Example:

A patent application contains claims directed to a method for prolonging the storage life of packaged meat products. A commonly owned patent contains claims directed to a method of preparing pork products. Since "meat" and "pork" are not the same thing—since a claim to "meat" could be infringed by a process that does not infringe a claim limited to "pork"—the claims are not for identical invention. The next question, then, is whether the claims to "meat" in the application are an obvious variation of the claims directed to "pork" in the issued patent. Since the term "meat" encompasses "pork," allowance of the application would extend the time frame of the monopoly with respect to the pork process and the claim directed to "meat" process should not be allowable in the absence of a terminal disclaimer.

Example:

A claim directed to administration of a compound to humans in an earlier-issued patent was invalid by virtue of obviousness-type double patenting over a claim directed to the administration of the compound to animals in a later-issued patent because humans are a species of the animal genus and thus the claim to animals is thus not patently distinct from the earlier issued human species claim (*Eli Lilly &Co. v. Barr Laboratories,* 251 F3d 955).

While species claims render later-issued genus claims obvious, genus claims do not render later-issued improvement claims obvious.

Example:

An earlier-issued patent included a claim directed to a chemical process "wherein the reaction is effected in the presence of an organic solvent." A patent application contained a claim directed to a similar process, "the improvement which comprises effecting said reaction in a solvent mixture of teraglyme and sulfolane." The solvent mixture is a species of the genus organic solvent in the issued patent. This would not constitute double patenting because the public would still be free to use the process in the earlier-issued patent when it expires, so long as the solvent mixture of the later-issued patent is not used. This result is the opposite of the situation where a species claim issues first, followed by issuance of a genus claim, preventing the public from using the entire genus, including the species of the earlier-issued patent for the entire term of the later-issued patent.

EXPERIMENTAL USE

Experimental use is a common law defense to patent infringement. This defense applies where your use of the patented invention constitutes research to understand or improve upon or modify the patented subject matter. The rationale for this rule is that the entire patent system is based on the premise that the rationale of patent protection is to encourage the disclosure of inventions so that others can improve upon the invention and thereby add to scientific knowledge.

The common law experimental use exception can arise under the following two circumstances:

1. for the mere purpose of intellectual curiosity, amusement, or philosophical experimentation, with no underlying business or commercial motive; and,

2. to confirm that an invention works the way it is disclosed in the patent specification.

Example:

Embrex was an exclusive licensee of a government patent for a method of inoculating birds against disease by injecting vaccines into a particular part of the egg prior to hatching. Embrex designed an injection machine to carry out the method on large scale chicken farms. SEC approached Embrex for a license to the technology, but Embrex refused. SEC tried to build in vivo injection machines by designing around the patent by injecting the chicken embryo in a region not covered by the government patent. In assessing the effectiveness of the new injection position, SEC used the Embrex method for control testing purposes. Embrex sued SEC for infringement of the licensed patent. SEC alleged that the tests did not infringe because they were scientific experiments with no resulting sales, and were exempt from patent infringement under either the merely deminimis exception or under the experimental use exception. The Federal Circuit Court disagreed, holding that SEC performed the experiments for commercial purposes and was merely cloaking its tests in the guise of scientific inquiry.

The *experimental use defense* to patent infringement typically arises in the case of pharmaceutical drug development. In fact, a separate experiment use statute has been created in this respect. It is known as the *FDA exemption,* which is legislated by 35 U.S.C. §271(e)(1). Under this statute, it is not an act of infringement for a manufacturer to use a patented drug or medical device so long as that use was reasonably related to the development and submission of information to the FDA. The primary motivation for this exemption is to enable generic manufacturers to sell generic equivalents of patented drugs immediately upon expiration of the patent. To do this, a generic manufacturer needs to test the generic equivalent of a patented drug for the purpose of obtaining approval from the FDA to sell that drug upon expiration of the patent.

However, 35 U.S.C. §271(e)(1) does not apply to preclinical research conducted to identify the best drug candidates, nor does it embrace all experimental activity that might at some point, however attenuated, may lead to an FDA approval process. The work must be solely for uses reasonably related to the development of information submitted to the FDA. Use of patented compounds in preclinical studies is protected, however, as long as there is a reasonable basis for believing the experiments will produce information that is relevant to an FDA submission, such as an investigational new drug application (IND) or new drug application (NDA).

INCORRECT INVENTORSHIP

You should keep an eye out for who the true inventors are of claimed inventions. Unfortunately this defense is not going to be something that is easy to determine, particularly at an early stage in court proceedings. This is because you will not have access to the plaintiff's records to determine who are the correct inventors.

However, you might be fortunate enough to find a disgruntled person who claims to have had a part in conceiving the invention. People who feel that they have been cheated out of recognition are usually quite willing to not only talk to you about this, but also to testify for you.

Patent applications must be applied for in the names of the correct inventors. (U.S.C., Title 35, Sec. 102(f).) The rule states that a person is not entitled to a patent if "he did not himself invent the subject matter sought to be patented."

If any of the claims in a patent application involve the inventive contributions of a person who was not named as a coinventor on the application, then the whole patent can be held invalid. Even if the missing inventor's contribution was to only one of the claims in the patent, that inventor should be listed as a coinventor. This is true even if the inventors did not work together, did not work on the invention at the same time, and even if each did not make the same contribution to the claimed invention. (U.S.C., Title 35, Sec. 116.) What is required is that the missing inventor:

- ✪ contributed in some significant manner to the conception or reduction to practice of the invention, and

- ✪ made a contribution to the claimed invention that is not insignificant in quality, when that contribution is measured against the dimension of the full invention, and have more than merely explained to the real inventors well-known concepts and/or the current state of the art. *(Fina Oil & Chem. Co. v. Ewen,* 123 F.3d 1466, 43 U.S.P.Q.2d 1935 (Fed. Cir. 1997).)

In order to determine correct inventorship, the court will first construe the claims. The court will then determine who contributed to the conception of at least one of the claims. Some examples of where incorrect inventorship might occur are listed below.

- ✪ The true inventor needs the help of his or her friend in financing the invention. To induce the friend, the inventor agrees to list the friend on the patent application as a coinventor. A patent is issued. The patent is invalid because it does not properly list the correct inventors.

✪ An inventor assigns his or her ownership to an employer. The employer mistakenly believes that he or she should be listed as the inventor on the patent application. A patent is issued. Again, the patent is invalid because it does not list the correct inventors.

✪ Inventor A, thinking that he or she can pull a fast one and get a patent issued in his or her name, files a patent application on an invention. Inventor B contributed to the inventive concept. This patent, too, is invalid because it does not list the correct inventors.

Reminder: Remember that incorrect inventorship can be corrected. (U.S.C., Title 35, Sec. 256.) A *certificate of correction* can be issued by the PTO that deletes an incorrectly named inventor or adds an inventor who should have been named, so long as the error was not made with deceptive intent of the person being deleted or added. This same statute also allows a court to order correction of inventorship on notice and hearing of all parties concerned. Thus United States Code, Title 35, Section 256 can be used as a saving provision by a plaintiff, even where the inventorship is incorrect. This saving provision clearly limits your use of this defense since the plaintiff can always invoke Section 256. You will need to prove deceptive intent if this occurs. However, errors in inventorship due to the deceptive intent of the named inventors can also render a patent unenforceable under the doctrine of inequitable conduct. What you will need to do is prove deceptive intent on the part of the person incorrectly listed or not named.

Example 1:

Perseptive sued Pharmacia for infringement. Pharmacia raised the defense that the patents were invalid for failure to name the correct inventors and that they were unenforceable due to inequitable conduct on the part of the named inventors during the prosecution of the patents. Since Section 256 authorizes correction of inventorship when there is no deceptive intent on the part of the omitted inventors and does not require inquiry into the intent of the originally named inventors, the court would allow a §256 motion. However, the court held that the named inventors had committed inequitable conduct when prosecuting the application because the named inventors intentionally misrepresented to the PTO the relationship between themselves and their collaborative research partner for the purpose of concealing the issue of inventorship and held the patents unenforceable.

Example 2:

Yoon collaborated with Choi in the development of safety rocars for endoscopic surgery. After the collaboration ended, Yoon applied for a patent on the invention, naming himself as the sole inventor. The patent issued, and Yoon granted an exclusive license to Ethicon. Ethicon later filed an infringement action against U.S. Surgical for infringement of the patent. U.S. Surgical learned of Choi's involvement in the development and obtained a retroactive license from Choi. U.S. Surgical then moved to correct inventorship of the patent under 35 U.S.C. §256, claiming that Choi was the coinventor of several claims in the patent. The district court found that Choi had contributed to two claims of the patent and granted U.S. Surgical's motion for dismissal of the infringement suit based on its valid license from Choi under the patent. Since under §116, joint inventors are joint and several owners of all claims of a patent regardless of whether the joint inventors contributed to all of the claims, Choi had the power to license rights in the entire patent and thus the court granted U.S. Surgical's motion for dismissal of the infringement suit based on its valid license from Choi under the patent.

chapter 24

Special Defenses to Patent Infringement

ANTITRUST VIOLATIONS

Antitrust violations is a separate area of law from patent law and beyond the scope of this book. You should be aware that a particularly monopolistic patent holder may run into problems with this area. You will need to consult with an attorney who specializes in this area of law.

STATUTE OF LIMITATIONS

This means that there are indeed penalties for not knowing what your competitors are up to. If you wait more than six years after infringing activity has occurred, you will not be able to recover damages on the infringing activity (U.S.C., Title 35, Sec. 286).

LACHES

Laches is not as clear as the statute of limitations. To prove laches, you must prove the following two things:

✪   that the patentee delayed filing suit for an unreasonable and inexcusable length of time after the patentee knew or reasonably should have known of its claim against you (the alleged infringer). A presumption of laches arises when the patentee delays bringing suit for more than six years after the date the patentee knew or should have known of the alleged infringing activity. (*Cobe Labs, Inc. v. Baxter Healthcare Corp.,* 34 U.S.P.Q.2d 1472 (D. Colo. 1994).) This rule is based on the statute of limitations discussed above; and,

✪   the delay resulted in material prejudice or injury to you. (*Gasser Chair Co. v. Infanti Chair Mfg. Corp.,* 60 F.3d 770, 34, U.S.P.Q.2d 1822 (Fed. Cir. 1995).)

INTERVENING AND PRIOR USER'S RIGHTS

Intervening rights was discussed earlier in Chapter 15 in our discussion of reissue patents. There are two classes of intervening rights that a court may apply when assessing damages for infringement. The first absolute class protects you with respect to a specific product that you used or sold but which was made, purchased, or used prior to the granting of say a reissue or reexamined patent (reexamination of patents is discussed in a later chapter). The second class of intervening rights is based on equity. *Equity* is a concept that means that a court has discretion in granting you intervening rights. This second class may allow your investment that began prior to say a reissue to be protected. To qualify, you must have engaged in the infringing activity, or made substantial preparations for the same, prior to the issuance of say a reissued or reexamined patent.

Another instance for this defense is when the patent was abandoned (e.g., by missing a maintenance fee deadline), but was later revived. During the time that such patent was not in force you are not liable for patent infringement. (U.S.C., Title 35, Sec. 41(c).)

Related to intervening rights is a defense called *prior user's rights.* This defense is based on a statute that says that if you have used a method commercially for over a year before a patent application was filed on the method, then you have a complete defense to any action for patent infringement on the method. (U.S.C., Title 35, Sec. 273.)

MEDICAL PROCEDURES

Healthcare providers, like doctors, are exempt from infringement for medical procedures under a special statute. (U.S.C., Title 35, Sec. 287(c).) This statute precludes the owner of a patent directed to a medical procedure from enjoining or obtaining damages from an infringer of that patent. Thus, the statute limits infringement damages as opposed to being an actual defense to infringement. You will probably not see patents covering medical procedures because of this statute.

This same statute has no effect on enforcement of a patent covering a medical device that is used to perform the procedure. In fact, patents on medical devices are a very fertile area for patent infringement cases.

OLD OR EXHAUSTED COMBINATION

When patent applicants draft patent claims, they often draft what are known as *combination* claims, where the new improved device is claimed as part of a combination with features already well known in the art. For example, if you were to make a new, improved carburetor for a car, you might want to claim the carburetor as part of the car (a combination claim). The reason for making the combination claim is that you anticipate that future infringers will be selling cars with your improved carburetor and royalties based on a car will be much greater than royalties based on the carburetor alone.

Claiming your improvement as part of a combination that performs no new function has in the past been held invalid by several courts under the theory that you are just trying to claim an old combination. The courts looked upon this as overclaiming. *(Great A. & P. Tea Co. v. Supermarket Equipment Corp.,* 340 U.S. 147 (1950).)

This old combination doctrine was rejected by the Federal Circuit court on the basis that the rule was not based on any statute. *(Steel and Mfg*

Co. v. MTD Products, Inc., 221 U.S.P.Q. 657 (1987).) However, at least one author has suggested that the rule may come back into the courts in light of a 2002 court ruling. (*Johnson & Johnston Associates, Inc. v. R.E. Service Co., Inc.,* 285 F.3d 1046, 62 U.S.P.Q.2d 1225 (Fed. Cir. 2002).) The *Johnson* case says that if a patentee discloses, but does not claim material in a patent, then that material is dedicated to the public. Based on Johnson, one could argue that where some improved device is disclosed, but not claimed, it would thereby be dedicated to the public. Moreover, its inclusion in combination with old elements (such as a car) would be obvious under United States Code, Title 35, Section 103(a). Now you could argue that the old combination rule does have a statutory basis.

This defense is novel, but worth raising with your attorney. Ask your attorney to research the issue.

PERMISSIBLE REPAIR

This defense was discussed in Chapter 6 in the sections on contributory infringement. In that context, you learned that where a purchaser of a component in a patented combination cannot have been said to infringe any claim of a patent, then one cannot argue that someone contributed to infringement of the patent.

Determining that contribution, however, can be difficult. Deciding when the replacement of some component of a combination invention constitutes permissible repair, which does not subject you to patent infringement, and when such replacement constitutes the actual making of the invention, is not always clear.

You are certainly not allowed to rebuild a patented invention using components sold by others. Such rebuilding would constitute reconstruction of the patented combination. But if there are components in the patented invention that wear out and the replacement of such components is necessary in order for your continued use of that patented invention, then your replacement of that component should not constitute patent infringement. You can argue that your replacement constitutes permissible repair of the patented combination.

ABANDONMENT

The basis for this defense comes from United States Code, Title 35, Section 102(c). That statute provides that a person shall be entitled to a patent unless he or she has *abandoned* the invention. This defense is rarely invoked. The reason for this is that it is highly unlikely that the patent holder has gone to the trouble to obtain a patent application on an invention that he or she would be considered to have abandoned. Even long periods of delay in filing a patent application for an invention have not been considered to constitute an abandonment.

In addition to expired patents, be on the lookout for patents that—although seeming in force at the present time—were at one time during their prosecution history abandoned. There have been cases where courts have held that patents that were improperly revived are invalid.

Example:

ATA filed its Australian provisional patent on July 8, 1997. Exactly one year later, ATA filed its international PCT application. Thirty months and one day later, ATA filed its national stage application in the United States. Under PCT foreign filing rules, this filing was actually late because an applicant has exactly thirty months to file its national stage application from the PCT filing. ATA was able to revive the application based on a procedure called *revival based on unintentional delay*. However, 35 U.S.C. §371 only allows for revival when a failure was "unavoidable," which is a much higher standard than that for "unintentional" abandonment. Years later, ATA sued IGT for patent infringement. IGT was successful in dismissing the patent as invalid on the basis that is had been abandoned and not lawfully revived.

LACK OF STANDING

A number of cases have been thrown out of court because the alleged patentee does not have standing to sue you. A situation where this might occur is where the plaintiff does not own the patent. Another case where it has occurred is where there are co-owners of the patent and one of the co-owners will not join in the suit against you.

Example:

Israel Bio-Engineering filed suit against Amgen, alleging patent infringement. The court dismissed the suit for lack of standing since one of the co-owners refused to join the patent lawsuit.

Note in the example above that ownership does not refer to inventorship. One can be owner of a patent and not an inventor. In fact this occurs commonly where employees come up with an idea and must be listed as inventors of the invention but the real owner is the company who the employees work for.

VIOLATION OF THE RECAPTURE RULE

You may recall earlier that a reissue patent application can not be made to "recapture" claimed subject matter that was surrendered in an application to obtain the original patent. If a reissue patent has done this and somehow the examiner has let the patent issue anyway, you can raise the defense that the patent is invalid in that it violates this rule.

SPECIAL DEFENSES AVAILABLE TO THE U.S. GOVERNMENT

Since the U.S. government creates patent laws, it might have the right to exempt itself from getting sued for patent infringement. In a sense, the U.S. government has done just that by restricting patent holders with respect to lawsuits against the U.S. government. A special statute (28 U.S.C. §1498) provides that whenever an invention described in and covered by a patent of the United States is used or manufactured by or for the United States without the license of the owner, the owner's remedy shall be by action against the United States in the U.S. Court of Federal Claims for the recovery of reasonable and entire compensation for such use and manufacture.

The statute goes on to say that, "the provisions of this section shall not apply to any claim arising in a foreign country." This is a particularly important part of the statute because it effectively bars any suit against the U.S. government where the act of infringement occurs outside the United States. You may recall that regular patent holders can make use of the statute that prevents would-be infringers from importing into the United States a product made by a person that is patented in the United States. This is not true when the United States or one of its subcontractors import such a product. In such a case, the U.S. government or its authorized subcontractor has a complete defense to patent infringement.

Example:

Zoltek's patent was directed to a method for processing carbon fiber sheet products. A defense contractor for the U.S. government used the method to manufacture fiber sheets in Japan, which were then imported into the U.S. and used to develop new fighter aircrafts for the U..S government. Both the U.S. government and subcontractor have a complete defense to patent infringement brought by Zoltek.

LICENSE OF THE PATENT

License of the patent is probably the easiest defense. If you have taken out a license to the patent, then there can be no infringement so long as you are not breaching the terms of your license. What if your licensor sends you a letter stating that a certain patent is covered by your license and you owe royalties under your license agreement? Further, suppose that you not only believe the patent is not covered by the license but that the patent that your patentee is trying to assert is invalid. In this case, your best option may be to seek a declaratory judgment that the patent is invalid under one of the other defenses in this chapter rather than risk not paying the alleged royalties due, getting sued for patent infringement, and possibly having to pay treble damages if your mistaken action is later to have been found willful. A declaratory action may be your best action since a recent decision holds that even licensees have standing to sue for a declaratory action that a patent is infringed. (See *MedImmune Inc. v. Genentech Inc.*)

INFRINGEMENT SUMMARY

In summary, you should carefully consider all of your patent infringe-ment defenses if someone accuses you of patent infringement. You should throw in as many defenses as you think could possibly apply. This approach will greatly assist you later if one of your defenses proves to be useless, but you are able to rely on some other defense that you have asserted. An interesting site that you can visit to see which party is prevailing on each of these defenses is www.patstats.org.

Alternative Dispute Resolution Techniques

Patent infringement suits last an average of 1.12 years and cost nearly $2 million dollars. With these delays and expenses, alternatives to traditional patent infringement actions are something that both plaintiffs and defendants should consider.

From a patent holder's perspective, a protracted patent infringement suit with the potentially worse outcome—an entire patent being declared invalid—will be much worse than agreeing to sell a license to a single infringer. This is particularly true where claim coverage is not that clear or where potential defenses can be asserted against the patent.

This chapter will look at ways that parties can resolve patent disputes through means that do not involve litigation. One very important mechanism is the *cross-license*. Sometimes the cross-license is the only choice for two competitors, because each party simply cannot practice their respective technologies without the permission of the other.

In this chapter you will also learn about such Alternative Dispute Resolution (ADR) techniques as *arbitration, mediation,* and *settlements* as ways to resolve patent disputes. These strategies can end disputes and avoid the emotional and financial burden that often comes from a long, drawn-out patent infringement lawsuit.

CROSS-LICENSING

Cross-licensing of each other's respective technology can often be the best business solution to a patent dispute. A cross-license can save you from an expensive drawn-out patent lawsuit. Perhaps even more important, a cross-license may be the only way that you get to practice your patented technology.

Take this scenario.

Example:

Alice just invented the desk. She obtained the following claim: "a desk comprising a top portion attached to one or more legs." This claim is very broad because it uses the open ended transition phrase *comprising* that in patent law means any product that has all of the elements of the desk (the top and attached legs) will be infringing.

Joe comes along years later and also is able to obtain a patent on a desk. Joe's claim reads as follows: "a desk comprising a top portion attached to one or more legs, and further comprising a shelf which is pivotally attached to said top portion." Joe's claim is also broad because it uses the "comprising" language. However, it is not quite as broad as Alice's claim, because Joe's claim contains the additional element, "pivotally attached shelf."

Two important questions arise from this scenario in the infringement context. The first question is does Joe's sale of his claimed invention amount to infringement of Alice's invention? The answer is yes, since Joe's product contains each and every element of Alice's invention (the top and attached legs).

Second, suppose that the desk with Joe's pivotal shelf is what consumers want to buy. Alice would now want to start selling Joe's desk with the pivotal shelf. Would her product infringe? It would as her new desk would contain each and every element of Joe's claimed invention (the top, attached legs, and pivotal shelf).

So a dilemma exists. Joe cannot manufacture his claimed invention without infringing Alice's claim. However, Alice cannot manufacture

Joe's product either. The best solution would probably be a *cross-licensing agreement,* in which both Alice and Joe license to each other their respective inventions. The actual mechanics of licensing an invention are discussed in Chapter 27.

ARBITRATION AND MEDIATION

Arbitration and mediation involve nonlitigation processes where patent disputes are decided not by a judge or jury, but rather by some specially designated person or persons. In arbitration, this specially designated person is called the *arbitrator.* Mediation is a process where the parties come together to see if they can come up with some type of settlement of the dispute. Usually this meeting will be coordinated by a special person, the *mediator,* who is trained in dispute resolution.

There are differences between arbitration and mediation. With arbitration, the arbitrator's decision is typically binding upon the parties, so there will be a winner and a loser of the case. In this respect, arbitration is somewhat akin to a lawsuit.

In contrast, mediation does not result in a decision that decides the dispute. In mediation, the mediator will leave it up to the parties to come to a resolution of their dispute. The mediator is only there to facilitate interaction between the parties. Mediators, unlike a judge or even an arbitrator, encourage parties to focus on their needs rather than positions. Mediation requires the parties to work together toward a resolution of their dispute. If the parties have a great deal of hostility toward each other to the extent a resolution is not possible, then arbitration may be a better way to go since arbitration involves a decision by the arbitrator.

Advantages of Arbitration Compared to Patent Litigation

The main reason for arbitration is that it provides an alternative to the immense expense and time of a patent litigation case. However, there are other advantages such as the following:

- ✪ In arbitration, knowledgeable professionals typically hear the case. This is sometimes not the case in patent trials where at the trial judges do not have a lot of experience in patent disputes. However, this can vary depending on the arbitrators chosen.

✪ Arbitration can avoid the possibility of huge punitive damage awards.

✪ Arbitration can avoid the prospects of a costly, lengthy appeals process, which saves substantial time and money.

Disadvantages of Arbitration/ Mediation Compared to Patent Litigation

There are some possible scenarios where it might not be advisable to use ADR.

✪ The quality of the arbitration will depend on the arbitrators chosen. Get an unqualified arbitrator, and you will likely get a bad arbitration process.

✪ There is a trend toward arbitrations taking longer and costing more, so you would be wise to write into your contract a clause that will expedite the process (see arbitration clauses below) if this is your objective.

✪ You are giving up protections inherent in the U.S. judicial system, such as rules of evidence, reasoned judgments, and the right to appeal. In other words, you are essentially stuck with the decision that your arbitrator hands down. Still this risk may be outweighed by the considerable savings in cost and time over a traditional patent litigation case in court.

✪ If you are a large, deep-pocketed company that is sued for patent infringement by another company, like a small patent-holding company, you may actually prefer litigation in order to set an example. In such an instance, the company with deeper pockets may have a strategic incentive to focus not only on the current lawsuit, but to take a broader view and send a message to all other such plaintiffs. If the company simply settles, others may view it as an easy target.

✪ Another example might be a patent owner who wants to enforce a new patent against an entire industry. Such an owner may want to fight his or her first case to obtain a clearly enforceable and final verdict that is upheld on appeal. Such a victory could encourage potential infringers to fall into line and either take a license or get out of the business.

✪ Mediation, as well as settlement, may offer some confidentiality that litigation does not offer. Confidentiality may be valuable to certain IP litigation. For example, a patentee who goes after a potential infringing defendant also risks that the defendant may find prior art that could potentially invalidate the patent owner's patent. A patentee will want to keep such prior art out of the public light so other competitors do not become aware of its existence. If the patent owner settles with the patentee, the patentee may also want to keep the prior art hidden so that its own competitors go through its own expense in uncovering such prior art. Mediation and settlement may offer such protection.

Author's Note: Arbitration

With respect to arbitration, 35 U.S.C. §294 requires arbitration decisions to be filed with the PTO, which places them in the corresponding patent file history. Thus, if your objective is confidentiality, which an ADR technique like an arbitration decision can provide, you may want to reconsider your posture in light of this rule.

It is important to see that patent litigation can be used as a tool against others. Also, given the appearance that one is ready and capable of going to battle may also result in a more favorable mediation or settlement by one's opponent who may start to balk at the expense of going into battle at court.

Arbitration Clauses in Contracts   When you enter into a transaction with another party, arbitration clauses are something you should put some thought into. If you decide on an arbitration clause, you should agree on the kinds of disputes to be arbitrated. Many companies incorporate *step clauses,* which provide an initial period of mediation. If mediation fails, the dispute goes to arbitration.

You should also specify which organization will handle the arbitration and where the arbitration will take place. This will determine the rules that will apply and the arbitrators who will hear the case.

You should also decide whether one or a panel of three arbitrators should handle the proceeding. Using a single arbitrator will make the arbitration go quicker. However, for larger, more-complicated disputes, using three arbitrators will mitigate the risk of an off-the-wall decision.

You should also consider time limits on the proceeding, as well as limitation on discovery. A growing concern, even with arbitration, is that the proceedings are taking too long and becoming expensive, much like a patent litigation case. Adopting expedited rules of the AAA may be a good bet.

How to Find and Select an Arbitrator

There are a number of organizations that administer all phases of mediation and arbitration. The most well-known organization of arbitrators is the American Arbitration Association (AAA), which can be found at www.adr.org. The AAA maintains a list called the *National Panel of Patent Arbitrators*. Parties can select an arbitrator from this list who has a technical background related to their dispute.

Other arbitrator organizations include JAMS (http://jamsadr.com/), the National Arbitration Forum (NAF) (http://arbitration-forum.com/), National Arbitration and Mediation (NAM) (http://namadr.com/), the International Chamber of Commerce (www.iccwbo.org/court), the Chartered Institute of Arbitrators (www.arbitrators.org), and the Institute for Conflict Prevention and Resolution (http://cpradr.org/).

Usually the fee of an arbitrator is determined by the size of your claim. Each organization has its own rules of procedure, which can vary dramatically on many important issues. These rules of procedure can typically be found at their websites. Your selection should obviously depend upon careful research of each of these possible arbitration organizations. At a minimum, the forum you select to arbitrate or mediate your case should understand IP disputes.

Court-Ordered Mediation

If your dispute results in a lawsuit, it is becoming common practice for there to be *court-ordered mediation*. In most jurisdictions, a court will order both parties to engage in mediation at some stage of the proceedings. Sometimes a court will order the parties to engage in mediation after the defendant files an answer to the complaint. Courts of other jurisdictions will order mediation after *dispositive motions* (hearings that can decide the outcome of a dispute) have been considered by the judge.

Settlement

Arbitration and mediation are processes used to help parties reach a settlement. As the name implies, a *settlement* relates to the resolution of a dispute. Settlement can occur at any point after you believe someone is infringing on your patent. Competitors may agree on how to resolve a dispute before going to court or the parties may resolve the dispute after litigation has started.

The terms of a settlement agreement will depend on the facts of your particular case. If you are the plaintiff, a favorable settlement agreement might, for example, be where you get the defendant to agree to pay you a certain amount of money for past infringement of your patent, acknowledge the validity and infringement of the patents involved, and enter into some type of licensing arrangement. The agreement should always be put in writing.

When to Arbitrate, Mediate, or Settle

Ideally, arbitration, mediation, or settlement should occur before litigation starts in your case. This is because both parties will save the most money at this stage of the proceeding. Complaints will not have to be filed and answers will not have to be prepared. This will result in savings of attorney fees. Moreover, parties will often become more adamant in their positions after large amounts of money have been spent on the litigation. This may make resolution of the case increasingly difficult without a decision from the court.

However, you simply may not understand the strengths and weaknesses of your case prior to the start of a court case. It will be hard for an arbitrator to decide or for you to come to a decision during mediation, without knowing the facts and circumstances of the case.

While you may be unable to have arbitration or mediation of your case before the case is filed, you often can get a pretty good idea of your case after discovery has occurred. *Discovery* is the phase of the case where both parties are required to exchange information regarding the matter. After such information has been gathered, exchanged, and analyzed, you often can come up with a pretty good idea about what the arguments of each side will be at trial. At this point, you should begin to see the strengths and weaknesses of your own case. This will enable you to have a better idea of what you would be willing to accept.

Even after your case has been decided, you should still consider mediation and settlement as a way to put an definitive end to your conflict. This should be an option, even if you are victorious at the district court level. The reason for this is that you can still lose your case on review before the appellate court. You will of course need to look at the particular strengths and weaknesses of your case before making any concessions. The point is there is still a place for settlement after a court decision has been rendered in the case.

Other Non-litigation Tools and Strategies

In this chapter you will also learn about other tools and strategies which may substitute for or supplement costly and prolonged litigation battles in a U.S. court. First, you will learn about a complex but important procedure called "an interference" to contest a competitor's patent or patent application on the basis that you believe yourself to be the first inventor.

You will also learn about a strategy called *reexamination*, which many people often do not consider from either an offensive or defensive patent strategy viewpoint. Reexamination is a procedure carried on before the U.S. Patent and Trademark Office (PTO). Defensively, it can be used to attack the validity of a patent based on prior art patents or written publications. Offensively, it can be used by a patent holder to strengthen a patent where some questions arise about the validity of a patent based on prior art patents or written publications, which were perhaps unknown to the patent holder when the patent was still in its application phase.

Finally, this chapter concludes with non-litigation strategies that you should always consider in opposing your competitor's activities abroad. Patent applicants will often file the patent applications in various foreign countries for the same invention filed in the United

States. You need to be aware of such applications and take steps to oppose such applications early on if warranted.

INTERFERENCE

Consider the following situation: You conceive an invention and spend years coming up with a working model of your invention. Finally, you obtain that working model and then decide to file your patent application for your invention. As you start to draft your patent application, you do a preliminary search for any other published patent literature that may already describe your invention. To your amazement you come across a published patent application of a competitor that claims your invention.

You could file your patent application, start to make your invention anyway, and then use the dates that you believe you invented your product as a defense if you are later sued by your competitor for patent infringement. However, instead of waiting for your competitor's patent to issue, you can go ahead and file your patent application, and then request that an *interference* be declared between your own patent application and the application filed by your competitor.

An interference is a proceeding held by the PTO to determine whether you or your competitor was the first inventor of the claimed subject matter. The proceedings are complex and quasi-courtlike, so you will need to hire an attorney who has expertise in interference proceedings.

An applicant of a patent can suggest an interference to the patent office. An interference can also be initiated by the PTO.

Interferences can be a great way to knock out the application of a competitor on the basis that you were the first to invent. However, costs are still quite high in an interference proceeding and typically approach about $500,000.

Prerequisites to an Interference   For interference to exist, there must be interference subject matter. *Interference subject matter* exists if the subject matter of a claim of one party would, if prior art, anticipate or render obvious the subject matter of an opposing party and vice versa. This is referred to as the *two-way party test*.

Example:

Party A claims a chair and Party B claims a chair with arms, which is not obvious in view of the chair. The chair is anticipated by the chair with arms because it has all the elements of a chair with arms. But the chair with arms is not anticipated by the chair so could not provoke an interference here. This situation often comes up with a genus versus species invention.

Another requirement for declaration of an interference is the need of two co-pending applications, or in the alternative, a pending application and issued patent. The PTO will not declare interference between two issued patents.

> ### Author's Note: Reissue and Interference
> If you do have an issued patent, you could turn it into an application by requesting a reissue and then file an interference.

Before an interference can be declared, you must also set aside rejected claims. The PTO will not allow an interference where rejected claims exist. This is easy to take care of. You can just cancel your rejected claims and file these rejected claims in a continuing application.

As soon as you discover a published patent on your invention, which you believe you came up with earlier, you must also copy those patent claims into your own application within one year from the date the application was published. Otherwise, you will be barred from getting into an interference contest with the patentee of that published application. Published applications for this purpose include not only U.S. applications but also WIPO publications (in any language) of an international application designating the United States.

> ### Author's Note: 35 U.S.C. § 135(b)
> This is an important requirement that is required by statute (35 U.S.C. § 135(b)), which states that "a claim which is the same as, or for the same or substantially the same subject matter as a claim of an application published under section 122(b) of this title may be made in an application filed after the application is published only if the claim is made before 1 year after the date on which the application is published."

The reason for this rule is to provide patentees with assurances that years after they file a patent application others will not claim the same subject matter in another application.

REEXAMINATION

Reexamination is a procedure where a patent is examined once again as if it were like a patent application rather than an issued patent. Indeed, prosecution of a patent in reexamination has many similarities to examination of a regular patent application. But there are large differences. For one, there is a three-member board that is experienced in reexamination matters that handles reexamination rather than a single examiner.

Reexamination is a procedure that is becoming an increasingly important patent strategy due to recent changes in the law that have expanded how one can use this procedure. At the same time, this procedure is probably still one of the most unfamiliar procedures around.

Reexamination can be used both as a defensive mechanism to challenge the validity of a patent, as well as an offensive strategy by a patent holder who wants to strengthen the claims of an issued patent.

There are two types of reexamination. The first type is referred to as *ex parte reexamination. Ex parte* is simply a legal term of art that denotes that the proceeding occurs without notice or involvement of one of the parties. When reexamination is carried on *ex parte,* the person whose involvement is limited is the person who requests the reexamination.

The second type of reexamination is referred to as *inter partes. Inter partes* is a legal term that denotes that all of the parties are involved in the proceeding. When reexamination is *inter partes,* the person who requested reexamination of the issued patent is involved in the proceeding. Involvement in the reexamination is advantageous in this respect, because the third party requester will get a chance to make arguments as to why the patent is invalid. In addition, the requester will be able to contest any arguments made by the patent holder as to why the patent is valid. However, *inter partes* reexamination is a more complex procedure, and hence, a more expensive one to conduct.

Ex parte reexamination is available for all pending patents, while *inter partes* reexamination is only available for patents that were filed after November 29, 1999.

Whether a reexamination is conducted *ex parte* or *inter partes,* there are three possible outcomes after the reexamination concludes. These possible outcomes are:

✪ the patent's validity is affirmed in its entirety;

✪ the patent is affirmed, but its scope is narrowed; or

✪ the patent is cancelled altogether.

The scope of a patent's claims cannot be enlarged by a reexamination. If you are a patent holder who wants to enlarge the scope of your patent claims, you will need to consider a *reissue* of your patent (see Chapter 15), rather than a reexamination.

Also, with respect to any claims that are added to the patent or that are amended as a result of the reexamination, a potential infringer will have an intervening rights defense with respect to those newly added, changed claims. (For a discussion of intervening rights, see Chapter 15.)

How to Know if a Patent Is Under Reexamination

You can find out whether a particular patent is subject to a reexamination using the USPTO's Public PAIR system. This can be useful, not only from knowing the status of that patent, but also because you can pull up all documents filed in such a reexamination to aid you in your own reexamination request. To do this you need to go to the USPTO's Public PAIR (discussed in Chapter 7), choose "patent number," enter the appropriate patent number, select "continuity data," and then scroll to the bottom of the resultant page and look for any entries under "child continuity data." If there is nothing listed, a reexamination request has not been received by the USPTO. If there is an entry, it is possibly a reexamination application and you will need to click on the entry to see. For example, if you follow these steps for U.S. patent No. 5969156, you will see that a reexamination certificate was issued for this patent on 09–26–2006.

Who Should Seek a Reexamination

Below are some common reasons why someone may want to request a reexamination.

1. To invalidate one or more claims of the patent.

2. To obtain prosecution history estoppel—Even if a party who attacks the validity of a patent claim loses with respect to the reexamination, such a reexamination may force the patent owner to make damaging prosecution history statements in order to obtain reallowance of the claims, which could potentially strengthen such third party's argument of non-infringement.

– Caution –

Be careful. Losing such a reexamination may very well have estoppel effects (discussed below) with respect to bringing those same arguments up again later in an infringement action.

---

3. To stay litigation—You are able to stay and stop a lawsuit. This might be an advantage depending on your viewpoint.

4. Litigation is much more expensive than reexamination— For example, one does not have motions and discovery in a reexamination.

5. To cast doubt on the validity of a patent—A patent carries a presumption of validity in a lawsuit. That presumption is provided by statute 35 U.S.C. §282. In court, a patent challenger has the burden of establishing the invalidity of an issued patent by clear and convincing evidence. In stark contrast, a patent does not carry any presumption of validity at the PTO. The PTO will examine that patent in an examination just as it would examine a patent application. This fact can be used to your defensive advantage if what you seek is to challenge the validity of patent. You may find it easier to make your challenge at the PTO rather than in the courtroom, at least with respect to the grounds that you can raise in a reexamination.

Of course for a patent holder, an interference is rarely desirable because you lose presumption of validity—not so in litigation—and often get claim construction, which is broader than in litigation and might lead to invalidity.

6. Influence of a jury—While a pending reexamination does not remove the presumption of the validity of a patent for a later court battle, a reexamination may be influential on the trier of fact in court. To know that the PTO considered that a substantial new question of patentability existed might get in front of the jury although some courts may not allow such information to reach the jury.

7. Reexamination may be of interest to patent holders in limited circumstances—For example, patent holders often want to use a reexamination to fix potentially invalid claims of an issued patent. A patent holder might do this, for example, by narrowing the claim so that he or she can pass muster with one of the defenses discussed back in Chapter 6.

Ex parte reexamination is also often used by a patent owner to run new prior art past the PTO (inter partes reexamination is not an option for owners). If the PTO affirms the patent after looking at such prior art, the patent gains additional strength, which can be used to convince competitors to shy away from attempting to challenge the validity of that patent later in court.

Ex parte Reexamination   *Ex parte* reexaminations came about in 1980, as the result of small businesses that complained to Washington that large corporations were using patents with questionable validity. The cost of patent lawsuits was being used as a way to drive smaller corporations out of business because they could not afford the costs.

In response, Congress passed a law that created *ex parte* reexamination. Under this procedure, any person may at any time file a request with the PTO to have an issued patent reexamined based on printed publications that constitute prior art (see Chapter 4). Such written publications are those that are published prior to a critical date, such as one year prior to the filing of a patent application. The publications must also disclose the invention. These same types of written publications can be used in a reexamination proceeding before the PTO.

If a party requests reexamination, the PTO has three months to determine whether or not the printed publication raises a *substantial new question of patentability* affecting any claim in the patent. A substantial new question of patentability will exist if a reasonable examiner would consider the publication material in deciding whether or not the claim is patentable.

If the PTO determines that a substantial new question of patentability exists, then the patent holder will have two months to file a reply in response to the reexamination request. The party who requested the reexamination then has two months to file an answer in response to this reply. But after this, reexamination no longer involves any more participation by the third party requester. The proceeding becomes one between the patent holder and the examiner at the PTO, just as it would in the application phase for a patent. This can be a disadvantage to the third party, who would like to know what is going on in the proceeding and perhaps present arguments in favor of invalidity of the claims.

Upon filing a request for ex parte reexamination, the PTO will reply with either a grant or denial within ninety days. The grant will identify which claims are subject to reexamination, and at least one reference supporting the grant of reexamination. If the reexamination has been granted, the patent owner optionally may file a response, or *statement,* to the grant, that can include the canceling or amending of any claims, or a correction of inventorship. If the patent owner files a response, the requester may then file a reply to this response. Otherwise, the requester is no longer able to participate in the reexamination, nor any appeals. Following the grant and any responses or replies, the examiner will issue an office action. Subsequent prosecution of an ex parte reexamination by the patent owner is similar to that of a utility patent application.

A patent holder who is disappointed in the results of an *ex parte* reexamination has the right to appeal this decision to the Board of Appeals and Interferences. If the Board renders an adverse decision, the patent owner may then appeal that decision to either the District

Court of the District of Columbia under United States Code, Title 35, Section 144 or directly to the U.S. Court of Appeals for the Federal Circuit under United States Code, Title 35, Section 145.

Inter Partes Reexamination

Inter partes reexamination is similar to an ex parte reexamination in that it is initiated by filing a request for reexamination that will be granted if the requester raises a substantial new question of patentability based on published prior art references. Issues of inventorship, inequitable conduct, enablement, written description, and best mode cannot be raised.

There are, however, significant differences between inter partes reexamination and ex parte reexamination. First, once the PTO orders an inter partes reexamination, the third party requester will be able to participate in the proceeding. This means that the third-party requester will have the right to rebut the patent holder's arguments with arguments and evidence of his or her own. Third parties who request inter partes reexamination are allowed to submit one written comment each time the patent owner files a response to the PTO. (U.S.C., Title 35, Sec. 315(a) and C.F.R., Title 37, Sec. 1.983.)

Second, the third party requester also has the right to participate in any appeal that the patent holder may take with respect to the decision of the PTO. If the third party requester is unhappy with the examiner's decision regarding the reexamination, the requester also has the right to appeal that decision to the PTO Board of Patent Appeals and Interferences. If the Board rules against the requester, then the requester can appeal that decision to the Court of Appeals for the Federal Circuit.

Another major difference is that the requester is estopped from asserting at a later time in litigation the invalidity of any claim finally determined to be valid on any ground raised or that could have been raised during the reexamination.

As an additional note about the use of inter partes reexamination, there is no opportunity for interviews with an examiner as to substantive issues. So a patentee may be at a disadvantage not being able to negotiate and try to overcome a rejection. Also, no continuations are allowed in inter partes reexamination. Typically, there is a first office action and final action (*action closing prosecution*).

When Can You Seek Reexamination/ Prerequisites

The following are prerequisites to initiation of a reexamination proceeding:

- ✪ Inter partes reexamination is available only against patents that have issued from applications filed after November 29, 1999. So a large majority of patents are not subject to reexamination. In addition, inter partes reexamination is only available to third-party requesters, not to patent owners.

- ✪ Documentary prior art only—In the case of both ex parte and inter partes reexamination, invalidity of a patent may only be challenged based on prior art patents and printed publications that can serve as a basis for anticipation rejections under 35 U.S.C. §102 or obviousness rejections under 35 U.S.C. §103. The third-party requester may not challenge the patent based upon other invalidity or unenforceability defenses such as non-patentable subject matter, prior use, on-sale bar, inadequate disclosure, inequitable conduct, and prosecution laches. Thus, you can not raise all theories of invalidity, as with a court challenge to a patent.

Author's Note: Locating Prior Art

The best prior art to locate is either printed publications, which were not considered by the PTO when examining the patent in question, or publications that the PTO may have missed. Naturally, if the PTO has already considered a reference during prosecution of the patent, your chances of a successful reexamination based on such reference is probably not going to be all that great. But the fact that prior art was previously considered by the PTO will now not necessarily preclude reexamination based on the prior art. The existence of a substantial new question of patentability is not precluded by the fact that a patent or printed publication was previously cited by or to the Office or considered by the Office. This means you can seek reexamination even based on prior art listed on the face of a patent.

How to Request an Ex Parte Reexamination

The rules for requesting an *ex parte* reexamination are specified in the Code of Federal Regulations, Title 37, Section 1.510. You will need to closely follow those rules if you want to request ex parte reexamination. A summary of what you must submit follows.

- ✪ Completed Form PTO/SB/57, *Request for Ex Parte Reexamination Transmittal Form* that can be found at the PTO website www.uspto.gov by clicking on "patents" on the main page and then clicking "forms."

- ✪ Attach to your request a statement pointing out each substantial new question of patentability based on prior written publications.

- ✪ Identify each claim for which you want reexamination and explain the pertinence and manner of applying the cited prior art to each claim for which you request reexamination.

- ✪ Attach a copy of each written publication that you are relying upon for your reexamination request. Any publication that is not in English must be translated.

- ✪ Submit a copy of each patent for which you are requesting reexamination.

- ✪ Certify in your request that you have mailed a copy of the request with its attachments to the attorney of record for the patent holder or to the patent holder. A space on the *Request Form* is provided to make this certification. (You will need to actually mail a copy to the appropriate person if you are making this certification. If service on the patent holder is not possible, you will need to include a duplicate copy of your request to the PTO.)

- ✪ Include the appropriate fee for your request.

See MPEP Chapter 2200 for more information on ex parte reexamination.

How to Request an Inter Partes Reexamination

The rules for making an inter partes request are governed by the Code of Federal Regulations, Title 37, Section 1.913. The rules are essentially the same as for making an ex parte request with the following difference:

✪   Your request form for an inter partes reexamination is Form PTO/SB/58, entitled *Request for Inter Partes Reexamination Transmittal Form*. You can obtain this form from the same site as you do for a request for ex parte reexamination.

✪   You will need to check the box listing the real party in interest who is filing the request. This should correspond to the person who is actually making the request. (An attorney who is representing the real party should not be listed here.)

✪   A third party requester will need to certify that the estoppel provisions of the Code of Federal Regulations, Chapter 37, Section 1.907 do not prohibit an inter partes reexamination. There is a box on your request to make this certification. All this means is that you are not bringing another request for reexamination concerning issues that were previously determined in a prior reexamination request.

✪   All documents that are filed by either the patent owner or the third party requester must be served on the other party. (U.S.C., Title 35, Sec. 314(b)(3) and C.F.R., Title 37, Sec. 1.951.)

NOTE: *Issues that are resolved in the inter partes reexaminations proceeding usually cannot be relitigated in a later court proceeding.*

What Is Better, Ex Parte or Inter Partes Reexamination?

Ex parte requests greatly outnumber inter partes request. For example, in 2006, there were 511 such requests, more than seven times as many as the seventy inter partes requests in that year. There may be some good reasons for this. For one, ex parte rexaminations may be conducted anonymously without identifying the requester. This may be good for startup companies that are in product design phase. One can file the reexamination without tipping off patentee as to who you are, which can force patentee to make estoppel amendments so you can more easily design around.

Your chances of success are higher with an ex parte reexamination with approval rates around 91%. Still, research indicates that even inter partes reexamination is quite successful if your goal is to damage the patent of another. According to one researcher, 59% of inter partes proceedings resulted in all claims rejected or cancelled and 39% had some claim amendments. Only 2% had all claims confirmed (Cohen, Joseph D., *What's Really Happening in Inter Partes Reexamination,* 87 J. Pat. & Trademark Off. Soc'y 207, 217 (2005).)

One potential advantage of inter partes reexamination as discussed is that ex parte reexamination offers fewer opportunities for the requester to participate actively, and the requester cannot participate in appeals. This will mean the request loses control over how the reexamination will progress. However, under some viewpoints this may be advantageous because it also means lower legal fees—at least in the short run—than in an inter partes proceeding.

As already mentioned, a major difference between ex parte and inter partes reexamination is that the requester is estopped from asserting at a later time in litigation the invalidity of any claim finally determined to be valid on any ground raised or that could have been raised during an inter partes reexamination. Estoppel is a concept covered in Chapter 24 with defenses to patent infringement. By statute, a third-party requester in an inter partes reexamination is estopped from later asserting, in any court action, that a claim in the patent is invalid based on any ground that the requester raised or could have raised during the reexamination proceeding. (35 U.S.C. §315.)

This estoppel does not apply to ex parte reexamination proceedings, which can be looked at as one possible advantage of pursuing ex parte reexamination where the third-party requester would not be precluded from relitigating any issues later on in court. The rationale for this difference is that inter parte reexaminations are by their procedure full participatory proceedings. It is thus deemed fair to require that one not be allowed to relitigate issues that could have been raised in the proceeding. So, if you are a third-party requester, you need to be aware that by pursuing the inter partes reexamination route, you will not be allowed to raise defenses like prior art, which you could have raised during the reexamination proceeding.

This estoppel effect, however, is dampened by the fact that one is, as a third-party requester, given full participatory rights in an inter partes reexamination much like one would in a court proceeding. Moreover, a third-party requester is not prevented from later asserting invalidity of a claim based on prior art that was unavailable to the third party requester and the USPTO. Despite this, the possible estoppel effect associated with inter partes proceedings is cited as a primary drawback with inter partes compared to ex parte reexamination. Clearly potential challengers still want the opportunity to be heard in court despite the much greater costs associated with protracted court litigation.

> ### Author's Note: Estoppel
>
> In some cases estoppel may actually be preferred. This is akin to prosecution history estoppel covered in Chapter 19, where what a patent owner says during prosecution can come back to haunt him or her in the form of a narrower construction of the patent claims. One strategy here with respect to inter partes reexamination may be to try to obtain a narrow construction of claims of a patentee through such an estoppel. This may serve you later on in litigation when a patent holder tries to claim that you are infringing the patent. So even if you cannot knock out the patent through reexamination, you might succeed later in litigation on the narrow claim construction.

In addition, any narrowing of the claims or amendments establish intervening rights. Thus, recovery of damages for an asserted infringement during the period between the date of issuance of the original patent and the date of issuance of the reexamination certificate requires that the original and reexamined claims be identical.

Cautionary Words about Reexamination

As already mentioned above, accused infringers and patent holders seek reexamination for a variety of reasons. However, some cautionary words are in order here, whether you are the accused infringer or patent holder. If you are the accused infringer, you need to be alert that the asserted patent may actually end up being stronger if a reexamination certificate issues. If you are a patent owner seeking reexamination, you face the risk of the cancellation of your patent.

Another cautionary word for patent holders is that you need to make sure any amendment you make during reexamination is done for a proper purpose. A reexamination amendment that fails to comply with the requirements of the reexamination statutes can result in the later invalidity of your affected claim. This can happen, for example, where you enlarge the scope of your claim during reexamination. Such enlarging of the scope of claims is prohibited by the reexamination statutes.

Even claims that are not impermissibly broadened during reexamination can be held invalid if they are added for an improper purpose. In this respect, it is important to keep in mind the reexamination statutes, particularly 35 U.S.C. §305, which states in pertinent part the following:

> *In any reexamination proceeding...the patent owner will be permitted to propose any amendment of his patent and a new claim or claims thereto, in order to distinguish the invention as claimed from the prior art cited under the provisions of section 301 of this title, or in response to a decision adverse to the patentability of a claim of a patent. No proposed amended or new claim enlarging the scope of a claim of the patent will be permitted in a reexamination proceeding under this chapter.*

In light of the above statutes, any of your reexamination amendments should be characterized, if at all, as distinguishing over the prior art or in response to a PTO rejection, and any unnecessary comments regarding other possible purposes should be omitted.

Example:

Dr. Freeman applied for and was granted a U.S. patent that was later reissued with additional claims. Dr. Freeman then sued an alleged infringer in U.S. district court. The court found the claims to be invalid and not infringed. Knowing about reexamination, Dr. Freeman applied for reexamination of his reissued patent and amended his claims in order to avoid the court's interpretation of the claims. The PTO examiner rejected the amendments as impermissibly broadened under §305. On appeal, the Federal Circuit Court affirmed the holding that the amendments were made neither to distinguish the invention from the prior art cited in his reexamination nor in response to a decision rejecting his claims, which are the only reasons permitted for amendments made under §305.

PUBLIC USE PROCEEDINGS

If you have information that a particular invention that is the subject of a patent application was in *public use,* you can submit your evidence to the PTO. To be in public use, the invention must either be in use or on sale more than one year prior to the filing date of the application.

You must submit your documents to the PTO before the patent application has been allowed by the PTO. Allowance of a patent application is when the PTO has mailed the applicant a notice that a patent will be granted based on the patent application.

Public use or sale of an invention more than one year prior to the filing of the claimed invention are arguments that can be made to invalidate a patent. (U.S.C., Title 35, Sec. 102(b).) They are equally good arguments to make to refuse the grant of a patent application. The strategy here is simply to use the arguments in the process before a patent is even issued. (See Chapter 10.)

After receiving the allegedly disqualifying information, the PTO has discretion to start a *public use proceeding*. This is an administrative hearing to determine whether the invention was actually in use or on sale more than one year prior to the filing of the application. (C.F.R., Title 37, Sec. 1.292.) You will need to submit a petition along with your documenting papers to the PTO. You should take a look at the MPEP Section 720 for the rules on how to do this. Following are some of the things you will need to do:

- ✪ Submit the appropriate fee as specified in the Code of Federal Regulations, Title 37, Section 1.17(j).

- ✪ Your petition must contain a sufficient description of the subject matter that you allege was in public use or on sale, including any necessary photographs, drawings, diagrams, exhibits, or flowcharts to enable the examiner to compare the claimed subject matter to the subject matter alleged to have been in public use or on sale.

✪ The caption of your petition will need to identify the pending patent application that is the subject of your petition. You will need to include information such as the name of the applicant, the application number, title of the invention, and filing date of the invention.

✪ The caption of your petition should also clearly identify itself as a "PETITION UNDER C.F.R., Title 37, Sec. 1.292."

✪ Serve (deliver) a copy of your petition upon the applicant of the patent application in any one of the ways specified in the Code of Federal Regulations, Title 37, Section 1.292. Include a certificate of service with your petition stating that you have made proper delivery.

Mail your petition to the Assistant Commissioner for Patents, Washington, D.C. 20231. Address it to the attention of the director of the particular technology center in which the application is pending. All inventions are assigned to a particular technology center with expertise in the particular field of the invention. For example, an application dealing with biotechnology would go to the biotechnology technology center. Use the PAIR system to help you locate the applicable technology center for the application for which you are interested. (See Chapter 4.)

PROTESTS

If you did not have evidence of prior use, but did have evidence as to some other disqualifying act that would make the grant of a patent inappropriate (see Chapter 10 for such arguments), you could possibly use a proceeding called a *protest*. Unfortunately, one of the requirements to filing a protest is that your petition must be filed before the patent application is either published or allowed, whichever occurs first. In all but a very few cases, this means you will have to file your protest with your disqualifying information before the patent application is published, because allowance will almost always occur after an application is published.

The problem with filing a protest before an application is published is that you will not have access to patent applications that are not published. There is simply no way for you to know about them unless somehow you learn through the grapevine that your competitor has filed one or unless one of the circumstances exist as discussed in Chapter 4. Pending applications that have not been published are generally held in confidence by the PTO. There is simply no data base to go to and search for such pending patent applications. This means that protests are probably not going to be something that you will be able to use under normal circumstances.

If you do know about a patent application before it is published and want to file a protest, consult the Code of Federal Regulations, Title 34, Section 1.291. It is also discussed in the MPEP at section 1900.

THIRD-PARTY SUBMISSION

A final procedure to consider is using the *third-party submission* procedure. (C.F.R., Title 37, Sec. 1.99.) This provides that any member of the public can submit patents or publications that are relevant to the patentability of published patent applications. Submission must be made within two months following the publication date of the patent application (or prior to notice of allowance, whichever is earlier). If you could not have made such a submission at that time, you can submit your documents while the application is still pending.

Since the vast majority of patent applications are published, a third party submission can be a useful way to get patents or publications before an examiner in order to prevent the patenting of an invention. Follow the procedures specified in Section 1.99. Your submission should include the following:

✪   The requisite fee specified in the Code of Federal Regulations, Title 37, Section 1.17(p). In addition, if you are making a late submission (not within two months from publication date), you must also include a processing fee specified in the Code of Federal Regulations, Title 37, Section 1.17(i).

✪   A list of the patents or publications that you are submitting, including the date of publication of each patent or publication.

Also include a self-addressed postcard (with postage on it) listing what you have sent to the PTO. This will serve as your notice that the PTO has received your papers. After this point, you will have no further contact with the PTO. Everything will now be in the hands of the examiner handling the patent application. At least you can rest assured that the examiner is now privy to the information that you knew. Hopefully, the examiner will use this information to deny allowance of the patent application.

These little-known procedures are useful in an attempt to get the PTO to reject the patent application if you believe that the PTO should not grant a patent. Striking before a patent application is allowed can be advantageous to you for a number of reasons. After a patent has been granted, your competitor can thereafter bring you into court for patent infringement based on the patent. Your competitor cannot do this prior to the date the patent is issued. If you are brought into court, you can still raise public use or sale of the invention more than one (1) year prior to the effective filing date of the patent application, but the whole process is going to be much, much more expensive.

PATENTS ISSUED ABROAD

Patents have really gone global. Back in the old days, corporations were probably not too concerned about foreign markets for their goods. This of course has all changed. All corporations now consider filing for patents not only in the United States, but also abroad in order to protect their inventions outside the United States. Two of the most important markets considered abroad are Europe and Japan. Both of those markets also offer an opposition procedure of which all patent strategists should be aware.

Europe   For Europe, a company will often file for a patent in the *European Patent Office* (EPO). At the time the patent is filed, the applicant will also designate any number of European countries where patent protection is desired. If the patent is granted by the EPO, the patent can turn into a host of patents that are enforceable in each of the

European countries selected by the applicant. Any third party has, however, nine months from the grant of that patent to file an *opposition* to the grant of the patent.

The key here is that you need to be aware of any patents that are issued by your competitors abroad. You can use one of the many competitive intelligence tools discussed in Chapter 3 to do this. If you become aware of a patent issued abroad by a competitor that you think could cause problems in the future, you should at least consider whether there are any grounds that can be used to oppose the grant of that patent. Such defenses will be very similar to any one of the defenses that you learned about in Chapter 10. A typical timeline of major events with a European opposition is shown below.

- The opponent to the patent must file a *Notice of Opposition* with the EPO within nine (9) months from the grant date of the patent. The grounds for opposition and issues to be resolved during the opposition must be set forth.

- A three member Opposition Division (OD) is chosen to conduct the substantive examination of the opposition.

- The patent owner is invited to file what are referred to as *observations* on issues raised by the opponent, or from the OD.

- The OD will issue a decision that revokes the patent, rejects the opposition, or maintains the patent in an amended form.

- Either side may appeal the decision of the OD by filing an appeal within two months to the Board of Appeal.

Japan The *Japanese Patent Office* (JPO) also affords third parties an opposition procedure similar to the EPO. However, the third party must file a written opposition to the grant of a patent within six (6) months after publication of the issued patent. If a decision is made to revoke the patent, the patent owner may appeal that decision to the Tokyo High Court. If the opposition is dismissed, the opponent may not appeal the decision, but a trial for invalidation of the patent may be filed with the JPO on the same grounds and using the same evidence as in the previous opposition.

Oppositions abroad are a good way to stop the issuance of a patent competitor. At the very least, you should be using your competitive intelligence tools to keep abreast of patent applications that your competitors are filing abroad and take steps in the form of an opposition where appropriate.

NOTE: *Even if you had the technical expertise to handle an opposition procedure yourself, you would still need the help of a foreign associate having experience in such matters to carry on the process abroad for you. You can go to the European Patent Office website at www.epo.co.at and click onto "search engines" and then click "European patent attorneys database" to help find a foreign associate. Another useful website to find patent agents in the United Kingdom (UK) can be found at www.cipa.org.uk.*

Another thing that you can do is to contact the patent department in a U.S. law firm. Firms that have intellectual property departments will also have foreign associates that they use for foreign filings. They will more than likely be delighted to give names or such contacts since they usually expect that any business they refer will be returned in their favor by the foreign firm.

SECTION VI

MAKING MONEY FROM YOUR PATENT

Licensing

As discussed, sometimes you will have no choice but to cross-license your invention. This often is true when your invention is an improvement over an existing patented technology. A great number of patented inventions are in fact improvements over inventions that have already been patented. If the patent on the existing technology has not yet expired, anyone who practices the invention, including yourself, may infringe the claims of the patent on the existing technology. Conversely, if the patent holder of the existing technology practices your improvement technology, the holder may also infringe your patent.

The solution to this perplexing problem is the *cross-license*. You and anyone else who wants to practice your invention will need to obtain a license on the existing patented technology. Similarly, the patent holder of the existing technology will need to obtain a license to use your improved technology patent. Both you and the patent holder give each other permission to use the respective patented technologies in the form of what is called a *license*.

In addition to cross-licensing, a more typical type of licensing arrangement will be when you grant another person the right to practice your invention in the form of a license in return for future royalties made from the sale of the licensed invention.

Licensing is important as it may be your only way to efficiently commercialize your patented invention. Most of us simply do not have the resources, nor the know-how, to manufacture and sell products. By licensing your invention to manufacturers who have the capability to produce and sell your patented invention, you are able to realize your ultimate goal of making money off your patented invention.

Even if you do have the ability to manufacture and sell your products yourself, licensing still may be the most efficient way to get your invention to the marketplace. In fact, large corporations enter into such licensing agreements all the time. Such corporations may decide that others are simply more efficient at making and selling their products.

Having a license will mean that you only get a small royalty on the revenues of your invention. But if your invention brings in a lot of revenues, this can actually amount to a lot of money. More importantly, by aligning yourself with a company or companies that have expertise in the manufacture and sale of your invention, you are probably going to get your invention into the marketplace a lot more effectively than if you try to do it yourself. In the end, this could mean the difference between success and failure.

As you read this chapter, remember that licensing is a separate subject in itself. Some of the important terms of a licensing agreement, as well as some sample licensing agreements are provided. However, this book is not meant to be a detailed discussion on the topic of licensing.

WHAT IS A LICENSE?

A patent license is, in effect, a contractual agreement that the patent owner will not sue the person who takes the license (the *licensee*) for patent infringement if the licensee makes, uses, offers for sale, sells, or imports the claimed invention, so long as the licensee fulfills its obligations and operates within the bounds delineated by the license agreement.

Licenses are very common in the patent world. Companies will often enter into licenses with other companies for patented inventions for a host of reasons. One important reason is that in return for the license, a company will typically gain revenue in the form of a *flat out payment* or in the form of *royalties* on the future sale of the patented invention. Companies also will enter into *cross-licenses* with other companies, so that each respective company is free to make and use the other company's patented invention.

NONEXCLUSIVE LICENSES

It is common for companies to also license a patented invention to more than one licensee. Such licenses are referred to as *nonexclusive licenses*. By licensing to more than one licensee, it is possible to increase your revenue because you now have more than one licensee paying you fees for the licensee. Even big corporations can make money licensing their inventions to hundreds of licensees who are willing to pay fees for the invention.

EXCLUSIVE LICENSES

The most valuable license a company can obtain is called an *exclusive license*. Although an exclusive license is not an *assignment* (discussed in Chapter 28) in the legal sense, it is pretty close. An exclusive license prevents even the patent owner (the one giving the license) from competing with the licensee as to the specified geographical region, length of time, and/or field of use set forth in the license agreement.

Deciding whether to grant an exclusive license over a nonexclusive license will depend upon your own unique circumstances. Having one very capable exclusive licensee who can manufacture and sell your products all over the world may earn you more money than a lot of less effective licensees. Moreover, your administrative costs in keeping track of all of your nonexclusive licenses may cut into your profits.

Further, from a licensor's perspective, exclusive licenses can be advantageous in that they can, if properly drafted, provide your licensee an incentive to commercialize you invention. If your exclusive licensee is required to give you up-front payments and meet minimum royalties, the exclusive licensee will be more inclined to do more to make as many sales as possible.

A licensee, such as a manufacturer, will generally prefer an exclusive license agreement. Since they are investing their own money into the commercialization of the licensed patented invention, they benefit more from the protection an exclusive license offers.

LICENSE FEES

In a license, what you get in return for giving the license is called a *royalty rate*. Typically, this royalty rate is based on sales made by the licensee of your invented product, and typically this royalty is in the range of 3%–8% of the value of the sale.

When negotiating a royalty rate for your invention, keep this in mind. If you insist on rates that are a lot higher than these typical rates, you risk the strong possibility that your potential licensor may decide it makes more business sense to try and design around your invention. Also, if your rate is so high that selling your product becomes unprofitable for your licensor, this will not do anyone any good. If your licensor cannot make any money off the sale, the licensor is not going to put a lot of effort into selling your product.

Also, remember this. If you go to court to enforce an infringement action against a company, reasonable royalties are typically the standard for measuring your damages. If all you can get in court is the prevailing royalty rate, it probably does not make sense for you to ask for more than this rate.

FINDING PROSPECTIVE LICENSEES

Finding prospective licensees will probably not be an easy task. One possible avenue to find potential licensees is companies that are infringing your patent. If you discover companies who are infringing your product, then your technology is obviously useful to them. Given this competitive knowledge, you are in a great position to demand a future royalty for their continued use of your invention. Some other sources include:

- publications;

- Small Business Administration;

- trade shows; and,

- PTO services.

Publications

There are a variety of ways to locate manufacturers, such as looking in the *Thomas Register* that lists manufacturers and their products in the United States. Another way to locate manufacturers on the Internet is through the AT&T website www.tollfree.att.net. Identify companies that have expertise in manufacturing products in your field. Those companies will be good potential licensees for your invention.

Small Business Administration

The Small Business Administration (SBA), and more particularly, its division called the Small Business Development Center (SBDC), has a listing of resources that you can use to locate manufacturers as potential licensees. Their website is www.asbdc-us.org.

Trade Shows

Trade shows in your particular field are a great way to find businesses that may be interested in licensing your patented invention. There is an international licensing show held in New York at the Jacob Javits Center www.javitscenter.com /content/events/webcast/main.htm each year, where individual inventors can show their products to prospective manufacturers who are interested in new products to license.

PTO Services

The Patent and Trademark Office publishes the *Official Gazette* (OG) every Tuesday that summarizes that week's patented inventions. The PTO will publish, for a $25 fee, a notice in the *Official Gazette* that your patent is available for licensing or sale. On the second Tuesday of each month, your patent for license or sale is published in the *OG*. You can access the *OG* electronically by going to the PTO website at www.uspto.gov, clicking on the "Index" icon at top, and then by clicking on "O" to find the "Official Gazette."

APPROACHING YOUR LICENSEE

You should come up with some type of marketing letter that you send to each of the prospective licensees you have identified. Try sending your letter to individuals in the company who you believe have the power to make decisions.

If your invention has been patented, attach to your letter a colored brochure about your invention. The brochure should detail how your invention works and list all of its advantages.

You want to get word out about your invention. This is more important than trying to keep it secret by insisting on confidentiality agreements. If you do not attract interest for your invention, it will be worth nothing to anyone. You have a patent, so you can be assured that anyone who tries to copy your invention will risk infringement of your patent.

If a color brochure is too expensive, reference a website that describes your invention. Websites are a very practical way to promote pictures and explanations about your invention.

Individuals of high rank in a corporation are probably going to be difficult to get an answer from right away. Follow up in a week or so, after you have sent your initial letter, to inquire as to whether there is any interest. Use the telephone or send an email to do this. Offer to come in at the officer's convenience to demonstrate how your invention works and to explain why you believe that it is a good fit with the company's products. Be persistent, but friendly.

The hardest part of your job will be obtaining interest from a company in licensing your invention. If you get "No" for an answer, do not dismay. Move on to your next targeted potential licensee. Approach as many companies about licensing your invention as you are able to. Moreover, there is no law against approaching several companies, simultaneously, about licensing your invention.

If after approaching several companies you are in the envious position of having more than one company interested in licensing your invention, then you have a couple of options. If you plan on entering into nonexclusive licenses, then your option is easy, simply enter into nonexclusive licensing agreements with each of the companies who are interested in taking such a license.

If you are interested in entering into an exclusive licensing agreement, then you will need to choose the best licensee out of the companies who are interested in taking a license with you. An obvious factor to consider in making your choice is which licensee will give you a better royalty rate. However, you should also consider which company you think would make a better partner. You may, for example, have a better working relationship with one company compared to another. You may also feel that one particular company is better able to make future sales of your products. Remember that greater future sales will equal greater royalties for you.

Sometimes your potential licensee will insist that you not approach other licensees about licensing your invention while that potential licensee evaluates your invention for licensing. In such a case, you should consider insisting that the potential licensee enter into something called an *option agreement* with you. Any time you agree to refrain from doing something, you are giving up value for which you should obtain something in return. For example, if you agree to give someone the right to buy your house ten years from now, then you should insist that you obtain something in value for giving that right. The agreement that governs such situations is called an *option agreement*. Your negotiations with potential licensees should be no different.

LICENSE AGREEMENT

If a company wants to license your patented invention, then you will need to finalize the deal with a *licensing agreement*. This section will point out some terms of particular importance to the patent license agreement. However, only a few key points are addressed as a complete licensing agreement is beyond the scope of this book.

The terms of a license will be similar with respect to whether you decide to enter into a nonexclusive or an exclusive licensing agreement, with the exception of the following major differences:

✪   An exclusive license agreement should provide for up-front payments to the licensor, as well as an obligation on the part of the licensee to meet some minimum royalties each year. One way to do this is to calculate what would be the minimum amount of money that you would accept when your royalty payments are due and put this amount right into your agreement as the minimum amount of royalty that your licensee must pay. However, there are many ways that you can incorporate this into your agreement ranging from the simple to very complex formulas.

✪   If your licensee is unwilling to agree to a minimum royalty, then as a licensor, you are better off insisting upon a non-exclusive licensing agreement. The reason for this is that an exclusive licensee will be your only source of revenue. If that revenue is low because the licensee does not make a lot of sales, then you are better off reserving the right to license to others, who may have a better shot at making sales.

✪   An exclusive license agreement will usually contain the right of the licensee to enter into *sublicenses*. Naturally an exclusive licensee will want to make as many sales as possible in order to meet their obligations to pay you minimum royalties and up-front payments. Therefore, your exclusive licensee will want the right to sublicense to enable itself to meet these demands.

Important Clauses   The following paragraphs are clauses that you should always pay particular attention to in a license agreement. While not every clause needs to appear in every type of licensing agreement, these clauses are some of the most important points that any licensor or licensee should consider.

Definitions
A license agreement will typically include a section that defines words of significance used in the agreement.

Net sales
Typically, royalty rates are based upon net sales made by a licensee. These sales are typically the invoice price of the product sold under the license agreement minus customary discounts or rebates allowed to a distributor or customer.

Products

When you enter into a license agreement, you need to do a little bit of thinking about what actually you are licensing. One answer to this question is that you are licensing the rights under your patent to your patented invention. However, claims of a patent are not something that a licensee will sell. What a licensee will typically sell are products that have been developed. These products will be covered by the claims of your patent. Therefore, license agreements typically have a definition for *products* that usually means the use, manufacture, or sale of any product covered by a claim of your patent. Your royalties will thereafter be based on a percentage of the net sales of these products.

Royalty rate

This is often the most difficult term to determine in a patent license. The rate you can get will depend on the worth of your invention to third parties. Typical rates hover around 5%, but they can go as high as 10%. Usually, high volume products bring more than smaller volume products.

Licensors will want to make sure that the royalty percentage is based on sales and never on profits. There should also be a provision that gives licensors the right to examine the books and records of the licensee.

Licensees, on the other hand, may want to base royalties on money actually received from the sale, rather than the sale itself.

One thing that you might insist on is a provision that states that you agree to a certain percentage as a royalty rate for a certain number of products sold, but that if a certain number of additional units are sold, you will be entitled to an increased royalty percentage rate.

A licensor may want to see if royalties can be based upon the product as a whole rather than the patented part. For example, if you invent an improved carburetor, you may want to see if you can base your royalty rate on the sale of the car in which your new carburetor will be used rather than the value of the carburetor itself. Your royalty rate will obviously be a lot larger since the value of the car is much larger. Licensees will probably object to such a provision, however.

Licensors may also want to consider royalties that increase in the event a licensee challenges validity and regardless of the outcome, or at least royalties that increase if a licensee challenges the validity of the licensor's patent and loses. The reason for this is due to the possibility that licensees will challenge the validity of the licensed patent even while the licensee agreement is in effect Such increases will help to cover the huge litigation costs that a licensor could face with such invalidity litigation and help deter the licensee from making such challenges.

Example:

Genetech granted Medimmune a license under an existing patent, as well as a patent that might issue from a pending application. The license called for royalties on "Licensed Products," and defined "Licensed Products" as a specified antibody, "the manufacture, use or sale of which would, if not licensed under the Agreement, infringe one or more claims of either or both of (the covered patents), which have neither expired nor been held invalid by a court or other body of competent jurisdiction from which no appeal has been or may be taken." A patent issued on the pending application and Genetech wrote Medimmune a letter saying that it believed a product sold by Medimmune was covered by this patent and expected Medimmune to pay royalties.

Medimmune believed the patent to be invalid and informed Genetech that it was paying royalties "under protest, and with reservation of all [its] rights and commenced an action against Genetech in federal court for a declaratory judgment that the patent was invalid. Medimmune alleged that it considered Genetech's letter a threat to terminate the license and sue Medimmune for patent infringement. The Supreme Court agreed that a court could determine whether or not the patent was invalid negating the obligation of Medimmune to pay royalties even though Medimmune (the licensee) was at the time paying royalties, and the licensor (Genetech) had no basis for commencing any type of action against the licensee.

Given this actual case, licensors should be careful about defining the products on which royalties are payable in some manner that refers to validity of the patent. Licensees, on the other hand, will be more interested in having that type of contract language.

Examples of possible contract language for licensors might include the following:

> *Licensed Products shall mean all products the making, use, importing, offering for sale, sale or supply of which would, in the absence of the license granted by this Agreement, infringe a patent of the licensed Patents.*

> *Products that would infringe a patent of the Licensed Patents is a Licensed Product without regard to and independent of whether the Licensed Patents are valid or invalid, or enforceable or unenforceable under the facts and the law, or as determined by a judgment of a court in any action binding on both parties.*

Reports and payments

A licensor will want to specify when the payment of royalties become due, as well as the requirement that licensee provide an accounting with respect to those royalties. Royalties are typically due on calendar quarters. However, other terms can be set forth.

Territory

The geographical location in which the licensee can operate should be defined. Clearly, a licensee will want the largest area possible. However, if a licensee has no intention of selling the products outside the United States, then the licensee should not insist upon worldwide territory. This is because the license agreement will typically also require that licensee use its best efforts to sell the products worldwide. This could lead to a breach on the part of the licensee, if the licensee has no intention to sell the product worldwide.

Up-Front payment

A licensor will want some type of up-front payment for the license, particularly for an exclusive license. The reasons for this is that if the invention fails, at least the licensor has obtained some compensation. For the exclusive license, a licensor will not only want an up-front license at the time the license agreement is entered into, but also periodically while the license is in force. Without such a guarantee, your exclusive licensee could just sit back and not even sell the invention. Your options are then limited since you cannot license to others under an exclusive license.

Most favorable terms clause

This clause is often insisted upon by licensees. It basically states that if the licensor offers a license on the same patent to anyone else on terms that are more favorable than the terms offered to the licensee, then the licensor must give those same favorable terms to the licensee.

Best efforts

Licensors should insist on a clause that covers the possibility that the licensee will not take steps to sell the licensed products. If a licensor has a licensee who is not making efforts to sell the product, then this obviously is not going to be much use to the licensor.

Bankruptcy

A bankrupt licensee may be useless to a licensor. A clause should probably be inserted giving the licensor a way out.

Representations and warranties

Certainly, a licensee will want the licensor to warrant that he or she owns or has the right to license the patents to be licensed. This is not an unreasonable request from a licensor's point of view.

The issue of validity of the patents to be licensed is another story. Licensors will want a clause stating that they do not guarantee the validity of the patent being licensed. Licensees will want a clause that licensors do guarantee validity. Given that no one can know for sure whether a patent is valid, a good trade-off is to provide that the license agreement will terminate if a patent is found invalid by a court.

Indemnity and insurance

Licensors will want a clause where licensee indemnifies licensor from any liability relating to the manufacture, distribution, and sale of the products. Proof of insurance should also be insisted upon.

Arbitration clause

Patent litigation is extremely expensive. It is probably in the interest of both parties that disputes over a license be resolved by arbitration. However, there are losers at arbitration, too. If you are confident in your position and ready for expensive litigation, you may not want an arbitration clause.

Sublicensing

There should be some language about whether the licensee can sublicense the license to others. A licensor usually does not want to give the right to sublicense. If such a right is granted, the licensor should insist that the licensee notify the licensor about any sublicenses. It should also be required that such sublicenses must be bound by all the terms of the original license agreement.

Infringement of patent by others

A licensor will want to specify that it has the right to bring suit for infringement and is entitled to all damages resulting from that infringement. The licensor should also require that the licensee bring to the attention of the licensor any known infringement by third parties.

Trademark, copyright, and patent notices

If you or your licensee wants to be able to recover damages for infringing activity under patent law, you will need to mark your products. Otherwise, you are going to be precluded from recovering damages until you provide an infringer actual notice of your patent rights. So make the marking of products a condition right in your license agreement. This way you will hopefully not have to worry whether or not your licensee is marking products sold under the coverage of your patent.

Trademarks are also an issue in the license. A licensor will want to ensure that only trademarks owned by the licensor are applied to the products. Trademarks take a long time to develop. If you have not come up with any trademarks for your products, you should include provisions as to what happens after the licensee agreement ends. A licensor does not want the licensee running off with ownership of a trademark after years have been spent in promoting the trademark.

Term of the license

The period that the license will remain in effect should be spelled out clearly. The licensee will want to ensure that any license agreement only lasts while the patent of the licensor is in force. This is because if a patent is not in force, the licensee really has no need for the license. Remember that the reason a licensee enters into a license is to avoid being sued for infringement by the patent holder. If the patent has expired or is otherwise not in force, the licensee can freely practice the invention without a license.

> ### *Author's Note: License Terms*
> Even a licensor should not object to a term extending beyond the time a patent is in effect since such a requirement is actually illegal and will make the license unenforceable.

Patent infringement

You will want to address this important issue, particularly in an exclusive licensing agreement. Exclusive licenses will typically insist upon at least the right to bring patent lawsuits against infringers. This is because these licensees are typically under an obligation to meet minimum royalties and up-front payments. Thus they will have an incentive to go after potential infringers who are cutting into their sales.

You should not object to giving your exclusive licensee the right to go after infringers because you will want your licensee's sales to be as big as possible. Letting others sell your products without giving you a royalty will reduce the royalty that you earn from your exclusive licensee. By allowing your exclusive licensee to pay for the cost of going after infringers, you will also not have to incur these costs up front, and you can sit back and relax while you let the bigger pockets of your licensee worry about everything.

Your agreement should also provide for what happens if your licensee obtains an award as a result of the litigation. Damages usually include lost profits on sales made by your infringer. Since this money represents sales that your licensee probably should have captured but for your infringer, it probably makes the most sense to divide these profits as if they were sales made by your licensee. Thus, one way that you can divide an award is to provide that your licensee is responsible for paying you the license royalty on these profits. Of course, you will want to let your licensee deduct any expenses it incurred in pursuing the litigation.

You also need to worry about the situation if others claim that your patents are invalid or that your sale or manufacture of the licensed products infringes upon some third party's patents. With an exclusive license, it makes sense to place the burden of defending such actions upon the licensee. Such licensees will typically have the bigger pocket and expertise to deal with the problem. In effect your licensing agreement acts like an insurance policy for you.

As already mentioned, you even need to be concerned that your own licensee may decide it wants to contest the validity of your licensed patent. In the past, licensees could not seek such invalidity determinations based upon patents covered under the license until the license was actually breached by the licensee. Only until that time would there be an actual threat of a patent infringement lawsuit by the licensor against the licensee making an actual case or controversy. An *actual case or controversy,* as you might recall, is a requirement for declaratory judgments, which are lawsuits seeking a court decision on an issue even before one is sued.

However, a new case called *Medimmune, Inc. v. Genetech, Inc.* has changed all of this. In *Medimmune,* the Supreme Court held that a patent licensee can go to federal court to seek a declaratory judgment that a licensed patent is invalid, unenforceable, or not infringed without having first to breach the license agreement. Thus, it now appears that licensees can continue to pay royalties under the license agreement while at the same time seeking a court declaration that a patent covered under the license is invalid or that a patent that the licensee is selling does not infringe the patent listed in the license.

Medimmune should be of concern to licensors and patentees. Given this case, licensors may want to consider some contract language designed to thwart such licensee behavior. Contract provisions that prohibit patent licensees from raising invalidity contentions are not allowed pursuant to a case called *Lear v. Adkins.* However, license provisions that might be allowed include procedural impediments such as mandatory arbitration, as well as substantive costs, such as increased royalties, associated with the right to challenge the propriety of the underlying patent. In the alternative, licensors may want to seek lump-sum, paid-up, or other front-loaded royalties. Reducing ongoing royalty payments in favor of higher up-front fees and periodic milestone payouts will maximize the patent owner's profits at the outset of the agreement and minimize the financial impact of a later challenge to the patent.

Other possibilities to deter licensees from raising such validity issues include provisions that, if the licensee alleges invalidity and pay royalties, the licensee becomes obligated as of the date of the challenge to make a lump sum payment approximating the patent owner's expected validity litigation costs or a series of payments over time roughly equal to the patent owner's costs of litigating validity.

Patent fees

You will want to have an agreement about who must pay maintenance fees to keep your patent in force. Having a patent go abandoned because these fees have not been paid will not be to anyone's advantage.

Right to terminate without cause

Licensees will probably want a way out of the agreement if they decide to no longer sell the licensed products. Licensors will generally want to keep the licensee under the obligation to finish selling the products for the duration of the agreement.

Licensors should keep in mind that with a right to terminate clause, licensees may have less incentive to invest in development and marketing activities that enhance the value of the licensed rights. This can be detrimental to both licensor and licensee. However, for products that do not require a large investment, a right to terminate clause can be best to end an unfavorable situation where two parties are not working well together. In such cases, it really makes no sense to have two parties who no longer want to work together be bound by a license

As was explained above in respect to the ability of licensees to potentially challenge the validity of licensed patents during the term of the license agreement itself, licensors will want to be careful making any royalty clause dependent on the validity of the patents. If there is such reference, licensees may be able to challenge the validity of a patent even during the license agreement, which is something they never had the right to do before. They could do this, for example, by sending the licensor a protest letter during the term of the license, which states they believe the patent that is the subject of the license agreement to be invalid. If the licensor then replies with any threat of a patent infringement lawsuit, the licensee can then file a declaratory judgment seeking to invalidate the patent.

Given this potential that licensees can challenge the validity of a patent while the license agreement is in effect, a termination at will clause in a license will be something that a licensor may now actually want to consider.

The problem with a termination at will as explained, however, is that it is not useful in situations where a patent owner is trying to provide incentives for the licensee to invest money in development and marketing activities that enhance the value of the licensed rights, such as in most situations where licenses are exclusive.

As alternatives to a termination at will clause, licensors may want to consider at least having a clause that terminates the license agreement in the situation where the licensee does challenge the validity of the patent subject to the license. A sample clause follows:

> *In the event Licensee, directly or indirectly, alleges in any action that any of the Licensed Patent is invalid, Licensor may terminate the license granted to Licensee in its entirety at any time by giving notice to the Licensee. Licensee's obligations, including, but not limited to, the obligation to pay royalties to Licensor shall continue as provided above or until such license has been so terminated.*

Which law governs.

It is always beneficial to have your home state law govern the terms of the license. This is so you do not need to go outside your state in order to hire an attorney to deal with disputes over the agreement. A jury may also favor a home-based company although that is theoretically not supposed to happen.

Technical expertise

Sometimes, license agreements involve more than a licensor giving the right to a licensee to manufacture and sell products covered by the claims of a patent. Sometimes what is exchanged is also technical expertise of the parties. For example, a licensee may not be able to easily manufacture a product without the technical assistance of its licensor. In such a case, a licensee will want a clause that requires the licensor to provide all of the necessary technical know-how that is needed by the licensee to manufacture the products.

A sample license agreement is included in Appendix C. It is important to remember that sample forms are just that. The language of forms need to be adjusted according to both your particular bargaining power and whether you are the licensor or licensee. There are many places were you can obtain license forms. One excellent site for such forms is the *Association of University Technology Managers* website at www.autm.net.

Whichever form you use, pay particular attention to the important clauses discussed in this chapter. You are also probably better off preparing the initial draft of a license agreement, if possible, since the first draft often shapes what follows. This may not, however, always be possible when dealing with a larger company than yourself.

Other Ways to Commercialize Your Invention

This chapter will discuss other options besides licensing to commercialize your patented invention. The first option is to manufacture and sell your product yourself. The second option is to sell your invention outright to a third party.

DO EVERYTHING YOURSELF

You always have the option to do everything yourself to get your product to the marketplace. In other words, you take care of the manufacturing, advertising, and distribution by yourself. The advantage of going this route is that you will be able to keep all the profits you make from the sale of your product. The disadvantage is that this route is very difficult to do if you do not have the necessary resources.

Sometimes commercializing your invention yourself will be your only option to make money off your invention. You simply may be unable to find anyone who is interested in licensing your invention. If you can neither find anyone who is willing to license or buy your invention, then you will have no alternative but to try to sell your invention to the public yourself.

Remember that doing everything yourself does not mean that you cannot rely upon other people to help you. In other words, you can find manufacturers who will manufacture your product just as you learned in the last chapter. However, instead of licensing your product to that manufacturer, you will need to enter into a contractual arrangement where you pay the manufacturer to make your work. You can enter into similar types of arrangements with salespeople and marketers. There are various books listed in Appendix A where you can find more information on helping you along each of the various facets of getting your product to the marketplace.

ASSIGNMENTS

Patent rights are property in the legal sense. As property rights, patent rights can be transferred. The way that you transfer your patent rights is through an *assignment*. An assignment can be the transfer to another of a party's entire ownership interest or of a percentage of that party's interest.

An *assignment* is the transfer by a party of all or part of its right, title, and interest in a patent or patent application. For an assignment to occur, the transfer to another must include the entirety of the bundle of rights that is associated with the ownership interest. This is because anything less than a transfer of entire rights would be a license, which was the subject of the last chapter.

This does not mean that you cannot assign a percentage of your interest in your patent, because it is entirely possible to do this. However, when you assign a portion of your interest, you must give up all rights associated with ownership of that interest.

Assignments are very common in the employer-employee relationship. An employer will usually insist that his or her employee assign any rights in inventions made while working at the company.

It is important to distinguish between an owner of a patent, and an applicant/inventor of a patent. While owners of patented rights and applicants of patent rights can be the same, they do not need to be. In fact, many of your patents will have different applicants and owners.

All patents must be applied for in the name of the actual inventors. To determine who is an inventor, you look at the claims of the patent. If any person has had any part in the conception of any claim listed in the patent, then that person must be listed as an applicant for the patent. Persons other than the inventors become owners of the invention typically through an assignment as in the employer-employee context.

Assignments vs. Licensing

Choosing between an assignment or license will depend on your own situation. However, commercialization of your patented invention through licensing is probably the more typical and better way to make money off your invention.

The reason for this is it will be hard to place a value on your patented invention. Both you, as the owner of the patent (patentee), and your prospective purchaser simply will have a difficult time determining the actual value of your patented invention until it has been manufactured and sold.

Given this difficulty in valuation, potential purchasers of your patent rights will probably be less willing to offer anything of great value for your patent unless it is a clear moncymaking bet. And even where your invention is a clear winner, such potential purchasers are probably going to offer you a lot less than what you will make if you take future royalties off sales over the term of your patent.

Therefore, unless you are pretty sure that what a prospective purchaser is offering you is close to what you will earn in future royalties through licensing, you are probably better off commercializing your invention through licensing.

When to Assign Patent Rights

There are several stages at which you can assign patent rights. You can assign your application:

- ✪ before you file it;

- ✪ after you file it, but before it issues as a patent; and,

- ✪ after it is issued as a patent.

NOTE: *Assignment of a patent application does not alter the fact that an application must be applied for in the names of the actual inventors. If you have taken assignment of rights to a patent application before the application has been filed, you still must file for the patent in the name of the inventors.*

A prospective purchaser of your patented invention will probably be more interested in purchasing rights to an already issued patent. This is because there are a lot of variables as to whether a patent will issue from an application. Patent prosecution can be an arduous and expensive process and a buyer will be much more interested in something that is more certain.

How to Assign Patent Rights

The requirements necessary to assign patent rights will depend at what stage in the patent process you are.

To assign a patent application prior to filing it, you must identify your patent application by its date of execution, the name of each inventor, as well as by its title.

To assign a patent after your have filed it, but prior to issue as a patent, you need to identify the application number in your assignment.

Assignment of an original application gives the assignee rights to any divisional, continuation, or reissue application stemming from the original application and filed after the date of assignment. However, this is not the case with a *continuation-in-part* (CIP). A CIP requires a new assignment. (MPEP 306 and 201.12.)

To assign rights in an issued patent, your assignment needs to identify your patent by its patent number. A form from the PTO that you can use to assign all of the rights to your patent is in Appendix D.

Recording

Any person who is assigned a patent should ensure that the assignment is recorded with the PTO. Recordation will ensure against any other possible assignment of the same patent rights.

If you record your assignment within three months from the date of assignment (or at least prior to the date of any subsequent purchase of the same patent rights), then your rights will be superior as to any subsequent purchaser of the same patent rights. If you fail to record your assignment, then you risk the possibility that a subsequent person could purchase your same patent rights, with those rights being superior to your own rights.

One can record either the original or a copy of an assignment with the PTO. There is a recording fee for each application or patent that is assigned. A recording cover letter form that you can use is in Appendix D. You should include the appropriate recordation fee and attach your assignment behind the cover sheet. You can also obtain the recordation cover sheet and assignment forms off the PTO website at www.uspto.gov.

The recordation cover sheet must contain the following information:

- the name of the party conveying the interest;

- the name and address for the party receiving the interest;

- a description of the interest conveyed (i.e., whether you are assigning a patent or some other document);

- each application number or patent number that you are recording;

- the name and address of the party to whom correspondence concerning the request should be mailed;

- the total number of applications or patents identified and the total fee;

- a statement that to the best of your knowledge and belief that the information contained is true;

- your signature; and,

- the date you signed the assignment.

Assignments can be faxed to 571–273–0140, electronically submitted to http://epas.uspto.gov, or mailed to:

Mail Stop Assignment Recordation Services
Director of the U.S. Patent and Trademark Office
P.O. Box 1450
Alexandria, VA 22313

Author's Note: Assignments
An assignment that is sent to the PTO through the mail will take about six months to get recorded. This means that if you are searching for assignments relating to a patent, it is possible that it will not show up for six months after the PTO receives it. However, once it is recorded, the recordation date will be the date the papers were received by the PTO.

One way to get around this delay is to electronically file your assignment. E-filed documents get recorded within about a day and are available in the assignment database immediately. To e-file your assignment, you should visit the PTO website and find the "electronic patent assignment system (EPAS)," which is listed under the "electronic business center (EBC)-Patents."

LICENSING COMPANIES

A number of companies are in the business of purchasing patented inventions from inventors. Companies such as ThinkFire and IPvalue are two examples (other sites can be found at www.ypatent.com in the licensing section). This is a relatively new approach. These companies buy or license patented inventions from a host of small inventors. By doing this, they are able to aggregate the patents and become more effective at commercializing and exploiting the technologies. Their expertise, as well as resources, make them a viable option for many small inventors who simply do not have the expertise, time, and resources to do this on their own.

Strategies for Commercialization

Have you ever wondered why some products are successful in the marketplace, while others are a complete flop? The quality of the product certainly plays a part, but there are a host of factors other than the novelty or usefulness of the features of the invention that make a product successful.

This chapter will take a look at simple things you can do to promote your invention and ensure that it is a commercial success. While big businesses spend millions of dollars promoting their products, the techniques in this chapter can be done quite inexpensively.

UNIQUE DESIGN

If you have a unique design or shape that you can add to your patented invention, consider doing this. As with trademarks, a unique, distinctive design or shape to a product can sometimes make all the difference in the marketplace.

If you do not believe that good designs can make winning products, here are three examples where distinctive designs have made huge successes.

- ✪ Motorola's RAZR cell phones are still cell phones. However, their thin design has boosted sales for Motorola to the extent of 50 million new phones sold.

- ✪ The sleek design of the iPod has resulted in Apple selling more than 58 million units.

- ✪ BMW's expected sales of its MiniCooper was twenty thousand per year at the most. Instead, it has become one of the most distinctive cars in the United States with sales over forty thousand in 2005.

There is a special type of patent, called a *design patent,* that you can file to protect unique designs and shapes in your patented invention. *Design patents* are not difficult to file. You should file one as soon as you come up with your unique design.

PRICING

If you can charge consumers a lower price for a product than your competitor, then you are usually on a road to success. Consumers love low prices and often make buying decisions with price in mind.

Sometimes the reason that retailers can charge a lower price for a product is due to some technical feature of the product itself. The product may simply be constructed out of some material that is less expensive to make or its design may make it less expensive to manufacture.

Hopefully, part of your patented technology is some technical feature that makes your product less expensive to bring to the consumer. Even if you do not have such a technical feature, you should still look for a variety of ways to keep the price of your products to a minimum. For example, you might partner with a manufacturer who has a track record of products more efficiently than its competitors. The end result will be a product that can be sold less expensively to the consumer.

LIMITED LIFE TERMS

There is a high correlation between your future profits and the life term of your product. The shorter the lifetime of your product, or the more need that buyers will have to replace your product and buy another one from you, the greater your sales will be.

A prime example of this is the company Intuit,® which sells three software products—*Turbo Tax*® (tax preparation software), *QuickBooks*® (accounting software for small businesses), and *Quicken*® (personal-finance software). Part of Intuit®'s success is due to the fact that Intuit's products require buyers to continually purchase a replacement product or upgrade, at least once a year.

CATCHY NAMES AND LOGOS

As you engage in the commercialization of your invention, you will inevitably be faced with the problem of coming up with unique names and logos for your products.

Choosing catchy names can often make the difference between success and failure. Many products lack any patent protection, yet are hugely successful in the marketplace because of their name. If you think that the brand name of your product does not matter, then consider this. There are actually companies out there that exist just to come up with names for products. Large corporations take the naming of new products seriously and so should you.

Whether you choose to have a professional assist you or you decide to come up with names and logos yourself, remember these useful tips.

- ✪ Consider the trademark implications of the name you choose. You will want to trademark any names and logos that you develop. (Review Chapter 1 for more information about trademarks.)

- ✪ Sometimes simple is good. Consider the "M" in the McDonald's® logo, or the red circle with a red dot in the middle of the Target® logo. Sometimes the simplest logos are the best and most memorable for the consumer.

✪   Consider getting the help of a professional. Coming up with good names can be difficult. One company you might take a look at is *Name Lab* (www.namelab.com), which is located in San Francisco. The American Institute of Graphic Arts (www.aiga.org) also offers a lot of information on finding qualified professionals.

✪   Use your chosen name and logo over and over. Only through continued use will you develop a strong brand identity.

✪   Consider any negative connotations that your names might have in foreign countries. This is sometimes referred to as a *connotation check*. If you do not do this, you may find that what you thought was a great name in the United States has a very negative connotation in a foreign country where you might want to sell your invention.

If you do use a professional to design your logo, have the creator assign his or her copyright rights to you. If you fail to do this, the creator could stop you from using your logo later on.

WEBSITES

The Internet has become increasingly important for businesses and the marketing of products. There are also many ways that you can use the Web to help you commercialize your patented invention. If you are not marketing your product yourself, you may at least find setting up a website useful for displaying the advantages of your invention to potential partners. As discussed, you can reference your website when you send out letters to prospective licensees. This can save you a lot of money in paper and printing costs. Instead of you having to provide detailed brochures, your potential licensee can find everything about your invention right on your website.

Domain Names

After you have designed a website that you feel pretty comfortable with, create a catchy name for your site. The name of your website is referred to as a *domain name*. An example of a domain name is www. Ypatent.com, which is the domain name I use for my website.

Refer to Chapter 1 for ideas on how to come up with a good domain name. Remember to do a quick check at the PTO website, www.uspto.gov, to make sure that your domain name is not trademarked.

Consider obtaining a trademark on your domain name. If it appears that your domain name is capable of trademark registration, register your name with a domain name registration service. Some of the more popular services are listed in Appendix A. You should not have to pay more than $10 per year to do this. Your hosting service will also register your name for you, but most hosting services charge you about double the price.

Hosting Services

After registering your domain name, obtain a web host for your site. Appendix A lists some web hosting services, but if you do a web search for website hosts, you will come across hundreds of more companies.

Email Campaigns

Email is still a great way to advertise your products. However, be careful with email campaigns because there are a number of ecommunication regulations—such as the CAN-SPAM Act—that you must comply with. One way to make sure that your marketing campaigns do not run afoul of the law is to use email marketing services that will send out your campaigns for you. Some of these services are very reasonably priced. A couple you might try are VerticalResponse (www.verticalresponse.com), Campaigner (www.Campaigner.com), and Constant Contact (www.constantcontact.com).

ALIGN YOURSELF WITH KEY PARTNERS

Even the largest companies around find that it may be more efficient to form partnerships when it comes to the commercialization of some technology. As a small inventor, you will probably find it an absolute necessity to form *strategic alliances*.

You form alliances in about everything you do when running a business. When you have a company supply you with photocopiers with a service contract, you are in effect forming a type of alliance. You may have simply found it to be more cost-effective to enter into such a contractual relationship, as opposed to buying the copiers yourself and servicing them when problems arise.

Another example of a small-time alliance that can help you on your website is what is called *affiliate programs*. This is simple to do and in fact can make you a little extra cash when someone goes to your website and clicks on a *banner advertisement* linking to the affiliate program that you have joined. Go to the website of just about any business and you will see a link to the company's *affiliate program* that you can join.

When it comes to choosing partners to help you commercialize your invention, remember what you learned in Chapter 27. Your licensee will be your most important partner in commercializing your invention. Here are some key points to consider as you choose your key partners.

Similar Technical Field

When you partner yourself with others, the most important thing to remember is to choose partners who are in the same technical field as yourself. For example, if you are selling products for the movie business, it would not make a great deal of sense to partner yourself with companies in the laundry business. A partner from a completely different field will simply not have the necessary contacts and skills to efficiently help you commercialize your invention. Your invention needs to somehow tie in with what your partner does.

Small Companies

Your initial view may be to try and align yourself with the biggest company around. This is usually not a great idea, particularly for the small inventor. First, large companies will often not give you the light of day when you try to present your invention. Larger companies also have in-house research and development teams and often have a bias against inventions that come from the outside, unless it is clear that such inventions have some great worth to the company.

FREE SAMPLES

Promoting your product and giving away samples of it is a great way to get consumers interested in your product. Clearly, not all products will be something that you can give away. You will also need to convince your advertising partner that your product will fit in nicely with the types of products that the partner sells.

STREET ADVERTISING

Street advertising is handing out pamphlets about your invention right on the street. A web design company noticed that business increased 200% by simply going to one of the busiest streets on Miami Beach and handing out little cards about the business. The owner did not hand out the cards himself. Instead, he found a model who agreed to do it for a couple of hours at about $50 an hour.

Conclusion

If you have made it this far, I congratulate you on a job well done. As I have said, patent law is not an easy subject, but I truly believe that inventors are in the best position to understand the technology of their own inventions. All they need is a little help understanding patent law, and to that end, I hope my book has helped you.

If you are the individual inventor or small company who is using this book to develop effective patent strategies, let me finally say that the work you are doing is important. Companies with fewer than five hundred employees account for more than 99% of businesses in the United States. These small businesses also employ 50% of the workplace. Moreover, the workforce at smaller companies is expected to grow by more than four times per year faster than larger companies. Employing strategies you have learned in this book will help you obtain a competitive advantage that can make your company a success.

If you have found my book useful in the prosecution of your patent or have questions or comments about my book, please let me know. I can be reached through my website, www.ypatent.com. This site also contains useful links to patent sites and other sites of interest.

Glossary

A

abandoned application. An application that is removed from the PTO docket of pending applications either: (a) through formal abandonment by the applicant, attorney, or agent of record; (b) through failure of applicant to take appropriate action at some state in the prosecution of the application; (c) for failure to pay the issue fee; or, (d) in the case of a provisional application, automatically after twelve months after the filing date of the provisional application.

advisory action. A form sent to you in response to your reply to a final office action from the PTO. This action will advise you of the disposition of your reply and why your application is still not in condition for allowance.

allowed application. This is an application that, having been examined, is passed to issue as a patent, subject to payment of the issue fee.

amendment. Opportunity to make changes to either your claims, a specification outside your claims, or arguments, in order to try to bring your application into condition for allowance.

antecedent basis. Referring back to something within your application.

anticipation. Art term used to describe a reference that teaches each and every element of your claimed invention. However, in order to anticipate your invention, the reference must also disclose all of your elements arranged in your claim.

application data sheet. A sheet that contains information about your patent application. The important pieces of information that it can contain include any claims of priority that you make to previously filed domestic or foreign applications.

assertion letter. The letter is written by a patent holder to another to inform the party about the patent holder's rights and to propose some resolution to the current infringing activity.

assignee. This is the owner of a patent application or patent.

B

body of claim. The portion of your claim that contains the elements or limitations of your invention.

C

cease and desist letter. *See assertion letter.*

claims. These are numbered sentences found in a utility patent. The scope of coverage for infringement purposes of the patent does not depend upon the number of claims, but rather on how the claims are written.

competitive intelligence. This term relates to knowledge about your competitors. Such knowledge might include information about your competitor's patent portfolio and their products.

continuation application. A second or even later filed application covering the same invention for which you previously filed a patent application. By filing a continuation, you maintain the ability to change the scope of your claims in case a competitor is successful in designing around the claims of your issued patent.

continuation-in-part application (CIP). Applications that are filed later to include new matter to your specification that was not included in your originally filed application.

continuity data. Information about all of the related applications, since more than one patent application may be filed for an invention.

D

declaration. A statement that warns you about willful false statements.

declaratory action. A special type of action used to resolve particular issues, such as whether a patent is valid or not. Typically, this type of action will be used strategically by a defendant to get a plaintiff onto the defendant's home court. A defendant can bring such an action as long as there is an actual controversy that will exist when a plaintiff threatens the defendant with a patent infringement lawsuit.

defendant. The parties against whom a lawsuit is brought.

dependent claim. A claim that refers back and further restricts a single preceding claim.

design patent application. This type of application protects the ornamental appearance of something. It is one of three types of patent applications, the others being utility and plant patent applications.

divisional application. A later application for an independent or distinct invention disclosing and claiming (only a portion of) only subject matter disclosed in the earlier or parent application.

docket number. A number that you create to identify your application.

doctrine of equivalents. This doctrine gives a patent holder a little more flexibility in being able to capture potential infringers who make, use, or sell products that have insubstantial modifications from a claimed invention. Under this doctrine, such insubstantial modifications are considered equivalents and fall within the scope of a claimed invention.

double patenting. A term used to describe the legal bar against claiming the same invention twice or claiming any inventions that are obvious from the one that you previously claimed in a patent application.

due diligence. The process of gathering information and assessing the merits, issues, and risks associated with a business transaction.

E

effective filing date. The date on which you file your patent application. If you have filed previous applications for the same invention, your effective filing date will be the earliest U.S. filing date so long, as you have made a claim of priority back to the earliest filed U.S. application.

enablement requirement. A statute requirement that demands your patent application teach one skilled in your art how to make and use your claimed invention.

extension of time. You can buy these in packages of up to five months in order to extend the time that you need to reply to an office action from the PTO.

F

filing date. This is the date you get when you file your patent application containing your specification, at least one claim, and any required drawings.

filing receipt. Obtained from the PTO when your application is complete.

final rejection. A second or subsequent office action that you may receive from your examiner that basically indicates that your examiner rejects your claims and wants to close your file. Your options after a final rejection become more limited.

foreign filing license. A prerequisite before you file a foreign application for your invention if your invention was made here in the United States. If you fail to obtain this license before your foreign file, the consequence can be loss of patent rights here in the United States.

freedom to operate. An inquiry to determine whether or not your activities may infringe the patents of some competitor, unless you want to risk the potential for a patent infringement lawsuit later.

I

incomplete application. An application lacking some of the essential parts and not accepted for filing by the PTO.

incorporation by reference. Instead of reciting all the information contained in a reference that you want to include in your specification, you are allowed to incorporate various types of references into your specification.

information disclosure statement (IDS). Completing an IDS fulfills your duty to let the PTO know about anything material to the patentability of your invention. If you neglect to fulfill this duty, any patent that you later obtain may be held unenforceable.

infringement. Unauthorized making, using, offering to sell, selling, or importing into the United States any patented invention.

interview. An appearance before your examiner for purposes of advancing your application toward allowance.

inventor. The person who has made any contribution to the conception of your claimed invention.

issue fee. A fee that you must pay after your application is allowed in order for you to be issued a patent. This fee is due three months from the date of your Notice of Allowance.

J

Jepson claim format. A particular style of writing a claim in which you use the phrase "wherein the improvement comprises...."

L

license. A contractual agreement that the licensor will not sue the licensee for infringement if the licensee makes, uses, offers for sale, sells, or imports the claimed invention, as long as the licensee fulfills its obligations and operates within the bounds delineated by the license agreement.

M

means-plus-function claim. A style of claim format that uses the word "means" followed by a specified function. Look to the specification to determine what types of means carries out the specified function.

multiple-dependent claim. A claim that depends on more than one claim. As with a dependent claim, a multiple-dependent claim must further restrict the claims on which it depends.

N

new matter. Any new material added to your patent application after the original patent filing.

notice of allowability. This form indicates that your examiner has allowed all of your claims and that your patent application is ready to be issued.

notice of appeal. File this type of notice if you disagree with the reasoning of your examiner.

O

oath. A notarized statement.

obviousness. A patent term of art used to describe the combination of prior art references to anticipate your invention, even though no one of the prior art references alone anticipates your invention.

office action. This is a written communication that you receive from the PTO concerning your patent application.

ordinary skill in the art. This refers to the level of skill that would be possessed by a person in the technology of the invention.

P

Patent and Trademark Office (PTO). The administrative agency charged with handling your application for a patent.

Patent Cooperation Treaty (PCT). The PCT allows you to file one international application in which you designate all the countries where you want to seek patent protection. After filing your PCT, you will need to enter national stage filings in each of those countries.

patent family. The first application that you file is your original application. If you later file a divisional application that claims priority to your originally filed patent application that divisional application is often referred to as a "child" of the original application. The original application and its child are also often said to be part of the same patent family.

patent term adjustment. Various situations in which the PTO will add extra days, months, or even years to your patent term.

Petition to Make Special. A petition that you can submit to the PTO in order to speed up examination of your patent application. You or your invention must fall into one of the categories that serve as the basis for such a petition.

plaintiff. The person or entity who initiates or starts a lawsuit.

preamble. The introductory portion of your claim.

preliminary amendment. An amendment that is received by the PTO on or before the mail date of your first office action.

prior art. A term of art to describe references that meet the criteria set forth in any one of the prior art sections of U.S.C., Title 35, §102. If a reference constitutes prior art and it anticipates your invention, your claimed invention will be rejected.

priority date. This date is usually when you file your patent application. However, if you have filed previous applications for the same invention (either domestic or foreign), then this date can become the date that any one of those earlier applications was filed, as long as you make a proper claim of priority to those earlier applications.

process claims. These claims define methods of making or doing something, and are characterized by their "-ing" active element steps.

product claims. These types of claims define discrete physical structures or materials.

product-by-process claim. A particular type of claim format in which you recite the product and a process of making that product.

prosecution history. The written record of an applicant's dealing with the Patent Office, including any actions taken by the examiner, and any statement, arguments, or modifications of the claims made by the applicant.

prosecution history estoppel. A term of art used to describe everything that goes on between you and the PTO after you file your patent application.

provisional application. An application for patent that allows filing without a formal patent claim, oath, or declaration, or any information disclosure (prior art) statement. It provides the means to establish an early effective filing date in a nonprovisional patent application filed under 35 U.S.C. §111(a), and automatically becomes abandoned after one year. It also allows the term "Patent Pending" to be applied.

R

rejected. This term is used in reference to the claims of your patent. It means that your claims are not allowable for some reason.

reply. *See response.*

Request for Continued Examination (RCE). An RCE is a later patent application that you file in order to keep alive the prosecution of your previously filed patent application. You usually file an RCE when you are up against a final rejection from your examiner and want a second chance to advance your arguments before your application becomes abandoned.

response. Your reply to an office action from the PTO, which must be made within the specified time period or else your application will go abandoned.

restriction. If two or more independent and distinct inventions are claimed in a single application, the examiner may require the applicant to elect (designate) single invention to which the claims will be restricted (limited to). This requirement is known as a requirement for restriction (also known as a requirement for division).

restriction requirement. Issued by your examiner if you claim more than one separate invention in your patent application.

S

shortened statutory period. The time period that the PTO sets for your response to an office action or other communication. The period is usually three months, although it can be shorter. There is a statute that provides an absolute six-month time limit for responding to all actions from the PTO.

small entity status. A determination that means an independent inventor, a small business concern, or a nonprofit organization is eligible for reduced patent fees.

specification. Everything that comprises your patent application, minus the drawings.

statute of limitations. A period of time in which you can make a claim in court. In patent law, you have six years to sue for infringement or be barred from recovering for that past infringement.

supplemental application data sheet. An application data sheet that you submit to correct any errors in the previous application data sheet submitted to the PTO.

supplemental reply. A subsequent response that you make after having previously responded to an office action from the PTO. You are allowed to make as many supplemental replies as you want, as long as they do not unduly interfere with your examiner's action on your prior responses.

T

terminal disclaimer. Form in which you agree that any patent issuing from your application must expire on the same date as another patent application that you also filed.

transition phrase. An introductory clause in your claim between the preamble and the body of the claim.

transmittal form. Form that must often be included with submissions that you make to the PTO. The form gives the PTO information about what you are submitting.

U

United States Patent and Trademark Office (PTO). See *Patent and Trademark Office.*

utility patent. One of three types of patents that are granted. This is the type of patent you will likely want to seek.

utility requirement. Requires that your invention as described in your patent application has a specific, substantial, and credible use.

W

written description requirement. A statute requirement that your patent application be detailed enough to show that you were in possession of your invention.

Important Addresses, Websites, and Telephone Numbers

USEFUL WEB LINKS

Recent changes to patent practice at the USPTO can be found at: www.uspto.gov/web/offices/pac/dapp/ogsheet.html.

Addresses, telephone numbers, and email addresses can be found on the PTO website (www.uspto.gov) by going to the "Contact Us" link. You can also email the PTO at usptoinfo@uspto.gov. Some of this important contact information is reproduced here.

IMPORTANT TELEPHONE NUMBERS

For general questions regarding patents, you can call 800–786–9199 or 703–308–4357, and 571-272–9950 for TTY.

PCT Help Desk: 703–305–3257.

Telephone number for assistance from the Electronic Business Center (EBC): 866–217–9197.

IMPORTANT FAX NUMBERS

1. Central Fax Number: 571–273–8300.

2. International Patent Applications

    An international application for patent or a copy of the international application and the basic national fee necessary to enter the national stage, as specified in 37 C.F.R. §1.495(b), may *not* be submitted by facsimile. Correspondence in an application before the U.S. Receiving Office, the U.S. International Searching Authority, or the U.S. International Examining Authority may be transmitted by facsimile, but the correspondence will *not* receive the benefit of any certificate of transmission (or mailing). (See 37 C.F.R. §1.6(d)(3) (referencing 37 C.F.R. §1.8(a)(2)(i)(D)-(F)).) Papers relating to international applications should be directed to one of the following numbers, if applicable:

    Facsimile number for papers in international applications: 703–305–3230

    Facsimile number for Response to Decisions on Petition: 703–308–6459

    Facsimile number for the PCT Help Desk: 703–305–2919

3. Office of Initial Patent Examination (OIPE)

    Other types of responses to notices from the Office of Initial Patent Examination (OIPE) and requests for corrected filing receipts may be transmitted by facsimile directly to the OIPE. The following is a list of official facsimile numbers for OIPE:

    Facsimile number for corrected Filing Receipt Requests: 703–746–9195

    Facsimile number for Response to Notice to File Missing Parts: 703–746–4060 (drawings may not be submitted by facsimile)

    Telephone number for Customer Service: 703–308–1202

4. Facsimile transmissions to the Office of Patent Publication

Payment of an issue fee and any required publication fee by authorization to charge a deposit account or credit card may be submitted by facsimile transmission. When drawings are submitted with payment of an issue fee, they may be submitted by facsimile. However, applicants are reminded that the facsimile process may reduce the quality of the drawings, and the Office will generally print the drawings as received.

The applicable facsimile number for payment of the issue or publication fees by facsimile transmission is as follows.

Facsimile number for Issue Fee (and any Publication Fee) Payments: 703–746–4000

Telephone number to check on receipt of payment (with Office of Patent Publication): 703–305–8283

5.   Facsimile transmissions to the Office of Pre-Grant Publication

Petitions for express abandonment to avoid publication under 37 C.F.R. §1.138(c), requests to rescind a nonpublication request, and notices of foreign filing should be directed to the Pre-Grant Publication Division. Questions regarding publication of patent applications (or rescissions of nonpublication requests) may also be directed by email to pgpub@uspto.gov.

Facsimile number for PG-PUB correspondence: 703–305–8568

Telephone number for the Pre-Grant Publication Division: 703–605–4283

6.   Facsimile transmissions to the Electronic Business Center

Requests for Customer Number Data Change (PTO/SB/124) and Requests for a Customer Number (PTO/SB/125) may be transmitted by facsimile to the *Electronic Business Center* (EBC).

The EBC may also be reached by email at: ebc@uspto.gov.

Facsimile number for the Electronic Business Center: 703–308–2840

7.   Facsimile transmissions of Assignment Documents

Facsimile transmission to record an assignment or other documents affecting title is also permitted. This process allows customers to submit their documents directly into the automated Patent and Trademark Assignment System and receive the resulting recordation notice at their facsimile machine. Credit card payments to record assignment documents are now accepted, and use of the credit card form (PTO-2038) is required for the credit card information to be separated from the assignment records. Only documents with an identified patent application or patent number, a single cover sheet to record a single type of transaction, and the fee paid by an authorization to charge a PTO deposit account or credit card may be submitted via facsimile.

Please refer to the PTO website, at www.uspto.gov/web/offices/ac/ido/opr/ptasfax.pdf for more information regarding the submission of assignment documents via facsimile.

Facsimile number for the Automated Patent and Trademark Assignment System: 703–306–5995

IMPORTANT ADDRESSES

For most correspondence (e.g., new patent applications), no mail stop is required because the processing of the correspondence is routine. However, certain correspondence with the PTO should be addressed to the proper *mail stop* if you want to ensure the fastest handling of your mail. The correct way to address your correspondence in such a case is as follows:

Mail Stop _____
Commissioner for Patents
P.O. Box 1450
Alexandria, VA 22313

A complete listing of mail stops can be found at the PTO website. Some of the more important mail stop designations are listed on the following pages. On the right side is a description of the type of correspondence you are interested in submitting, and on the left side is the corresponding mail stop you should place on your address labels.

Mail Stop Designations	Explanation
Mail Stop AF	Amendments and other responses after final rejection, other than an appeal brief.
Mail Stop Amendment	Information disclosure statements, drawings, and replies to office actions in patent applications with or without an amendment to the application or a terminal disclaimer. (Use Mail Stop AF for replies after final rejection.)
Mail Stop Appeal	For appeal briefs or other briefs under part 41 of title 37 of the Code of Federal Regulations (e.g., former 37 C.F.R. §1.192).
Mail Stop EBC	Mail for the Electronic Business Center, including: Certificate Action Forms, Request for Customer Numbers, Requests for Customer Number Data Change (Forms PTO-2042, PTO/SB/124A and 125A, respectively), and Customer Number Upload Spreadsheets and Cover Letters.
Mail Stop Expedited Design	Only to be used for the initial filing of design applications, accompanied by a request for expedited examination under 37 C.F.R. §1.155.
Mail Stop Express Abandonment	Requests for abandonment of a patent application pursuant to 37 C.F.R. §1.138, including any petitions under 37 C.F.R. §1.138(c) to expressly abandon an application to avoid publication of the application. (This new mail stop should be used instead of Mail Stop PGPUB-ABD. Applicants are encouraged to transmit the requests by facsimile to 703–305–8568.)
Mail Stop Issue Fee	All communications following the receipt of a PTOL-85, Notice of Allowance and Fee(s) Due, and prior to the issuance of a patent should be addressed to Mail Stop Issue Fee, unless advised to the contrary. Assignments are the exception. Assignments (with cover sheets) should be faxed to 703–306–5995, electronically submitted, or submitted in a separate envelope and sent to Mail Stop Assignment Recordation Services, Director—U.S. Patent and Trademark Office.
Mail Stop Missing Parts	Requests for a corrected filing receipt and replies to OIPE notices, such as the Notice of Omitted Items, Notice to File Corrected Application Papers, Notice of Incomplete Application, Notice to Comply with Nucleotide Sequence Requirements, and Notice to File Missing Parts of Application, and associated papers and fees.
Mail Stop Patent Ext.	Applications for patent term extension and any communications relating thereto.
Mail Stop PCT	Mail related to international applications filed under the Patent Cooperation Treaty in the international phase and in the national phase under 35 U.S.C. §371, prior to mailing of a Notification of Acceptance of Application under 35 U.S.C. §371 and 37 C.F.R. §1.495 (Form PCT/DO/EO/903).

Mail Stop Designations	Explanation
Mail Stop Petition	Petitions to be decided by the Office of Petitions, including petitions to revive and petitions to accept late payment of issue fees or maintenance fees.
Mail Stop Post Issue	In patented files, requests for changes of correspondence address, powers of attorney, revocations of powers of attorney, withdrawal of attorney, and submissions under 37 C.F.R. §1.501. Designation of, or changes to, a fee address should be addressed to Mail Stop M Correspondence. Requests for Certificate of Correction need no special mail stop, but should be mailed to the attention of Certificate of Correction Branch.
Mail Stop RCE	Requests for continued examination under 37 C.F.R. §1.114.
Mail Stop Sequence	Submission of the computer readable form (CRF) for applications with sequence listings, when the CRF is not being filed with the patent application.

Additional Resources

There are many other resources available to assist you through the patent process. Some are listed here.

BOOKS

Business Listings and Products

International Yellow Pages
(R.H. Donnelley Corp.)
Thomas Register of American Manufacturers
(Thomas Pub. Co.)

Business Plans

Complete Book of Business Plans, 2nd Edition
Joseph Covello and Brian Hazelgren
(Sourcebooks, 2006)

Complete Business Plan with Software
Bob Adams
(Streetwise, 2002)

Your First Business Plan, 5th Edition
Brian Hazelgren
(Sourcebooks, 2005)

Competitive Intelligence

Competitive Strategy: Techniques for Analyzing Industries and Competitors
Michael E. Porter
(The Free Press, 1980)

Millennium Intelligence: Understanding and Conducting Intelligence in the Digital Age
(Cyber Age Books, 2000)

The New Competitor Intelligence: The Complete Resource for Finding, Analyzing, and Using Information About Your Competitors
(John Wiley & Sons, 1995)

Proven Strategies in Competitive Intelligence: Lessons from the Trenches
John E. Prescott & Stephen H. Miller
(John Wiley & Sons, Inc., 2001)

Copyright Law

How to Register Your Own Copyright
Mark Warda
(Sphinx, 2004)

E-commerce/ Internet

Best of the Internet
Joe Kraynak
(Que, 2003)

e-Patent Strategies
Stephen Glazier
(Law & Business)

What's on the Web
Eric Gagnon
(Internet Media Corp)

Financing/ Venture Capital

Angel Investing
Mark Van Osnabrugge and Robert J. Robinson
(Jossey-Bass Publishers, 2000)

Financing Your Small Business
James Burke and Richard Lehmann
(Sourcebooks, 2006)

SBA Loans
Patrick D. O'Hara
(John Wiley & Sons, Inc., 2002)

Negotiation

Getting to Yes: Negotiating Agreements Without Giving In
R. Fish & W. Ury
(Penguin)

Marketing and Promoting Your Product

Communicating Globally: An Integrated Marketing Approach
Don E. Schultz and Philip J. Kitchen
(NTC Business Books)

Guerrilla Marketing On-Line
Jay C. Levinson & Charles Rubin
(Houghton Mifflin Co.)

Guerrilla Publicity
Jay Levinson, Rick Frishman & Jill Lublin
(Adams Media Corporation, 2002)

How to Invent Your Way to Wealth
Tony L. King
(Knolls West Press, 1989)

How to Make Big Money from Your Inventions & Patents
Steve S. Barbarich
(U.S. Inventorship Books, 1993)

Instant Marketing for Almost Free
Susan Benjamin
(Sourcebooks, 2007)

Inventing & Patenting Sourcebook
Richard C. Levy
(Gale Research, Inc., 1992)

The Inventor's Bible: How to Market and License Your Brilliant Ideas
R. L. Docie, Sr.
(Ten Speed Press)

The Tipping Point: How Little Things Can Make a Big Difference
Malcolm Gladwell
(Little, Brown & Company, 2002)

Patent Law   *Biotechnology and the Law*
Iver P. Cooper

Deller's Patent Claims
Ernest Bainbridge Lipscomb, III

General Information Concerning Patents
(This is a booklet that can be purchased from the Superintendent of Documents,
U.S. Government Printing Office, Washington, D.C. 20402. The booklet is also available from the PTO Web page at www.uspto.gov)

Lipscomb's Walker on Patents
Ernest Bainbridge Lipscomb, III

Patent Application Practice
James E. Hawes

Patent Applications Handbook
Stephen A. Becker
(West Group)

Patent Law: A Practitioner's Guide
Ronald B. Hildreth
(Practicing Law Institute, Second Edition)

Patent Law Basics
Peter D. Rosenberg

Patent Law Fundamentals
Peter D. Rosenberg

Patent Law Handbook
Glenn Rhodes

Patent Law: Legal and Economic Principles
John W. Schlicher

Starting Your Own Business

Big Vision, Small Business
Jamie S. Walters
(Berret-Koehler Publishers, Inc., 2002)

Business: The Ultimate Resource
(Perseus Publishing, 2002)

The Small Business Start-Up Guide, 4th Edition
Hal Root and Steve Koenig
(Sourcebooks, 2006)

The Small Business Survival Guide, 3rd Edition
Robert E. Fleury
(Sourcebooks, 1995)

The Weekend Small Business Start-Up Kit
Mark Warda
(Sourcebooks, 2007)

Trademark Law

How to Register Your Own Trademark
Mark Warda
(Sphinx, 2000)

Trademarks
Tom Blackett
(Macmillan Business/Interbrand, 1998)

POPULAR PATENT LAW JOURNALS/ MAGAZINES

Intellectual Property Today
(a version of this can also be found at www.iptoday.com)

The Journal of Patent and Trademark Office Society
(a version of this can also be found at www.jptos.org)

WEBSITES

Arbitration

The Patent Board
www.PatentBoard.org
(has services for settling patent disputes)

Competitive Intelligence

Society of Competitive Intelligence Professionals
www.scip.org
(a global nonprofit organization that helps companies achieve and maintain a competitive advantage)

Domain Naming

www.register.com

Financing, Funding, and Venture Capital

www.clickey.com

Venture Capital Resource Library
www.vfinance.com

Insurance

www.infringeins.com
(covers costs of patent infringement enforcement)

www.lloyds.com
(writes policies that will cover the high costs of patent infringement enforcement in court)

Marketing

American Marketing Association
www.marketingpower.com
(a powerhouse of information for your marketing needs)

Licensing

www.pl-x.com
(patent and licenses exchange where you can both buy and sell patent rights)

Patent Law

Yahoo!
http://dir.yahoo.com/Business_and_Economy
(intellectual property information and listings of websites that cover this area of law)

American Intellectual Property Law Association
www.aipla.org
(a top legal association for intellectual property attorneys)

www.bustpatents.com
(a site devoted to helping you find prior art to invalidate software patents)

www.cipa.org.uk
(a site that you can use to locate patent agents in the UK)

www.ipo.org
(Intellectual Property Owners Association)

www.lexisnexis.com
(a commercial database for prior art)

www.micropatent.com
(allows you to search for patents)

www.patents.ibm.com
(website where you can search for patents)

Inventor Sites

www.frompatenttoprofit.com
(a good site for inventors with respect to commercializing inventions)

www.gibbsgroup.com
(a comprehensive site for the inventor on everything from patents to marketing)

www.inventionconvention.com
(online source for the individual inventor)

www.inventions.org
(offers assistance for the individual inventor)

www.inventnet.com
(online forum and mailing list so you can contact other inventors)

www.inventored.org
(links for the inventor)

www.inventorsdigest.com
(site for the individual inventor)

www.patentcafe.com
(inventor organizations and links)

www.qpat.com
(another commercial site to search for patents)

Software Patent Institute
www.spi.org
(this organization maintains a prior art database for software inventions)

United Inventors Association
www.uiausa.org

www.uspto.gov/web/offices/com/iip
(PTO's office for independent inventor support)

Sale of Your Invention

National Technology Transfer Center
www.nttc.edu
(has a wealth of information on commercialization of inventions)

www.willitsell.com
(useful in determining whether your invention will be marketable before you invest time and money in the patent process)

ww.yet2.com
(a marketplace Internet site where you can both buy and sell patent rights)

Patent Office Websites

European Patent Office
www.european-patent-office.org

Japan Patent Office
www.jpo.go.jp

UK Patent Office
www.patent.gov.uk

(UK Patent Office)
U.S. Patent and Trademark Office
www.uspto.gov

World Intellectual Property Organization
www.wipo.int

Trademarks   www.tmcenter.com
(a company that does trademark searches and has information about trademarks)

www.tmexpress.com
(trademark company that does searches and offers other services)

www.uspto.gov/web/offices/tac/doc/basic
(the trademark fact page at the uspto.gov site)

Trade Secrets   www.rmarkhalligan2.com/tshp
(trade secret law)

Sample Patent Application

This is a complete patent application for a folding carrier that was discussed throughout this book. This application is here for you to examine in order to become more familiar with what each part of your application will look like.

FOLDING CARRIER

Background of the Invention

1. Field of the Invention

[0001] The present invention relates to carriers that are configured to be attached to motor vehicles for carrying such objects as bicycles, skis, luggage, and the like, and more particularly, is directed toward foldable carriers of the foregoing type, in which the weight of the object is distributed on the carrier's feet.

2.   Description of the Prior Art

[0002] In recent years, the popularity of bicycle riding for sport, recreation, and transportation has increased. Bicycle carriers of various configurations have been designed that enable the bicycle owner to transport one or more bicycles from place to place by means of an automobile. Carriers of the type in which the weight of the bicycles is distributed on feet are shown in U.S. Pat.Nos. 3,710,999; 3,927,811; 4,290,540; and 4,332,337. Such carriers have been introduced with varying degrees of success. A need has arisen for an automobile carrier of the foregoing type that can be mounted and demounted easily and that can be collapsed into a flat configuration for easy shipment and storage.

3.   Summary of the Invention

[0003] It is an object of the present invention to provide a folding carrier of the type in which the weight of the object being carried is distributed over upper and lower carrier feet. In addition, the folding carrier can be easily mounted to and demounted from a motor vehicle and folded into a relatively flat configuration for easy shipment and storage. The carrier includes a main frame, to which a carrying member and a supporting member are pivotally mounted for movement between a collapsed position and an extended position. The carrying member is substantially U-shaped, having a front foot bar and a pair of extending arms, and the supporting member is a substantially U-shaped member, having a rear foot bar and a pair of extending legs. The carrying member is held in its extended position by a pair of braces and the supporting member is held in its extended position by bearing against the main frame. Straps are provided for holding the supporting member and for securing the carrier to the motor vehicle in its extended position. In the extended position, feet on the foot bars of the carrying and supporting members are in contact with the motor vehicle. As the supporting member is rotated from the collapsed position into the extended position, it bears against the main frame and is prevented from further rotation in that direction.

Other objects of the present invention will in part be obvious and will in part appear hereinafter.

The invention accordingly comprises the apparatuses and systems, together with their parts, elements, and interrelationships that are exemplified in the following disclosure, the scope of which will be indicated in the appended claims.

4.   Brief Description of the Drawings

[0004] A fuller understanding of the nature and objects of the present invention will become apparent upon consideration of the following detailed description, taken in connection with the accompanying drawings, wherein:

FIG. 1 is a perspective view of a foldable carrier, embodying the invention in a collapsed or folded position;

FIG. 2 is a perspective view of the carrier of FIG. 1 in its extended position; and,

FIG. 3 is a side view of the carrier of FIG. 2 in its extended position and mounted on an automobile trunk.

5.   Detailed Description of the Preferred Embodiments

[005] Referring now to the drawings, in FIG. 3 there is shown a folding carrier 12 embodying the present invention mounted on an automobile trunk lid. As hereinafter described, folding carrier 12 is movable between a flat collapsed position and an erect extended position. The flat collapsed or folded position is shown in FIG. 1, and the erect or extended position is shown in FIGS. 2 and 3.

[006] Folding carrier 12 includes a main frame 14, a carrying member 16, and a supporting member 18. A pair of bracing members 20 are provided for holding carrying member 16 at a selected angular position with respect to main frame 14. Attaching hardware, such as a rear strap 22 and front straps 24, secure carrier 12 to the automobile. Rear strap 22 is placed

over both main frame 14 and supporting member 18. Front straps 24 are attached to opposite sides of carrying member 16. Main frame 14, a substantially U-shaped member, for example, a hollow metal pipe, includes a first side leg 26, a cross member 28, and a second side leg 30. Protective covers 32 are provided on main frame 14. Carrying member 16 is pivotally mounted to an upper portion of side legs 26 and 30 by means of pins or fasteners 34, for example, screws with lock nuts. Supporting member 18 is pivotally mounted to a lower end of side legs 26 and 30 by means of pins or fasteners 36, for example, screws with lock nuts. Carrying member 16 is mounted on the outside of side legs 26, 30, and supporting member 18 is mounted on the inside of side legs 26, 30.

[007] Carrying member 16, a substantially U-shaped member, for example, a hollow metal pipe, includes a pair of arms 40, 42, and a base member or front foot bar 44. The ends of arms 40 and 42 are bent upwardly to form stops 50 and 52. Opposite ends of braces 20, for example, bent rods, are received in holes 51 and 53, formed in carrying members 40, 42, and side legs 26, 30, respectively. The ends of braces 20, which are received in holes 53, are reversely bent to hold the braces therein. The other ends of the braces 20, which are received in the holes 51, are bent greater than ninety degrees to prevent the braces from inadvertently coming out of the holes when a heavy load is being carried on the carrying arms. A suitable protective covering, such as a plastic tubing or the like, may cover all of or a portion of arms 40, 42, and stops 50 and 52. A pair of feet 54, for example, resilient feet such as molded rubber members with flat bottoms 56, and a split circular portion 58, are mounted on front foot bar.

[008] Supporting member 18, a substantially U-shaped member, for example, a hollow metal pipe, includes a pair of legs 60, 62, and a base member or rear foot bar 64. The end portions 66 and 68 of legs 60 and 62, respectively, are bent so that the corner formed at the bend acts as a stop to hold the supporting member 18 in its extended position. Rear foot bar 64 is long enough so that it rests against side legs 26 and 30 when the supporting member 18 is in its collapsed position. The corners

of base member 64 and legs 60, 62 are bent greater than ninety degrees to permit the end portions 66 and 68 to be fastened to the inside of the side legs 26 and 30. The corners of base member 64 and legs 60, 62 are bent in the manner described so as to form a rear foot bar, which is sufficiently long to prevent it from passing between the side legs when the supporting member 18 is in its collapsed position. That is, the length of the rear foot bar 64 is greater than the length of cross member 28. A pair of feet 70, for example, resilient feet such as molded rubber members with flat bottoms 62, and a split circular portion 74 are mounted on base 64.

[009] When carrier 12 is mounted on an automobile as shown in FIG. 3, feet 54 press against the trunk lid 76 and feet 70 press against the lower body panel 78. Strap 22 is threaded about both the cross member 28 and the rear foot bar 64. Strap 22 is also threaded through a clamp 80 having a hooked end portion 82 which is secured to the rear bumper 84. A buckle 86 is provided to tighten strap 22. Each strap 25 is threaded through a buckle 88 which is secured to one fastener 34. A clamp 90 having a hooked end portion 92 is attached to each strap 24 and the hooked end is secured to the top of the trunk lid 76.

[010] Movement of the folding carrier 12 from its extended position shown in FIG. 2 to its folded or collapsed position shown in FIG. 1 is accomplished by merely removing the ends of braces 20 from holes 51 and pivoting carrying member 16 and supporting member 18. When carrier 12 is in the extended position shown in FIGS. 1 and 3, the major part of carrying arms 40, 42 and the major part of supporting legs 60, 62 extend in opposite directions from opposite ends of frame 14 in a substantially parallel relationship to one another and in substantially perpendicular relationship to the frame. Carrying member 16 is held generally perpendicular to frame 14 when in its extended position by braces 20. The corner formed between the end portion 66 and leg 60, and the corner formed between the end portion 68 and leg 62 define stops, which limit rotational movement of supporting member 18 and hold the supporting member in its extended position. When a bicycle is positioned on carrying arms 40, 42, the weight of the

bicycle is distributed over feet 54 and feet 70, which are fitted over front foot bar 44 and over rear foot bar 64, respectively. The flat bottoms of the feet 54 and feet 70 distribute the weight of the bicycle over a greater area than the weight distribution provided by feet in the form of caps on the ends of the tubular members. Side legs 60, 62 and the parts of arms 40, 42 below frame 14 are sufficiently long to keep the bicycle pedals from hitting the automobile.

[011] When the carrier 12 is in its collapsed position, frame 14, carrying member 16, and supporting member 18 are substantially in side-by-side relationship to one another. Initially, carrying member 16 is rotated counterclockwise from the extended position shown in FIG. 2 to the collapsed position shown in FIG. 1. Then, the ends of braces 20 are inserted into holes 51. It is to be noted that carrying member 16 is mounted to main frame 14 in such a manner that front foot bar 44 passes over the top of side legs 26 and 30 when carrying member 16 is rotated from its collapsed position to its extended position. That is, the distance from screw 34 to front foot bar 44 is greater than the distance from screw 34 to the ends of side legs 26, 30 of frame 14. When supporting member 18 is rotated from its collapsed position (FIG. 1) to its extended position (FIG. 2) by moving it in a counterclockwise direction, the corners of legs 60 and 62 engage the corners of side legs 26, 30, thereby preventing further rotation of the supporting member. The carrying member 16 is held rigidly by braces 20, and the supporting member 18 is now braced against frame 14, thereby providing a rigid support for articles such as bicycles, for example, which are to be carried on carrying arms 40 and 42. Carrying member 16 is moved from its extended position shown in FIG. 2 to its collapsed position shown in FIG. 1 first by pulling bracing members 20 out of holes 51, and then by rotating carrying member 18 clockwise to its collapsed position. Supporting member 18 is moved to its collapsed position by merely rotating it clockwise. When the folding carrier is mounted on the automobile, the supporting member 18 is held in its extended position by the strap 22, which passes over it, and the cross member 28.

[012] Since certain changes may be made in the foregoing disclosure without departing from the scope of the invention herein involved, it is intended that all matter contained in the above description and depicted in the accompanying drawings be construed in an illustrative and not in a limiting sense.

What is claimed is:

1. A folding carrier mountable on an automobile or the like, said carrier comprising of:

    (a) a frame;

    (b) a carrying member pivotally mounted to said frame, said carrying member movable about a first axis between an operative extended position and a collapsed position, said carrying member and said frame being in a substantially side-by-side relationship when said carrying member is in its collapsed position, a foot of said carrying member positioned to contact the automobile when said carrying member is in its operative extended position;

    (c) bracing means mounted to said frame and configured to engage and disengage said carrying member, said carrying member fixed in its extended position when said bracing means is in engagement with said carrying member; and,

    (d) a supporting member pivotally mounted to said frame and constrained for limited rotational movement relative thereto between an extended position and a collapsed position about a second axis, said first axis being parallel to said second axis, when said supporting member is in its extended position, a portion of said supporting member is pressed against said frame and said supporting member is prevented from further movement relative to said frame, said supporting member and said frame being in a substantially perpendicular relationship to one another when said supporting member is in its extended position, said supporting member and said frame being in a substantially side-by-side relationship when said carrying member is in its collapsed position, a foot portion of said supporting member positioned to contact the automobile when said supporting member is in its operative extended position.

2. The folding carrier as claimed in claim 1, wherein said frame includes a first side leg, a second side leg, and a cross member, said carrying member and supporting member pivotally mounted to said first and second side legs.

3. The folding carrier as claimed in claim 1, wherein said carrying member is mounted on the outside of said frame and said supporting member is mounted on the inside of said frame.

4. The folding carrier as claimed in claim 3, wherein said carrying member includes a pair of arms and a front foot bar, one of each said arms pivotally mounted to one of each said side legs of said frame, said front foot bar is positioned to contact the automobile when said carrying member is in its operative extended position.

5. The folding carrier as claimed in claim 4, wherein said supporting member includes a pair of legs and a rear foot bar, each said leg being bent adjacent to its end to form a corner, which bears against said frame when said supporting member is in its operative extended position, said rear foot bar is positioned to contact the automobile when said supporting member is in its operative extended position.

6. The folding carrier as claimed in claim 5, wherein said rear foot bar is longer than said cross member.

7. The folding carrier as claimed in claim 4, including feet mounted on said front and rear foot bars, the weight of an object carried on the folding carrier being distributed over said feet.

8. The folding carrier as claimed in claim 6, wherein said feet includes a pair of resilient feet mounted to each said front and rear foot bars, each said resilient foot having a substantially flat bottom.

9.   A folding carrier mountable on an automobile or the like, said carrier comprising of:

(a) a frame;

(b) a supporting member pivotally mounted to said frame, said supporting member having stop means that constrain said supporting member against full rotational movement relative to said frame, said supporting member rotatable about a first axis between an operative extended position and a collapsed position, said supporting member rotated in a first direction from said extended position to said collapsed position and in a second direction from said collapsed position to said extended position, said first direction opposite said second direction, said supporting member and said frame being substantially perpendicular to one another when said supporting member is in its extended position, said supporting member and said frame being in a substantially side-by-side relationship when said carrying member is in its collapsed position, a foot portion of said supporting member positioned to contact the automobile when said supporting member is in its operative extended position;

(c) a carrying member pivotally mounted to said frame said carrying member movable about a second axis between an extended position and a collapsed position, said first axis being parallel to said second axis, said carrying member and said frame being in a substantially side-by-side relationship when said carrying member is in its collapsed position, a foot portion of said carrying means positioned to contact the automobile when said carrying member is in its operative extended position; and,

(d) bracing means mounted to said frame and configured to engage and disengage said carrying member, said carrying member and said frame being in a fixed relationship when said bracing means is in engagement with said carrying member.

10. The folding carrier as claimed in claim 9, wherein said frame includes a first side leg, a second side leg, and a cross member, said frame having a substantially U-shaped profile.

11. The folding carrier as claimed in claim 10, wherein said supporting member includes a pair of legs and a rear foot bar, said legs having bent end portions, each said leg end portion pivotally mounted to one of each said side legs of said frame, said supporting member having a substantially U-shaped profile, said rear foot bar positioned to contact the automobile when said supporting member is in its operative extended position.

12. The folding carrier as claimed in claim 10, wherein said carrying member includes a pair of arms and a front foot bar, one of each said arms pivotally mounted to one of each said side legs of said frame, said carrying member having a substantially U-shaped profile, said front foot bar positioned to contact the automobile when said carrying member is in its operative extended position.

ABSTRACT

A folding carrier for carrying objects on an automobile or the like has a frame to which a carrying member and a supporting member are pivotally mounted for movement between collapsed and extended positions. The carrying member is held by a pair of braces in its extended position for carrying objects and the supporting member is held in its extended position by bearing against the frame. The carrying member is a substantially U-shaped member, having a front foot bar and a pair of extending arms, and the supporting member is a substantially U-shaped member, having a rear foot bar and a pair of extending legs. When the carrier is in its operative extended position, the weight of an object being carried is distributed on feet mounted on the foot bars of each carrying and supporting members.

Inventor: Allen, Richard A.
Title: Folding Carrier
Sheet 1 of 3

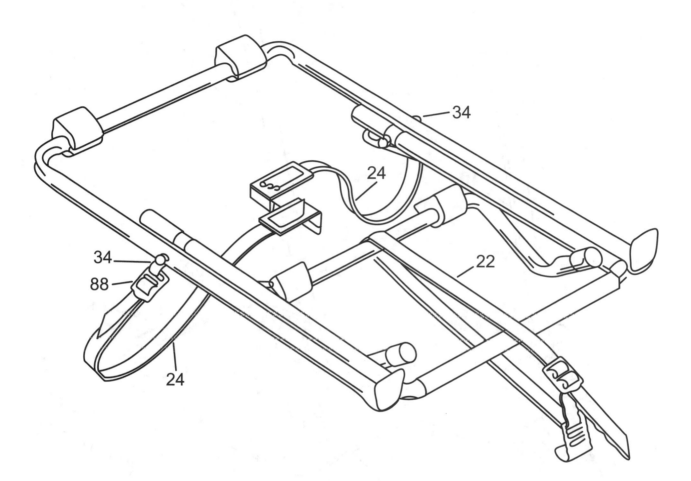

FIG. 1

Inventor: Allen, Richard A.
Title: Folding Carrier
Sheet 2 of 3

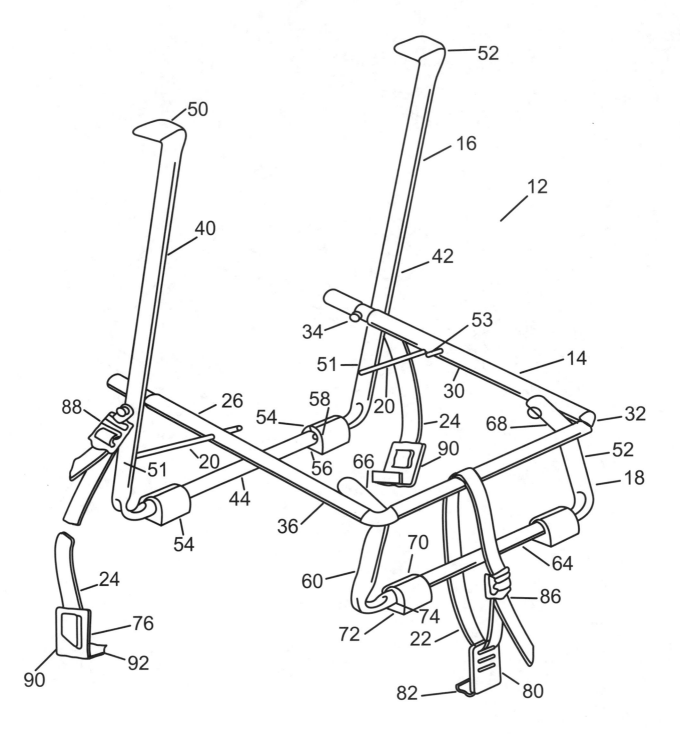

FIG. 2

Inventor: Allen, Richard A.
Title: Folding Carrier
Sheet 3 of 3

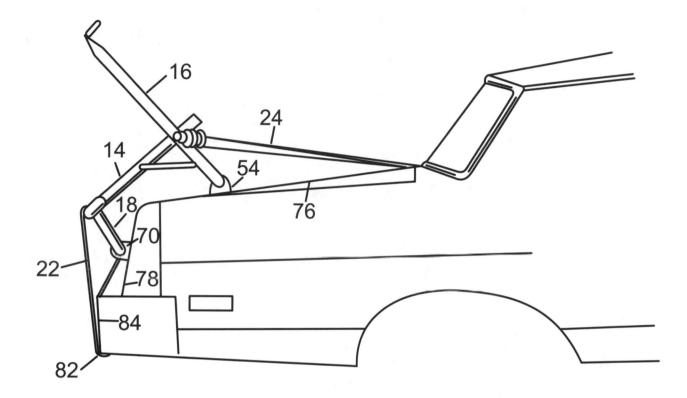

FIG. 3

This is a sample design patent, as discussed in Chapter 8. You may access the original by searching for and downloading patent number D296,039 on the PTO website. Reviewing this sample will help you draft your own design patent.

Inventors LIN, Fang-Chuanand SALTET, Philippe
Title: GRILLER
Sheet 1 of 4

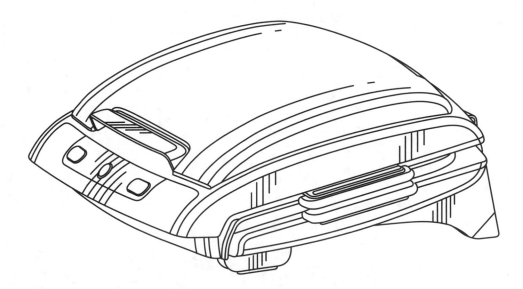

FIG. 1

Inventors LIN, Fang-Chuanand SALTET, Philippe
Title: GRILLER
Sheet 2 of 4

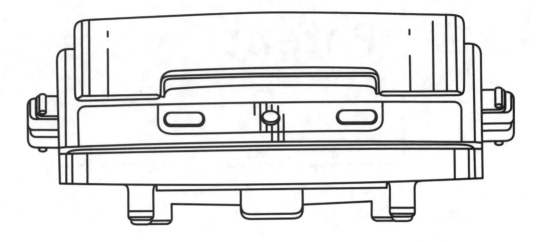

FIG. 2

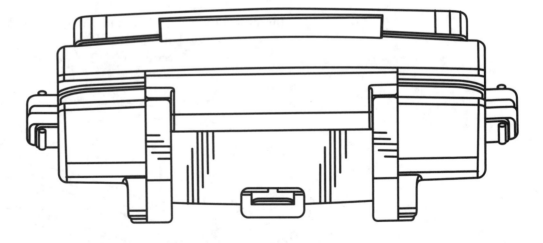

FIG. 3

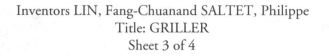

Inventors LIN, Fang-Chuanand SALTET, Philippe
Title: GRILLER
Sheet 3 of 4

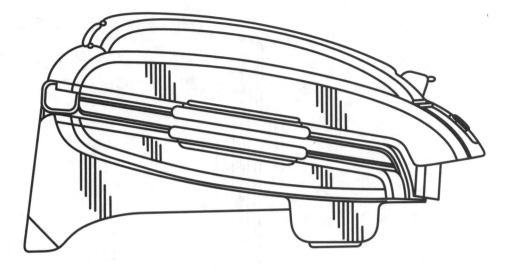

FIG. 4

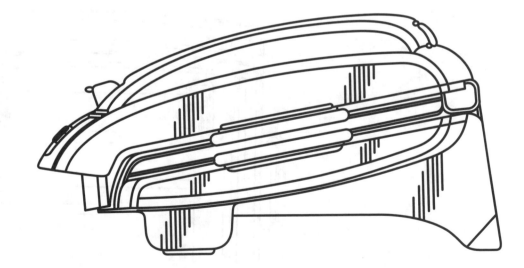

FIG. 5

Inventors LIN, Fang-Chuanand SALTET, Philippe
Title: GRILLER
Sheet 4 of 4

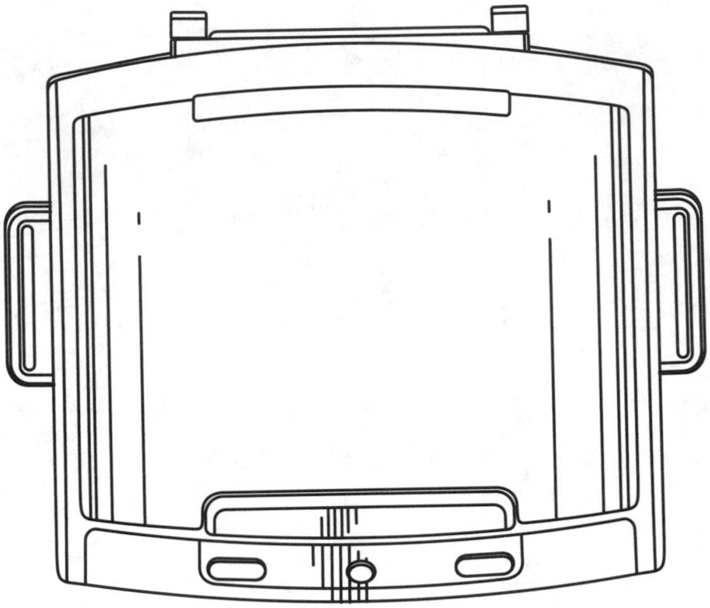

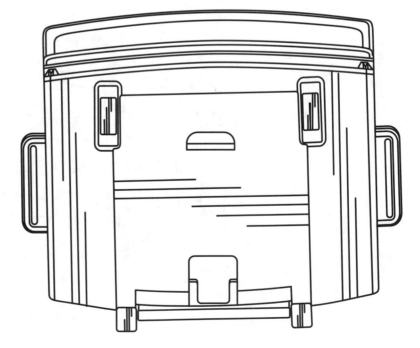

FIG. 6

FIG. 7

Sample Confidentiality Agreements

This appendix contains two sample confidentiality agreements. The first is a One-Way Short Form and the second is a Two-Way Mutual Form.

CONFIDENTIALITY AGREEMENT (ONE-WAY SHORT FORM)

This is a very simple confidentiality agreement that can be used with respect to a product that you are developing and that you want to reveal to third parties, such as prospective licensees. You will need to substitute the actual names of the parties for "COMPANY 1" and "COMPANY 2" in the agreement.

CONFIDENTIALITY AGREEMENT (TWO-WAY MUTUAL FORM)

This is a more complex licensing agreement. It is a two-way mutual agreement where both parties agree to keep confidential proprietary information disclosed by each party. You will need to substitute the actual names of the parties for "COMPANY 1" and "COMPANY 2" in the agreement.

CONFIDENTIALITY AGREEMENT

This Agreement, effective as of the _____ day of _____, 200___, ("COMPANY 1"), by and between _____, a _____ corporation having its principal place of business in _____ ("COMPANY 2"), and _____, a corporation having its principal place of business in _____ ("Licensee").

WHEREAS, COMPANY 1 possesses proprietary expertise and technical expertise in _____, as represented by COMPANY 1's following pending patent application(s) _____ And/or patent(s) _____ (hereinafter "COMPANY 1's Confidential Information")

WHEREAS, COMPANY 1 AND COMPANY 2 wish to evaluate whether there is a basis for a potential business relationship between the parties concerning the Confidential Information.

NOW, THEREFORE, for and in consideration of the mutual promises, covenants, provisions and agreements contained herein, COMPANY 1 AND COMPANY 2 do hereby agree that any Confidential Information disclosed will be used, in whole or in part, only to evaluate whether there is a basis for a potential business relationship between the parties concerning the technology, and it will not be used or disclosed to others, without the express written permission of COMPANY 1.

I am authorized to make this commitment:

By: _____

Name

Title: _____

Date: _____

CONFIDENTIALITY AND NON-USE AGREEMENT

This Agreement, effective as of the _____ day of _____, 200___, ("COMPANY 1"), by and between _____, a _____ corporation having its principal place of business in _____ ("COMPANY 2"), and _____, a corporation having its principal place of business in _____ ("Licensee").

WHEREAS, COMPANY 1 possesses proprietary expertise and technical expertise in _____, as represented by COMPANY 1's following pending patent application(s) _____ And/or patent(s) _____ (hereinafter "COMPANY 1's Confidential Information")

WHEREAS, COMPANY 1 AND COMPANY 2 wish to exchange proprietary, secret and confidential data, information and materials, with respect to their products, patents, technology, trade secrets, finances, distribution, manufacturing processes and capabilities (collectively "Confidential Information") for the purpose of allowing the parties to evaluate said Confidential Information for business purposes and for potential commercial interactions;

NOW, THEREFORE, for and in consideration of the mutual promises, covenants, provisions and agreements contained herein, COMPANY 1 AND COMPANY 2 do hereby agree to the following terms under which Confidential Information will be exchanged:

The Confidential Information will be sued for the sole purpose of allowing the parties to evaluate same for business purposes and for potential commercial interactions.

The Confidential Information shall mean any and all information disclosed, developed or otherwise derived in accordance with this Agreement including, but not limited to, proprietary, secret and confidential data, information, and materials, relating to the disclosing parties' business

The Confidential Information includes communications or data in any form, including, but not limited to oral, written, graphic or electromagnetic forms, which information, if disclosed, could adversely affect the disclosing parties' business.

The Parties agree that any Confidential Information disclosed, developed or otherwise derived in accordance with this Agreement shall be maintained in secrecy and confidentiality and each Party will use all reasonable diligence to prevent disclosure except to its own personnel on a "need to know" basis and to its professional advisors who are under a similar obligation of confidentiality and non-use.

The obligations of confidentiality and non-use under this AGREEMENT shall be limited to a period of five (5) years from the effective date of this AGREEMENT.

The following Confidential Information shall be excepted from the obligations imposed by this Agreement:

such Confidential Information was already and rightfully known by the receiving party prior to receipt hereunder;

such Confidential Information which at the time of disclosure to the receiving party was in the public domain at the time of its receipt from the disclosing party or which, after disclosure thereunder, becomes generally available to the public through no fault attributable to the receiving party;

such Confidential Information as is hereunder made available to the receiving party for its use or disclosure from any third person who is not under a non-disclosure obligation to COMPANY 1 and/or to COMPANY 2;

prior to the receiving party's receipt of the Confidential Information from the disclosing party, such Confidential Information was independently developed by an employee of the receiving party who was not privy to the Confidential Information; or,

is required by law to be disclosed, provided that the receiving party takes reasonable care and lawful actions to avoid or otherwise minimize the degree of such disclosure, and advises the disclosing party in writing, reasonably in advance of such disclosure.

Either party may at any time terminate this Agreement with respect to the disclosure and evaluation of Confidential Information. Upon its receipt of written notice of such termination, the receiving party will promptly return to the disclosing party all documents and tangible items received by or generated on behalf of the other or otherwise derived, pertaining, referring to or in relation to the Confidential Information. The provision of this Agreement regarding the non-disclosure and non-use of Confidential Information shall survive such termination of this Agreement for a period of five (5) years from the effective date of this Agreement.

It is understood that no patent right or license is hereby granted by this Agreement and that disclosure of Confidential Information does not result in any obligation to grant either party any rights in or to such Confidential Information or its transfer hereunder.

The parties agree to maintain in confidence the existence of this Agreement and the existence of any Confidential Information or its transfer hereunder.

This Agreement may not be assigned by either party without the prior written consent of the other party.

Any notice given pursuant to the terms and provisions hereof will be in writing and will be sent by (return receipt requested), postage pre-paid, if

To COMPANY 1, to: _____

_____

To COMPANY 2, to: _____

_____

The parties hereto agree that all matters arising under this Agreement is made under and shall be governed by the laws of the Sate of _____. Any dispute arising out of this Agreement or the parties' relationship thereunder shall be heard in the state or federal courts located in _____ County, _____, to the exclusion of any other courts.

The foregoing constitutes the entire Agreement between the Parties with respect to the subject of this Agreement, and any and all written or oral agreements, proposals or understandings heretofore existing between the Parties pertaining to the specific subject matter of this Agreement are expressly canceled.

This Agreement shall not be modified, amended, canceled or superseded except by an instrument in writing signed by COMPANY 1 AND COMPANY 2.

IN WITNESS WHEREOF, the parties hereto have executed this Agreement by their respective representatives, each of whom is duly authorized to execute the same, as of the day, month and year signed below.

COMPANY 1   COMPANY 2

By: _____.   By_____.

Name   Name

Title: _____.   Title: _____.

Date: _____.   Date: _____.

Sample Licenses

NOTE: *One form can never capture all possible fact situations that will be unique to your own situation. Thus, these forms are a starting point only. You will need to adapt these forms as the case requires for your own situation. Consultation with an attorney is highly recommended.*

You should carefully review points of significance contained in Chapter 10, as well as other license books, before using any of these forms. The types of clauses that you may want to insist upon will depend upon your own unique factual considerations and whether you are the licensor or the licensee.

This appendix contains two sample licensing agreements. This first is for a non-exclusive license and the second is for an exclusive license.

NON-EXCLUSIVE LICENSE AGREEMENT

Use this type of license agreement when you want to license your patented invention, but want to reserve the rights to use and license it to others. In other words, you want more control over your patented invention.

EXCLUSIVE LICENSE AGREEMENT

Use this type of license agreement when you want to give only one licensee the exclusive use of your patented invention.

NOTE: *In these agreements, you will see the words* Licensor *and* Licensee. *Usually the names of the actual parties is substituted in the agreement where these words appear in the text of the agreement.*

NON-EXCLUSIVE LICENSE AGREEMENT

This Agreement, effective as of the _____ day of _____, 200___, by and between _____, a _____ corporation having its principal place of business in _____ ("Licensor"), and _____, a corporation having its principal place of business in _____ ("Licensee").

1. Definitions.

1.1 "Affiliate" shall mean any corporation or other business entity that directly or indirectly controls, is controlled by, or is under common control with the Licensee, Control means ownership or other beneficial interest in 50% or more of the voting stock or other voting interest of a corporation or other business entity.

1.2 "Net Sales" shall mean the total of all fees and other consideration charged by the Licensee and any Affiliate for the manufacture, use, sale, rental, or lease of Products, less returns and customary trade discounts actually taken, outbound freight, value added, sales or use taxes, and custom duties. In the case of transfers or Products to an Affiliate by the Licensee for sale, rental, or lease of such Products to third parties by such Affiliate, Net Sales shall be based upon the greater of the total fees and other consideration charged by the Affiliate to third parties or the total fees and consideration charged by the Company to the Affiliate. If Product is sold in combination with another active component or components, Net Sales for purposes of determining royalties on the combination shall be calculated by multiplying Net Sales of the combination by the fraction $A/(A+B)$, where A is the total invoice price of Product if sold separately and B is the total invoice price of any other active component or components in the combination if sold separately.

1.3 "Patent" shall mean United States Patent No. (_____), entitled "_____," issued _____, 200___, corresponding patent application or related patent document, including any provisional, divisional, continuation, continuation-in-part, substitute, renewal, reissue, extension, confirmation, reexamination or registration thereof and any patent issuing there from including any substitute, renewal, reissue, extension, confirmation, reexamination or registration thereof.

1.4 "Product" or "Products" shall mean any Product, the development, manufacture, use, sale rental or lease of which is covered by a claim of a Patent.

1.5 "Calendar Quarter" means the last business day of January, April, July and October of each year of this agreement.

1.6 "Territory" shall mean the United States.

2. Grant of License

2.1 Licensor grants to the Licensee, upon and subject to all the terms and conditions of this Agreement:

a non-exclusive license with no right to sublicense throughout the Territory under Patents to develop, manufacture, have manufactured, use, sell, have sold, rent, or lease Products.

3. Royalties and Payment

In consideration of the license granted under Section 2.1 of this Agreement, Licensee shall pay to Licensor a royalty of _____ percent of Net Sales of all Products.

4. Reports, Payments and Records

4.1 Payment Reports. Within forty-five (45) days after the end of each calendar quarter, Licensee shall submit to Licensor a written report with respect to the preceding calendar quarter (the "Payment Report") stating:

(a)   Net Sales made by the Licensee and any Affiliate during such calendar quarter;

(b)   In the case of transfers of Products to an Affiliate by the Licensee for sale, rental, or lease of such Products by the Affiliate to third parties, Net Sales by the Licensee to the Affiliate and Net Sales by the Affiliate to third parties during such calendar quarter;

(c)   A calculation under Section 3 of the amounts due to Licensor, making reference to the application subsection thereof;

4.2 Payments. Simultaneously with the submission of each Payment Report, the Licensee shall make payments to Licensor of the amounts due for the calendar quarter covered by the Payment Report.

4.3 Records. The Licensee shall maintain at its principal office usual books of account and records showing its actions under this Agreement. Upon reasonable notice, such books and records shall be open to inspection and copying, during usual business hours, by an independent certified public accountant to whom the Licensee has no reasonable objection, for two years after the calendar quarter to which they pertain, for purposes of verifying the accuracy of the amounts paid by the Company under this Agreement. The inspection shall be limited to entries and information relating to this Agreement and Products hereunder.

5. Patent Notices
LICENSEE agrees that on the product, its packaging and collateral material there will be printed the number of the licensed patent in compliance with 35 U.S.C. § 287.

6. Reservation of Rights
Licensee reserves all rights not expressly granted to Licensee, including but not limited to the right to grant non-exclusive licenses and other rights under the Patent(s), whether such be commercial entities, academic institutions, or other persons, and Licensor reserves the right to use the Patent(s) in any manner it deems fit.

7. Best Efforts.
The Licensee shall use its best efforts to develop and market Products for commercial sale and distribution throughout the Territory. The Licensee's efforts shall include but not be limited to telemarketing, direct sales visits, direct mail, trade shows, and presence on the worldwide web.

8. Bankruptcy
In the event LICENSEE files a petition in bankruptcy, or if the LICENSEE becomes insolvent, or makes an assignment for the benefit of creditors, the license granted hereunder shall terminate automatically without requirement of a written notice.

9. Infringement.
Licensor will use reasonable efforts to protect its Patents from infringement and prosecute infringers at its own expense when in its sole judgment such action may be reasonably necessary, proper, and justified.
In the event Licensor initiates legal proceedings to enforce any Patent against an alleged infringer, Licensee shall use its best efforts to cooperate fully with and shall supply all assistance reasonably requested by Licensor initiating such proceedings.

10. Representations and Warranties.
10.1 Licensor's Warranties.
Licensor warrants that:

(a)   It owns or has the right to license to Licensee all Patent(s) licensed to Licensee, free and clear of all liens, encumbrances and contractual or other restrictions.

(b)   Licensor is not presently aware of any pending or threatened claims or litigation contesting Licensee's rights with respect to any of the Patent(s);

(c)   This Agreement has been duly authorized, executed and delivered by Licensor and is a valid, binding, and legally enforceable obligation of Licensor, subject (as to the enforcement of remedies) to applicable bankruptcy, insolvency, moratorium and other laws now or hereafter in effect affecting the rights of creditors generally and to equitable principles;

(d) The execution, delivery and performance of this Agreement will not result in a breach or violation, or constitute a default under, any agreement or instrument to which Licensor is a party, or any order of any court or governmental agency or body having jurisdiction over Licensor or any of its properties;

(e) No consent, approval, authorization, or order of any court or governmental agency or body is required for the consummation by Licensor of the transactions contemplated by this Agreement.

10.2 Licensee's Representations and Warranties.

(a) Licensee represents and warrants that:

(b) There are no pending or, to the best of its knowledge, no threatened claims or litigation contesting, or which would otherwise affect, its ability to enter into this Agreement or to consummate the transactions contemplated hereby;

(c) This Agreement has been duly authorized, executed and delivered by Licensee and is a valid, binding, and legally enforceable obligation of Licensee, subject (as to the enforcement of remedies) to applicable bankruptcy, insolvency, moratorium and other laws now or hereafter in effect affecting the rights of creditors generally and to equitable principles;

(d) The execution, delivery and performance of this Agreement will not result in a breach or violation or, or constitute a default under, any agreement or instrument to which Licensee is a party, or any order of any court or governmental agency or body having jurisdiction over Licensee or any of its properties;

(e) No consent, approval, authorization, or order of any court or governmental agency or body is required for the consummation by Licensor of the transactions contemplated by this Agreement.

11. Indemnity.

The Licensee shall indemnify, defend and hold harmless the Licensor, agents and their respective successors, heirs and permitted assigns (the "Indemnities"), against any liability, damage, loss, or expense (including reasonable attorneys' fees and expenses of litigation) incurred by or imposed upon the Indemnities or any one of them in connection with any claims, suits, actions, demands or judgments arising out of the design, production, manufacture, sale, use in commerce, lease, or promotion by Licensee, affiliate or agent of licensee of any product, process or service relating to, or developed pursuant to, this Agreement, or any representation made or warranty given by the Licensee or its Affiliates with respect to Products or Patents. This Paragraph shall survive expiration or termination of this Agreement.

12. Insurance.

The Licensee shall maintain, during the term of this Agreement, comprehensive general liability, including product liability insurance, with reputable and financially secure insurance carriers acceptable to Licensor to cover the activities of the Licensee and Affiliates for minimum limits of $2,000,000 per incident and $2,000,000 annual aggregate. Such insurance shall include Licensor, agents and their respective successors, heirs and permitted assigns (the "Indemnities"), as additional insureds.

The Licensee shall furnish a certificate of insurance evidencing such coverage, within thirty days written notice to Licensor. Licensee shall provide the Licensor with written notice at least fifteen (15) days prior to the cancellation, non-renewal or material change in such insurance; if Licensee does not obtain replacement insurance providing comparable coverage within such fifteen (15) day period, the Licensor shall have the right to terminate this Agreement effective at the end of such fifteen (15) day period without notice or any additional waiting periods.

The Licensee's insurance shall be primary coverage; any insurance Licensor may purchase shall be excess and non-contributory. Such insurance shall be written to cover claims incurred, discovered, manifested, or made during or after the expiration of this Agreement.

13. Term of Agreement.

This Agreement shall be effective as of the date first set forth above and shall continue in full force and effect until expiration of Patents.

14. Right to Terminate without Cause.
The license granted under this Agreement may be terminated without cause by the Licensor or the Licensee with six (6) months written notice, and upon payment of amounts due Licensor through the effective date of termination.

15. Notices.
Any notice required or permitted to be given under this Agreement shall be sufficient if sent by certified mail (return receipt requested), postage pre-paid, if

       To Licensor, to: _____

                          _____

       To Licensee, to: _____

                          _____

16. Assignment.
This Agreement may not be assigned without the written consent of the other party. Both parties agree such consent shall not be unreasonably withheld.

17. Governing Law.
This Agreement shall be governed by _____ law applicable to agreements made and to be performed in _____.

IN WITNESS THEREOF, Licensor and the Licensee have caused this Agreement to be executed by their duly authorized representatives as of the day and year first written above.

_____ (Licensor)

By: _____
     (Insert name and Title above)

_____ (Licensee)

By: _____
     (Insert name and Title above)

EXCLUSIVE LICENSE AGREEMENT

This Agreement, effective as of the _____ day of _____, 200____, by and between _____, a _____ corporation having its principal place of business in _____ ("Licensor"), and _____, a corporation having its principal place of business in _____ ("Licensee").

1. Definitions.

1.1 "Affiliate" shall mean any corporation or other business entity that directly or indirectly controls, is controlled by, or is under common control with the Licensee, Control means ownership or other beneficial interest in 50% or more of the voting stock or other voting interest of a corporation or other business entity.

1.2 "Net Sales" shall mean the total of all fees and other consideration charged by the Licensee and any Affiliate for the manufacture, use, sale, rental, or lease of Products, less returns and customary trade discounts actually taken, outbound freight, value added, sales or use taxes, and custom duties. In the case of transfers or Products to an Affiliate by the Licensee for sale, rental, or lease of such Products to third parties by such Affiliate, Net Sales shall be based upon the greater of the total fees and other consideration charged by the Affiliate to third parties or the total fees and consideration charged by the Company to the Affiliate. If Product is sold in combination with another active component or components, Net Sales for purposes of determining royalties on the combination shall be calculated by multiplying Net Sales of the combination by the fraction $A/(A+B)$, where A is the total invoice price of Product if sold separately and B is the total invoice price of any other active component or components in the combination if sold separately.

1.3 "Patent" shall mean United States Patent No. ((_____), entitled "(_____," issued (_____, 200( ), corresponding patent application or related patent document, including any provisional, divisional, continuation, continuation-in-part, substitute, renewal, reissue, extension, confirmation, reexamination or registration thereof and any patent issuing there from including any substitute, renewal, reissue, extension, confirmation, reexamination or registration thereof.

1.4 "Product" or "Products" shall mean any Product, the development, manufacture, use, sale rental or lease of which is covered by a claim of a Patent.

1.5 "Calendar Quarter" means the last business day of January, April, July and October of each year of this agreement.

1.6 "Sub licensee" means: any entity which, subject to the terms of Section 2 below, is granted by Licensee the right to develop, manufacture, have manufactured, use, sell, have sold, rent, or lease any Products.

1.7 "Territory" shall mean the United States.

2. Grant of License.

2.1 Licensor grants to the Licensee, upon and subject to all the terms and conditions of this Agreement:

An exclusive license to develop, manufacture, have manufactured, use, sell, have sold, rent, or lease Products.

The right to sublicense to third parties under terms and conditions no greater than those acquired by Licensee under this agreement. Each permitted sub licensee shall enter into an agreement with Licensee containing, to the extent applicable, all of the rights and obligations due to Licensor as are contained in this Agreement.

3. Royalties and Payment.

<u>Up-Front Payments:</u> In consideration of the license granted under Section 2 of this Agreement, Licensee shall pay to Licensor a non-refundable payment of $_____, payable upon execution of this Agreement and at the end of each calendar quarter hereinafter.

<u>Royalties:</u> In consideration of the license granted under Section 2.1 of this Agreement, Licensee shall pay to Licensor a royalty of _____ percent of Net Sales of all Products. However, in order to maintain the exclusivity of the license, said royalties must be greater than $_____ per calendar quarter.

4. Reports, Payments, and Records.

4.1 Payment Reports. Within forty-five (45) days after the end of each calendar quarter, Licensee shall submit to Licensor a written report with respect to the preceding calendar quarter (the "Payment Report") stating:

(a)   Net Sales made by the Licensee and any Affiliate during such calendar quarter;

(b)   In the case of transfers of Products to an Affiliate by the Licensee for sale, rental, or lease of such Products by the Affiliate to third parties, Net Sales by the Licensee to the Affiliate and Net Sales by the Affiliate to third parties during such calendar quarter;

(c)   A calculation under Section 3 of the amounts due to Licensor, making reference to the application subsection thereof;

4.2 Payments. Simultaneously with the submission of each Payment Report, the Licensee shall make payments to Licensor of the amounts due for the calendar quarter covered by the Payment Report.

4.3 Records. The Licensee shall maintain at its principal office usual books of account and records showing its actions under this Agreement. Upon reasonable notice, such books and records shall be open to inspection and copying, during usual business hours, by an independent certified public accountant to whom the Licensee has no reasonable objection, for two years after the calendar quarter to which they pertain, for purposes of verifying the accuracy of the amounts paid by the Company under this Agreement. The inspection shall be limited to entries and information relating to this Agreement and Products hereunder.

5. Patent Notices.

LICENSEE agrees that on the product, its packaging and collateral material there will be printed the number of the licensed patent in compliance with 35 U.S.C. § 287.

6. Best Efforts.

The Licensee shall use its best efforts to develop and market Products for commercial sale and distribution throughout the Territory. The Licensee's efforts shall include but not be limited to telemarketing, direct sales visits, direct mail, trade shows, and presence on the worldwide web.

7. Bankruptcy.

In the event LICENSEE files a petition in bankruptcy, or if the LICENSEE becomes insolvent, or makes an assignment for the benefit of creditors, the license granted hereunder shall terminate automatically without requirement of a written notice.

8. Infringement.

Licensor will use reasonable efforts to protect its Patents from infringement and prosecute infringers at its own expense when in its sole judgment such action may be reasonably necessary, proper, and justified.

In the event Licensor initiates legal proceedings to enforce any Patent against an alleged infringer, Licensee shall use its best efforts to cooperate fully with and shall supply all assistance reasonably requested by Licensor initiating such proceedings.

9. Representations and Warranties.

9.1 Licensor's Warranties.

Licensor warrants that:

(a)   It owns or has the right to license to Licensee all Patent(s) licensed to Licensee, free and clear of all liens, encumbrances and contractual or other restrictions.

(b)   Licensor is not presently aware of any pending or threatened claims or litigation contesting Licensee's rights with respect to any of the Patent(s);

(c)   This Agreement has been duly authorized, executed and delivered by Licensor and is a valid, binding, and legally enforceable obligation of Licensor, subject (as to the enforcement of remedies) to applicable bankruptcy, insolvency, moratorium and other laws now or hereafter in effect affecting the rights of creditors generally and to equitable principles;

(d)   The execution, delivery and performance of this Agreement will not result in a breach or violation or, or constitute a default under, any agreement or instrument to which Licensor is a party, or any order of any court or governmental agency or body having jurisdiction over Licensor or any of its properties;

(e)   No consent, approval, authorization, or order of any court or governmental agency or body is required for the consummation by Licensor of the transactions contemplated by this Agreement.

9.2 Licensee's Representations and Warranties.

(a)   Licensee represents and warrants that:

(b)   There are no pending or, to the best of its knowledge, no threatened claims or litigation contesting, or which would otherwise affect, its ability to enter into this Agreement or to consummate the transactions contemplated hereby;

(c)   This Agreement has been duly authorized, executed and delivered by Licensee and is a valid, binding, and legally enforceable obligation of Licensee, subject (as to the enforcement of remedies) to applicable bankruptcy, insolvency, moratorium and other laws now or hereafter in effect affecting the rights of creditors generally and to equitable principles;

(d)   The execution, delivery and performance of this Agreement will not result in a breach or violation or, or constitute a default under, any agreement or instrument to which Licensee is a party, or any order of any court or governmental agency or body having jurisdiction over Licensee or any of its properties;

(e)   No consent, approval, authorization, or order of any court or governmental agency or body is required for the consummation by Licensor of the transactions contemplated by this Agreement.

10. Indemnity.

The Licensee shall indemnify, defend and hold harmless the Licensor, agents and their respective successors, heirs and permitted assigns (the "Indemnities"), against any liability, damage, loss, or expense (including reasonable attorneys' fees and expenses of litigation) incurred by or imposed upon the Indemnities or any one of them in connection with any claims, suits, actions, demands or judgments arising out of the design, production, manufacture, sale, use in commerce, lease, or promotion by Licensee, affiliate or agent of licensee of any product, process or service relating to, or developed pursuant to, this Agreement, or any representation made or warranty given by the Licensee or its Affiliates with respect to Products or Patents.

This Paragraph shall survive expiration or termination of this Agreement.

11. Insurance.

The Licensee shall maintain, during the term of this Agreement, comprehensive general liability, including product liability insurance, with reputable and financially secure insurance carriers acceptable to Licensor to cover the activities of the Licensee and Affiliates for minimum limits of $2,000,000 per incident and $2,000,000 annual aggregate. Such insurance shall include Licensor, agents and their respective successors, heirs and permitted assigns (the "Indemnities"), as additional insureds.

The Licensee shall furnish a certificate of insurance evidencing such coverage, within thirty days written notice to Licensor. Licensee shall provide the Licensor with written notice at least fifteen (15) days prior to the cancellation, non-renewal or material change in such insurance; if Licensee does not obtain replacement insurance providing comparable coverage within such fifteen (15) day period, the Licensor shall have the right to terminate this Agreement effective at the end of such fifteen (15) day period without notice or any additional waiting periods.

The Licensee's insurance shall be primary coverage; any insurance Licensor may purchase shall be excess and noncontributory. Such insurance shall be written to cover claims incurred, discovered, manifested, or made during or after the expiration of this Agreement.

12. Term of Agreement.

This Agreement shall be effective as of the date first set forth above and shall continue in full force and effect until expiration of Patents.

13. Notices.

Any notice required or permitted to be given under this Agreement shall be sufficient if sent by certified mail (return receipt requested), postage pre-paid, if

To Licensor, to: _____

_____

_____

To Licensee, to: _____

_____

_____

14. Assignment.

This Agreement may not be assigned without the written consent of the other party. Both parties agree such consent shall not be unreasonably withheld.

15. Patents.

15.1 Fees. Licensor shall pay as and when due, all fees and annuities and do such other things as may be necessary or advisable to maintain the Patents and any patent issuing from any application constituting part of the Patents. If Licensor elects to forgo maintenance on any patent constituting part of the Patents, then Licensor shall so notify Licensee at least sixty (60) days prior to the time such maintenance payment is due or such longer period as shall reasonably permit Licensee to so maintain such patent under applicable law, and Licensee may in its sole judgment and at its own expense, do so. All costs so incurred by Licensee may be offset against Royalties due Licensor.

15.2 Enforcement of Patents.
   (a)   By Licensee: Upon learning of the possible infringement of any of the Patents by a third party, each party hereto shall inform the other party of that fact, and shall supply the other party with any evidence available to it pertaining to the infringement. Licensee may, at its sole expense and discretion, take all necessary steps to enjoin the infringement and recover damages therefore, including the institution of appropriate legal action in the name of Licensor (or as its assignee), and shall be entitled to retain all damages recovered, except that Licensee shall pay Licensor Royalties as if such damages (less all attorneys' fees and other litigation expenses) were Net Sales of Products. All costs and expenses (including attorneys' fees) incurred by Licensee in such action may be deducted from any Royalties payable to Licensor hereunder. If Licensee so assumes the obligation of enforcing the Patents and Licensor does not undertake to assume the enforcement obligation within thirty (30) days after notice by Licensee, then Licensee shall have the right to settle such alleged infringement with the third party in any manner it deems reasonable, including the granting of a sublicense without Licensor's consent. In the event a sublicense is granted, Licensee may retain all royalties obtained in connection therewith, except that Licensee shall pay Royalties as if such third party royalties (less all attorneys' fees and other litigation expenses) were Net Sales of Products.

(b) By Licensor: If Licensee fails or refuses within one hundred eighty (180) days after receipt of written notice to institute legal action against any alleged infringer, Licensor shall then have the right, but not the obligation, at Licensor's own expense to institute appropriate legal action, in which case Licensor shall retain all sums recovered in such legal action.

15.3 Patent Defense

(a) Infringement: Except to the extent arising out of a breach of Licensors representations under Section 9.1 above, Licensee shall defend at its own expense any actions brought against it, its sublicensees or Licensor alleging that the manufacture, sale or use of any Product infringes any claim of any patent and Licensee shall pay all damages and costs payable by Licensee in said actions (whether by settlement, judicial order or otherwise). All costs and expenses (including attorneys' fees) incurred by Licensee in such action may be deducted from any Royalties payable to Licensor hereunder. If any claim or proceeding is made or brought against Licensee or a permitted sublicense, based on any of their infringement or alleged infringement of any third party's patent incident to the manufacture, having manufactured, use, or sale of any Product, then Licensee may, in its sole judgment, settle such claim or proceeding by purchasing or taking a license under such third party's patent. Licensee may offset up to 50% of the cost of such purchase or license from any Royalties payable, or which may become payable, to Licensor.

(b) Revocation or Invalidity Actions. Licensee shall have the right to defend at its own expense, in the name of Licensor, all suits or proceedings seeking to have any of the Patents revoked or declared invalid. Licensor shall give Licensee prompt notice in writing of the institution of such suits or proceedings and shall permit Licensee, through counsel of its own choice, to defend the same, and shall give Licensee such information as it has in regard to such suit. Licensee shall also give Licensor prompt notice of such suits or proceedings commenced against Licensee. If Licensee fails to take such action in either case at least thirty (30) days prior to the time Licensee is required to respond to such suit or proceeding, Licensor shall have the right to take whatever action it deems appropriate to defend such suit or proceeding. All costs and expenses (including attorneys' fees) incurred by Licensee in such action may be deducted from any Royalties payable to Licensor hereunder from the sale of Products in the country where said revocation or invalidity suit or proceeding is pending.

15.4 Cooperation. In any suit, action or proceeding referred to in Sections 15.2 and 15.3 (regardless of which party commences or defends), each party shall, at its own expense, cooperate with the other party by providing such witnesses, documents and records and other evidence as may be reasonably provided.

16. Governing Law.

This Agreement shall be governed by _____ law applicable to agreements made and to be performed in _____

.

IN WITNESS THEREOF, Licensor and the Licensee have caused this Agreement to be executed by their duly authorized representatives as of the day and year first written above.

_____ (Licensor)

By: _____
    (Insert name and Title above)

_____ (Licensee)

By: _____
    (Insert name and Title above)

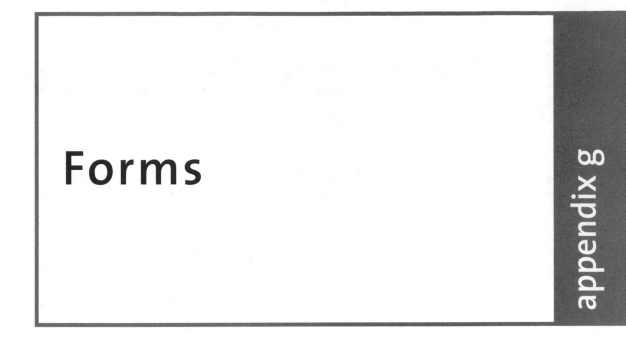

Forms

I would encourage you to use the forms that the PTO uses rather than forms you create yourself or find in patent law textbooks. Most, if not all, of the forms that you will need for patent prosecution are on the PTO website (www.uspto.gov). Click on the "Site Index" icon at the top of page and then hit "F" for forms. Finally, click the "Forms, USPTO" icon.

Not every form you may need to carry out prosecution of a patent application before the PTO is cross-referenced in this appendix. These other forms not cross-referenced can similarly be found on the PTO website. The PTO forms are listed by form number and title. Using the forms from the PTO website is in your best interest because you are more likely not to miss any updated changes or required information.

Since most of the forms that you will need are contained at the PTO site, they are not reproduced here. Instead, a list of the forms by title, form number, and use is given. If the PTO does not provide a form, a blank form that you can photocopy and use is provided. Each of the forms that you will need from the PTO's website are itemized according to the chapters of the book where instructions and explanations are given.

All of the forms listed in this appendix are also contained on the CD-ROM attached to the back cover. See "How to Use the CD-ROM" for more instructions for using the forms on the CD-ROM.

NOTE: *Some chapters do not have forms listed. These chapters discussed concepts, as opposed to specific forms.*

FORMS FOR CHAPTER 5

FORM 1. PETITION FOR SUBMITTING COLOR PHOTOGRAPHS OR DRAWINGS.
Use this form if you have decided that your invention requires the submission of color photographs or drawings.

FORMS FOR CHAPTER 7

FORM 2. COVER LETTER.
It is a good idea to start off the package of materials that you are sending to the PTO with a cover letter that lets the PTO know what you have included in your package.

FORM 3. UTILITY PATENT APPLICATION TRANSMITTAL (PTO/SB/05).
A transmittal is a form that indicates what you are sending to the PTO. You should always fill out a transmittal for any application that you send to the PTO.

FORM 4. FEE TRANSMITTAL (PTO/SB/17).
This form is used to calculate how much money you will need to include with your application.

FORM 5. PATENT APPLICATION FEE DETERMINATION RECORD (PTO/SB/06).:
Fill out Part I of this record and attach this right behind your Fee Transmittal.

FORM 6. MULTIPLE DEPENDENT CLAIM FEE CALCULATION SHEET (PTO/SB/07).
If you are presenting any multiple dependent claims in your application, you should fill out this form. Remember that multiple dependent

claims count for the numbers of claims that are directly referenced in your multiple dependent claim.

FORM 7. CREDIT CARD PAYMENT FORM (PTO-2038).
If you are paying by credit card, you should fill out this form. Attach it behind your multiple fee calculation sheet or your patent application fee determination record (if you have no multiple dependent claims).

FORM 8. APPLICATION DATA SHEET.
This form should be attached directly behind your fee transmittals and fee worksheets (and credit card payment form if you use one). If a section is not applicable to you, simply leave the section blank.

FORM 9. DECLARATION (PTO/SB/01A).
Use this form for your utility patent application declaration if you have submitted an Application Data Sheet. Your declaration should be attached after your specification and drawings.

FORM 10. INFORMATION DISCLOSURE STATEMENT COVER LETTER.
You should submit a cover letter similar to this before the PTO IDS forms in item (1) to disclose to the PTO any prior art references that you consider material to your invention. You will see that the numbering starts with the number "1." You can continue to number according to how many references you are going to list. There is more space to list references at the top of the second page. If you need more space to list your references beyond the pages here, simply insert an additional blank page between pages 1 and 2 of the form here.

FORM 11. INFORMATION DISCLOSURE STATEMENT (PTO/SB/08).
In addition to your IDS cover letter in item (9), you must list each of your prior art references on this form. You can attach this form right behind your IDS.

FORMS FOR CHAPTER 8

FORM 12. DESIGN PATENT APPLICATION TRANSMITTAL (PTO/SB/18).
Whenever you submit a new patent application to the PTO, you will

need to include a transmittal. Design patent applications are no exception to this rule.

FORM 13. PROVISIONAL APPLICATION COVER SHEET (PTO/SB/16).
Start off your provisional application package materials with a cover sheet that tells the PTO exactly what you are enclosing in your envelope.

FORM 14. FEE TRANSMITTAL (PTO/SB/17).
Attach your Fee Transmittal form behind your cover sheet.

FORM 15. REQUEST FOR CONTINUED EXAMINATION (RCE) (PTO/SB/30).
Use this form as your transmittal for an RCE.

FORM 16. SUPPLEMENTAL DECLARATION (PTO/SB/04).
Use this form if you have previously submitted a declaration and now you need to submit another declaration because you have made changes to you specification. A common situation where you want to execute a Supplemental Declaration is when you file a CIP.

FORMS FOR CHAPTER 9

FORM 17. COVER LETTER WITH EXPRESS MAILING.
You can use this form as your cover letter for your PCT application.

FORM 18. TRANSMITTAL LETTER (PTO-1382).
Use this form for your Transmittal Letter to the PTO.

FORM 19. PCT REQUEST (FORM PCT/RO/101).
You can use this form for your request. The notes that accompany this form tell you how to fill out the form item by item and should not be included with the request that you will send to the PTO.

FORM 20. PCT FEE CALCULATION SHEET (FORM PCT/RO/101 (ANNEX)).
This form must be completed to figure out how much you owe the PTO. Do not forget to include your check payable to the Commissioner of Patents and Trademarks. If you are paying by credit card instead

of check, you should fill out a Credit Card Payment Form PTO 2038 from Chapter 7. Notes on how to fill out the form are included but are not to be submitted along with the form.

FORM 21. DEMAND (FORM PCT/IPEA/401).
If you want to enter Chapter II and obtain a preliminary examination of your PCT, then you need to elect such countries in a Demand no later than nineteen months from your priority date. You can use this blank form for your demand.

FORM 22. PCT FEE CALCULATION SHEET (FORM PCT/IPEA/401 (ANNEX)).
There is a fee for your Demand and this form is what you need to fill out to determine the fee that you owe.

FORM 23. TRANSMITTAL LETTER TO THE UNITED STATES DESIGNATED/ELECTED OFFICE (DO/EO/US) CONCERNING A FILING UNDER 35 U.S.C. §371(FORM PTO-1390).
If the United States is one of your designated states in your Request, then you will need to enter the national stage in the United States within thirty months of your priority date. To enter the national stage, you need to include a transmittal letter with your papers. You can use this form for your transmittal.

FORMS FOR CHAPTER 10

FORM 24. PETITION TO MAKE SPECIAL.
You can use this form for your Petition to Make Special your application based on any one of the grounds listed in MPEP 708.02. This particular petition is geared toward the ground of infringement. You will need to pay the requisite fee under 37 C.F.R. §1.17(h) and also include a declaration by you as the inventor or your attorney.

FORM 25. DECLARATION IN SUPPORT OF PETITION TO MAKE SPECIAL.
You will need to attach this declaration behind your Petition to Make Special.

FORMS FOR CHAPTER 11

FORM 26. COVER LETTER.

You should include a cover letter and transmittal before your amendment. If you are adding more than claims that what you have previously paid for, then you will also need to include the appropriate fee for such added claims.

FORM 27. SUPPLEMENTAL APPLICATION DATA SHEET.

Use this form if you want to make changes to the original Application Data Sheet. You cannot simply use Form 8 (Application Data Sheet) on the PTO website because a supplemental data sheet has to be labeled a "supplemental application data sheet," and it must identify the information that is being changed.

FORM 28. AMENDMENT.

You can either type in the necessary information to this form as your amendment, or reproduce this form onto your word processor with your necessary information organized on the hard drive of your computer. If you are making your amendment after a final rejection, you should address this form to Mail Stop AF rather than Mail Stop Amendment.

NOTE: *This form is only a skeleton of how your amendment should look. The arguments you make and changes you make to your claims require thoughtful review of what you have read in this book.*

FORM 29. SUBMISSION OF CORRECTED DRAWINGS.

Use this form to submit corrected drawings to your Official Draftsperson. You can submit corrected drawings even after you have received a Notice of Allowance.

FORMS FOR CHAPTER 13

FORM 30. DECLARATION UNDER 37 C.F.R. §1.131.

This is a bare-bones Rule 1.131 declaration, which you will need to adapt to your particular situation.

FORM 31. DECLARATION UNDER 37 C.F.R. §1.132.

This is a bare-bones Rule 1.132 declaration used to rebut a prima facie case of obviousness. Again, you will need to make adaptations to this form to fit your own unique situation.

FORMS FOR CHAPTER 14

FORM 32. TERMINAL DISCLAIMER TO OBVIATE A PROVISIONAL DOUBLE PATENTING REJECTION OVER A PENDING SECOND APPLICATION (PTO/SB/25).

This form can be used as your terminal disclaimer in order to obviate a double patenting rejection based on a pending second application.

FORM 33. TERMINAL DISCLAIMER TO OBVIATE DOUBLE PATENTING REJECTION OVER A PRIOR PATENT (PTO/SB/26).

This form can be used as your terminal disclaimer in order to obviate a double patenting rejection based on a prior patent.

FORM 34. PETITION FOR REVIVAL OF AN APPLICATION FOR PATENT ABANDONED UNAVOIDABLY UNDER 37 C.F.R. 1.137(A).

Use this form to revive a patent application that has been abandoned unavoidably. You must accompany the application with adequate showing as to why your application was unavoidably abandoned, the necessary petition fee, any required terminal disclaimer and any reply you should have submitted before you application became abandoned.

FORM 35: PETITION TO REVIVE UNINTENTIONALLY ABANDONED APPLICATION (PTO/SB/64).

Use this petition to revive your application that you unintentionally abandoned. You will need to include a cover letter with your petition as well as the appropriate fee under 37 C.F.R. §1.17(m). In addition, you will need to include a reply to your last office action that you failed to respond to on time.

FORMS FOR CHAPTER 15

FORM 36: COVER LETTER FOR CERTIFICATE OF CORRECTION.
You will need to figure out your appropriate fee for the Certificate of Correction by going to the PTO website and looking for "Certificate of Correction." If the mistake was due to the fault of the PTO, then delete the sentence referring to your check and insert instead "Since the noted error(s) arose through the fault of the Patent and Trademark Office, no fee is believed to be due."

FORM 37: CERTIFICATE OF CORRECTION (PTO/SB/44).
Use this form for making any correction to your issued patent.

FORM 38: MAINTENANCE FEE TRANSMITTAL FORM (PTO/SB/45).
Use this form to submit your required maintenance fees.

FORM 39: COVER LETTER FOR PETITION TO ACCEPT UNAVOIDABLE DELAYED PAYMENT OF MAINTENANCE FEE. Use a cover letter like this before your Form PTO/SB/65.
You will need to calculate the appropriate fees (both petition fee and maintenance fees) to include with your submission. Send by first class mail with Certificate of Mailing.

FORM 40: PETITION TO ACCEPT UNAVOIDABLY DELAYED PAYMENT OF MAINTENANCE FEE IN AN EXPIRED PATENT UNDER 37 C.F.R §1.378(B) (PTO/SB/65).
Complete this form and include it in back of your cover letter with the appropriate fee. You will also need to attach a declaration stating why your submission was unavoidable.

FORM 41. DECLARATION IN SUPPORT OF PETITION TO ACCEPT UNAVOIDABLY DELAYED PAYMENT OF MAINTENANCE FEE IN AN EXPIRED PATENT UNDER 37 CFR §1.378(B)
Use a form like this as your declaration in support of form 39 above. In the body of the declaration state the reasons why your failure to pay maintenance fees was unavoidable.

FORM 42. FORM PTO/SB/66: PETITION TO ACCEPT UNINTENTIONALLY DELAYED PAYMENT OF MAINTENANCE FEE IN AN EXPIRED PATENT UNDER 37 C.F.R. §1.378(c)

Complete the form, include the necessary fee, and include it in back of a cover letter similar to the one in item (4) above except replace "Unavoidably" with "Unintentionally." Your cover letter also does not need to reference a supporting declaration because a declaration is not required with this type of petition.

FORMS FOR CHAPTER 28

FORM 43: ASSIGNMENT OF PATENT (FORMER PTO/SB/41).

This form can be used to assign a patent.

FORM 44: RECORDATION FORM (PTO-1595).

This form from the PTO website can be used to record your assignment. Instructions for completing the form are also included but should not be submitted to the PTO.

IN THE UNITED STATES PATENT AND TRADEMARK OFFICE

Applicant(s): (   )

Serial No.: (   )

Filed: (   )

Title: (   )

Group Art. Unit: (   )

Examiner: (   )

Docket No.:

FILED BY EXPRESS MAIL
Commissioner for Patents
P.O. Box 1450
Alexandria, VA 22313

EXPRESS MAIL CERTIFICATE

"Express Mail" Label No. _____

Date of Deposit: _____

I hereby certify that this paper and the attachment herein are being deposited with the United States Postal Service as "Express Mail Post Office to Addressee" service under 37 C.F.R. §1.10 on the date indicated above and is addressed to Commissioner for Patents, P.O. Box 1450, Alexandria, VA 22313.

_____

[type or print name of person making deposit]

_____

[signature of person making deposit]

Petition for Submitting Color Photographs or Drawings

Dear Sirs:

Applicant respectfully petitions that the color photographs filed herewith be accepted as formal drawings. The applicable fee under 37 C.F.R. Sec. 1.17(i) is enclosed.

These color photographs or drawings are necessary because:

Respectfully submitted,

By _____
(Applicant)

IN THE UNITED STATES PATENT AND TRADEMARK OFFICE

Applicant(s): (   )

Serial No.: (   )

Filed: (   )

Title: (   )

Group Art. Unit: (   )

Examiner: (   )

Docket No.: (   )

FILED BY EXPRESS MAIL
Commissioner for Patents
P.O. Box 1450
Alexandria, VA 22313

EXPRESS MAIL CERTIFICATE

"Express Mail" Label No. _____

Date of Deposit: _____

I hereby certify that this paper and the attachment herein are being deposited with the United States Postal Service as "Express Mail Post Office to Addressee" service under 37 C.F.R. §1.10 on the date indicated above and is addressed to Commissioner for Patents, P.O. Box 1450, Alexandria, VA 22313.

_____

[type or print name of person making deposit]

_____

[signature of person making deposit]

Express Mail Cover Letter

Dear Sirs:

Enclosed and attached hereto are the following documents:
(1) Utility Patent Application Transmittal;
(2) Fee Transmittal (in duplicate);
(3) Fee Determination Record.
(4) Credit Card Payment Form;
(5) Application Data Sheet;
(6) Specification (__ pages);
(7) Formal drawings (__ sheets);
(8) Executed Declaration;
(9) Information Disclosure Statement;
(10) Citation of references included in IDS (__ pages); and,
(11) Self-addressed, stamped postcard.

It is respectfully requested that the attached prepaid postcard be stamped with the date of filing of these documents and that it be returned as soon as possible.

Respectfully submitted,

Docket No. _____   By _____

(Applicant)

IN THE UNITED STATES PATENT AND TRADEMARK OFFICE

Applicant(s): (   )

Serial No.: (   )

Filed: (   )

Title: (   )

Group Art. Unit: (   )

Examiner: (   )

Docket No.: (   )

FILED BY EXPRESS MAIL
Commissioner for Patents
P.O. Box 1450
Alexandria, VA 22313

EXPRESS MAIL CERTIFICATE

"Express Mail" Label No. _____

Date of Deposit: _____

I hereby certify that this paper and the attachment herein are being deposited with the United States Postal Service as "Express Mail Post Office to Addressee" service under 37 C.F.R. §1.10 on the date indicated above and is addressed to Commissioner for Patents, P.O. Box 1450, Alexandria, VA 22313.

_____
[type or print name of person making deposit]

_____
[signature of person making deposit]

Information Disclosure Statement under 37 C.F.R. §§1.56 & 1.97–1.98

Dear Sirs:

Pursuant to the provisions of 37 C.F.R. §§1.97–1.98, and in full compliance with their duty of disclosure under 37 C.F.R. §1.56, Applicant(s) are bringing the following ( ) documents to the attention of the U.S. Patent and Trademark Office and the Examiner handling their above-identified application:

1.

Copies of the above-listed ( ) documents are being submitted herewith as Exhibits ( ). A completed Form PTO-1449 is also attached herewith.

By this voluntary citation of art, Applicant(s) are requesting that the documents be made of record in the instant application.

The filing of this information disclosure statement shall not be construed to be an admission that the information cited in the statement is, or is considered to be, material to patentability as defined in Sec. 1.56(b).

Applicant(s) respectfully request that the Examiner make the above-submitted documents of record in the instant application.

This IDS is being filed in accordance with 37 C.F.R. §1.97(b)(3), that is, prior to issuance of a First Office Action on the merits. Applicant(s) believe that no fee is required.

Respectfully submitted,

By _____
(Applicant)

IN THE UNITED STATES PATENT AND TRADEMARK OFFICE

Applicant(s): (   )

Serial No.: (   )

Filed: (   )

Title: (   )

Group Art. Unit: (   )

Examiner: (   )

Docket No.: (   )

FILED BY EXPRESS MAIL
Commissioner for Patents
P.O. Box 1450
Alexandria, VA 22313

EXPRESS MAIL CERTIFICATE

"Express Mail" Label No. _____

Date of Deposit: _____

I hereby certify that this paper and the attachment herein are being deposited with the United States Postal Service as "Express Mail Post Office to Addressee" service under 37 C.F.R. §1.10 on the date indicated above and is addressed to Commissioner for Patents, P.O. Box 1450, Alexandria, VA 22313.

_____
[type or print name of person making deposit]

_____
[signature of person making deposit]

Cover Letter with Express Mail Certificate

Dear Sirs:

Enclosed and attached hereto are the following documents:

(1) Cover letter with Express Mail Certificate;

(2) Transmittal Form;

(3) PCT Request;

(4) Specification (__ pages);

(5) Formal drawings (_____ sheets);

(6) Executed Declaration;

(7) Check for $ _____ ; and,

(8) Self-addressed, stamped postcard.

Respectfully submitted,

Docket No. _____   By _____
                                                        (Applicant)

IN THE UNITED STATES PATENT AND TRADEMARK OFFICE

Applicant(s): (	)	<u>EXPRESS MAIL CERTIFICATE</u>

Applicant(s): (   )

Serial No.: (   )

Filed: (   )

Title: (   )

Group Art. Unit: (   )

Examiner: (   )

Docket No.: (   )

FILED BY EXPRESS MAIL
Commissioner for Patents
P.O. Box 1450
Alexandria, VA 22313

<u>EXPRESS MAIL CERTIFICATE</u>

"Express Mail" Label No. _____

Date of Deposit: _____

I hereby certify that this paper and the attachment herein are being deposited with the United States Postal Service as "Express Mail Post Office to Addressee" service under 37 C.F.R. §1.10 on the date indicated above and is addressed to Commissioner for Patents, P.O. Box 1450, Alexandria, VA 22313.

_____
[type or print name of person making deposit]

_____
[signature of person making deposit]

Petition to Make Special

Pursuant to 37 C.F.R. §1.102(d), Applicant hereby petitions the Commissioner to make the subject application special so that it may be taken out of turn for immediate action.

Attached to this Petition to Make Special is a declaration of Applicant in support of the Petition to Make Special under Rule 102(d).

Due to the fact the Applicant's claims are being infringed (see appended Declaration of Applicant's attorney) and Applicant requires a patent in order to terminate such infringement, this Petition to Make Special is being filed.

The required petition fee required under 37 C.F.R. §1.17(h) has been calculated as $_____.

A check in payment of the petition fee required under 37 C.F.R. §1.17(h) is enclosed. Applicant respectfully requests that this Petition be granted.

Respectfully submitted,

Date _____   By _____
                                          (Applicant)

IN THE UNITED STATES PATENT AND TRADEMARK OFFICE

Applicant(s): (   )

Serial No.: (   )

Filed: (   )

Title: (   )

Group Art. Unit: (   )

Examiner: (   )

Docket No.: (   )

FILED BY EXPRESS MAIL
Commissioner for Patents
P.O. Box 1450
Alexandria, VA 22313

EXPRESS MAIL CERTIFICATE

"Express Mail" Label No. _____

Date of Deposit: _____

I hereby certify that this paper and the attachment herein are being deposited with the United States Postal Service as "Express Mail Post Office to Addressee" service under 37 C.F.R. §1.10 on the date indicated above and is addressed to Commissioner for Patents, P.O. Box 1450, Alexandria, VA 22313.

_____

[type or print name of person making deposit]

_____

[signature of person making deposit]

Declaration in Support of Petition to Make Special

I, _____, declare as follows:

1. I am the Applicant in the above-indicated application, which covers a _____.

2. On or about _____, it came to my attention that _____ of _____ was distributing _____ under the name "_____."

3. I have compared the claims in the above-indicated application with the specimen, _____, distributed by "_____" and it is my opinion that Claims _____ of this application would be infringed by the manufacture, use, or sale of said specimen.

4. I have made a careful search of the prior art and have concluded that the claims in the above-indicated application would not be anticipated or be obvious over any of the prior art references discovered.

5. One copy of each of the references that I deemed most closely related to the subject matter encompassed by the claims of the above-indicated application are attached behind this declaration. These references are the following: _____.

6. As a result of reviewing this application and the prior art, I believe that all of the claims in this application are allowable.

I declare that all statements made herein of my own knowledge are true and that all statements made on information and belief are believed to be true and, further, that these statements were made with the knowledge that willful false statements and the like so made are punishable by fine or imprisonment, or both, under 18 U.S.C. §1001 and that such false statements may jeopardize the validity of this document and the application to which it relates.

Respectfully submitted,

Date _____

_____
(Applicant)

IN THE UNITED STATES PATENT AND TRADEMARK OFFICE

Applicant(s): ( )	EXPRESS MAIL CERTIFICATE
Serial No.: ( )	"Express Mail" Label No. _____
Filed: ( )	Date of Deposit: _____
Title: ( )	I hereby certify that this paper and the attachment herein are being deposited with the United States Postal Service as "Express Mail Post Office to Addressee" service under 37 C.F.R. §1.10 on the date indicated above and is addressed to Commissioner for Patents, P.O. Box 1450, Alexandria, VA 22313.
Group Art. Unit: ( )	
Examiner: ( )	
Docket No.: ( )	

FILED BY EXPRESS MAIL
Commissioner for Patents
P.O. Box 1450
Alexandria, VA 22313

_____
[type or print name of person making deposit]

_____
[signature of person making deposit]

Dear Sir:

Enclosed please find the following documents for lining with the PTO in the above-captioned matter:

(1) Transmittal Letter;
(2) Fee Transmittal;
(3) Amendment; and,
(4) Self-addressed, stamped postcard.

Respectfully submitted,

_____
(Applicant)

SUPPLEMENTAL APPLICATION DATA SHEET

Application Information

Application Type: _____

Subject Matter: _____

Suggested Classification: _____

Suggested Group Art Unit: _____

CD-ROM or CD-R?: _____

Title: _____

Attorney Docket Number: _____

Request for Early Publication?: _____

Request for Non-Publication?: _____

Suggested Drawing Figure: _____

Total Drawing Sheets: _____

Small Entity: _____

Petition included?: _____

Secrecy Order in Parent Appl.?: _____

Applicant Information

Applicant Authority Type: _____

Primary Citizenship Country: _____

Status: _____

Given Name: _____

Middle Name: _____

Family Name: _____

City of Residence: _____

State or Province of Residence: _____

Country of Residence: _____

Street of Mailing Address: _____

City of Mailing Address: _____

Country of Mailing Address: _____

Postal or Zip Code of Mailing Address: _____

Applicant Authority Type: _____

Primary Citizenship Country: _____

Status: _____

Given Name: _____

Middle Name: _____

Family Name: _____

City of Residence: _____

State or Province of Residence: _____

Country of Residence: _____

Street of Mailing Address: _____

City of Mailing Address: _____

State or Province of Mailing Address: _____

Postal or Zip Code of Mailing Address: _____

Correspondence Information

Correspondence Customer Number: _____

Name: _____

Street of Mailing Address: _____

City of Mailing Address: _____

State or Province of Mailing Address: _____

Postal or Zip Code of Mailing Address: _____

Telephone: _____

Email Address: _____

Domestic Priority Information
Application: Continuity Type: Parent Application: Parent Filing Date:

Foreign Priority Information
Country: Application Number: Filing Date: Priority Claimed:

Assignee Information: _____

Assignee Name: _____

Street of Mailing Address: _____

City of Mailing Address: _____

State or Province of Mailing Address: _____

Country of Mailing Address: _____

Postal or Zip Code of Mailing Address: _____

IN THE UNITED STATES PATENT AND TRADEMARK OFFICE

Applicant(s): (   )

Serial No.: (   )

Filed: (   )

Title: (   )

Group Art. Unit: (   )

Examiner: (   )

Docket No.: (   )

FILED BY EXPRESS MAIL
Commissioner for Patents
P.O. Box 1450
Alexandria, VA 22313

EXPRESS MAIL CERTIFICATE

"Express Mail" Label No. _____

Date of Deposit: _____

I hereby certify that this paper and the attachment herein are being deposited with the United States Postal Service as "Express Mail Post Office to Addressee" service under 37 C.F.R. §1.10 on the date indicated above and is addressed to Commissioner for Patents, P.O. Box 1450, Alexandria, VA 22313.

_____
[type or print name of person making deposit]

_____
[signature of person making deposit]

Dear Sirs:

In response to the Office Action of _____ , 200____, please amend the above-identified application as follows:

☐ Amendments to the Specification begin on page _____ of this paper.

☐ Amendments to the Claims are reflected in the listing of claims that begins on page _____ of this paper.

☐ Amendments to the Drawings begin on page _____ of this paper.

☐ Remarks/Arguments begin on page ____ of this paper.

Respectfully submitted,

_____
(Applicant)

IN THE UNITED STATES PATENT AND TRADEMARK OFFICE

Applicant(s): (   )

Serial No.: (   )

Filed: (   )

Title: (   )

Group Art. Unit: (   )

Examiner: (   )

Docket No.: (   )

FILED BY EXPRESS MAIL
Commissioner for Patents
P.O. Box 1450
Alexandria, VA 22313

EXPRESS MAIL CERTIFICATE

"Express Mail" Label No. _____

Date of Deposit: _____

I hereby certify that this paper and the attachment herein are being deposited with the United States Postal Service as "Express Mail Post Office to Addressee" service under 37 C.F.R. §1.10 on the date indicated above and is addressed to Commissioner for Patents, P.O. Box 1450, Alexandria, VA 22313.

_____

[type or print name of person making deposit]

_____

[signature of person making deposit]

Submission of Corrected Drawings

Dear Sirs:

Attached please find replacement drawing sheet(s) _____
for the above application. Please substitute this/these sheet(s) for the corresponding sheet(s) on file.

A copy of the replacement sheet(s) is/are also attached and marked up to indicate the changes being made.

Respectfully submitted,

_____

(Applicant)

IN THE UNITED STATES PATENT AND TRADEMARK OFFICE

Applicant(s): ( )

Serial No.: ( )

Filed: ( )

Title: ( )

Group Art. Unit: ( )

Examiner: ( )

Docket No.: ( )

FILED BY EXPRESS MAIL
Commissioner for Patents
P.O. Box 1450
Alexandria, VA 22313

EXPRESS MAIL CERTIFICATE

"Express Mail" Label No. _____

Date of Deposit: _____

I hereby certify that this paper and the attachment herein are being deposited with the United States Postal Service as "Express Mail Post Office to Addressee" service under 37 C.F.R. §1.10 on the date indicated above and is addressed to Commissioner for Patents, P.O. Box 1450, Alexandria, VA 22313.

_____
[type or print name of person making deposit]

_____
[signature of person making deposit]

Declaration under 37 C.F.R. §1.131

Dear Sirs:

I, _____, declare that I am the inventor for the above-identified patent application and that I conceived the invention claimed in the above-identified patent application in the United States prior to _____, the filing date of the cited U.S. Patent No. _____ to _____.

Attached Exhibit A is a copy of notebook records relating to this conception wherein Pursuant to this conception, I actually reduced to practice in the United States, the invention claimed in the above-identified patent application prior to _____, the filing date of the cited _____ patent.
Attached Exhibit B is a copy of a memorandum relating to this reduction to practice wherein.

Exhibits A and B, which relate to the aforementioned conception and actual reduction to practice, correspond to the invention broadly disclosed and claimed in the above-identified patent application.

I hereby declare that all statements made herein of my own knowledge are true and that all statements made on information and belief are believed to be true; and further that these statements were made with the knowledge that willful false statements and the like so made are punishable by fine or imprisonment, or both, under Section 1001 of Title 18 of the United States Code, and that such willful false statements may jeopardize the validity of the application or any patent issued thereon.

Respectfully submitted,

_____
(Inventor/Applicant)

IN THE UNITED STATES PATENT AND TRADEMARK OFFICE

Applicant(s): (   )

Serial No.: (   )

Filed: (   )

Title: (   )

Group Art. Unit: (   )

Examiner: (   )

Docket No.: (   )

FILED BY EXPRESS MAIL
Commissioner for Patents
P.O. Box 1450
Alexandria, VA 22313

EXPRESS MAIL CERTIFICATE

"Express Mail" Label No. _____

Date of Deposit: _____

I hereby certify that this paper and the attachment herein are being deposited with the United States Postal Service as "Express Mail Post Office to Addressee" service under 37 C.F.R. §1.10 on the date indicated above and is addressed to Commissioner for Patents, P.O. Box 1450, Alexandria, VA 22313.

_____

[type or print name of person making deposit]

_____

[signature of person making deposit]

Declaration under 37 C.F.R. §1.132

Dear Sirs:

I, _____ , declare and say:

That I am a citizen of _____ reside at

_____ ;

That I was graduated in _____ from _____

located in _____ with a _____

Degree in _____. I was also graduated in _____

from _____ located in _____

with a _____ Degree in _____ ;

That since _____ I have been working in the field of

_____. I have been employed by _____

since _____, and part of this time has been spent in this

field. Since _____, I have been _____ in the

_____ Department of _____ ;

That I have been granted _____ patents in the _____ field, and I am the author of _____ papers in the _____ field;

That I am familiar with the above-identified patent application Serial No.: _____ and with the following references cited by the Examiner: _____;

That a test was performed (by me) (on behalf of applicant) described in detail hereinafter to compare _____ employed in the invention described and claimed in the above-identified patent application;

That in accordance with the invention, _____;

That the results of this test are summarized in the following table:

[Insert Table]

That the above test demonstrates clearly the (superiority of, criticality in, or synergism with) _____ as claimed in the above-identified patent application;

That, in my opinion, the aforementioned (superiority, criticality, or synergism) with respect to _____ of the claimed invention is unobvious to one skilled in the art.

I hereby declare that all statements made herein of my own knowledge are true and that all statements made on information and belief are believed to be true; and further that these statements were made with the knowledge that willful false statements and the like so made are punishable by fine or imprisonment, or both, under Section 1001 of Title 18 of the United States Code, and that such willful false statements may jeopardize the validity of the application or any patent issued thereon.

Respectfully submitted,

_____
(Applicant/Patentee)

IN THE UNITED STATES PATENT AND TRADEMARK OFFICE

Applicant(s): (   )

Serial No.: (   )

Filed: (   )

Title: (   )

Group Art. Unit: (   )

Examiner: (   )

Docket No.: (   )

FILED BY EXPRESS MAIL
Commissioner for Patents
P.O. Box 1450
Alexandria, VA 22313

EXPRESS MAIL CERTIFICATE

"Express Mail" Label No. _____

Date of Deposit: _____

I hereby certify that this paper and the attachment herein are being deposited with the United States Postal Service as "Express Mail Post Office to Addressee" service under 37 C.F.R. §1.10 on the date indicated above and is addressed to Commissioner for Patents, P.O. Box 1450, Alexandria, VA 22313.

_____
[type or print name of person making deposit]

_____
[signature of person making deposit]

Request for Certificate of Correction

Dear Sirs:

Enclosed and attached hereto is a Form PTO-1050 indicating errors in the above-identified patent.

A check for $_____ for the Certificate of Correction is enclosed.

It is respectfully requested that the Certificate of Correction be issued.

Respectfully submitted,

_____
(Applicant)

About the Author

James L. Rogers received his law degree from Suffolk University Law School. He received an MS degree in biology from New York University with an emphasis on DNA recombinant technology and a PhD in molecular medicine from the University of South Florida College of Medicine with an emphasis on immunology. He is a member of the New York and Massachusetts bars, as well as admitted to practice before the United States Patent and Trademark Office and several U.S. District Courts. He has been a university instructor on the subject of patents and has written extensively on a wide range of legal subjects. He has authored or coauthored several books including *The Complete Patent Book* and *Profit from Intellectual Property*. He currently resides in New York City.